Racism, Sexism, and the Media

4 edition

This book is dedicated in memory of the vision and energy of
Dr. Lionel C. Barrow Jr.
a trailblazing leader, mentor, scholar, teacher, and advocate for women and men of every color in their efforts to advance mutual respect and understanding of all people through all forms of communication.

Racism, Sexism, and the

4 edition

Media

Multicultural Issues Into the New Communications Age

Clint C. Wilson II *Howard University*

Félix Gutiérrez *University of Southern California*

Lena M. Chao *California State University, Los Angeles*

Los Angeles | London | New Delhi
Singapore | Washington DC

Los Angeles | London | New Delhi
Singapore | Washington DC

FOR INFORMATION:

SAGE Publications, Inc.
2455 Teller Road
Thousand Oaks, California 91320
E-mail: order@sagepub.com

SAGE Publications Ltd.
1 Oliver's Yard
55 City Road
London EC1Y 1SP
United Kingdom

SAGE Publications India Pvt. Ltd.
B 1/I 1 Mohan Cooperative Industrial Area
Mathura Road, New Delhi 110 044
India

SAGE Publications Asia-Pacific Pte. Ltd.
3 Church Street
#10-04 Samsung Hub
Singapore 049483

Copyright © 2013 by SAGE Publications, Inc.

Printed in the United States of America

A catalog record of this book is available from the Library of Congress.

978-1-4522-1751-2

This book is printed on acid-free paper.

Acquisitions Editor: Matthew Byrnie
Editorial Assistant: Stephanie Palermini
Production Editor: Libby Larson
Copy Editor: Melinda Masson
Typesetter: C&M Digitals (P) Ltd.
Proofreader: Victoria Reed-Castro
Indexer: Molly Hall
Cover Designer: Scott van Atta
Marketing Manager: Liz Thornton

12 13 14 15 16 10 9 8 7 6 5 4 3 2 1

Brief Contents

Detailed Contents

Preface to Fourth Edition

This volume reflects and encompasses more than 40 years of its authors' observations and scholarship on the relationship between American mass communications media and the largest racial and cultural minority groups in the United States. Beginning with the first edition titled *Minorities and the Media* (1985), we have chronicled how general audience media have marginalized these groups and in the process reflected the hegemonic attitudes that have prevented the full realization of a society that has historically proclaimed its constitutional foundation to be equality of opportunity in a participatory democracy. The study of any nation's mass media—and of those who determine its content as overseers, managers, and producers—tells us much about the core values and objectives of that society. The United States has developed a general media operational pattern that is wholly consistent with the principle of "free market enterprise." That notion has traditionally allowed the hegemonic political and economic power structure to determine and reinforce the social roles of racial and cultural "minorities" for both marketing and socioeconomic purposes.

We have come now, however, to a new era wherein the forces of technology and demographic evolution appear to be changing the dynamics of media communication. Mass media corporations and conglomerates are struggling to adapt to an American marketplace that has seen "social media"—through the use of smartphones, tablet computers, and other electronic devices—shift the emphasis from corporate to individualized personal communication platforms. These social media technologies have transformed people who have been the audience of media content into creators of pictures, videos, and messages that are sent to many others. Despite the major technological impact being made in the "new media age," this volume carries a cautionary message that acknowledges the strong lingering effects of more than two centuries of racial, cultural, and gender stereotyping and denigration of peoples of color perpetrated by mass media in the United States. Of foremost concern is the extent of the historical damage inflicted upon marginalized groups over time and whether the pervasiveness of stereotypical imagery has led them to generally "buy in" to the notions of otherness and inferiority that will prevent them from being viable participants in a pluralistic society. Meanwhile, although new media platforms have emerged, the continuing replay of the old images of the past is still used to consume time and space across the increasing numbers of communication channels and serves to introduce new generations to the old media's damaging messages.

The past 40 years have also necessitated other changes in our approach to this effort. In this edition of our work on the relationship between mass communications media in the United States and non-Anglo Americans, the accelerated pace of racial and cultural diversity has required the addition of two groups that have not been addressed in previous volumes. First, discussions of Asian American, Pacific Island, and East Asian (Chinese, Japanese, and Korean) people have been broadened to include South Asians, such as Asian Indians defined as those descending from or being from India, a group now including nearly 3 million residents in the United States.

Second, throughout this work, sections have been added to address the media portrayals of people of Arab or Middle Eastern descent and those of various ethnicities who practice the Islamic faith. The 21st century not only saw dramatic changes in communications technology but also was an era in which the United States engaged in unconventional wars against extremist religious groups spread across several nations in the Middle East. Against this backdrop some confusion exists in the United States concerning whether persons of Middle Eastern descent who reside in the United States should be considered a distinct racial group. As a category, some ethnologists list the people of Egypt, Iran, Iraq, Israel, Jordan, Kuwait, Lebanon, Qatar, Saudi Arabia, United Arab Emirates, and Yemen (among others) as being primarily of Caucasoid (White) racial origin.

However, a March 2009 article in the *Los Angeles Times* discussed a movement among some Middle Eastern American college students against declaring themselves as "White" on U.S. Census forms:

> For years the federal government has classified Arab Americans and Middle Easterners as white. But confusion and disagreement have led some students to check "Asian" or "African," depending on what part of the Middle East they came from . . . The Arab American Institute estimates that including Middle Easterners in the white category on the census has led to a population undercount of more than a million, said Helen Samhan, who works at the institute. There are more than 3 million Arabs in the United States, the institute says.[1]

Significantly, the article noted that the students generally resented declaring themselves as White because they were not treated as such in American society and were often marginalized and not socially accepted as equal citizens. Superficial and stereotypical media coverage has led to confusion among Americans who are often unable to distinguish differences between the cultural issues and the religious practices of persons of Middle Eastern heritage. Moreover, persons of all races who practice the Islamic faith encompass a wide range of diverse thought and levels of orthodoxy in much the same manner as those who profess Catholicism or Judaism.

In this work, the Middle East is defined as the nations of Algeria, Bahrain, Egypt, Iran, Iraq, Israel, Jordan, Kuwait, Lebanon, Libya, Morocco, Oman, Palestine, Sudan, Syria, Tunisia, Turkey, Qatar, Saudi Arabia, United Arab Emirates, and Yemen.

Despite the advent of the new millennium, we continue to live in conflicting and complex times with regard to issues of race, gender, class, and culture. On the one hand, marginalized groups and minorities have made significant—even historical—strides toward greater equality including the 2008 election of Barack Obama as the first African American president of the United States.

Yet, at the same time, we've witnessed renewed attacks against cultural diversity and the promotion of ethnic and racial equity both in the United States and abroad. According to a 2011 report issued by the National Coalition of Anti-Violence Programs, hate crimes rose 13% from 2009, with 70% of those killed being minorities and 44% transgender women (Romney, 2011). In one of Europe's worst terrorist attacks, a radical right extremist in Norway killed 87 people in 2011 in a raging backlash against those the perpetrator believed were allowing the "cultural suicide" that led to demographic changes and the rise of multiculturalism in his once homogeneous nation. And despite the fact that the attack was committed by a "right-wing Christian fundamentalist," the initial response was to point the finger at Muslim extremists or "jihadis." This volume examines the role of communications media in the multicultural landscape of the United States.

As we have noted in previous editions, the scholarship and general interest documentation of the racial and cultural groups addressed here is uneven and varies widely among the groups and their representation across the range of mass media platforms. Research data have, in some cases, been extrapolated from different available sources and compiled to provide readers with a general comparative overview. In other instances, data on specific groups are nonexistent and therefore have not been included.

In this volume, chapters have been reconfigured to better assess the historical perspective that the passage of time has provided. For example, the use of the Second World War as a frame of reference has been discarded in favor of a more useful millennial assessment. At the same time, the authors have noted the importance of imagery in early commercial radio to the perpetuation of racial stereotypes and have added content that emphasizes the role that important medium played for generations of American citizens.

Other major changes in this edition include updating of census figures and employment data of the subject groups in the workplaces of major mass media industries and their participation as faculty and students in higher education institutions where persons are prepared to become professional practitioners.

We note also that in the wake of Barack Obama's election to the presidency of the United States the concept of the nation as a "postracial" society has emerged. That notion is challenged in this work through a variety of racist incidents promulgated through and by mass media following Obama's election. This volume, therefore, encourages the reader to make an assessment of the current status and viability of the ideal notion of a postracial America.

Limitations

As noted in previous editions, limitations in this work exist in several respects. The text concerns itself generally with the largest racial/cultural minority groups in the United States. Other groups sometimes categorized as "minorities" (the physically challenged, gays, lesbians and White women in the workforce, etc.) are not subjects of this work, although some parallels may be seen in their relationships to general audience media. Similarly, this book does not attempt to address every general audience public communication medium. Therefore, music recording, book publishing, magazine fiction, and other media forms are not within the scope of this work.

Although scholars continue to contribute new knowledge about media relationships to the subject groups, the authors still find that research material on the various groups remains uneven. Thus, it was not possible to tell the complete story of each group in every chapter. The gaps in research literature continue to suggest areas for future study by students and scholars who are seriously interested in documenting the role of media as they have related to racial groups in the United States. We hope that this book encourages further work in this important field so that more knowledge gaps are addressed and filled.

Definition of Terms

In this book, the terms *Asian Pacific American* and *Asian American* (sans hyphen) are used interchangeably to describe people who trace their origins to the Asian continent, as well as those from the Pacific Islands.

The term *Black* is used to describe African Americans and others who trace their origins to the sub-Saharan part of the African continent.

Latino or the feminine form, *Latina*, is used along with *Hispanic* as inclusive terms for persons of Latin American or Spanish background, including the Caribbean region.

The term *Native American* is used to describe the indigenous peoples of the continent that Europeans and other immigrants have called America.

The terms *White* and *Anglo* are used as applied by the U.S. Bureau of the Census and describe persons of European background who are not Latinos. All terms are capitalized in the text when referring to people of different races and cultures.

The authors acknowledge, however, that the use of terms such as *Asian, Latino, African American,* and *White* to describe a diverse group of people is often inadequate, and the hyphenation of two continents—to create, for example, *Asian-American*—is problematic.

Finally, the authors would be remiss if they did not acknowledge the contributions of many persons who have assisted them over the years in making this series a groundbreaking work that has influenced the development of an area of study in mass communications scholarship that did not exist before 1985.

Acknowledgments

The authors wish to reiterate acknowledgements of persons, and their affiliations at the time, who provided assistance during preparation of the previous editions of this work. They include graduate research assistants Carey Jue and David Tomsky. Also Luther Luedtke who provided support when he served as Interim Director of the University of Southern California School of Journalism. Appreciation is also extended to Erwin Kim, a former USC colleague, whose assistance with the historiography of film portions of the text was invaluable. Other colleagues at USC who made important contributions included Stanley Rosen, of the USC East Asian Studies Center, who assisted in translating portions of the first Asian American newspaper along with graduate student Stanley Chung. Students in our courses at Howard University, USC, and California State University, Los Angeles brought enthusiasm for the subject of race and the media and were a source of inspiration and encouragement as was Alice Marshall of Wave Publications.

Important in the development of historical information in the first edition were Michael Emery and Tom Reilly of the journalism faculty at California State University, Northridge. Jorge Reina Schement, then on the faculty of the University of California, Los Angeles, and Hugo Garcia of the Northeast Newspapers in Los Angeles provided much of the stimulation for sections on audience segmentation. Also Armando Valdez of Stanford University and Don Carson and Edith Auslander of the University of Arizona provided speaking opportunities and comments that led to some of the concepts developed in those sections. Carolyn McIntosh, research librarian at USC, provided valuable assistance in locating material on topics covered in the book, and staff members of the Margaret Herrick Library, Academy of Motion Picture Arts and Sciences, assisted in obtaining photographs.

Gratitude is extended to those who have been gracious with their time and expertise during preparation of previous editions of the book. They include Vernon Stone, formerly research director for the Radio-Television News Directors Association, Brenda Alexander of the Howard University Department of Journalism, and numerous colleagues in the Minorities and Communication division of the Association for Education in Journalism and Mass Communication who consistently reinforced the need for this volume. Also Elena Gutièrrez of the University of Michigan for her editing and comments on the first chapter and Bunty Anquoe and Tim Giago of *Indian Country Today* and Mark Trahant of the *Salt Lake Tribune* for their insights into coverage of Native Americans. Jon Funabiki of San Francisco State University provided good counsel on issues relating to diversity in the media and journalism education, and Aissatou Sidime of Xavier University provided research for the chapter on advertising.

Special thanks for their specific contributions to Ping Lien Chao, Monterey Park, California; Thelma Grayson, Los Angeles; Yumi Wilson, San Francisco State University; Rick Mastroianni, Freedom Forum Library; Sandy Close, New America Media; Sandra Ball-Rokeach, Michael J. Cody, Elisia Cohen, Geoff Cowan, Stella Lopez, Michael Parks, and Ernest Wilson, Annenberg School for Communication and Journalism, University of Southern California; Mercedes Lynn de Uriarte and Maggie Rivas-Rodriguez, School of Journalism, University of Texas at Austin; Monty Roessel, Rough Rock Community School, Chinle, Arizona; Nicolas Kanellos, Arte Publico Press, University of Houston; Kuei Chiu, University of California, Riverside Library; Andrea Shepherd, Newseum; Steve Montiel, Institute for Justice and Journalism; Dennis McAuliffe, *The Washington Post*; Joellen El-Bashir, Moorland-Spingarn Research Center, Howard University; and Frank Wood, Frank & Marie-Therese Wood Print Collections, Alexandria, Virginia. Additional thanks are extended to Raul Ibarra, Erik Jimenez, Jenkij Satyapan, and Melissa Tindage—an exceptionally promising group of graduate students in the Department of Communication Studies at California State University, Los Angeles—for their assistance in researching updated resources in the areas of women and people of color in the media.

Most important, we must again recognize the support, encouragement, and sacrifices made by those closest to us: Mary Julia Wilson and Clint C. Wilson III; Marìa Elena, Elena Rebeca, Anita Andrea, and Alicia Rosa Gutiérrez, along with granddaughters Rosa Amalya and Mae Elena; and Julian Lee Benedict. Without their sustaining presence and nurturing expressions, the authors could not have completed the task.

Clint C. Wilson II

Félix F. Gutiérrez

Lena M. Chao

Note

1. Raja Abdulrahim, "Students Push UC to Expand Terms of Ethnic Identification: Middle Easterners Want Alternatives to 'White' and 'Other,'" *Los Angeles Times*, March 31, 2009, accessed March 22, 2012, http://articles.latimes.com/2009/mar/31/local/me-arab31.

PART I

Majority Rules

"Minorities" and the Media

1 Demographics

The U.S. Census Bureau made headlines in 2008 when it announced that minorities "are expected to become the majority in 2042."[1] Digital, broadcast, and print news media in the United States and beyond reported the Census Bureau's projection that the people it called Asians, Blacks, Hispanics, American Indians, Alaska Natives, Native Hawaiians, and Other Pacific Islanders would grow to 54% of the U.S. population by 2050.

"Minorities Will Be in Majority," the *Chicago Tribune* reported. CNN's website posted a story headlined "Minorities Expected to Be Majority in 2050." In England *The Guardian*'s headline ran "Ethnic Minorities to Form Majority by 2050."

The prospect of the United States becoming a majority minority nation in which all people are members of a racial or ethnic minority group also stirred controversy and comments across the nation. Some examined the role of Whites in a nation in which people of other colors collectively composed the majority. In 2009 the blog Digital Journal noted "White people continue to be the largest identifiable group in the U.S. This fact will continue well into the future, regardless of whether or not it's above 50%."[2] *Newsweek* ran a column by Ellis Cose headlined "Red, Brown, and Blue: America's Color Lines Are Shifting." A review in *The New Yorker* asked "Beyond the Pale: Is White the New Black?," then explored possible changes in White identity and interests as Whites become a minority in a multiracial nation. Author Kelefa Sanneh concluded by observing that the racial change "doesn't mean that white is the new black ... and never will be." But the racial changes from White majority to White minority were seen as portending the "the slow birth of a people" in which Whiteness would become "a work in progress" as Whites developed an awareness of their own history and future in a multiracial nation.[3]

The projected growth of people of color from different races and cultures in the United States to more than 50% of the population and the Census Bureau's 2011 recognition of Hispanics, also called Latinos, as the largest of those groups also rocked the nation's race relations mind-set. Moving beyond a focus on Black and White, the nation became more aware of its multiracial and multicultural future. This soul searching heightened as racial and ethnic issues across society became more focused, clearer, and sometimes divisive.

Figure 1.1 U.S. Minorities Becoming the Majority

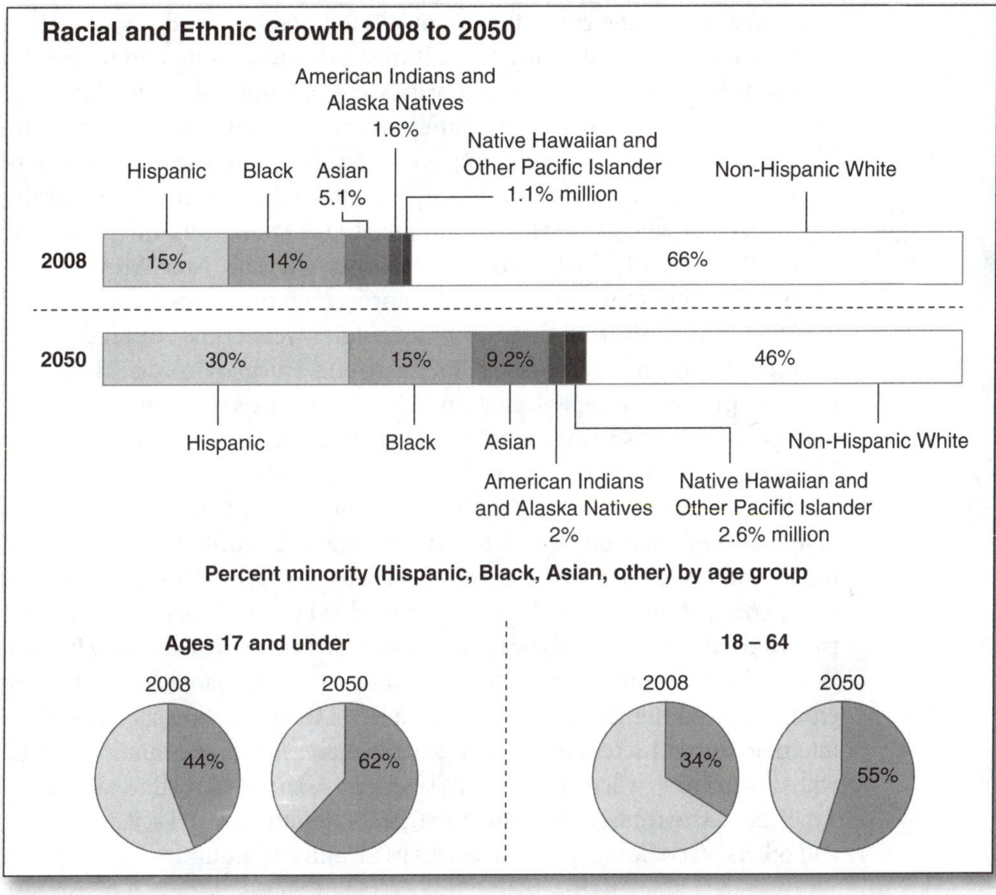

Racial and Ethnic Growth 2008 to 2050

American Indians and
Alaska Natives
1.6%

Native Hawaiian and
Other Pacific Islander
1.1% million

Hispanic   Black   Asian
5.1%

Non-Hispanic White

2008   15%   14%   66%

2050   30%   15%   9.2%   46%

Hispanic   Black   Asian

Non-Hispanic White

American Indians
and Alaska Natives
2%

Native Hawaiian and
Other Pacific Islander
2.6% million

Percent minority (Hispanic, Black, Asian, other) by age group

Ages 17 and under

2008   2050

44%   62%

18 – 64

2008   2050

34%   55%

Source: Data from U.S. Census Bureau.

As Figure 1.1 shows, the United States is quickly moving from being a nation that has a White majority and minority groups of different races and ethnicities to one in which no single racial or ethnic group will be in the majority. As this happens, the nation and its media will need to change how people of diverse races and cultures are seen and treated. No one group will be the majority, and everyone in the United States will be a member of a minority group.

Who Are the Minorities?

When used in its statistical sense, the term *minorities* refers to things that are small in number, less than the majority. In the past the term was often applied to people of color in the United States because the total number of Blacks, Latinos, Asians, and Native Americans was smaller than the White majority. Arabs, South Asians, and some other groups were considered so small that they were not counted at all or were placed under one of the existing catego-ries. In the late 20th century the term *minorities* became a convenient umbrella label under which any group that is not White could be placed.

However, it is a misleading label. It misleads those using and seeing the label to think of people called minorities as small not only in number, but also in importance. In a democratic nation based on majority rule, the label can make the interests and issues raised by minorities seem less important than those of the majority. Increasingly, it is not a statistically accurate term when referring to the racial and ethnic mix of the United States. By the early 21st century, California, Hawaii, New Mexico, and Texas were states in which people of color were in the majority. Analysis of the 2010 census revealed that eight more states were at the "tipping point" of becoming majority minority by 2020: Arizona, Florida, Georgia, Maryland, Mississippi, Nevada, New Jersey, and New York. The same census revealed that 341 of the 3,143 counties (11%) were majority minority, and another 225 were at the tipping point of being so classified by 2020.[4]

These projections make it clear that the United States will continue to grow as a nation of color through the next generation. In 2010, Asian Americans, Blacks, Latinos, and Native Americans made up 36% of the U.S. population and had accounted for 92% of the nation's population growth since 2000. As this pattern continues, they will continue to grow at a faster rate than non-Hispanic Whites due to immigration, birthrate, and larger average family sizes. As these groups grow in number and percentage of the U.S. population, factors such as intermarriage between groups and generational, gender, and ethnic diversity within each group will make umbrella labels like Asian, Black, Latino, and Native American less useful. At the same time, Arabs, South Asians, Pacific Islanders, and others will become more important as identifiable groups.

The WASP Melting Pot

These changes continue an evolving racial and ethnic mix that has been part of the land that is now the United States since the arrival of the first Europe-ans in the early 1600s. It is a natural evolution and one that is more inclusive than earlier "Whites preferred" policies that governed the nation's popula-tion policies and practices when immigrants came primarily from Europe.

"The region changed from predominantly Native American to predomi-nantly White Anglo-Saxon Protestant (WASP) in large part due to high mor-tality on the part of the former and high immigration and fertility on the part of the latter group," wrote population analysts Leon F. Bouvier and Cary B. Davis. "In 1800 close to 20 percent of what, by then, was the United States of America was Black—in large part, the result of high levels of immigration, albeit forced. By 1900, more significant changes had occurred. Blacks were only 10 percent of the population, but among Whites the proportion coming from southern and eastern Europe had grown substantially."[5]

As Bouvier and Davis pointed out, the influx of southern and eastern European immigrants challenged the nation's WASP identity early in the 20th century and led to the vision of the United States as a "melting pot" society in which newcomers became Anglo Americans by shedding the culture, language, foods, and identities of their homelands and ancestors. In reality, the melting pot is a high-heat fusion process that melts metals into liquids to force out impurities and unessential elements. The Americanization process was seen as subjecting newcomers to a similar process to disassociate them from their pasts, lose their individual and group identities, then forge a new identity closer to the Anglo American model.

"A popular way of getting hold of the assimilation idea has been to use a metaphor, and by far the most popular metaphor has been that of the 'melting pot,' a term introduced in Israel Zangwill's 1908 play of that name," wrote Hunter College professor Peter Salins. He quoted the play:

> There she lies, the great Melting-Pot—Listen! Can't you hear the roaring and the bubbling? . . . Ah, what a stirring and a seething! Celt and Latin, Slav and Teuton, Greek and Syrian, black and yellow . . . Jew and Gentile . . . East and West, and North and South, the palm and the pine, the pole and the equator, the crescent and the cross—how the great Alchemist melts and fuses them with his purifying flame! Here shall they all unite to build the Republic of Man and the Kingdom of God.[6]

Though the play's text included "Latin . . . Syrian . . . black and yellow . . . the crescent and the cross" in a multiracial and multicultural melting pot, in practice the assimilation process of American society was less inclusive of non-White people and some Europeans such as Jews, Italians, and Irish. Their marginalization was examined in Nathan Glazer and Daniel Patrick Moynihan's 1963 book *Beyond the Melting Pot*,[7] which also examined practices keeping Blacks and Puerto Ricans from fully assimilating into American life.

Nevertheless, the melting pot became an idealized and popular way of describing the assimilation of European immigrants coming to the United States in the early 20th century. Proponents of the model held that those who came to the United States would cast aside the identities, cultures, and languages of home countries such as Germany, Poland, Ireland, or Sweden as they either adopted, or were forced to adopt, the identities, loyalties, customs, and language of their new homeland.

The melting pot theory held that it was necessary to forget, or at least submerge, the culture of a person's roots in order to be allowed to participate in the benefits of the United States. In essence, assimilation to the WASP standard was the price of participation in U.S. society.[8] It was thought that within a generation or so the children of European immigrants would "melt" into the working class of the United States and no longer be identifiable by the national origin of their homeland. Many shared the white skin of the British and other earlier European arrivals. By adopting the English language, changing their names to sound more

When most newcomers to the United States came from Europe, the immigrants were urged to shed their home country language and customs and "melt" into Anglo American society. The melting pot graduation ceremony of the Ford English School for immigrant automobile factory workers in Michigan in 1916 idealized this with a steamship background and symbolic melting pot.

Source: Henry Ford Museum and Greenfield Village.

Anglo, and adopting the customs of their new nation, they would appear to be like those who arrived before them.

Leaving the ways of the old country behind and adopting the WASP norms of their new land of opportunity had its advantages for the immigrants. The WASP founders of the United States envisioned a land where people had "inalienable rights . . . of life, liberty and pursuit of happiness" in a nation where all men were created equal, could participate in electing leaders, and could move up based on merit, hard work, and opportunity.

The melting pot concept was so dominant that the Ford Motor Company in Michigan established the Ford English School in 1913. The goal of the school, which in three years had 2,200 students from 33 nationalities studying under 150 English-speaking Ford workers, was to teach the immigrants to read, write, and speak English in eight months. The graduation ceremony ended with graduates standing on stage alongside a huge symbolic melting pot under the Latin words printed on U.S. currency, "E Pluribus Unum" (From Many, One).

"All commencements were held at the school, and every class had to go into this large cauldron in a foreign costume holding a symbol indicating the country he or she came from," wrote Boris Sanchez de Lozada and Robert Armoush. "The ceremony ended by emerging students coming out of this cauldron with American clothing and American flags waving in their hands. The school's objective here was to break language and cultural barriers ... to increase productivity."[9]

Today the melting pot's legacy is found among White Americans who know little of their family history, other than that their ancestors came from Germany, Sweden, Denmark, Poland, or some other European country. But while the descendants of those who blended into the melting pot may not be able to speak the language or share the customs of their European ancestors, many have shown an increased interest in connecting with family roots, national heritage, and past customs, particularly as political changes and ethnic strife occurred in Eastern Europe.[10]

U.S. Grows Beyond the Melting Pot

At the same time, the members of groups who were left "beyond the melting pot" because their racial skin color, eye shape, hair texture, or other characteristics made it impossible for them to fully "melt" into Anglo identities by merely changing their last names are growing in number in the United States. Because of differences in race, legal status, or geographic proximity to the home country, they were never fully blended, or allowed to blend, into the melting pot of the United States in spite of efforts by many to approximate Whites in appearance, values, and lifestyle. Rather than a melting pot, people in these groups experienced the United States as a stew pot. As in a stew, each element retains its identity while contributing its own flavor to those of others and absorbing some of the flavors of other groups onto itself. Many today have become Americans by living a daily life of more than one culture, language, or identity as they build on their homeland roots, rather than cutting them off.

As a nation whose population growth has historically been fueled by immigration, the United States has always had racial, national, and ethnic minorities beyond the melting pot available to many European immigrants. People whose racial or ethnic groups fell outside of the melting pot have been counted separately since the first U.S. census of 1790. From the nation's beginning they were considered separate and oftentimes unequal to Whites.

The nation's first census categories reflect the racial and gender priorities as the new

People of color were long subject to legal and social segregation that limited their educational, political, and social opportunities in the United States. This 1942 NO DOGS, NEGROES, MEXICANS sign attributed to the Lonestar Restaurant Association in Texas marked such segregation.

Source: Lonestar Restaurant Association 1942.

Laws prohibiting Native Americans from voting at the same time that immigrants, identified by their European attire, and newly freed Blacks cast their votes were questioned by *Harper's Weekly* political cartoonist Thomas Nast in 1871. Women were not allowed to vote at that time.

Source: Harper's Weekly, 1871.

nation began: free White males, age 16 and older; free White males, age 16 and younger; and free White females. Non-Whites were designated as "all other persons" and "slaves." Black slaves counted as three fifths of a White person for purposes of determining representation in Congress. The 1790 census counted 757,000 Blacks, 92% of them living as slaves. They composed nearly one fifth of the nation's population. Native Americans were not included in 1790 census figures for congressional representation because they were considered citizens of separate nations.[11]

In 1910 census takers visited homes and classified people as "White," "Black," "Mulatto," "Chinese," "Japanese," "American Indian," and "Other." The 1960 census was the first time people were asked to self-identify their race, rather than rely on the observations of census takers. A Spanish/Hispanic question wasn't introduced on the census short-form questionnaire until 1980, and the 2000 census was the first to allow people with multiracial backgrounds to select more than one race.[12] Since Hispanics are an ethnic group whose members can be of any race, the census has evolved into asking for both race and ethnicity to determine the nation's population composition of Hispanics and non-Hispanics. Further reflecting the nation's racial and ethnic complexity, the census also provides more label options and asks more details about national origin of people of color than of Whites.

The 2010 census question "What is this person's race?" offered Whites only one possible response: White. In comparison, the census asked about Hispanic origin and race in separate questions. Those reporting they were of Hispanic, Latino, or Spanish origin were then asked to check a separate box indicating whether they were Mexican, Mexican American, or Chicano; Puerto Rican; or Cuban, or to write in their other Hispanic, Latino, or Spanish origin, such as Argentinean, Colombian, Dominican, Nicaraguan, Salvadoran, or Spaniard. People once simply called Black by the census could check one of three boxes marked Black, African American, and Negro. Others could check a box labeled American Indian or Alaska Native and mark their tribe. Persons of Asian or Pacific Islander race could check Asian Indian, Chinese, Filipino, Japanese, Korean, Vietnamese, Native Hawaiian, Guamanian or Chamorro, Samoan, Other Asian (Hmong, Laotian, Thai, Pakistani, Cambodian, etc.), or Other Pacific Islander (Fijian, Tongan, etc.).[13] The census of 2000 revealed more than 1.6 million Asian Indians living in the United States, a population that grew to more than 2.8 million by 2010, a growth rate of 69% that was highest among all Asian American communities.

Although the Census Bureau in 2003 issued a separate report on "The Arab Population: 2000,"[14] it did not include Arabs as a category in the 2010 census and did not list Arabs in its *Overview of Race and Hispanic Origin: 2010* census report issued in 2011. The 2003 report counted 1.2 million Arabs in the United States in 2000, up from 860,000 in 1990 and double the 610,000 counted in 1980. The census report included all who reported being Arab, Egyptian, Iraqi, Jordanian, Lebanese, Middle Eastern, Moroccan, North African, Palestinian, Syrian, and so on. The report cautioned that not all people from these countries consider themselves Arabs and noted Arabs are found in other parts of the world. About 60% of reported Arabs in the United States in 2000 traced their ancestry to Lebanon, Syria, or Egypt.

Because Islam is the religion most associated with many of the countries to which the Arab Americans traced their roots, Muslims in the United States have often been portrayed racially as Arabs, North Africans, and Middle Easterners. This association has given Muslims a racialized identity in the U.S. media portraying Muslims as Arabs. In fact, Muslims are the most racially diverse religion in the United States, with 28% of the members White, 35% African American, 18% Asian, and 18% other races.[15] The Census Bureau does not report the number of Muslims because they are members of a religion and questions about religion are not part of the census. In 2011 advertisers and companies seeking Muslim customers estimated the Muslim population in the United States at between 6 million and 8 million.

As the Arab report and racial diversity of Muslims illustrate, reporting the nation's racial and ethnic makeup is further complicated by attempts to categorize people by labels that may not really describe who or what they are. Though Asians were counted separately for the first time in 2000, data for

Asians and Pacific Islanders are often combined, putting people from such disparate nations as Japan, Vietnam, Indonesia, and India under the same umbrella. By the same token, American Indians are combined with Alaska Natives, combining people who may appear similar to others, but may have important differences between groups combined together. Hispanics—people who trace their roots to Spain, Latin America, or the Caribbean—can be of any race. The 2010 census forms used the terms *Hispanic, Latino,* and *Spanish* origin to identify people it categorized as Hispanic in its reports. *Hispanic* can be used interchangeably with *Latino,* the term most often used in this book.

The Browning of America

The 2010 census also reported the continuation of what others have called "the browning of America" as people of color increased their share of the nation's population. Between 2000 and 2010 the U.S. population grew by 9.3%, an increase of 27.3 million people, and most of the growth was driven by people of color.

The 2010 census reported non-Whites and Latinos were 36% of the U.S. population of 308.7 million in 2000, up from 30% of the population in 2000 and 25% 10 years earlier. As the percentage of non-Hispanic Whites in the United States dropped between 2000 and 2010, the growth rates for other racial and ethnic groups continued to rise, continuing a trend going back at least 40 years. Blacks, American Indians or Alaska Natives, Asian or Pacific Islanders, Hispanics, and those marking "Other" all grew in number and percentage of the population between 2000 and 2010.

The only group that lost ground was non-Hispanic Whites, declining from 69% of the people in the United States in 2000 to 64% in 2010. Persons indicating they were more than one race, a category used for the first time in 2000, increased from 1.6% of the population in 2000 to 3% in 2010.[16]

"The vast majority of the growth in the total population came from increases in those who reported their race(s) as something other than White alone and those who reported their ethnicity as Hispanic or Latino," the Census Bureau reported in its *Overview of Race and Hispanic Origin: 2010.* "More than half of the growth of the total population in the United States between 2000 and 2010 was due to the increase in Hispanic population."[17]

The Census Bureau reported that Hispanics, who can be of any race, numbered 50.5 million or 16% of the U.S. population in 2010, an increase of 43% since 2000. The Black or African American population was 38.9 million, 13% of the population. Asian Americans numbered 14.7 million, about 5% of the population. American Indians and Alaska Natives were 2.9 million, slightly less than 0.9% of the population. Native Hawaiians and Other Pacific Islanders were half a million, 0.2% of the population. Those reporting they were of some other race numbered 19.1 million, 6% of the population. People who reported being of more than one race numbered 9 million, 3% of the population.

Though all reported groups representing people of color continued to grow in numbers between 2000 and 2010, the Census Bureau reported

In some elections, White mobs kept Blacks from voting, as illustrated by *Harper's Weekly* political cartoonist Thomas Nast's drawing of violence at Atlanta, Georgia polling places during the 1872 presidential election.

Source: Harper's Weekly, 1872.

their growth rates varied from group to group, and some saw a decline in their percentage of the nation's population.

"The Asian alone population experienced the fastest rate of growth and the White alone population experienced the slowest rate of growth, with the other major race groups' growth spanning the range in between," the Census Bureau noted. Between 2000 and 2010 the Asian population grew by 43%; Native Hawaiians and Other Pacific Islanders grew by more than 33% in population; those reporting "Some Other Race" grew in number by about 25%, mainly due to Hispanics who did not respond to the racial categories listed; American Indians and Alaska Natives experienced an 18% rate of growth; and Blacks had a 12% growth rate.

Although the African American numerical growth from 34.7 million to 38.9 million people in the United States was larger than for any other single minority racial group except Asians, the African Americans' percentage growth rate was lower because their population base is larger. The number of Whites grew by 12 million, but their share of the population dropped from 75% in 2000 to 72% in 2010 because of the growth of other racial groups.

"The only major race group to experience a decrease in its proportion of the total population was the White alone population," the Census Bureau reported in 2011. Perhaps an even more important indicator of the nation's future racial makeup was the number of people reporting they were of "Two or More Races," increasing by one third between 2000 and 2010.

Undercounting Racial and Ethnic Diversity

"The U.S. population has become more racially and ethnically diverse over time," the Census Bureau concluded in its closing paragraph on the 2010 census. But the growth in diversity "over time" was probably greater than the Census Bureau reported. One reason is because the Census Bureau has admitted undercounting the nation's people of color for decades.

"The census has historically missed a higher percentage of minorities and children, and this trend continued in 2010," the Population Reference Bureau reported in 2011.[18] The independent research organization cited an analysis of the 2010 census revealing that African Americans had been undercounted by 2.5%, that Hispanics were "disproportionately missed," and that more than 1 million children under 18 "may have been missed." The miscounting pendulum swung both ways: "For other racial groups, there was a slight net overcount of 0.5 percent."

The Census Bureau reported that the 2000 census undercounted people of color while Whites, according to the acting director of the census, may have been overcounted in 2000.[19] The Census Bureau admitted in 2000 it had missed 2.17% of the non-Hispanic Blacks, 2.85% of the Hispanics, 4.74% of the American Indians and Alaska Natives living on reservations, 3.28% of the American Indians and Alaska Natives off reservations, and 4.60% of the Native Hawaiians and Other Pacific Islanders.[20] These were all a higher percentage not counted than the national undercount rate of 1.2%, or about 3.2 million people who the census didn't count.[21] Despite the admitted undercount of people of color, the Census Bureau refused to adjust its 2000 population figures to accurately reflect the number of people in the United States and provide better baseline data for 2010 census comparisons.

Adding to the census controversies, people who completed their census forms in 2000 and 2010 claimed the Census Bureau's race, ethnicity, and national origin categories caused their groups to be undercounted. In 2000 some Hispanic groups noted that while Mexicans, Puerto Ricans, and Cubans had their own boxes to check, people with roots in other countries were asked to check the "Other Spanish/Hispanic/Latino" box and then write in the name of their group. Though more options were offered in 2010, some people were confused as to which box to check, didn't see a label they felt described them, or had problems translating the census terms. Those asked to write in their group often didn't know the appropriate Census Bureau labels and thus were not correctly counted. Problems with racial and ethnic labels were further illustrated by an analysis of the 2006 Census Bureau American Community Survey, conducted by sociology professors Amon Emeka and Jody Agius Vallejo of the University of Southern

California. The analysis found that 12% of U.S.-born people who declared Hispanic or Latin American ancestry did not check the box saying they were Spanish/Hispanic/Latino, resulting in an undercount of the number of Latinos.[22]

"When you are trying to predict the size of a population, those projections depend on how that population sees itself and how they answer the ethnicity and race questions on the U.S. Census," said Emeka. Since Latinos can be of any race, some people may check the "White," "Black," or "Asian" box because their racial identity may be more important in their daily lives, the researchers suggested. Another factor may be a desire to have a single racial identity.

"There's still this tendency to pick one race, especially among African Americans, when you must claim more than one on the U.S. Census surveys," Agius Vallejo said. One example was President Barack Obama, who is half White and half Black, checking the "Black" box instead of indicating his true multiracial background in the place provided on the 2010 Census Bureau form.

This 1871 *Harper's Weekly* drawing by political cartoonist Thomas Nast shows a White mob moving from burning a Colored Orphan Asylum to attacking a Chinese immigrant who seeks protection from Columbia (a U.S. symbol) alongside a wall of anti-Chinese slogans. Eleven years later, the U.S. enacted the Chinese Exclusion Act, versions of which were in force until 1943.

Source: *Harper's Weekly*, 1871. The Bancroft Library, University of California, Berkeley.

Similarly, it was reported that some multiracial students applying to college mark the race that they think will be of more help in gaining admission. A 2011 Associated Press story cited Lanya Olmstead, a Florida-born student whose mother immigrated from Taiwan and whose father is of Norwegian ancestry.[23] Though she considers herself half Taiwanese and half Norwegian, she checked "White" when applying to Harvard.

"I didn't want to put 'Asian' down," Olmstead was reported as saying, "because my mom told me there's discrimination against Asians in the application process." The story cited studies showing Asian Americans "often need test scores hundreds of points higher than applicants from other ethnic groups" to gain admission because the proportion of Asian Americans meeting college admission standards is "far out of proportion to their 6 percent representation in the U.S. population."

In addition to those who might check incorrect boxes, other people are not accurately classified by race or ethnicity because their groups were not listed by the Census Bureau. This is a criticism that has also been raised by Assyrians, Chaldeans, Arabs, and Afghans.

"I've checked 'White' all my life," Dearborn attorney Ziad A. Fadel told *The Detroit News* after the 2000 census. "There is no category for who I am," said Fadel, an Arab American.[24] In California, the San Francisco Bay Area Afghan American community, estimated at between 30,000 and 60,000 people, was reported as numbering only 7,000 in the 2000 census, one sixth of its estimated size. Said Sohaila Hashimi, an Afghan American in San Jose, "It's going to be a problem for us. Numbers count in order to be effective and to stand up for a statement or a view."[25]

Further confusing racial and ethnic identity figures in the future is the increase in mixed-race marriages and the growing number of children with parents of different races. By 2010, 15% of all marriages were between people of different races or ethnicities, the Pew Research Center reported. The study revealed that Hispanics and Asians were more likely to marry someone of a different race or ethnicity than Blacks and Whites.[26]

In 2010, 26% of Hispanic and 28% of Asian newlyweds had "married out" to someone of a different race or ethnicity. Seventeen percent of non-Hispanic Blacks and 9% of non-Hispanic Whites married someone of a different race or ethnicity. Since Whites are the largest racial group, most intermarriage involved Whites and members of a minority group.

When comparing race and gender, the Pew study found that 36% of Asian females and 17% of Asian males married non-Asians. In comparison, 24% of Black males and 9% of Black females married outside of their race. There were no gender differences in Hispanic and White intermarriages with people of different races or ethnicities. The study also found growing acceptance of intermarriage, with 63% saying it "would be fine" if a member of their family married someone of a different racial or ethnic group. In 1986, only 28% of those surveyed said people marrying out of their race was not acceptable.

Building a More Colorful United States

But even with the shortcomings of census count and increasing racial and ethnic blending, the reported growth of Blacks, Asians, Native Americans, and Latinos has moved steadily upward over the past four decades. There are many reasons cited for the steady "browning of America" when compared with overall population trends.

One reason is that most racial and ethnic minority groups have a younger median age than Whites and, thus, are more likely to be within the childbearing, family-rearing ages. Their children are also likely to have their own children and families in the near future. The impact of this trend was reinforced by a 2011 study revealing that for the first time non-Hispanic White children were less than half of the babies born in the United States. The study by William Frey of the Brookings Institution found that slightly more than 50% of the children under 3 years old were either Hispanics or children of color, up from less than 40% in 1990.[27]

Much of this growth was driven by an increase in what Frey called "new minorities": Hispanics, Asians, and people of more than one race. From 2000 to 2010 the population of White children in the United States dropped by 4.3 million, while the number of Hispanic and Asian children grew by 5.5 million. Non-Hispanic Whites composed 80% of the U.S. population over age 65, and "with a rapidly aging White population, the United States depends increasingly on these new minorities to infuse its youth population—and eventually its labor force," Frey reported.

A second reason was increased immigration from Asia and Latin America. While in earlier decades Europe had supplied large numbers of immigrants to the United States, during the 1970s immigration to the United States from Asia and Latin America increased sharply. Some of this was spurred by a 1965 change in U.S. immigration regulations. Another factor was warfare and political turmoil in certain countries in these regions. Other immigrants were driven by the desire for an improvement in their economic status. But, for whatever reason, the United States continued to be the land of opportunity for these new residents, just as it had been for the earlier European immigrants.

The Population Reference Bureau reported in 1982 that, between 1977 and 1979, immigrants from Latin America and Asia accounted for 81% of the immigrants to the country, while those from Europe accounted for only 13% percent in that period. In contrast, between 1931 and 1960, Europeans composed 58% of the immigrants, Latin Americans 15%, and Asians 5%.[28] The Asian and Latin American trends continued through the end of the 20th century. Although the number of European immigrants increased from 1981–90 to 1991–98, more immigrants came to the United States from Asia and the Americas than from Europe, and the number from Africa also increased in the same period.[29]

The first decade of the 21st century saw even more immigrants coming from regions other than Europe. In 2009 the Department of Homeland Security Yearbook of Immigration Statistics reported that only 9% of the legal immigrants to the United States came from Europe and the rest came from Asia, Africa, South America, and North America, which included Mexico, the Caribbean, and Central American nations. A Pew Research Center analysis of the 39.9 million people living in the United States in 2010 who were born in another country revealed only 14.5% were born in Europe or Canada, compared with 85% in Latin America, the Caribbean, South or East Asia, the Middle East, Africa, or Oceania. More than 50% were born in Mexico or other parts of Latin America, and 25% percent were born in South and East Asia.[30]

U.S. intervention in the affairs of Latin American and Caribbean nations has long been accompanied by people moving to the United States from that region. This 1920 political cartoon in the British magazine *Punch* shows Uncle Sam pondering whether to once again intervene as he watches a Mexican revolutionary.

PUNCH, OR THE LONDON CHARIVARI.—MAY 26, 1920.

HIS OWN BUSINESS.

UNCLE SAM. "IF I WEREN'T SO PREOCCUPIED WITH IRELAND I MIGHT BE TEMPTED TO GIVE MYSELF A MANDATE FOR THIS."

Source: Punch, May 26, 1920.

A third factor spurring the growing racial and ethnic diversity of the United States was the difference in the number of children born to White and non-White parents. Blacks, Native Americans, and Asian and Pacific Islanders all had a higher birthrate than Whites through the 1980s and 1990s. In 2001, the Census Bureau projected those groups and Hispanics would have higher birthrates than Whites through 2010.[31] In the past, the Census Bureau assumed that the childbearing rates for all racial and ethnic groups would eventually be the same and that there would be a steady decline in the number of children each woman would bear. However, noting "a dramatic rise in total fertility levels to almost 2.1 births per woman" and finding no historical evidence to support the assumption that childbearing rates would become equal, the bureau abandoned both positions in 1992.[32]

As predicted, women of color had higher birthrates than non-Hispanic Whites through the early years of the 21st century. In 2008, non-Hispanic White women between the ages of 15 and 44 had 59.4 births per 1,000 women, called their fertility rate by the Census Bureau. Both Hispanics at 98.8 births per 1,000 women and non-Hispanic Blacks at 71.1 births per 1,000 women had substantially higher fertility rates. The Census Bureau also reported an Asian or Pacific Islander fertility rate of 71.3 births per 1,000 women and an American Indian, Eskimo, and Aleut rate of 64.6 births per 1,000 women.[33] All four groups had higher fertility rates than non-Hispanic Whites.

Analysts of population trends cited other possible causes of the population boom. These included a possible increase in the number of persons willing to designate themselves as members of minority groups, a change in the racial categories used on census forms, and a stepped-up effort to accurately count members of different minority groups by the Census Bureau. But, whatever the reason, the bottom line was clear. People of color had grown at a substantially higher rate than the rest of the nation's population and, as a result, composed a larger percentage of the United States than ever before. Even more important are the projections for the future.

It is clear that people of color will continue to grow both in actual numbers and as a percentage of the U.S. population for the foreseeable future. The projected growth rate for people of color and its relationship to the White population's trends are a matter of debate among demographers. But, while they may argue over the slope of the ascending racial and ethnic growth rate, they all agree about its upward direction.

The projected continuation of these trends promises to dramatically alter the racial and cultural mix of the United States through the 21st century. But the "new" America as a nation where everyone is a minority should not come as any surprise. Signs of the changes, as well as spirited debate and discussion of their implications, had put issues of race and ethnicity into the headlines long before the first decades of the 21st century.

From Melting Pot Minorities to Multiculturalism

The racial and cultural trends making a more colorful America may have been news to some in 1992 when a front-page *USA Today* story was head-lined "Minorities Are Headed Toward the Majority."[34] But racial and ethnic changes were not news to demographers and others who had been tracking the nation's changing racial and cultural makeup. In 1982, the independent Population Reference Bureau reported the racial growth trends and commented on the changes they could bring to American society.

"There are those who would prefer a 'status quo' society. That is to say a continuation of the present racial and ethnic composition under an Anglo-conformity umbrella," demographers Leon F. Bouvier and Cary B. Davis wrote. "There are those who see the future demographic changes as marking the onset of a new phase in the ever changing American society—a 'multicultural' society. In the late 19th century and early 20th century the United States successfully changed identity from WASP to multi-ethnic culture within the White community . . . It may once again change towards being the first truly multi-racial society on the planet earth, a multi-cultural society which while still predominantly English speaking would tolerate and even accept other languages and other cultures."[35] The projected changes caused some rethinking and discussion among those who became accustomed to the melting pot model of assimilation in the United States. The rise of multiculturalism raised sharp debates over issues of race and culture that had long concerned members of racial and ethnic minority groups and forced others to reassess their vision of race and culture in the United States.

In a 1981 interview Daniel Levine, acting director of the U.S. Bureau of the Census, commented that he no longer saw the United States as a melting pot. Instead, he said, he saw the nation developing as a "confederation of minorities" from different groups, each demanding to be counted by the census and, in his words, demanding attention addressing its needs or redressing discrimination against it.

In the same interview, Bruce Chapman, director designate of the Census Bureau, sounded a more optimistic note. He argued that values long seen as "traditional American values" were also part of the value structure of the nation's newest immigrants, particularly Asians and Latinos. He cited the strong family relationships of members of these groups and predicted they would become assets to the nation. "They may want to retain some cultural identification with the old country, but they also want to be unhyphenated Americans," he said.[36]

The debates over the impact of the new America's racial and cultural mix sharpened into the 21st century, particularly in the field of education. Universities, colleges, and school systems debated over the best ways to educate students and prepare them for a multicultural world, including whether standardized admissions tests such as the SAT and ACT were unfair for students who did not come from a standardized background or who attended schools that did not focus on preparing students for college. As the nation's school-age population grew more racially and ethnically diverse, students who were members of groups that traditionally had not been prepared for college became more numerous.

Along with the admissions issues, other educators discussed the best ways to prepare all students to live and work in a multicultural nation. Some argued for the traditional Anglocentric approach as the best way to equip young people to succeed in America, contending that the ways of other cultures are less important in the United States. Others recognized the need for multicultural curricula, as long as the traditions and influence of England and other European nations were recognized as making the greatest contributions to the shaping of the United States. A third approach argued for a multicultural curricula, recognizing the contributions of all groups to the United States and affording special attention to the advances of groups that had traditionally been underrepresented in the curricula. A fourth alternative called for educating students in the learning styles and content of people of their own race, such as an Afrocentric approach to education.

Reacting against racially inclusive instruction, some school boards limited or eliminated ethnic studies and multicultural textbooks and attacked bilingual education programs designed for children from homes where a language other than English is spoken.

"There has always been resistance to my books," said Professor Rudy Acuña of California State University, Northridge, the author of several textbooks about Latinos in the United States, including one "banned" from Tucson schools in 2011. "I published three children's books before *Occupied America* [in 1972], and two were banned in Texas. Some teachers in California threw the books in the waste basket. Censorship in Tucson did not begin recently. I hark back to the banning of bilingual education."[37]

Perhaps most importantly, the debates raised the importance of culture as a part of racial and ethnic identity. Issues of language, food, lifestyle, and values became more important as people either reclaimed or reinforced cultural elements of their lives that ran counter to the melting pot ideology. And, as intermarriage continued to become more prominent, it became clear that pure racial categories would be less useful in the future.

RACIAL AND ETHNIC MINORITIES: A WORLDWIDE PHENOMENON

The United States is not the only country with substantial and growing racial and ethnic minority populations. Nor is it the only one that has recently experienced racial and ethnic turmoil. During the late 1980s through the early 21st century, racial, ethnic, and religious conflicts between groups tore apart nations on all continents. The contests ranged from disputes that had long had international attention, such as conflicts between Jews and Muslims in the Middle East, Catholics and Protestants in Northern Ireland, and Hindus and Christians in India, to smoldering tensions that flared up after political changes, such as battles between Serbs, Slovenes, and Muslims in what had once been Yugoslavia. Conflicts suddenly sharpened between groups that had long contended for the same territory, such as Pakistan and India's claims to Kashmir.

In addition, passions inflamed by new immigration, such as demonstrations for and against immigrant workers from Third World countries coming to England, France, Germany, and other European nations. New workers coming from South to North from Turkey, Morocco, and elsewhere to Europe often found their race, religion, and cultures were not welcome when they arrived in their new homelands, and the job opportunities were less than expected.

Violent conflicts much like the racial riots in the United States in the 1960s broke out in France and England in the years around the end of the first decade of the 21st century. A *New York Times* correspondent covering riots and fires in the London neighborhood of Tottenham in 2011 reported "frustration in this impoverished neighborhood" and a community where law enforcement was not trusted because "a large Afro-Caribbean population has felt singled out by the police for abuse."[38]

Like the United States, most nations have different religious, ethnic, cultural, or racial minority groups within boundaries that have changed over the years. The treatment of members of these groups varies from nation to nation, depending on the political, religious, and economic systems of the country, as well as the historical relationship between the dominant and subordinate groups.

In most colonial situations in which one country conquers or colonizes the people of another land, there are rigid social separations based on class and race. England, the country to which U.S. political and social institutions are most linked, colonized much of North America, as well as parts of Africa, Oceania, and Asia. The British assumed what it called the "White man's burden" of bringing civilization to uncivilized people, often forcing it on them through a rigid colonial system that put Whites at the top. The British colonial system maintained strict lines of distinction between the predominantly White Anglo colonizers and the people of "colour" whose territory they came to occupy. The United States followed the thinking, if not the strict colonization, of Great Britain's model as it became an international power in the late 19th and 20th century.

During the era of the 1898 Spanish-American War, the United States' Uncle Sam was pictured in *Judge* as following Great Britain's John Bull in picking up "The White Man's Burden" by carrying Cubans and other dark-skinned people up from oppression, barbarism, and ignorance to civilization.

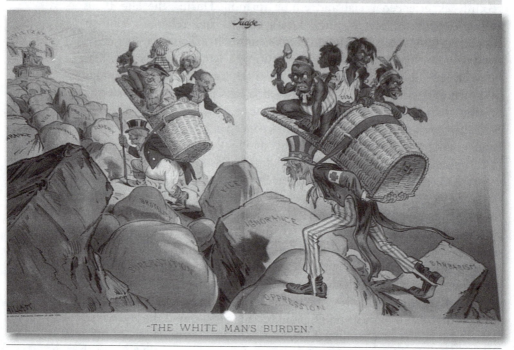

"THE WHITE MAN'S BURDEN."

Source: Judge, 1898.

"The British colonial code draws the most rigid color line of all," wrote Raymond Kennedy in 1945, when Britain still maintained much of its colonial empire. "The British have been in contact for a longer time with more dark peoples than any other western nation, yet they hold aloof from their subjects to an unequalled degree. They refuse to associate freely or make friends with other races, and their exclusiveness had engendered a reciprocal feeling toward them on the part of their colonial peoples."[39]

In England and elsewhere, the children's stories, literature, movies, news coverage, and other media during the era of the British Empire reinforced images of English colonizers bringing civilization to the uncivilized people they colonized before the United States also picked up the White man's burden in the Third World in the early 20th century.

The links between popular British and U.S. stereotypes of people of color outlasted the British Empire. From 1958 to 1978, one of the British Broadcasting Company's most popular television programs was *The Black and White Minstrel Show,* which featured White entertainers in blackface. The program was set in "the Deep South where coy White women could be seen being wooed by docile, smiling black slaves. The black men were, in fact, White artists 'Blacked-up,'" wrote British media scholar Sarita

Malik. She added that the "racist implications of the premise of the pro-gramme" were what "largely led to the programme's eventual demise."[40]

As the 21st century loomed, the British Empire's media images of peo-ple of color were still being addressed by journalists and media scholars in England[41] and in other lands still part of the British Empire, such as Australia.[42] A study in the mid-1990s found only 12 to 20 Black journalists among the 3,000 workers on Britain's national newspapers, leading to charges that England's news media were "blind to Blacks" and other reports that "Black and Asian faces are rare among Britain's 'news breed.'"[43]

Spain colonized most of Latin America, including what is now the U.S. Southwest from Texas to California and as far north as parts of Wyoming. In the Spanish and Portuguese colonies of Latin America, the racial situation was less clearly defined for those indigenous people who survived the conquest and colonial missions. In all countries the European nation expropriated the lands of the indigenous peoples, making them slaves or peons working the lands in some countries and importing African slaves in others. But, although there were class distinctions between the Spanish Europeans and the indigenous people, there were also intermarriage and elaborate classification systems to label and identify offspring by their racial mixture, with European-born Whites at the top.

As a result, mixed racial populations emerged in Mexico and other places, where Spanish mixed with native populations to blend into mesti-zos, and in Brazil and the Caribbean, where Spanish and native people mixed with Black slaves brought from Africa to form mulattos. In contrast to English colonists, who marginalized the identity of the offspring of White and indigenous parents by calling them "half-breed," the Spanish term *mestizo* indicates a mixture and blending of races and cultures.

Colonialism in Asia and Southeast Asia was shared by several nations, including Britain, France, the Netherlands, Portugal, and Spain, each with different policies toward the indigenous residents of the area. Like the Portuguese in Brazil, some colonizing nations also brought in laborers from other areas: Indians from India to Burma and Malaysians and Chi-nese to most of Southeast Asia. As a result, these colonized areas became stratified on three levels: Europeans, immigrant workers, and the natives.[44] English and Portuguese colonies in Asia continued into the 1990s, long after European nations had given up their African and American colonies.

In the American, African, and Asian colonies of European nations, the relationship between minorities and majorities was the opposite of what racial minorities have experienced in the United States. In the colonial situa-tion, the numerical minority groups were the European colonizers, who conquered and then governed the native people who outnumbered them. In this case, the term *minority* could be applied to the Europeans who, though smaller in number, exerted military, political, economic, and social control over the native populations. Thus, while the Europeans may have been a numerical minority, they were not a power minority. A legacy of this relation-ship, and the fight of indigenous people to regain their rights, could still be seen in the relationship of Whites over Blacks in South Africa, where Nelson Mandela, the first Black to head the government, was not elected until the

As the 19th century ended, the magazine *Puck* showed Uncle Sam trying to teach unruly dark-skinned Filipinos, Hawaiians, Puerto Ricans, and Cubans in the front row of a class with neatly groomed children representing lands previously conquered by the United States behind them. Pictured, but not participating in the class, are a Black man washing windows, a Native American boy in the corner reading a book upside down, and a Chinese girl hopefully looking in from the outside.

SCHOOL BEGINS

Source: Puck January 25, 1899, pp. 8–9, Louis Dalrymple, copyrighted by Keppler & Schwarzmann.

mid-1990s; in Hong Kong, which was not transferred from British to Chinese rule until 1997; and in Macau, which was held by Portugal until 1998.

The legacies of colonialism and distinctions based on race are found throughout the world. As Charles F. Marden and Gladys Meyer point out in their book *Minorities in American Society,* nations as diverse in political and economic structure as South Africa, Israel, Soviet Russia, and the People's Republic of China have substantial differences based on ethnic and racial divisions between dominant and subordinate groups.[45] The heated conflicts between Blacks and Whites in South Africa and between Jews and Arabs in Israel and other parts of the Middle East have been widely reported. Less well known in the United States is what Marden and Meyer call "the virtual destruction of small tribal people in Asiatic Russia"[46] and the annexation of Tibetan people by the People's Republic of China in the late 1940s.

Except for the Native Americans, who were subjected to colonization by the Spanish and extermination by the English, minority groups in the United States have followed patterns that are different from those of other nations. This is because the predominantly White Europeans who were to dominate the country were themselves immigrants who became the numerical majority. Rather than exert their control only through a rigid class system, they exterminated or confined the Native Americans; waged war to take lands held first by Native Americans and then by Mexicans; imported and restricted the rights of Blacks, Asians, and Latinos as needed; and encouraged more European immigrants to come, settle, and develop a new society of White European immigrants in the United States. Between 1820 and 1970, 45 million immigrants entered the United States, 75% of them from European nations.[47] It is these immigrants, their children, and their grandchildren who consolidated their identity through the melting pot and became the new majority in the United States, leaving people of color to be designated as racial and ethnic minorities.

RACIAL AND ETHNIC DIVERSITY: PROBLEM OR OPPORTUNITY?

Growing racial and ethnic diversity will drive the nation's population through the foreseeable future. The census and projected growth figures clearly show where the United States is headed in the future. How the media and other institutions react to these demographic changes will, to a large extent, determine whether the United States is still considered the land of opportunity for all.

The question is: How will people adapt to a society in which everyone is in a minority group? The answer probably lies in changing the dialogue on race and ethnicity from a focus on sociology to a focus on psychology. Until the early 21st century, race and ethnicity in the United States were dominated by sociology: numbers, demographics, and statistical analyses of the different groups. In the next era the discussion should focus more on psychology. While the numbers set the stage, the importance of these statistics will be known only as people make individual decisions regarding their own attitudes and behavior amid growing diversity. Will they withdraw into their own group, perhaps with more people than before? Will they interact with members of other groups, also more numerous than before? Will they intermarry? Will they learn to appreciate new kinds of music, food, and cultures? How will the media prepare people for the changing society, and how will people use media targeted to them and to other groups?

MEDIA AND DIVERSITY: MAXIMIZING OPPORTUNITY?

The growth of racial diversity in the United States has forced the media to reexamine the ways they have traditionally dealt with people of color. As these groups grow at a rate that outstrips the Anglo population both in number and as a percentage of the population, the media executives have looked for new ways to deal with them.

Too often the growth of a racially and ethnically diverse population has been portrayed as a problem for the media and other institutions, forcing them to change their methods of doing business and making them cater to groups that tenaciously hang on to their cultural roots in a nation in which other immigrants have willingly shed theirs. These differences in physical appearance, language, culture, religion, and lifestyle are sometimes seen as threats to Anglo American values, not assets, as the United States seeks to build relationships with countries around the world.

Some media, while professing concern over the changing populations, consciously adopted strategies that appear to be an attempt to avoid minority groups as they moved into the nation's cities. They moved from building audiences based on *geography*, focusing on readers, viewers, and listeners living or working nearest the media outlet, to building audiences based on *demography*, focusing on readers, viewers, and listeners who fit a desired age, education, income, race, or gender profile. In the long run, this has led to more ethnic class media targeted to people of color. But earlier, this change was characterized by general audience mass media efforts to avoid or bypass growing numbers of people of color.

In the 1970s and 1980s, at the same time that the inner cities were becoming increasingly racially diverse, some big-city newspapers looked for ways to avoid the potential readers living closest to their offices, but chase those who were living in suburban cities and counties. Denying any racist intentions, the newspaper managers said they were merely following the more affluent readers who moved to the suburbs.

The strategies of newspapers in avoiding the inner city were described by Ben Bagdikian of the University of California, Berkeley, in a 1978 article.[48] He cited newspapers in different parts of the nation that consciously adopted circulation and news reporting strategies that avoided the growing numbers of minorities and low-income residents in central city areas, while reaching out to readers in the predominantly Anglo and more affluent suburbs of those cities.

"The blackout of news to the central city is usually justified by publishers on grounds that it is harder to sell papers there, that it is harder to hire and keep delivery people on the job and there is a higher rate of nonpayment of bills," Bagdikian wrote. "That is true, and it has always been true. The difference now is that advertisers don't want that population so now the publishers don't either."

Because advertisers wanted affluent readers, newspapers and broadcast media targeted their content to audiences in the more affluent, and predominantly Anglo, suburban areas. Circulation percentages and actual numbers declined in the cities whose names the newspapers proudly wore on their front pages, and ratings dropped in cities that television stations were awarded federal licenses to serve. Broadcasters, while they could not control who watched or listened to their stations and bore no additional costs for having low-income people tuned into their broadcasts, tried to target news and entertainment programming to more affluent viewers and listeners. The ABC network issued a demographic analysis of its audience in the 1970s titled "Some People Are More Valuable Than Others."

This mentality apparently continued into the 21st century. In 2002, *San Francisco Chronicle* television critic Tim Goodman wrote a front-page article headlined "Un-Reality TV: Few Minority Actors in S.F. Shows," noting the absence of non-White lead characters in the growing number of television programs based in San Francisco, one of the nation's most racially diverse cities.[49] After a yearlong study of television news practices, longtime TV network news executive Av Westin reported in 2001 his "project's most sobering discovery: Every week—every day—stories about African-Americans, Hispanics, and Asians are kept off the air . . . I feel confident in declaring that racism is alive and well in many television newsrooms around the country." As in the 1970s, Westin cited broadcaster desires to achieve certain viewer demographics as driving race-based news decisions. One former news executive told him, "[Blacks] don't get the demo."[50]

In 1978, *Los Angeles Times* publisher Otis Chandler admitted to an interviewer that the *Times* had "a way to go" in adequately covering Los Angeles' minority communities. But he added that it "would not make sense financially for us" to direct the newspaper to those readers because "that audience does not have the purchasing power and is not responsive to the kind of advertising we carry."[51]

"So we could make the editorial commitment, the management commitment, to cover these communities," Chandler said. "But then how do we get them to read the *Times?* It's not their kind of newspaper: it's too big, it's too stuffy. If you will, it's too complicated." In a 1979 *Columbia Journalism Review* article by two authors of this book, Chandler and other *Times* executives denied that the newspaper approached coverage and circulation from a racial standpoint, although one did admit the strategy meant the newspaper was directed at a predominantly Anglo audience. John Mount of the *Times*'s marketing research department said, "We don't approach marketing from a racial standpoint. It just happens that the more affluent and educated people tend to be White and live in suburban communities."[52]

"Our major retail advertisers have said to us that 'We want a certain class of audience, a certain demographic profile of reader, whether that person be Black, White, or Brown or Chinese or whatever. We don't really care what sex or race they are. But we do care about their income,'" Chandler said. He also expressed optimism that more minorities would begin to read the *Times* "as their income goes up and their educational level comes up and they become interested in a paper like the *Times.* Then they become prospects for our advertisers."

Unlike earlier newcomers to the United States, 21st-century immigrants stay in close touch with their home country through daily news reports, such as Korean-language KBS World live television news with English-language news running at the bottom of the screen. Cultural ties are transferred from generation to generation through language, music, and food, as illustrated by this grandmother and granddaughter shopping at a California grocery store specializing in Mexican food.

By the 21st century, it was clear that Chandler's dream would not come true. Los Angeles and Southern California were growing as one of the nation's most racially and ethnically diverse regions. Yet, *Los Angeles Times* circulation, whether measured by the numbers of readers or by the percentage of Southern Californians who read the paper, was lower than when he made the projection in 1978. Instead of turning their attention to the *Times,* many members of racial and ethnic groups turned to broadcast, print, and digital ethnic media that covered them and things they cared about. The highest-rated local newscast in Los Angeles and many other major cities was the Spanish-language Univision news. The *Times* had to compete for readers against strong regional newspapers, more radio and television stations, and print, broadcast, and digital media targeting racial and ethnic audiences. The *Times* couldn't afford to sit back and wait for people of color to fulfill Chandler's hope they would "become interested in a paper like the *Times.*"

The lesson that the *Los Angeles Times* and other media learned is that a growing racially and ethnically diverse population is not a problem for the media, but an opportunity. Instead of trying to bypass non-White readers and coverage, news organizations that made the greatest gains are those that have seen the growing opportunities presented by racial diversity not as a problem to be solved. Some general audience media, such as English-language daily newspapers and television news programs, had a hard time learning that, if they wanted people of color to pay more attention to them, they had to pay more attention to people of color.

Notes

1. "An Older and More Diverse Nation by Midcentury," News Release, U.S. Census Bureau, August 14, 2008.

2. "The New Minority-Majority," Digital Journal, May 22, 2009, Newstex ID: 35154054.

3. Kelefa Sanneh, "Beyond the Pale: Is White the New Black?," *New Yorker,* April 12, 2010, 69–74.

4. Analyses of data from the 2010 chapter are largely drawn from Mark Mather, Kevin Pollard, and Linda A. Jacobsen, *First Results From the 2010 Census* (Washington, DC: Reports on America, Population Reference Bureau, July 2011).

5. Leon F. Bouvier and Cary B. Davis, *The Future Racial Composition of the United States* (Washington, DC: Demographic Information Services Center of the Population Reference Bureau, August 1982), 1, 3.

6. Peter D. Salins, "Assimilation, American Style," accessed May 18, 2012, reason.com/9702/fe.salins.shtml, excerpted from Peter D. Salins, *Assimilation, American Style* (New York: Basic Books, 1997).

7. Nathan Glazer and Daniel Patrick Moynihan, *Beyond the Melting Pot: The Negroes, Puerto Ricans, Jews, Italians, and Irish of New York City* (Cambridge, MA: MIT Press, 1963).

8. For an analysis of this phenomenon see Milton Gordon, *Assimilation in American Life* (New York: Oxford University Press, 1964).

9. Boris Sanchez de Lozada and Robert Armoush, *Henry Ford & The Five Dollar Day,* http://web.bryant.edu/~ehu/h364proj/summ_99/armoush/index.htm.

10. For more information see Mary Waters, *Ethnic Options: Choosing Identities in America* (Berkeley: University of California Press, 1990).

11. Paul Muschick, "Census Raising New Racial Questions," *Greensboro News & Record,* April 16, 2001, B1; "Understanding the Data," *The Orange County Register,* March 30, 2001.

12. Mather et al., op. cit., 8–9.

13. Figure 1, *Overview of Race and Hispanic Origin,* 2010 Census Briefs (U.S. Census Bureau, March 2011), 1.

14. *The Arab Population: 2000,* Census 2000 Brief (U.S. Census Bureau, December 2003).

15. *Muslim Americans: A National Portrait* (Muslim West Facts Project, a Partnership Between Gallup's Center for Muslim Studies and the Coexist Foundation, 2009), 20–21.

16. See *Overview of Race and Hispanic Origin,* op. cit., 3–7, for tables and descriptions of these data.

17. Ibid., 22.

18. Mather et al., op. cit., 6.

19. Janet Elliott and Julie Mason, "Democrats Say Census Costs State; Using Only Raw Data Affects Federal Dollars," *The Houston Chronicle,* October 18, 2001, A29.

20. Donald L. Evans, *Prepared Testimony of Honorable Donald L. Evans Secretary of Commerce Before the Senate Committee on Commerce, Science and Transportation* (Washington, DC, March 28, 2001).

21. Elliott and Mason, op. cit., A29.

22. Amon Emeka and Jody Agius Vallejo, "Non-Hispanics With Latin American Ancestry: Assimilation, Race and Identity Among Latin American Descendants in the U.S.," *Social Science Research* (November 2011): 1547–1563.

23. Jesse Washington, "Identity Crisis for Asian-Americans," *Oakland Tribune: Bay Area News Group,* December 4, 2011, A8.

24. Gordon Trowbridge, "Arab Americans Lose Out in Census; No Ethnic Box Costs Political, Economic Clout," *The Detroit News,* March 26, 2001, 1.

25. Jack Chang, "Bay Area Afghan-American Members Dispute Statistics," *Contra Costa Times,* November 21, 2001, A1.

26. Tony Pugh, "Mixed Marriages on the Rise in U.S: Racial, Ethnic Barriers Abating as Country Becomes More Diverse," *The Houston Chronicle,* March 25, 2001, A12; Wendy Wang, "The Rise of Intermarriage: Rates, Characteristics Vary by Race and Gender" (Pew Research Center Social & Demographic Trends, February 16, 2012).

27. William H. Frey, "America's Diverse Future: Initial Glimpses at the U.S. Child Population From the 2010 Census," *State of Metropolitan America* 29 (Brookings Institution, April 6, 2011).

28. Bouvier and Davis, op. cit., 2.

29. "No. 7. Immigrants by Country of Birth: 1981–1998," *Statistical Abstract of the United States: 2001* (Washington, DC: U.S. Census Bureau), 11.

30. "Origin of Legal Immigrants, 2009," *Yearbook of Immigration Statistics,* accessed May 18, 2012, http://www.dhs.gov/files/statistics/publications/yearbook .shtm; Jeffrey Passel and D'Vera Cohn, "U.S. Foreign-Born Population: How Much Change From 2009 to 2010?" (Pew Research Center, Pew Hispanic Center, February 21, 2012).

31. "No. 70. Births and Birth Rates by Race, Sex, and Age: 1980 to 1999" and "No. 74. Projected Fertility Rates by Race, Origin and Age Group: 2000 and 2010," *Statistical Abstract of the United States: 2001* (Washington, DC: U.S. Census Bureau), 60, 62.

32. Robert Pear, "New Look at the U.S. in 2050: Bigger, Older and Less White," *New York Times,* December 4, 1992, A1, D18.

33. "Table 79. Live Births, Birth Rates, and Fertility Rates by Hispanic Origin: 2000 to 2008" and "Table 81. Births, Birth Rates, and Fertility Rates by Race, Sex, and Age: 1980 to 2008," *Statistical Abstract of the United States: 2012* (Washington, DC: U.S. Census Bureau), 65–66.

34. Margaret Udansky, "Minorities Are Headed Toward the Majority," *USA Today,* December 4–6, 1992, 1A.

35. Bouvier and Davis, op. cit., 57.

36. "What Does the 1980 Census Show? Looking Ahead and Looking Back," *Public Opinion,* 15–16, 1981.

37. Michelle Chen, "Acuna: The New Culture Wars," *CultureStrike,* accessed January 21, 2012, http://wordstrike.net/acuna-ethnic-studies-and-the-new-culture-wars.

38. Ravi Somaiya, "London Neighborhood Smoldering," Morning Report, *Oakland Tribune,* August 8, 2011, AA1.

39. Raymond Kennedy, "The Colonial Crisis and the Future," in Ralph Linton (Ed.), *The Science of Man in the World Crisis* (Columbia University Press, 1945), 320, as cited in Charles F. Marden and Gladys Meyer, *Minorities in American Society* (D. Van Nostrand Company, 1978), 5. For an analysis of the role of the media

in Great Britain and their relationship to racial minorities, see Paul Hartmann and Charles Hubbard, *Racism and the Mass Media* (Rowman & Littlefield, 1974).

40. Sarita Malik, "The Black and White Minstrel Show," accessed 2002, www .mbcnet.org/archives/etv/B/htmlB/blackandwhim/blackandwhim.htm, 2.

41. See Sarita Malik, *Representing Black Britain: Black and Asian Images on Television* (Thousand Oaks, CA: Sage, 2001); "What Colour Is the News? Minority Journalists Hold Key to Media's Role in Multicultural Britain," *Chronicle World*, accessed 2002, www.chronicleworld.org.

42. See Andrew Jakubowicz, *Racism, Ethnicity and the Media* (Australian Cultural Series, Allen & Unwin, 1994); Michael Meadows, *Voices in the Wilderness: Images of Aboriginal People in the Australian Media* (Greenwood Press, 2001).

43. "What Colour Is the News?," op. cit.

44. Marden and Meyer, op. cit., 6–7.

45. Ibid., 10–15.

46. Ibid., 14.

47. Ibid., 63–64.

48. Ben H. Bagdikian, "The Best News Money Can Buy," *Human Behavior* (October 1978): 63–66.

49. Tim Goodman, "Un-Reality TV: Few Minority Actors in S.F. Shows," *San Francisco Chronicle*, July 24, 2002, A1.

50. Av Westin, "The Color of Ratings," *Brills Content* (April 2001).

51. Félix Gutiérrez and Clint C. Wilson II, "The Demographic Dilemma," *Columbia Journalism Review* (January/February 1979): 53.

52. Ibid.

2 Media Matter

How much do you know about the people who first lived on what is now called North America?

Think about it. How much do you know about the people who lived in nomadic tribes and permanent villages across what is now the United States? Do you know what languages they spoke? What they liked to eat? Can you describe how they dressed? Or what their villages looked like? Or how they defended themselves against the Europeans who invaded their homelands? How about their lives today? What are their prospects for the future?

If you're like most people in the United States, you probably know some, but not all, answers to those questions. You know some things about Native Americans but not as much as you might think you should know. And, unless you're Native American yourself, much of what you know you probably learned from the media. At some time or another, you've seen a movie, viewed a television program, or read a news article about Native Americans.

Now, try to remember what you learned about Native Americans from these media: from movies, television, newspapers, and magazines. Chances are, you won't remember much factual information. Aside from their presence in Western movies, appearances as sports team mascots, and coverage in an occasional news report, Native Americans are invisible in the media of the United States. The squaws, warriors, and chieftains featured often are images from the 19th century that portray Native Americans as they were seen by Whites, not as they saw themselves. Movies and television programs have traditionally treated Native Americans as savages vanquished by a superior civilization whose people now tell the stories. Team mascots that use heroic or warlike images of indigenous people to strike fear into their opponents use war paint, tomahawks, and battle cries evoking images of the "Redskins" and "Braves" as seen by Whites in the past, not the present-day lives of Native Americans. When Native Americans are covered by the news media, the stories often fall into one of two categories: "zoo stories" and "problem people stories." The *zoo stories* feature colorful powwows with costumed Native American drummers and dancers displaying people who are apparently frozen in a past that has little connection with modern life. The *problem people stories* show Native Americans either as overburdened by problems of their own, such as poverty and alcoholism, or as the source of problems for others, such as operating casinos on reservation lands. Although both types of stories merit some coverage, neither provides adequate coverage of Native Americans today.

All of us depend on the media to portray and define those things that we have not personally experienced. We "learn" about others through radio, websites, television, movies, video games, newspapers, and magazines. The portrayals and news coverage of Native Americans and other groups in those media can become reality in our minds, especially if we have personal experiences with Native American people to balance them against. The impact of media images of people of color and other underrepresented groups on society has been amply described and documented by scholars who have examined how the media affect society.[1]

The Functions of Media in Society

Over the years, many scholars have described the functions of the media in modern society. While they disagree on some details, they all agree on the media's pervasive influence on American society. In a 1948 essay that is often cited by other researchers, Harold Lasswell described the three major functions of communication:

1. *Surveillance* of the environment, disclosing threats and opportunities affecting the value position of the community and of the component parts within it.

2. *Correlation* of the different parts of society in responding to environment.

3. *Transmission* of the social heritage from one generation to the next.[2]

Examined as part of a society with many racial and ethnic minority groups and a majority group that, to a large extent, controls the dominant media, Lasswell's *surveillance* function of the media assigns to the media the lookout role of scanning the society to define and describe the different racial and ethnic groups within it. The *correlation* function of the media helps the consumers of the media take stock of those groups and determine how and where they fit into the society. Finally, the *transmission* function of the media both defines what the social culture and heritage of the society are and transmits them to other members of the society. This process, whether those with the power have consciously engineered it or not, includes some cultures, excludes others, and redefines all the cultures for the audience.

Although the United States prides itself on being a democratic society built on rational public opinion formed through broad dissemination of information, Lasswell (1948) noted that communication can be altered when the ruling elements of the society sense a threat from an inside or outside group.

> In society, the communication process reveals special characteristics when the ruling element is afraid of the internal as well as the external environment. In gauging the efficiency of communication in any given context, it is necessary to take into account the values at stake, and the identity of the group whose position is being examined.[3]

Lasswell reinforces the importance of the fact that the media behave differently when leaders perceive a threat, especially when a particular group is linked to that threat. The group could be identified by its politics, religion, race, ethnicity, age, gender, or any other characteristic linked to it by the media. In these cases, the media must provide a consistent message that communicates a cohesive opinion of that threat or group to others in the society.

If we apply Lasswell's media functions to portrayals of Native Americans, it is not surprising that most people in the United States have little accurate information about native people. The news media have historically treated native people through the surveillance function, watching the horizon and reporting on them as heathen savages when they defended their lands, people, and culture from European intruders. As part of their correlation function, the media defined Native Americans as primitive people who stood in the way of the progress of the Whites who were fulfilling their Manifest Destiny to "civilize" and populate North America. Native people were often portrayed as unable to adapt to the ways of the Whites and worthy only of annihilation, subjugation, or confinement to reservations. Finally, the transmission function of the media defined the culture of the continent as the culture developed by and for European newcomers rather than the culture of Native American people.

Most of us may have limited knowledge about the cultures and civilizations of Native Americans, but not because what we know about them is derived from the way they were covered in the newspapers and magazines published during the White westward expansion of the 19th century. For the most part, our images of the people the Europeans called "Indians" have been shaped by the movies, television programs, and Western novels we have seen or read over the years.

These media are primarily designed not to be informative but to entertain. That is why in 1959 Charles Wright added a fourth dimension to Lasswell's three functions: the *entertainment* function, which emphasized that communication can also entertain the society.[4] The entertainment images and portrayals of Native Americans have become reality in the minds of many who have seen Native Americans in movies and on television but nowhere else.

Later, others noted that in addition to these four functions, the media perform an important *economic* function in society. Communication scholars Wilbur Schramm and William Porter wrote in 1982 that although no economist had as yet outlined the economic functions of the media with the specificity of Lasswell's functions, it was possible to describe the economic roles of the media.

> For one thing, communication must meet the need for an economic map of the environment so that each individual and organization can form its own image of buying and selling opportunities at a given moment. For another, there must be correlation of economic policy, whether by the individual, the organization, or the nation. . . . Finally, instruction in the skills and expectations of economic behavior must be available.[5]

Other scholars took a more bottom-line approach to describing the economic role of the media. In a 1972 textbook, Peter Sandman, David Rubin, and David Sachsman described the economic function of the media as "to make money."[6] In another edition of the book 10 years later, they broadened their description to read "to serve the economic system" and emphasized the central role of business in the operation of media in the United States.

> The fundamental economic purpose of the mass media in the United States is to sell people to advertisers. Economically, the articles in your newspaper and the programs on your radio and TV sets are merely "come-ons" to catch and hold your attention. Advertisers buy that attention from the media, and use it to sell you their products and services. In the process, both the media and the advertisers earn substantial profits.[7]

Today, almost all the media, including those that do not depend on advertiser support—such as movies, blogs, social media, CDs, DVDs, many digital sites and applications, and some cable television channels— also serve the economic system. Increasingly, corporations pay to have their products placed in movies, push advertising e-mail to World Wide Web users, and copromote their products with movie and music productions. Most media are owned and operated by corporations that sell a product to an audience or advertisers, are privately held, issue stock, and generate profits or losses for their shareholders.

This role of the media in the economy has become even more important in the last two decades as media have been bought, sold, and merged in multibillion-dollar deals. As the United States has developed into an information economy, these mergers and purchases have served the economic system by concentrating media ownership in fewer corporations, all positioning themselves to become more profitable by creating, buying, selling, and distributing news, entertainment, and information. Some of what they provide is fresh, such as the content of daily news sites and prime-time network television programs. But other content is taken off

the shelf, recycled, and sold over and over again, such as many cable programs, DVDs of movies, and downloaded digital music featuring actors
and artists who are no longer alive.

The media must serve the economic system because they are private
businesses, rather than publicly supported institutions such as public
schools or libraries. Because they are part of the private enterprise system, the media must behave as other corporations and businesses do,
seeking income and profits by maximizing the number of people consuming their products while lowering the costs of production and
distribution.

Thus we find that scholars have described five central functions for the
media in the United States.[8] These are as follows:

1. *Surveillance:* the sentinel or lookout role of the media, that is,
   watching the society and horizon for threats to the established order
   and information on people or places of public interest and reporting
   these to the audience.

2. *Correlation:* the interpretation and linking function of the
   media, which helps the audience to understand, interpret, and
   comprehend what is happening in and out of the society (and
   how these events affect each other) and to stay in touch with others in the society.

3. *Transmission:* the socialization function of the media, in which the
   media define the society and its norms and values to the audience
   and, through their portrayals and coverage, assist members of the
   society in adopting, using, and acting on those values.

4. *Entertainment:* the function of the media for diversion and enjoy-
   ment, in which the media provide stories, features, music, and films
   designed to make the audiences laugh, cry, relax, or reflect rather
   than gain information.

5. *Economic service:* the role of the media within the economic system
   of the society, which in the United States means that most media
   function as businesses serving the needs of shareholders and other
   corporations by selling a product that they either produce or attract.

The Mass Media and the Mass Audience

The U.S. media could fulfill all of these functions without treating
members of racial and ethnic minority groups any differently than they
treat the majority. However, in the early 19th century the development of
communication media changed course as the American political, economic,
and racial identity was being formed. Earlier, the framers of the U.S.
Constitution foresaw a system in which the media would operate in a free

marketplace of ideas. They hoped for a society in which every political group, every interest group, or anyone else with the money, message, and motivation would print and disseminate newspapers, books, and pamphlets to promote their views.

It was hoped that the new republic's voters, at that time limited to some White males, would choose from the wide variety of diverse media and, after weighing different versions of information and opinions, would make an informed choice at the polling place. The media were seen both as the public's watchdogs on the government and as important communication links on which the new democratic society would depend for information. For this reason, the First Amendment to the U.S. Constitution prohibits Congress from making laws limiting the freedom of the press—the only private business sector with constitutional protection from government.

But the First Amendment also had what some say is a "fatal flaw." In freeing the press from governmental restraints, the framers of the Constitution also withdrew the government licenses and financial subsidies that had been given to official government or sanctioned media in Europe and America. The press, while freed from the laws of Congress, was forced to function as a business within the unwritten economic laws of capitalism governing business in the United States. For several decades after the First Amendment was ratified in 1791, newspapers and magazines focused on specialized content in class media for targeted audiences. Political parties subsidized their own party newspapers, ethnic media in different languages targeted non-English-language readers, and business publications were published for merchants. But in the 1830s, there emerged a new formula that dominated the development of the media in the United States through the end of the 20th century: the penny press.

The penny press first gained success with the *New York Sun,* which appeared in 1833 and sold for only one cent. The newspaper made a profit through a new form uniquely adapted to the free enterprise system. Unlike competing newspapers, its primary income did not depend on subsidies from a political party, government placed public notices, or reader subscriptions. Benjamin Day, founder of the *New York Sun,* envisioned the penny press as a newspaper for the mass audience of city residents who would be drawn by the newspaper's lively content, low price, and promise that "It Shines for ALL."[9] The newspaper's formula, which was widely imitated, was successful in attracting readers. But readers were not the only ones interested in the penny press.

> Another person began to take a special interest in the newspaper for the masses. This was the advertiser, who was impressed by the amazing circulation of the new medium. Putting an ad in every publication bought by small splinter groups was expensive and ineffective sales promotion. The large circulation of the penny papers now made it feasible to publicize articles for sale that formerly would not have warranted advertising expense.[10]

Given the successful formula developed by the penny press, the most successful media in the United States were not *class* communication media, attracting audience segments for many competing views, but *mass* communication media, attracting a large audience to a few mass circulation media outlets. The space for the advertisement in the newspaper or time on the television screen has no economic value by itself. Its worth is based on the size of the audience attracted by the news or entertainment content of the print or broadcast media. As media strove to accumulate larger and larger audiences, they developed content that would attract the widest audience possible and offend the fewest people.

Rather than class media, a variety of small outlets addressing the needs of different segments of society, the dominant media in the United States became mass media seeking a large audience drawn from all groups. As a result, the class media serving political, religious, or racial and ethnic minorities were consigned to a second-class media status because they did not attract a mass audience. The activities of those groups, as well as of women, were either ignored by the mass media or portrayed in a way that made them palatable to the mass audience. Mass media in the United States were meant not to serve all the groups in the masses but to amass people into a large audience as consumer targets for advertisers.

In an effort to amass the largest possible audience in a nation of immigrants and their descendants, the mass media tried to cultivate broad common interests and address the media content to those interests, whether in news, entertainment, or information. The media that most successfully attracted the mass audience could charge the highest rates to print and broadcast advertisers or, in the case of records, DVDs, and movies, sell the most products. The advertisers, with their seemingly insatiable appetite for larger audiences for their advertisements, fueled the media's chase of the mass audience. But advertising's important role in shaping mass media content was not always appreciated by scholars describing how the U.S. media developed.

Historian David Potter wrote in 1954 that

> histories of American periodicals and even of the mass media deal with advertising as if it were a side issue. Students of the radio and of the mass-circulation magazines frequently condemn advertising for its conspicuous role, as if it were a mere interloper in a separate, pre-existing, self-contained aesthetic world of actors, musicians, authors, and script-writers; they hardly recognize that advertising created modern American radio and television, transformed the modern newspaper, evoked the modern slick periodical, and remains the vital essence of each of them at the present time.[11]

Although the variety of media has greatly increased in the decades since Potter wrote, and the media now offer a wider range of content for different segments of American society, the fundamental relationship that he described between advertising and the media has not changed. In the era when the mass media dominated all the media, this relationship dictated that racial and ethnic minority groups were treated in ways that did not challenge but, rather, reflected and reinforced the majority society's attitudes toward these groups in order to attract the largest audience possible.

The Mass Media and the Collective Consciousness

As advertisers demanded mass audiences for their products, media corporations responded by adopting news and entertainment strategies that would attract the largest numbers of people. At that time, the people targeted by the mass media in the United States were White, many of them European immigrants looking to the media to learn about the people of their new nation. Men and women of color, such as Blacks, Latinos, Native Americans, and Asian Pacific Americans, were treated by the media as fringe audiences, not large enough in number to influence the content directed to the mass audience. If the media offended people of color by omitting or misrepresenting them, the favorable response of the majority White audience more than made up for the dissatisfaction of the minority.

However, the mass audience was by no means homogeneous, especially in a nation of immigrants from different countries, with different religions, and speaking many languages. In fact, the people in the predominantly White mass audience were not identical to each other. The mass audience included rich and poor, young and old, city and country, men and women: all with different needs and interests. The challenges facing the mass media were to find common themes and content that would attract people from all the desired groups and to look for things they could share.

The media thus shaped and reinforced the collective consciousness needed to attract large numbers of people in a heterogeneous society. The mass media's mission was to find common interests among members of the audience: themes, images, interests, and ideas that would attract the mass audience. To draw the largest possible audience, the media developed content that would attract the lowest common denominator of shared interests in the audience. This meant that the mass media reinforced, rather than challenged, the attitudes and practices of the society. If they would have done otherwise, they would have risked offending significant audience segments and losing the mass audience demanded by the advertisers.

Most immigrants came from Europe in varying shades of White and could be expected to blend together within a generation or two without physical differences separating them. Driven by a melting pot mentality, the U.S. media often treated as outsiders the members of groups that had not assimilated or had not been allowed to assimilate. Racial and ethnic minorities identifiable by color or facial features were placed beyond the melting pot, unable to completely blend because of physical characteristics.

People who could not easily melt into society often were not targeted as audiences by the mass media. Movies, broadcast programs, newspapers, and news magazines generally overlooked the daily issues confronting people of color in the United States, as well as their culture and traditions. Instead, people of color became targets of the media. When they did appear in the media, it was often in stereotypical roles that catered to White society's images of people of color, such as the camel-riding Arab, bandana-wearing Black mammy, Indian chief in feathered war bonnet, greasy Mexican bandito, and South Pacific maiden wearing a grass skirt. Although all stereotypes have some elements of truth, these gross characterizations were based on the preconceptions outsiders had of the groups rather than on the realities of the groups themselves. They were pictures filtered through Anglo eyes, rather than honest reflections of the people portrayed. Seen through a microscope, they may have been part of the people portrayed. But the media became a magnifying glass that enlarged these images out of proportion and presented to the audience a distorted image of the people portrayed.

Symbols, Stereotypes, and the Mass Media

The mass media came to rely on symbols and stereotypes as shorthand ways of communicating to the diversity of people in the mass audience through newspaper headlines, movie characterizations, and television pictures. Images of rich bankers, heroic cowboys, or old spinsters were used so that audiences would understand the character the first time he or she appeared on the screen or in the story. Newspapers used terms such as *right wing, leftist,* and *moderate* in headlines as symbols that characterized people or groups along different points of the political spectrum.

These symbols were a useful shorthand for the mass media, since they allowed the entertainment and news media to portray even complex personalities and issues with a shortened character or term. Thus, when the audience at a Western movie saw a man come on the screen wearing a white hat, they knew that he was the hero. Or when the term *leftist* was used in a headline, it meant that the group that the term symbolized was on the liberal extreme, bordering on communism. The terms became *symbols* that made complex matters easier to handle by triggering recall of preconceived *stereotypes* that Walter Lippmann, in his 1922 book *Public Opinion,* described as "pictures in our heads."[12]

Media symbols are like digital screen icons. When using a computer, laptop, tablet, or cell phone, we have learned that when we see an icon and

Symbolic images of people of color featured in early-20th-century travel stickers and food labels triggered stereotypes held by many Whites in the United States and also reinforced false images of the people portrayed, including sexualized images of women of color.

point to it, a click or tap will bring something we want to the screen. The *symbol* is the icon we see on the screen, and the *stereotype* is the function the computer brings to the screen when we click on the icon. In the same way, media images of people of color, such as fat Mexican maids, fast-talking Black street hustlers, noble Indian chiefs, and karate-chopping Asians, have become symbols that trigger stereotypes of the people portrayed and of others who look like them.

Racial and ethnic minorities have been among the people portrayed by symbols and stereotypes in mass entertainment and news media through much of this nation's history. As discussed in subsequent chapters, through the 1960s, unrestricted stereotypes of Native Americans, Blacks, Asian Pacific Americans, and Latinos made up nearly all of the portrayals of the people in these groups in the entertainment media of movies, radio, fiction, and television.

Similarly, news media rarely covered the activities of the people in these communities unless, in accordance with their surveillance function, they perceived them as *problem people* who were posing a threat to the established order or, in accordance with their correlation function, they covered them in *zoo stories* on display for colorful cultural festivals. Thus, the predominantly White mass audience saw only a slice of minority communities, one that did not jar their preconceptions of these groups and probably helped legitimize and reinforce their lower social and economic standing. The people on both sides of this biased coverage were shortchanged. People of color were denied accurate representation, and Whites were denied the opportunity to become better acquainted with groups different from their own.

In the absence of personal contact, alternative portrayals, and broadened news coverage, such one-sided stereotypes and news coverage could easily become reality in the minds of the White mass audience. Whites were seen in a wide range of roles in movies, ranging from villains to heroes. In contrast, until the late 1960s there were no government or industry-wide efforts to provide alternative media portrayals and coverage to counteract the mass media stereotypes of people of color in a society where they had less than equal standing with Whites.

Do Media Matter?

It was once thought that the mass media were a "magic silver bullet" that entered the minds of the audience and could convert them to any opinion or attitude. However, scholars who have examined the effects of the media on members of society have found that the influence of the media is much more limited and complex. Instead of being a mere target for a bullet, the audience is more accurately described as a complex set of groups and individuals who actively make decisions about which media to use, what to remember from the media, and how to interpret what they remember. The media have their greatest effect when they reinforce and channel existing attitudes and opinions consistent with the psychological makeup of individuals and the social structure of the groups with which they identify, not when they try to change opinions.

While the "magic bullet" theories saw the audience as a target for media messages, researchers established later that media audiences are active, not passive. Rather than sit back and take whatever the media offer, people seek out the media that fulfill their needs and gratify their desires. In today's world of multimedia, people have more choices of media than ever, and can quickly change media channels. All at the same time, they may be reading, listening to music, and using a tablet, laptop, or mobile phone.

Because of the wide range of social and psychological factors that affect how a person thinks and acts, it is difficult to pinpoint the specific effects of the media on individuals. However, what we know of the reinforcement and channeling effects of the media, coupled with the content analyses of coverage and portrayal of minorities in the news and entertainment media, provides insight into the negative effects of one-sided media images on both Whites and the members of the racial and ethnic groups portrayed.

Media effects research is less definitive than other areas of communication research. Nevertheless, studies have shown that negative, one-sided, or stereotyped portrayals and news coverage in the media very often reinforce racist attitudes in prejudiced members of the audience and can channel mass actions against the group that is portrayed stereotypically. The studies also show that bigots watching television programs that ridicule bigotry interpret the program to reinforce their preexisting beliefs. Children in both minority groups and the majority are particularly affected by entertainment characters portraying minority groups. In contrast to the effects of negative portrayals, programs portraying better interracial understanding and cooperation among people of different races can stimulate positive attitudes and behavior, especially among children.

To better understand the different ways news and entertainment media can affect racial attitudes and behavior, it is helpful to examine the findings of three studies examining this issue at different points over more than 70 years.

The Zoot Suit Riots of 1943

In the midst of World War II, the streets of downtown Los Angeles were the scene of violent attacks by mobs of battle-trained American servicemen on Mexican American, Black, and Filipino youths. The attacks targeted civilians with well-greased hair wearing "zoot suits," which were suits with long coats and pants with deep pleats at the waist that were pegged at the cuff. The servicemen cut off their clothing, whether they were wearing zoot suits or not. The police officers, who responded to reports of the violence, arrested and jailed the civilian youths, not the servicemen who attacked them. The attacks followed and were accompanied by a campaign in the news media that characterized the zoot suited youths, most of them of

Negative newspaper coverage of zoot suit-wearing youths helped shape public support for the battle-trained U.S. servicemen who attacked and stripped clothing from Mexican American, Black, and Filipino youths during Los Angeles's zoot suit riots in 1943.

Source: Los Angeles Times.

Mexican origin, as antisocial elements whose dress was out of step with the nation's war effort.

In 1956, sociologists Ralph Turner and Samuel Surace analyzed the press coverage of Mexicans in the Los Angeles press to see if it might have affected the violent attacks on the predominantly Mexican American zoot suiters.[13] Turner and Surace hypothesized that the period before the riots would be characterized by steady negative news coverage of Mexicans in Los Angeles and studied the portrayal of Mexicans in the *Los Angeles Times* from 1933 to 1943.

Articles covering persons of Mexican descent were categorized five ways:

1. *Favorable:* stories that emphasized the area's Old California tradition; the romantic, brave, dashing image of Mexicans; religion in the Mexican community; or Mexican culture.

2. *Unfavorable:* articles on delinquency and crime or Mexicans as a public burden.

3. *Neutral:* miscellaneous articles including people with Spanish surnames, but not identified as Mexicans in the article.

4. *Negative-favorable:* articles that stated and then refuted accusations against Mexicans, such as "Not all zoot suiters are delinquents."

5. *Zooter theme:* articles identifying the zoot suit dress with crime, sex, violence, or gangs.

Turner and Surace (1956) thought that crowd behavior, such as the organized attacks by military personnel stationed in the area, would be preceded by newspaper coverage in which the term *Mexican* was used as an unambiguous negative symbol. They also hypothesized that because of the negative behavior ascribed to Mexicans by the newspaper, the mass society would sanction mob violence that would not be tolerated in other circumstances.

The sociologists felt that both favorable and unfavorable feelings toward people of color could be triggered by ambiguous symbols, noting that "even the most prejudiced person is likely to respond to the symbol 'Negro' with images of both the feared invader of white prerogatives and the lovable, loyal Negro lackey and 'mammy.'" But unambiguous negative symbols representing people outside the boundaries of normal, accepted behavior would trigger "the dictum that 'you must fight fire with fire' and the conviction that a person devoid of human decency is not entitled to be treated with decency and respect." Turner and Surace wrote that when the media symbol of a group triggers a strictly negative stereotype, the people associated with it can become targets for mob violence.

Therefore, in looking at the news coverage, Turner and Surace expected to find a decline in the number of times the term *Mexican* was used in favorable news coverage in the period preceding the zoot suit riots. This would result in the development of a clearly negative image for the predominantly Mexican zoot suiters.

Their hypothesis was only partially supported by the *Times* coverage for the 10 years before the 1943 riots. In fact, between 1933 and 1943, favorable Mexican themes (primarily those romanticizing Mexican culture) made up between 80% and 90% of the stories in which the term *Mexican* was used. However, in taking a closer look at the data, Turner and Surace discovered the importance of an unambiguous negative symbol in news coverage before the mob violence against Mexican youths.

While the percentage of favorable mentions of *Mexican* in the three-year period preceding the 1943 riots did not decrease, there was a sharp decline in the number of articles using the term *Mexican* at all. The term was used in 27 articles sampled between January 1933 and June 1936, and it was used 23 times in articles between July 1936 and December 1939. But it was used in less than half that number, only 10 articles, between January 1940 and June 1943. Turner and Surace found what they described as "a shift away from *all* the traditional references to Mexicans during the period prior to the riots."[14] This shift was not the result of less news coverage of those of Mexican descent in the *Los Angeles Times*—in fact, the number of articles about this group rose steadily in three periods studied between 1933 and 1943. However, there was a decline in the number of articles using the term *Mexican* and an increase in the percentage of articles classified as neutral, negative-favorable, and zooter theme. In the first period, articles coded as favorable constituted 80% of the articles coded, but in the last period those coded as favorable accounted for only 25% of the articles. The percentage of articles coded as neutral increased sharply to 32%, and Turner and Surace noted that the category "actually consists chiefly of unfavorable presentations of the object 'Mexican' without overt use of the symbol 'Mexican.'"[15] The percentage of articles in the negative-favorable category also increased, although it was smaller than the others, and also was based on an overall negative image of Mexicans, such as reporting that not all Mexicans are lazy.

The most startling shift was the sharp increase in the *Times* use of the term *zoot suit* as a strictly negative symbol. The zoot suit theme, which was not used before 1940, accounted for one third of all the articles from 1940 to June 1943. The authors concluded that the introduction of the term and its heavy use in unfavorable circumstances resulted in a strictly negative symbol that triggered no unambiguous or positive stereotypes. It was the association of that symbol with Mexican American youths portrayed as having antisocial behavior that helped spur the indiscriminate attacks of servicemen on them, including those not wearing zoot suits.

Turner and Surace wrote that

> unlike the symbol "Mexican," the "zoot-suiter" symbol evokes no ambivalent sentiments but appears in exclusively unfavorable contexts. While, in fact, Mexicans were attacked *indiscriminately* in spite of apparel (of two hundred youths rounded up by the police on one occasion, very few were wearing zoot suits), the symbol "zoot-suiter" could become a basis for unambivalent community sentiment supporting hostile crowd behavior more easily than could "Mexican."[16]

The researchers found that in the period just before the violent attacks on Mexican teenagers, the newspaper's coverage of the Mexican American community in the issues sampled was dominated by the zoot suiter theme in unfavorable coverage, less use of the term *Mexican* in favorable coverage, and increased coverage of Mexicans in articles in which the term *Mexican* was not used but the community was portrayed unfavorably. In the month just before and during the attacks by servicemen on Mexican youths, 74% of the 61 articles on the Mexican community concerned zoot suiters, 23% were negative-favorable, and 3% were neutral. While not holding the *Times* entirely responsible for the violent attacks on civilian youths, the researchers felt that news coverage contributed to the violence and general public support of the servicemen by introducing a new symbol, the zoot suiter, and using it in a strictly unfavorable context. Turner and Surace wrote that the new symbol

> provided the public sanction and restriction of attention essential to the development of overt crowd hostility. The symbol "zoot-suiter" evoked none of the imagery of the romantic past. It evoked only the picture of a breed of persons outside the normative order, devoid of morals themselves, and consequently not entitled to fair play and due process. The "zooter" symbol had a crisis character which mere unfavorable versions of the familiar "Mexican" symbol never approximated. And the "zooter" symbol was an omnibus, drawing together the most reprehensible elements in the old unfavorable themes, namely, sex crimes, delinquency, gang attacks, draft-dodgers, and the like and was, in consequence, widely applicable.[17]

Turner and Surace's research is valuable because of the link it makes between the symbols that trigger commonly accepted stereotypes in the minds of the mass audience, which are used often in news coverage of Latinos and other racial and ethnic groups, and the psychological, social, and even physical damage caused to those being stereotyped. Symbols are often used at a time when the surveillance and correlation functions of the media are called on to describe a change in the environment posed by minorities or to define how and where members of minorities fit into the society.

A survey of national magazine coverage of Mexicans in the United States from 1890 to 1970 revealed an almost complete absence of news coverage—except when elements of the Mexican population were seen as a threat to society, which then triggered discriminatory acts by the public or law enforcement officials. In these periods, terms such as *zoot suiters,* border-crossing *wetbacks,* and militant *Chicanos* dominated the headlines of national magazines.

More recently, the term *illegal alien* has been used to symbolize a person who enters the country illegally and is said to constitute a burden on public resources. A survey of 114 randomly selected articles from California newspapers on undocumented immigration from January 1977 through March 1978 found that nearly half used the term *alien* or *illegal alien* in the headlines. The largest categories of headlines treated the immigrants as a law enforcement problem or drain on public resources.[18] Use of the term *illegal alien* continued in news headlines and coverage into the early 21st century, most often referring to Latino immigrants. More recently, some news organizations referred to the same people simply as *illegals.* The news media have used terms—such as *savages* during the 19th century battles against Native Americans, *Japs* in World War II, and *Black Power militants* in the 1960s—as shorthand symbols to trigger stereotypical images in the minds of readers, listeners, and viewers. Following the September 11, 2001, hijacked airliner crashes that destroyed New York City's World Trade Center towers and damaged the Pentagon, the news media used negative symbols of Arabs, Muslims, and other Middle Easterners to trigger stereotypes of terrorists and troublemakers.

Bigotry and Archie Bunker

When the situation comedy program *All in the Family* hit the airwaves in 1971, it immediately triggered a debate over its barrier-breaking use of racial and ethnic humor on network television. The story line of the program pitted Archie Bunker, a rascally but hardworking bigot, against his liberal son-in-law, Mike, a graduate student living in the Bunker household with Archie's daughter. Mike engaged in lively and humorous debates with Archie, who had dropped out of high school and had a blue-collar job. Archie's lines in the show's script featured derogatory racial, ethnic, religious, and gender slang terms that were not then used in polite company or on television. Some lauded the program for tackling racial prejudice and exposing the foolishness of bigotry through the use of comedy. Others

Archie Bunker's use of racial slurs and bigotry when arguing with son-in-law Michael in the 1970s television sitcom *All in the Family* was shown by researchers to reinforce prejudice in some viewers. The program continued to be seen in syndication and on cable into the 21st century.

Source: © Bettmann/CORBIS.

argued that the program, by portraying Archie as a lovable bigot, had the effect of sanctioning and even encouraging prejudice.

Norman Lear, the producer of the program, answered critics by arguing that the comedy's story line countered bigotry because Mike effectively rebutted Archie and that Mike was the one "making sense." Lear wrote in 1971 that the audience saw Archie as an advocate of "convoluted logic."[19] He contended that the program's dependence on racial themes would bring bigotry out into the open and would allow parents to answer children's questions about bigotry. CBS, which aired the program, commissioned a study that showed that the program could lessen racial bigotry by humorously exposing its shortcomings. Others defended the program for using a comedy format to belittle those with prejudiced opinions. The Los Angeles chapter of the National Association for the Advancement of Colored People (NAACP) gave its 1972 Image Award to *All in the Family* for contributing to better race relations.

The program appeared on network television for more than a decade and continued on local and cable stations for more than 40 years. Although several research projects examined the impact of the program on viewers, one of the most important studies was one of the first. In 1974, psychologist Neil Vidmar and sociologist/psychologist Milton Rokeach published a study analyzing the impact of *All in the Family* on viewers in the United States and Canada. Noting the debate then taking place over the effect of Archie Bunker on bigotry and prejudice, the researchers tested the audience reaction to the program in terms of previous studies showing how audiences use selective perception and selective exposure when using media.

Under the selective perception hypothesis, Vidmar and Rokeach theorized that viewers with different degrees of prejudice or racism would have different reasons for watching the program, would identify with different characters, and would find different meanings in the outcomes of the programs. Under the selective exposure hypothesis, the researchers proposed that low prejudiced and high prejudiced viewers would not watch *All in the Family* to the same extent.

To test these hypotheses, Vidmar and Rokeach (1974) surveyed 237 high school students in a small Midwestern town in the United States and 168 adults in London, Ontario, in Canada.[20] Those surveyed were asked to respond to a questionnaire with eleven items designed to probe their reactions to the program and six items designed to measure their ethnocentrism or prejudice. The initial data showed that more than 60% of the respondents liked or admired Archie more than they did Mike, 40% of the American respondents felt Archie won at the end of the show, 46% named Mike as the one most made fun of, and 35% saw nothing wrong with Archie's use of racial and ethnic slurs. The responses of the Canadians who were surveyed followed the same pattern.

The researchers then compared the exposure to and interpretations of the program of respondents who were rated as high prejudiced and low prejudiced on the six items measuring ethnocentrism and prejudice. While both groups enjoyed the program equally, people at different levels of prejudice drew different conclusions from watching the same television characters. Vidmar and Rokeach wrote that "high prejudiced persons in both the U.S. and Canadian samples were significantly more likely than low prejudiced people to admire Archie over Mike and to perceive Archie as winning in the end."[21] High prejudiced American adolescents were also more likely to report that Archie made better sense than Mike and to report that in 20 years their attitudes would be similar to Archie Bunker's. High prejudiced Canadian adults also condoned Archie's racial slurs more often and saw the show as poking fun at Archie less often than did low prejudiced viewers.

Vidmar and Rokeach summarized that the findings "tend to support the selective perception hypothesis—namely, that prejudiced persons identify more with Archie, perceive Archie as making better sense than Mike, perceive Archie as winning."[22] Furthermore, high prejudiced viewers noted things they disliked about Mike, and low prejudiced viewers noted things they disliked about Archie.

Vidmar and Rokeach also found support for the selective exposure hypothesis, but in a different direction than that proposed by CBS. Network researchers, assuming that the program would be interpreted as satirizing bigotry, speculated that low prejudiced people would be the most avid viewers. But Vidmar and Rokeach found that American teenagers who were in the high prejudice group were *All in the Family*'s most frequent viewers. The study showed that the most frequent viewers admired Archie more than Mike and condoned Archie's ethnic slurs more than infrequent viewers did. The researchers concluded that the selective exposure meant that "*All in the Family* seems to be appealing more to the racially and ethnically prejudiced members of society than to the less prejudiced members."[23]

Vidmar and Rokeach wrote that

> the findings surely argue against the contention that *All in the Family* has positive effects, as has been claimed by its supporters and admirers. We found that many persons did not see the program as a satire on bigotry and that these persons were even more likely to be viewers who scored high on measures of prejudices. Even more important is the finding that high prejudiced persons were likely to watch *All in the Family* more often than low prejudiced persons, to identify more often with Archie Bunker and to see him winning in the end. All such findings seem to suggest that the program is more likely reinforcing prejudice and racism than combating it.[24]

The findings of Vidmar and Rokeach, as well as those of subsequent scholars who examined the impact of *All in the Family*, were consistent with previous studies showing that preexisting social and psychological factors influence people's choices of which media to use and how to interpret what they see, hear, or read. In the classic "Mr. Biggott" studies in the late 1940s, prejudiced individuals were shown cartoons in which the bigoted attitudes of Mr. Biggott were portrayed unfavorably. However, instead of seeing the shortcomings of bigotry, the respondents reinterpreted the cartoons to reinforce their existing prejudices or to avoid ridiculing Mr. Biggott.[25]

These and other studies have shown that the impact of the media is to reinforce attitudes already held by members of their audience rather than to convince people to change them. When the content of the media plays on negative racial images, even if these themes are ridiculed, prejudiced persons interpret the message as supporting their bigoted attitudes rather than rejecting or changing them.

Media Images of Muslims: Impact on the People Portrayed

Media images and coverage of people of color have a double impact. They help frame and shape what others think of the people whose images they see in the media. They also have an impact on the self-image of the people portrayed and what they think of the United States and its media. The effect of this double-edged media sword was reinforced in the years following the September 11, 2001, attacks on New York City's World Trade Center and the Pentagon as the nation's media increased their attention to Arabs and Middle Eastern people and painted a racialized image of followers of Islam.

"Most Muslim-Americans believe that the news media's portrayal of Muslims and their religion is unfair, negative, stereotypical, and not at all reflective of the true nature of Islam, and the vast majority of its followers," wrote Brigitte L. Nacos and Oscar Torres-Reyna in a 2007 book analyzing stereotyping, media coverage, and public opinion of Muslim Americans.[26] The book's opening chapters reported on studies and experiences in coverage of Muslim Americans before and after the 9/11 attacks, the visual portrayls of Arabs and Muslims, and how Americans viewed Islam and Muslims in the United States and abroad. But the most compelling findings were in the final chapter describing the impact of the news coverage and media portrayals on Muslims in the United States.

Using focus group discussions with American Muslims and citing polls reporting the post-9/11 opinions of Muslim Americans, the authors drew a picture of people who were generally positive about their own experiences in the United States, but somewhat dissatisfied with American society's understanding and attitudes regarding Muslims. Many of the comments reflected a distrust and dissatisfaction with the way the media portrayed Muslims in this era and reflected a growth in dissatisfaction in the years following the attacks as the United States waged war on Muslim-dominated countries. For instance, a few months after the 9/11 events, 41% of American Muslims reported that in their own experience and overall they felt Americans had been respectful and tolerant of Muslims. But three years later the percentage reporting respect and tolerance of Muslims by Americans had dropped from 41% to 32%. Similarly, in 2001, 8% of the respondents reported they felt Americans were disrespectful and intolerant of Muslims. Three years later that percentage grew from 8% to 12% reporting disrespect and intolerance of Muslims.[27]

The source of this growing dissatisfaction could be linked to the media coverage. A few months after the 9/11 events two thirds of the Muslim Americans polled felt the mainstream media were unfair in covering Muslims and Islam. In less than two years the fraction grew to three fourths, and just as many felt Hollywood entertainment media were unfair to Muslims and their religion. Even more compelling than the numbers were the focus group comments of American Muslims as they described their feelings about the American news coverage and portrayal of Muslims in the early 21st century.[28]

"The media portrays us like all Muslims are like fanatics and we go along with bombs in our hand, pockets and stuff like that," a Muslim man said in a 2003 focus group session cited by Nacos and Torres-Reyna. A Muslim woman called some of the American news media's coverage of Muslims "shameless" and added, "It's very, very scary thinking how much they can

Media coverage and portrayals of Arabs, Middle Easterners, and Muslims in the years before and after the first decade of the 21st century often focused on terrorism, extremism, and violence. These images and their impact were analyzed by Brigitte L. Nacos and Oscar Torres-Reyna in their book *Fueling Our Fear: Stereotyping, Media Coverage, and Public Opinion of Muslim Americans*.

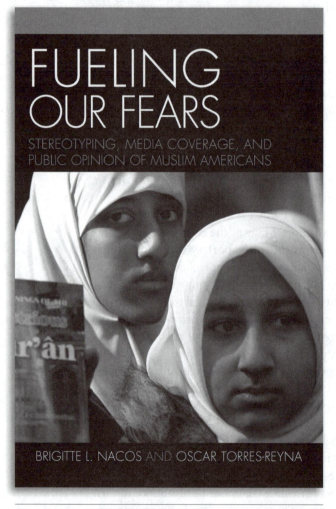

Source: Fueling Our Fears, by Brigitte L. Nacos and Oscar Torres-Reyna, 2007, Rowman & Littlefield Publishing. Group.

manipulate the general American population. Some of those (news organizations) are a lot worse than the others, but they're all in general bad."

One teenage girl observed that "You don't see them (the media) saying good things about Muslims 24–7, and then, if we ever did say anything wrong, oh, it would be on ABC, NBC—every single channel," and a female college student complained about the media's "bashing of Islam."

"The picture that has been given about the Muslims and the Arabs is—of course, in the media, you—they are made out to be monsters . . . and camel herders, and nothing else. I mean, every picture that they bring you, they don't even bring you a decent place or a decent street to see. They bring you just stone-throwing kids and people behind jack-asses . . . They don't give you anything that is of value to the Arabs, or the Muslims," she said.

By linking Muslims and Islam to terrorism, while not identifying others fighting around the world by their religion, the focus group participants felt the news media "brainwashes" the American public to think of "Muslims as fundamentally bad people," Nacos and Torres-Reyna reported.[29] Still others felt the one-sided news images had a negative effect on Muslims themselves as they looked for ways to influence the nation and its media.

"What I don't like to see is us always portraying ourselves as poor victims," said one woman, "It annoys me to no end when we constantly portray ourselves as victim, victim, victim. I think that we have to give ourselves a certain sense of empowerment and—just take the bull by the horns and do what we have to do. I don't like being portrayed as the underdog."[30] The importance of influencing media coverage and portrayals as an early step in achieving better public understanding of Muslims and Islam was identified as an early priority.

"Following the 9/11 attacks, nine of ten members of this minority felt that Muslims should be involved with the American media and educational system in order to improve the image of their religion," Nacos and Reyna-Torres reported. In the focus groups participants identified strategies for advancing more accurate coverage of Muslims and Islam.

One woman observed that things would not change "until we infiltrate the media, until we infiltrate politics." A man felt "the media will not cover good stories (about us)," but encouraged fellow Muslims to "minimize the impact of negative stereotyping of Islam and Muslims" by presenting counter images in the media. A college student observed that media coverage of Muslims has "a lot to do with discrimination and fear" and urged others to "speak out and stand up for ourselves" in dealing with the media.

The focus group participants reported mixed success in dealing with media in a nation where the major media voices are not owned or controlled by Muslims or people who have a long-standing interest in Muslims or Islam. A woman felt that the coverage and portrayals could best be influenced by "leaders out there who have access to the media that we don't have."

"I've gotten involved with my local newspaper. I've gone to meet the editor. I have written letters-to-the-editor. I have written op-ed pieces, and I have gotten involved and I am encouraging others to get involved . . . Don't fight it at the higher level (but) the grass root level," said one lawyer in describing his experiences.

Others advocated the development of media directed to, for, and about Muslims in America and around the world, including Bridges TV, the first channel by and for American Muslims, and newspapers, magazines, digital sites, and radio programming targeting that audience. This would continue the growth of class media targeting other groups that have faced racial or ethnic discrimination in the United States and its media and provide multiple voices for the American Muslim communities. This media growth could "brand Muslim Americans in a positive way," Nacos and Reyna-Torres reported.

Working toward the goal of more complete and accurate news coverage of Muslims and Islam, professional journalism organizations such as the Society of Professional Journalists, media foundations such as the Poynter Institute, and equal rights groups such as the Council on American-Islamic Relations (CAIR) have developed and made available guidelines and resources to help journalists in their coverage of a group that received too little attention and understanding in the American media prior to the events of September 11, 2001.

How Do Media Matter?

The findings of the studies cited above and of other studies show that the coverage and portrayal in the media of minorities have an effect on members of both minority and majority groups. But it is a complex effect, one that is mediated by each person's psychological makeup, social status, age, and use of the media. It is unlikely that scholars will ever be able to make definitive conclusions regarding the effects of the media on racial and ethnic minority groups or on any other segments of society.

Communication, unlike chemistry or physics, is a behavioral and social science. It involves human beings and society, not physical elements in laboratory experiments. The role and effect of the media are not as predictable as the outcome when the same chemicals are repeatedly mixed in the same proportions in a laboratory. Furthermore, laboratory findings do not always reflect reality. While the laboratory may be the best setting to observe physical experiments under controlled conditions, it may be the worst setting for observing social happenings. People encounter the media not in a sterile setting but in homes, waiting rooms, bars, and so on. They may watch a television program alone one week, then see the same show the next week with a group. What they see, hear, and read in those settings is influenced by the people around them and by their own psychological makeup.

Although it is difficult to assess the effects of mass communication on society, the research findings make it clear that certain types of people, including the young, those with predispositions to view members of racially different groups in a certain way, and members of minority groups that are not well integrated into the coverage and programming of the media, are affected to a greater extent than others.

From Mass Media to Class Media

The increased racial and ethnic diversity in the United States and the increased diversity in technologies available for the public to use have radically changed the nation's landscape of communication media. As people have more choices of media, they are able to select from more media targeted to their own interests, age, race, or sex. With more choices of media, people go to more places for media. More people are spending more time with media, but less than before with mass media such as general circulation newspapers and prime-time network television. The television audience, once divided among only three networks and a few local channels, now chooses from a wide range of cable and broadcast outlets, DVDs, and videos. The media are moving from *mass media* to *class media,* with the sharpest growth in class media that target segments of the population rather than catering to a general audience. More media target more subgroups in the population with news and entertainment for their specific interests. As this occurs, the system of diverse media voices envisioned by the authors of the First Amendment to the U.S. Constitution more than 200 years ago is coming close to reality.

In a multimedia and multicultural society, people pay attention to the media that pay attention to them. In the past, the mass media often ignored or stereotyped people of color, who were too insignificant in number to matter. Now that both the media and society offer more diversity in content than ever before, more people of more races have more media to choose from that target them as an audience class. Whether more choice leads to a better understanding of ourselves and those not like us is not yet known. What is known is that people of color have not been treated adequately or accurately in the mass audience media that have been the dominant mass media in the United States for almost 200 years.

Notes

1. For books with readings on racial, ethnic, and gender issues in the media, see S. Biagi and M. Kern-Foxworth, eds., *Facing Difference: Race, Gender and Mass Media* (Thousand Oaks, CA: Pine Forge, 1997); S. Cottle, ed., *Ethnic Minorities and the Media* (Buckingham and Philadelphia: Open University Press, 2000); E. E. Dennis and E. C. Pease, eds., *The Media in Black and White* (New Brunswick, NJ: Transaction, 1997); G. Dines and J. M. Humez, eds., *Gender, Race and Class in Media: A Text-Reader* (Thousand Oaks, CA: Sage, 1995); Y. R. Kamalipour and T. Carili, eds., *Cultural Diversity and the U.S. Media* (Albany: State University of New York Press, 1998).

2. Harold Lasswell, "The Structure and Function of Communication in Society" (1948), reprinted in Wilbur Schramm and Donald F. Roberts, eds., *The Process and Effects of Mass Communication* (Urbana and Chicago: University of Illinois Press, 1971), 84–99.

3. Ibid., 99.

4. Charles Wright, *Mass Communication: A Sociological Perspective* (New York: Random House, 1959), cited in Wilbur Schramm and William E. Porter, *Men, Women, Messages, and Media: Understanding Human Communication* (New York: Harper and Row, 1982), 27.

5. Wilbur Schramm and William Earl Porter, *Men, Women, Messages, and Media: Understanding Human Communication* (New York: Harper and Row, 1982), 27.

6. Peter M. Sandman, David M. Rubin, and David B. Sachsman, *Media: An Introductory Analysis of American Mass Communication*, 3rd ed. (Englewood Cliffs, NJ: Prentice Hall, 1982), 14.

7. Ibid., 9.

8. For a further elaboration of these functions in contemporary media, see Joseph R. Dominick, *The Dynamics of Mass Communication* (Reading, MA: Addison-Wesley, 1983), 33–49.

9. For more on the *New York Sun* and its influence, see J. E. Steele, *The Sun Shines for All* (Syracuse, NY: Syracuse University Press, 1993).

10. Michael Emery and Edwin Emery, *The Press and America*, 8th ed. (Boston: Allyn and Bacon, 1996), 102.

11. David Potter, *People of Plenty* (Chicago: University of Chicago Press, 1954), 167–168.

12. Walter Lippmann, *Public Opinion* (New York: Free Press, 1997; original work published 1922).

13. Ralph H. Turner and Samuel J. Surace, "Zoot-Suiters and Mexicans: Symbols in Crowd Behavior," *American Journal of Sociology* 62(1) (July 1956): 14–20.

14. Ibid., 18.

15. Ibid., 18–19.

16. Ibid., 19.

17. Ibid., 20.

18. Félix Gutiérrez, "Making News-Media Coverage of Chicanos," *Agenda* 8(6) (1978): 21–22.

19. Norman Lear, "As I Read How Laura Saw Archie," *New York Times*, October 10, 1971, D17.

20. Neil Vidmar and Milton Rokeach, "Archie Bunker's Bigotry: A Study in Selective Perception and Exposure," *Journal of Communication* 24(1) (Winter 1974).

21. Ibid., 42.

22. Ibid., 43.

23. Ibid., 45.

24. Ibid., 46

25. Eunice Cooper and Marie Jahoda, "The Evasion of Propaganda: How Prejudiced People Respond to Anti-Prejudice Propaganda," *The Process and Effects of Mass Communication*, ed. Wilbur Schramm and Donald F. Roberts (Urbana: University of Illinois Press, 1971), 287–299.

26. Brigitte L. Nacos and Oscar Torres-Reyna, *Fueling Our Fears: Stereotyping, Media Coverage and Public Opinion of Muslim Americans* (Lanham, MD: Rowman & Littlefield, 2007), 101.

27. Ibid., 117.

28. Ibid., 101–103.

29. Ibid., 106.

30. Ibid., 108–110.

Disparaging the "Other" 3

Any discussion of the depictions of people of color in hegemonic American culture must include the concept of stereotyping. The *American Heritage Dictionary* has defined stereotyping as "a conventional, formulaic, and oversimplified conception, opinion, or image." In the broadest sense, stereotyping has been employed as a literary and dramatic device from the earliest beginnings of those art forms. It is a means of quickly bringing to the audience's collective consciousness a character's anticipated value system and/or behavioral expectations. Audience members are then able to assess the character against their own value systems and categorize the character as, for example, "the villain" or "the heroine." Stereotypes, therefore, are shortcuts to character development and form a basis for entertainment and literary fare.

Stereotyping can be a useful device when used without prejudice. A simplistic example would find a White villain brought to justice by a White hero in an entirely White social environment. The message transmitted to the audience would be that good overcomes evil. However, negative stereotyping of non-White cultural groups in a White-dominated environment transmits a far different message when done historically and persistently with prejudice.

Because the concept of prejudice is central to our discussion, let's use the term as James M. Jones has defined it in his book *Prejudice and Racism*. Prejudice, he wrote, "is a negative attitude toward a person or group based upon a social comparison process in which the individual's own group is taken as the positive point of reference."[1] In that context our example would transmit the notion not only that good (the dominant cultural group) overcomes evil (the socially subjected culture) but that the latter *is* evil. Thus, while stereotyping *per se* may have merits in popular literature and the arts, when combined with prejudice it poses a devastating obstacle to human development and understanding in a multicultural society.

Before examining racial portrayals in American mass entertainment, we will look at the social historic context and attitudes in which certain stereotypes were cultivated. This will provide insight into whether the stereotypes were prejudiced and the degree to which social historic factors have been influential in their development and use. We shall consider the social historic experiences of several racial and cultural groups with hegemonic Whites in the United States to illustrate the causal relationship between those experiences and their marginalization in communication media.

Native Americans as Barriers to "Civilization"

Native Americans (colloquially known as "Indians") were the first peoples of a different ethnicity to confront European settlers on the American continent. Anglo European settlers were at once faced with a dilemma of how to coexist with people they saw as primitive but who also had some qualities they admired. Writings of early settlers referred to what they considered to be the natives' primitive innocence, their willingness to share food and other essentials of life in a communal environment, and their dark, handsome physical appearance. To the White settlers these attributes were "noble." At the same time the settlers also observed the natives' proclivity for nudity, open sexual relationships, and incidents of cannibalism. These traits were considered "savage." Thus emerged in colonial era literature the concept of the "noble savage."

Initially the English colonists decided to convert the natives to Christianity in an attempt to assimilate them while the process of creating a European-style society was under way. Religious conversion was eventually seen, however, as an impossibility, and the colonists rationalized that the natives had to be removed as a barrier to the "civilization" of the continent.

By the mid-1800s the policies for dealing with the "Indian problem" had found their justification in popular literature, which helped to establish the myth of the monolithic "Indian" without regard for the distinctions of more than 2,000 different cultures, languages, and value systems that the concept represented. The literary stereotype was part of the Western frontier writing formula developed after the Civil War. Writers of this genre included Francis Bret Harte and Mark Twain. Readers of this fare were

Harvard professor Frederick Jackson Turner popularized his "Frontier Thesis" that included the notion that Native American Indians were merely obstacles that tested the mettle of White settlers during westward expansion and fulfillment of "Manifest Destiny."

Source: Used by permission, Utah State Historical Society,

already conditioned to see the natives portrayed in a manner that justified their elimination as a barrier to Western expansion. Twain, Harte, and others wrote of the picturesque scenery and romantic lifestyles of the frontier in contrast with the "savages" who occupied the land. In *Roughing It* Twain described the Gosiute Indians as "scrawny creatures," "treacherous-looking," and "prideless beggars." It remained only for dime novel author Edward S. Ellis to write during the 1880s and 1890s of Native American Indians as merely a prelude to a more enlightened White civilization.

Stories of actual and exaggerated atrocities by Indians upon White settlers, who pushed ever westward into the frontier, firmly established a hatred against them that clearly made them an enemy both in warfare and of the progress of civilization. Literature during the Indian wars is rife with tales of natives burning, looting, raping, and scalping the pioneers who were fulfilling the fervor of "Manifest Destiny." It was against this backdrop that Frederick Jackson Turner's "Frontier Thesis," presented in 1893, argued that American (White) character had been molded by the experience of the Western frontier. Turner's ideas were accepted to the extent that they pervaded history textbooks into the middle of the 20th century. Elimination or subjugation of Native Americans was seen as merely an evolutionary step in the development of industrial America.

Legendary American novelist Mark Twain was among writers who created literary stereotypes that denigrated Native American Indians and other cultural minority groups.

Source: A.F. Bradley, New York, 1907.

Justifying African Enslavement

In 1619, a year before the arrival of the *Mayflower* on the shores of the American continent, 20 Africans were brought to Jamestown aboard a Dutch pirate ship. The ship's captain offered to exchange his human cargo for a supply of foodstuffs. The young Black men and women with Spanish names such as Isabella and Pedro were probably originally headed for the West Indies on a Spanish vessel before being intercepted by the Dutch ship.[2] The 20 Africans became the genesis of a Black population that was to have a major impact on the development of the future United States.

Although the facts of slavery in America and its legacy of human indignity have been well chronicled, the roots of its underlying psychosis have been less explored in popular literature. The general notion regarding the treatment of Blacks and their African ancestors has tended to focus on slavery as a phenomenon of Southern White culture based upon geographic and economic factors. What is often overlooked is that slavery was a part of the Northern experience in America from colonial times. It is clear that racism against darker-skinned people was a factor in English Calvinist and Puritan religious ideology even before those influences were brought to the New World. This affected colonial-era attitudes toward Black people in two ways. First was the Anglo Saxon belief that the color white represented things that were pure, clean, good, and reflective of the spiritual light. The color black, on the other hand, represented impurity, filth, evil, and spiritual darkness. Both concepts persist to this day. Second, the Puritan concept of predestination relied upon observation to distinguish the "elect" from the "damned." Those who seemed relatively prosperous and self-sufficient were deemed superior to those who were enslaved. Against this religiously seated and strongly held attitude the posture of the English colonists toward Blacks in the New World is predictable even among inhabitants of the Northern seaboard. In fact, the trading of slaves was the predominant commodity on New York's Wall Street into the 1700s partly because Puritan law was ambiguous on the subject. One such law enacted in 1641 is revealing:

> There shall never be any bond-slavery, villenage or captivitie amongst us; unlesse it be lawfully captives taken in just warrs, and such strangers as willingly sell themselves, or are sold to us: and such shall have the libertyes and Christian usages which the law of God established in Israel concerning such persons doth morally require, provided this exempts none from servitude who shall be judged thereto by Authoritie.[3]

Whites in New England were first to establish what later would be called "Jim Crow" laws in the South as a means of codifying their prejudices against Blacks although slavery never became a widespread practice there for economic reasons. In the South the mythology of the "happy slave," who was content to serve his or her master as the ultimate fulfillment of life, grew as a justification for the exploitation of Blacks. Much of the post–Civil War literature paints a negative image of Black people designed to reinforce institutional and social racism. Many of the accusations against Black integrity that emerged during Reconstruction are now too familiar: laziness, slow wit, loose standards of morality, fondness for alcoholic beverages, and so on. Lynching and other acts of violence against Blacks and those sympathetic to them are ample evidence of the attitudes held by White Americans toward them at the dawning of the 20th century.

Fighting Mexicans for "Independence"

There was little mention of colonial Mexico in North American literature until the 19th century. Spain ruled Mexico for 300 years (1521–1821) before Mexico won its war for independence. In 1803, however, the Louisiana Purchase removed the vast buffer of territory between the United States and Mexico. The expansionist movement by U.S. settlers into the West and Southwest not only precipitated conflict with Native Americans, as discussed previously, but also led to war with Mexico in 1846.

Central to the development of relations between Mexico and the United States was the Santa Fe Trail, which was legally opened as a commercial trade route in 1821. The trail ran from Independence, Missouri, to Santa Fe, New Mexico, and became the focal point of friction between White settlers and Mexicans. When some inhabitants of the newly formed Republic of Mexico became disenchanted with their new government, Anglo American settlers were there in significant numbers to spur the movement for independence by the mid-1830s. In fact, there is much to suggest that American literature of the period was primarily designed to stir up local sentiment for overthrow of the Mexican government in Texas and New Mexico. Thus, Whites engaged in hostilities against Mexicans with Mexican allies during the war for Texas independence. At the same time popular literature portrayed in vivid terms the perception of a "cruel" massacre by General Antonio López de Santa Anna of the "gallant" defenders of the Alamo in 1836, who included folk heroes David Crockett and James Bowie. Americans were generally persuaded to visualize the Mexican as an inhuman enemy a decade before war with Mexico was officially declared.

Cruelty was not the only negative trait ascribed to Mexicans. Cecil Robinson, in his 1977 book *Mexico and the Hispanic Southwest in American Literature,* chronicled the origins of several stereotypes, which began to appear in Anglo writings before and during the U.S.-Mexican War.[4] During that war American naval Lieutenant H. A. Wise wrote that Mexicans were "beyond comparison the laziest and most ignorant set of vagabonds the world produces."[5] George Wilkins Kendall penned: "Give them but tortillas, frijoles, and chile colorado to supply their animal wants for the day, and seven-tenths of the Mexicans are satisfied; and so they will continue to be until the race becomes extinct or amalgamated with Anglo-Saxon stock."[6]

When Mexicans were not being portrayed in Anglo American literature as lazy and indolent, they were assailed for uncleanliness. Texas romance writer Jeremiah Clemens gave his version of the origin of the term *greaser* and why he felt it was appropriate: "The people look greasy, their clothes are greasy, their dogs are greasy—everywhere grease and filth hold divided dominion, and the singular appropriateness of the name bestowed by the western settlers, soon caused it to be universally adopted by the American army."[7] In the 1834 short story "The Inroad of the Nabajo" by Albert Pike, the women of Santa Fe are described as "scudding hither and thither, with their black hair flying, and their naked feet shaming the ground by their superior filth."[8] It should be noted, however, that several American writers found Mexican women quite charming and wrote at length about their feminine virtues that contrasted sharply with puritanical customs of American women of the era in dress and social demeanor.

A major factor in the attitude of Whites toward Mexico and its people was the negativism toward Mexican ethnicity. Most of the population was either full-blooded native (Indian) or mestizo (mixture of Spanish ancestry and Indian). Anglo American writers routinely referred with disdain to Mexicans as "these mixed races." But it was the sizeable body of popular literature that grew out of the lore of the Santa Fe Trail that set the tone for American imagery of Mexicans and the Southwest. Works such as *The Time of the Gringo* by Elliott Arnold, *Anthony Adverse* by Hervy Allen, and *Adventures in the Santa Fe Trade* by James Josiah Webb established the basic stereotypes by 1900.

Importing "Peril" From Asia

The Asian experience in America has a short history prior to 1900 because Chinese immigration didn't begin until the California gold rush in 1848. Japanese people didn't begin to arrive formally until after 1855 when the Japanese government passed laws enabling its citizens to emigrate. We are concerned in this discussion with the Chinese and Japanese because other Asian and Pacific island peoples were less a social factor in the United States before 1900 and because American attitudes toward the two groups were similar enough as to be virtually indistinguishable. In fact, many Americans never bothered to take note of any differences between Chinese and Japanese people and later came to prejudiciously lump them together as simply the "Yellow Peril."

Since the overwhelming majority of Asian immigration was to California and other states on the West Coast, their social history in America during the 19th century is focused there. By 1870 there were more than 60,000 Chinese in California who had settled into farming, mining, factory work, and domestic labor after railroad jobs became scarce. Whites, who had come west to seek quick wealth in the gold rush, came to resent the Chinese because they had jobs while many Whites were unemployed. Denis Kearney, leader of the California Workingmen's Party, orchestrated an anti-Chinese movement with the backing of the *San Francisco Chronicle*. Kearney ended every speech with the slogan "The Chinese Must Go." Kearney and his followers stirred a sentiment of prejudice against Chinese workers who were highly visible because of their adherence to traditional customs of dress, pigtail hairstyle, and communal living. Suddenly after 20 years of serving as a welcome source of cheap labor and having enjoyed a reputation for industry, honesty, thrift, and peaceful disposition the Chinese were the object of scorn. Whites now saw them as debased, clannish, and

Chinese laborers called "coolies" were brought to the United States during the California gold rush era to work farms, build railroads, and perform domestic tasks. Soon, however, they were denigrated as the "Yellow Peril" in American newspapers.

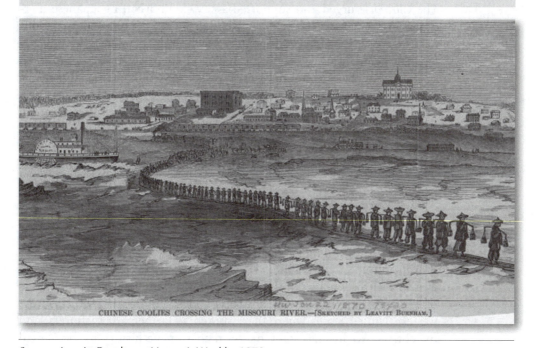

CHINESE COOLIES CROSSING THE MISSOURI RIVER.—[Sketched by Leavitt Burnham.]

Source: Leavitt Burnham, *Harper's Weekly,* 1870.

deceitful. In the 1870s a series of racially motivated incidents of violence occurred in several western towns resulting in the deaths of numerous Chinese inhabitants.

Finally, in 1882 the first Chinese exclusion law was passed, and in 1887 only 10 Chinese people immigrated to the United States. Ironically, the Chinese Exclusion Act of 1882 made possible the increase in Japanese immigration. The decline in Chinese immigrant labor proved the fact of White racism because those jobs went unfilled and a serious farm labor shortage developed in California and other western states. Soon there was a demand for Japanese immigrants who had proven farming skills and were willing to work for low wages. Between 1899 and 1904 nearly 60,000 Japanese came to America to meet the labor demand that had previously been met by Chinese workers.

History repeated itself when, between 1901 and 1906, the corrupt administration of San Francisco Mayor Eugene Schmitz and his political boss Abraham Ruef used the Japanese as scapegoats when public attention was turned on their own dubious activities. Schmitz's regime was backed by organized labor, which claimed the Japanese worked for lower wages and were driving Whites out of the job market. At the same time, Japan was quickly defeating the Russians in the Russo-Japanese War (1904) and going on to eventually seize Korea. Japan's military successes created apprehension in America that Asians were a threat to Western civilization.

Once again it was the *San Francisco Chronicle* that crusaded in front-page articles against immigration, this time with the Japanese as objects. The *Chronicle* urged and supported a citywide boycott of Japanese merchants in San Francisco. The paper charged the immigrants with maintaining loyalty to the Emperor of Japan. Mass meetings were held denouncing Japanese immigrants, and acts of assault and other violence soon followed against them. The official reaction to what became known as the Yellow Peril was a series of laws restricting Japanese immigrant rights in America. This culminated with passage of the Immigration Act of 1924 banning entry to the United States for all aliens not eligible for citizenship although the legislation was clearly targeted at the Japanese.

During the height of Yellow Peril hysteria Chinese and Japanese persons were viewed as devious and vicious. Popular literature warned of the dangers of intermarriage with Asians and charged openly that Asian men purposefully sought White women. These attitudes also found their way into entertainment media, as we shall see.

Asians from India did not officially arrive as U.S. immigrants in significant numbers until 1946 with passage of the Luce-Celler Act. However, as early as the turn of the 20th century, about 2,000 Sikhs (members of a religious group from the Punjab region of India) had settled in the western United States where they worked as farmers, day laborers, and merchants. Accordingly, they have a media image history in the United States that dates from virtually the beginning of the motion picture industry.

The Middle Eastern Presence in America

The history of Middle Eastern peoples in the United States dates back to the turn of the 20th century. New York's Ellis Island was then a major point of entry into the United States for immigrants who were mostly from Europe. But a significant number of Christian Arab immigrants from the Middle East also came to America to escape religious discrimination they experienced under rule of the Ottoman Empire. The new arrivals came mostly from the greater Syrian region of the empire that encompassed what is now modern Syria, Lebanon, Jordan, Israel, and the Israeli-occupied West Bank. The Ellis Island Immigration Museum has archived photographs of the newly arrived immigrants wearing turbans and burnooses.

The first wave of immigration from the Middle East ended in 1924 with passage of the National Origins Act, legislation that severely restricted non-European immigration to the United States. By the time the National Origins Act was terminated in 1965, Middle Easterners had long since taken their place among other cultural minority groups as fodder for stereotypical representations in the U.S. media. Much as was the case with people of African descent, the Anglo European notion of Arab people was cultivated long before White settlers came to America. History reveals that in the 18th and 19th centuries European writers and artisans categorized people of the Middle East through colonization of their lands and presented an image of a culture rife with bearded thieves, corrupt leaders, and practitioners of a heathen religion.

In modern times, many thousands of Middle Easterners have come to America and contributed to society as professionals in the fields of medicine, science, and academia as well as semiskilled workers, retail clerks, and small business owners. But their media stereotypes have ranged from villainous sheiks, to violent thieves, to exotic "belly dancers," to wealthy scions of the desert, and, worse, to purveyors of sinister acts of terrorism. Much of the earlier media content concerning Middle Easterners centered on stereotypical portrayals of them within their own nations and created an image of inferior but exotic cultures. But the 21st-century versions have generally shifted into more brutal and sinister characterizations.

An American media staple among ethnic stereotypes is the Arabian "belly dancer," an image that dates from at least the early 20th century.

Source: Photos.com/PhotoObjects.net/Thinkstock.

Racial Legacy of the Live Stage

The historic social relationships between Anglo European Americans and the marginalized groups under consideration in this volume reveals hegemonic attitudes were molded negatively toward each of the groups from the earliest stages of intercultural contact. In each case the definition of prejudice (a negative attitude toward the groups based upon a comparison process using the dominant White society as the positive point of reference) was operative. We shall now see how these prejudicial attitudes became the fiber of mass entertainment and popular culture in America.

It is no accident that the rise of American mass entertainment coincided with the populist movement that began in the 1820s and 1830s. The election of Andrew Jackson to the Presidency in 1828 marked the ascension of the "common man" as a political and social force if not general economic prosperity. Cities became population centers, and laborers

The minstrel show, featuring White entertainers in blackface, was a pop-culture fixture that rendered caricatures of Black people in 19th-century America.

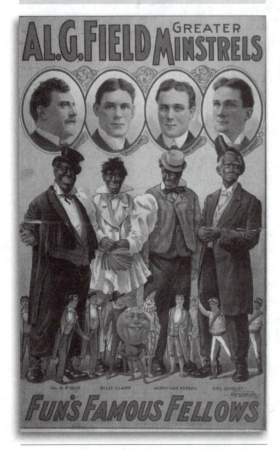

Source: The Courier Co. of Buffalo, 1907.

moved there from the farms to become wage earners. Upper-class, socially elitist Americans with refined cultural tastes were inundated by the onrushing tide of the populist movement.

The pivotal year 1833 marked the beginning of the penny press newspaper ushered in by Benjamin Day's *New York Sun* and its symbolic motto "It Shines for ALL." Just as Day's unsophisticated newspaper became the reading fare of an audience that clamored for "news" of gossip, sensationalism, and crime, so did live entertainment change to accommodate the tastes of the working class. It was also 1833 in New York City's Bowery Theatre when an uninhibited audience shouted down the orchestra's symphonic overture and hollered instead for a rendition of "Yankee Doodle"; the audience got its wish. Just as the penny press made newspapers affordable for the masses, ticket prices for live entertainment plummeted from several dollars to 25 cents or less.

From the middle of the 19th century to the 1920s, the live stage became the first major mass entertainment medium in America. People in the cities were filling large, ornate theaters, and rural dwellers attended traveling shows housed in tents. Theatrical agents quickly came to understand the imperative of catering to the public's taste. Their reward was a full cash box and lusty cheers; those who failed suffered the wrath of hostile catcalls, hisses, and financial loss. People of color played a figurative, if not literal, role in the development of mass entertainment because the populist audience demanded their inclusion in theatrical performances. The terms of that inclusion, however, were accommodating to the attitudes and values of the prejudiced masses. In general, the audience wanted plays with common people (themselves) portrayed as heroes. They wanted foot-tapping music and dance and maintained a strong desire to see anything that fulfilled their perceptions of Black American culture. Perhaps above all, they wanted comedy, and people of color were a convenient foil. "Leave 'em laughing" became an early show business axiom.

One early favorite play had a Native American theme and was titled "The Original, Aboriginal, Erratic, Operatic, Semi-Civilized and Demi-Savage Extravaganza of Pocahontas." Stereotypical myths of Native Americans, which had been spread by writers such as James Fenimore Cooper and pulp novelists, easily made the transition to the stage. After the Civil War live entertainment took to the outdoor theater arena with "Buffalo Bill" Cody and his "Wild West" show leading the way. Cody played out the American myth of the taming of the West and its Native American Indian population to Eastern audiences while the real Indian wars were being fought across the country. Cody legitimized himself by periodically returning to the West to serve as a scout and Indian fighter. His show played to packed audiences in the United States and Europe for several decades. Other traveling shows including circuses and variety acts spread racial stereotypes across America by 1900.

Minstrel shows featuring Anglo American actors in blackface appeared in the 1830s after an itinerant White actor, Thomas Dartmouth Rice, borrowed a song and dance routine from a little Black slave boy he had seen perform on a street corner. Billing himself as "Daddy" Rice, he applied burnt cork to his face, dressed in tattered clothing, and performed the borrowed routine as the "Jump Jim Crow" dance to the delight of audiences from New York's Bowery Theatre to the London stage.

Edwin P. Christy, a traveling salesman from Buffalo, New York, launched his career as a show business promoter after his travels took him through the South in the 1830s and 1840s. In Louisiana, Christy saw Blacks perform at a public gathering where they were allowed to gather for the amusement of Whites. Impressed with the musical and dance variations he saw, Christy went back to Buffalo and developed his own caricatures of Black personalities for an entertainment variety act, and the minstrel show was born. For decades Blacks could neither perform in nor attend these shows, which were based on their musical and dance traditions. Ironically, when Black minstrel troupes did become acceptable to White audiences, they, too, were compelled to perform in blackface.

For 80 years the minstrel show was the most popular form of live American entertainment. In its classic form the minstrel show consisted of two acts. Part one employed a minimum of 15 men on stage in a semicircular seating arrangement with gaudily dressed comedians at the end seats. A nattily attired "interlocutor" stood in the center, and a comedic exchange took place between him and the comedians. Singers and banjo and tambourine players composed the rest of the troupe, and songs, dances, rapid-fire jokes, and gags came without pause. Part two of the show (often called the "olio") was composed of recitations, monologues, specialty songs, comedy skits, and burlesque routines. After minstrel shows faded in popularity the olio concept was expanded into a separate group of acts and became known as vaudeville. Vaudeville launched the careers of some of America's most honored performers including George Burns, Bob Hope, Jack Benny, and Abbott and Costello. It remained only for Al Jolson to refine minstrel show affectations to indelibly stereotype Black people in American entertainment. With renditions of "Mammy," "Rock-a-bye Your Baby with a Dixie Melody," "Swanee," and others, Jolson was being called "Mr. Show Business" as early as 1915, but he had been a popular fixture since the turn of the century. Jolson was unquestionably the most popular entertainer in America during the period. By the time motion pictures began to supplant the live stage show in popularity, the quintessential stage musical *Show Boat* opened the Broadway season in 1927 with a favorite White American theme at its core: the interplay of Blacks and Southern Whites set against an idyllic romantic background along the Mississippi River.

Although there are many differences between and among the racial and cultural groups under consideration here, a close examination of their treatment in American mass entertainment reveals remarkable similarity. Our review earlier in this chapter of the social historic experiences of these groups shows that in most instances Whites held negative prejudicial attitudes against each of them well before those attitudes manifested themselves in popular media. This notion of disparaging other racial and cultural groups in popular media established a pattern that continued—as we shall see—into and through the 20th century.

Notes

1. James M. Jones, *Prejudice and Racism* (Reading, MA: Addison-Wesley, 1972), 3.

2. Lerone Bennett, *Before the Mayflower* (New York: Penguin, 1966), 30.

3. Cited in W. D. Jordan, *White Over Black: American Attitudes Toward the Negro, 1550–1812* (New York: Penguin, 1969), 7.

4. Cecil Robinson, *Mexico and the Hispanic Southwest in America Literature* (Tucson: University of Arizona Press, 1977).

5. H. A. (Henry Augustus) Wise, *Los Gringos* (New York: Baker and Scribner, 1849), 148.

6. George Wilkins Kendall, *Narrative of the Texan Santa Fé Expedition, Vol. II* (New York: Harper and Brothers, 1844), 46.

7. Jeremiah Clemens, *Bernard Lile: An Historical Romance: Embracing the Periods of the Texas Revolution and the Mexican War* (Philadelphia: J. B. Lippincott & Co., 1856), 214.

8. Albert Pike, "The Inroad of the Nabajo," *Prose Sketches and Poems Written in the Western Country* (Boston: Light and Horton, 1834), 150.

PART II

Racism and Sexism in American Entertainment

4 "Bamboozling" Stereotypes Through the 20th Century

I n the new millennium year 2000, a film by African American director Spike Lee was released and quickly became a center of controversy because of its use of Black stereotypes from a supposedly bygone era. The film, *Bamboozled*, depicted minstrel shows with Black actors in blackface and parodied a cast of stereotypical characters ranging from mammies to pickaninnies and virtually every other vile portrayal of Blacks ever exhibited in the guise of American entertainment. The target of Lee's satire was the network television industry of the early 21st century. The message: Film and video producers were continuing to "bamboozle" American audiences with distorted image displays of all peoples of color and pass them off as marginalized caricatures in society. To understand how entertainment and popular culture in the United States could enter the 21st century under the shadow of antiquated notions of racial and cultural insensitivity, we must review those aspects of the historical development of mass media in America.

Motion Pictures Bring Racism to a New Medium

Although the live stage remained the primary entertainment venue as the United States entered the 20th century, it would only be a matter of a few decades before motion pictures would captivate American audiences. Thomas Edison is generally credited with the development of motion picture technology with his invention of the Kinetoscope in 1889. In 1903, one of his assistants produced the first motion picture with a story line, *The Great Train Robbery*. Movies were projected without sound until 1927 when Al Jolson starred in *The Jazz Singer,* the first "talking" (and, of course, "singing") movie.

Not surprisingly, portrayals of people of color appeared very early in motion picture history. As early as 1894, one could view the *Sioux Ghost Dance* on one of Edison's contraptions. By 1898, Buffalo Bill's Wild West show had been committed to film complete with its imagery of the Native American Indian's collapse before White "civilization." Perhaps the first film to openly proclaim the doctrine of White supremacy over Native American Indians was William S. Hart's *The Aryan,* which was released in 1916. One of the titles projected across the screen of this silent movie also played to the fear of miscegenation and read in part, "Our women shall be guarded." As was most commonly the practice in early movies, Whites portrayed all of the non-White characters in both films. (It is interesting to note, however, that genuine Native American Indians were sometimes employed to play minor roles, but the practice was not without problems. Directors found it difficult to teach them how to act "Indian," prompting one observer to write an article on "The Dangers of Employing Redskins as Movie Actors.")

Al Jolson was one of many White entertainers who performed in blackface on stage and in movies.

Source: © Bettmann/CORBIS.

African American characterizations likely first appeared on film in 1904 when Biograph released a one-reel feature (*A Bucket of Cream Ale*) depicting a Black maid employed by a White man. A White actress in blackface played the maid. Other films soon followed including *The Wooing and Wedding of a Coon* (1905), *The Masher* (1907), and *The Nigger* (1915). The most notorious of early Black stereotypes, however, appeared in the cinematic technical epic *The Birth of a Nation* by D. W. Griffith (1915). Griffith established a pattern, which would endure for decades, of portraying American Blacks as intellectually and morally inferior to Whites and perpetrated a strong message against sexual contact between the races.

Latinos fared no better in the first two decades of American cinema. Between 1910 and 1914, several films projected Mexican stereotypes including a series of works with the term *greaser* in the titles. These included *Tony, the Greaser* (1911) and *The Greaser's Revenge* (1914). During this era, Mexicans in American film were presented as vile characters that indulged in banditry, pillage, plundering, rape, and murder. The portrayals were so severe that the Mexican government banned such films in 1922 after filing a written protest in 1919 that went unheeded. Hollywood's response was to transport the "greaser" role to other nations or to invent locales with pseudo Latin names. In a perverse manner, these films set the stage for the popularity of the mysterious, forbidden "Latin lover" roles that became a movie staple in the 1920s and 1930s. Rudolph Valentino was Hollywood's biggest star in that role.

Japanese actor Sessue Hayakawa was involved in at least two early films in which he portrayed Asian characters. In *The Typhoon* (1914), Hayakawa plays a young Japanese diplomat in Paris who, among other things, becomes romantically involved with a French actress. During the course of an argument, the woman hurls racial epithets including "whining yellow rat" at the diplomat, and he kills her. In *The Cheat* (1915), Hayakawa is cast as a deceitful Asian who schemes to obtain the sexual favors of a naive, but married, White socialite. Again, in both *The Typhoon* and *The Cheat,* the message is clear: Interracial love leads to tragedy.

Consistent with the White perception of Asian peoples at the turn of the century, they appeared stereotypically as diabolical personalities with the 1916 release of *The Yellow Menace.* Interestingly, in *The Yellow Menace,* Asians and Mexicans are portrayed as combining forces in a subversive plot against the United States.

In 1897, Edison produced a short film titled *Fatima* that depicted "Arab" women dancing provocatively to seduce a White male audience. A 1917 film *The Sultan's Wife* in which an evil raja tries to force a White girl (Gloria Swanson) into his harem was among the early depictions of Middle Eastern people. Rudolph Valentino, the silent film romantic star, ventured away from Latino characterizations to portray an "Arabian" in two films, *The Sheik* (1921) and *The Son of the Sheik* (1926), in which Arab characters were seen as thieves and murderers, thus paving the way for 21st-century Middle Eastern–themed images now pervading American movie screens.

Generally, characterizations of people of color in early American films projected an attitudinal posture of White superiority. That attitude revealed itself on screen through the portrayal of "minority" groups as inferior in two major capacities: intellectual and moral. Given the low socioeconomic status of working-class Whites during the heyday of the industrial age, movie producers of the era capitalized on audience insecurities by using racial stereotypes to bolster their self-esteem and reinforce racial attitudes. Anglo European insecurities, as reflected in the first 40 years of American popular cinema, were revealed to be a fear of miscegenation and the threat that numerical minority cultures would have an impact on hegemonic White social values. Thus, as live stage producers and entertainers profited

Silent screen idol Rudolph Valentino (shown here with Agnes Ayres) twice portrayed an Arabian sheik in the 1920s and paved the way for a movie stereotype that persisted into the 21st century.

Source: The Sheik, Paramount Pictures, 1921.

financially by giving the masses what they wanted, moviemakers quickly developed a symbiotic relationship with their patrons often at the expense of foreign cultures and Americans of color.

Several basic movie themes derived from the attitudinal premises of White intellectual and moral supremacy (see Table 4.1), and they were applied at various times to all of the groups addressed in this book.

Table 4.1   Some Traits Commonly Applied to People of Color in Early Movies

Intellectual Traits	Moral Traits
Preoccupation with simple ideas.	Low regard for human life.
Inferior strategy in warfare/conflict situations.	Criminal behavior.
Low or nonexistent occupational status.	Sexual promiscuity.
Poor speech patterns/dialect.	Drug/alcohol abuse.
Comedic foil.	Dishonesty.

Hollywood's Heyday, Comics, and Radio Racism: 1930–1945

The fact that stereotypes can, and do, change is evidenced by shifts in racial portrayals during the 15-year period from 1930 to 1945. Although basic attitudes held by Whites toward peoples of color did not undergo significant change, the passage of time altered social relationships between Whites and non-Whites. The result was that Hollywood had to make changes to conform to new realities. Unfortunately, the portrayals did not become more accurate and sensitive to the realities of the non-White experience in America but were merely adjusted to conform to more credible representations. For example, Blacks could not continue to be seen as only criminals and undesirables of various types (the primary theme of the years 1900–1920) because it was clear they had other dimensions of character that were easily observed in "real life." The movie industry response to social reality was simply to shift to new stereotypes that were still consistent with prejudicial notions.

About the same time a new mass medium, commercial radio, emerged and began to captivate American audiences. By 1930, the most popular radio show was "Amos 'n' Andy," a program that featured two White men, Charles Correll and Freeman Gosden, portraying the comedic adventures of two Black men and their associates. The show was the first to be nationally syndicated in the United States and was attracting 40 million listeners each week.

Portrayals of Native American Indians changed very little between 1930 and 1945 probably because of their unique place in American lore. They symbolized the fulfillment of the American dream—the White immigrant's ability to conquer the obstacles presented by a new continent and its existing inhabitants and to harvest its seemingly endless riches as a reward. Hollywood adopted the Indian as a living monument to the ideals of Manifest Destiny and created a stereotype that barely managed to be a facsimile of Native American culture. Examples include *Drums Along the Mohawk* (1939) and *Northwest Passage* (1940). No distinction was made in the movies between Indian cultures of the Northeast, the Plains, and the Southeast. Feathered headdresses, beads, fringed pants, pinto ponies, and halted English dialects were applied indiscriminately to represent the concept of "Indian" to movie audiences. Those stereotypical notions played well across the United States as moviegoers seemingly could not get their fill of "cowboy and Indian" movies and serials.

Radio audiences also got full doses of the stereotypical Indian when the "Lone Ranger" and his native sidekick Tonto rode across the airwaves in 1933. The Lone Ranger successfully crossed over into motion pictures and comic books and ultimately was an easy choice for television programmers when that medium came to fruition in the 1950s. Similarly, "Red Ryder," a Western cowboy comic strip, began in 1938 featuring the title character and his juvenile Indian sidekick Little Beaver. The comic strip gravitated to radio in 1942 and also had a run as a movie serial before its appearance on television the following decade.

Hattie McDaniel earned an Oscar for her portrayal of the faithful mammy to Vivien Leigh's Scarlett O'Hara in *Gone With the Wind* (1939). Hollywood usually depicted Black slaves as being delighted with their servile roles.

Source: MGM Studios/Handount/Moviepix/Getty Images.

Generally, however, the Native American's role was to constantly help audiences relive his defeat at the hands of the U.S. Calvary and other assorted "good guys." Thus, the major change in Native American movie portrayals from 1930 to World War II was the crystallization of an image. The Native American Indian became a cliché. Clichés die hard, and the movie Indian remained so throughout the heyday of Hollywood cinema.

A more pronounced stereotypical shift took place in the movie characterization of Black Americans during the boom period. The venomous, hate-filled disparagement of Blacks epitomized in *The Birth of a Nation* and other films of its era evolved into less threatening characterizations. The new stereotype played to White perceptions of Black personalities who, in the vernacular of the era, "knew their place" in American society. Blacks now appeared in movies for the purpose of entertaining White audiences within the context of social limitations. They had roles in musicals where they could demonstrate their "rhythmic" talents as singers and dancers.

Meanwhile, the supposed inferior mental capacities of Blacks made for hilarious comedy. When in movie character, Blacks were subservient to Whites as maids, mammies, domestics, and sidekicks. The pre–World War II era brought to the screen Stepin Fetchit, Mantan Moreland, and Willie Best. It also produced the "Our Gang" series with the characters of Buckwheat, Farina, and Stymie. When the old days of the antebellum South were recalled by Hollywood, as in *Gone With the Wind* (1939), Blacks played the happy, faithful, and sometimes lazy slaves. Hattie McDaniel received the first Oscar awarded to a Black actor for her portrayal of the dutiful and protective mammy to Scarlett O'Hara in the screen classic. Ms. McDaniel's award for "Best *Supporting* Actress" was, therefore, doubly symbolic.

Perhaps the primary reason for the change in Latino stereotyping during the 1930s was economics. The formal protest and subsequent banning of American moviemaking and distribution in Mexico by the Mexican government in 1922 did not go unnoticed in other Latin American countries. Although Hollywood intended the "greaser" stereotype to be its vision of Mexicans, Central and South American nations took equal offense when filmmakers began to create euphemisms for the roles in an attempt to placate Mexico. Film distribution sales in the affected countries were lucrative, so Hollywood eventually imported Latino actors and actresses to star in sizzling romantic features in an attempt to appeal to the foreign market. It took the film industry awhile to learn how to effectively cope with the problem. In the late 1920s and 1930s, filmmakers promoted Latinos to a more sophisticated level of "greasery." The Latino male had yet to attain personal integrity and social acceptability, but he did, in the words of one movie critic, at least dress well. At the same time, it was non-Latino actors such as Noah Beery and Paul Muni who played the Latino roles in *The Dove* (1928) and *Bordertown* (1935), respectively. Alas, the "Latin lover" wasn't even Latino.

One of the traits Hollywood ascribed to Mexicans was a quick temper, and films of this era almost always allowed for a display of irrational Latino temperament. The concept was soon incorporated into female roles, and by the mid-1930s and early 1940s Hollywood had recruited a number of sensuous, tempestuous leading ladies for the purpose. The idea was to appeal to both U.S. and Latin American audiences. Among the new female stars were Dolores del Rio (*The Red Dance,* 1928) and Lupe Velez (*Hot Pepper,* 1933; *Strictly Dynamite,* 1934; *Mexican Spitfire,* 1940). One concept in the tradition of Hollywood racial portrayals was unchanged, however; interracial movie romances were virtually never successful between Latinos and their White lovers.

By this time, relations with Latin America were vital also for political reasons because the United States could ill afford to offend potential allies at a time when war was imminent. This circumstance paved the way for other Latino actors who virtually flooded Hollywood shortly before the outbreak of World War II. The display of Hollywood goodwill and profit motive produced Carmen Miranda, Cesar Romero, and Desi Arnaz, and film titles began to reflect a Latin American flavor (*Down Argentine Way*, 1940; *Week-End in Havana*, 1941). Concurrently there was a conscious attempt to acquaint American audiences with Latin American history through movies on Benito Juárez and Simón Bolívar. Although political and economic pressures combined to accord Latinos the largest degree of change in stereotype among people of color between 1930 and 1945, certain prejudices lingered on screen. In general, Latinos were not seen as people with family values or stable romantic relationships; nor were they seen as in pursuit of honorable careers. Moreover, Latino men still had an uncomfortable (for Anglo American audiences) proclivity for romantic interest in White women.

With the passage of the Immigration Act of 1924, the presence of Japanese characters in popular films effectively ceased until they were brought to the American conscience again with the arrival of World War II. The "Yellow Peril," insofar as the

Lupe Velez, who was born in Mexico, was cast in a series of movies including *Mexican Spitfire* (1940) as the sexy, tempestuous Latina.

Source: Hulton Archive/Stringer/Getty Images.

Japanese were concerned, was no longer a threat to White American sensibilities during the 1930s. Instead, China and its people became the center of American attention in the Far East. China was in the midst of civil war and had been since 1911. Negative racial imagery had been popularly established with the appearance around 1910 of Sax Rohmer's fictional character, Dr. Fu Manchu, in several stories and novels. Fu Manchu soon became a diabolical movie villain and provided Hollywood with an entree into new stereotypes based upon Chinese warlords. Movies of the genre proved to be highly successful. Among the most profitable of these films that exploited the "mysterious Orient" were *The Bitter Tea of General Yen* (1933), *Oil for the Lamps of China* (1935), and *The General Died at Dawn* (1936).

On the domestic front, the decade of the 1930s belonged to Charlie Chan who was the Chinese American's cinematic representative, although no Chinese or other Asian actor portrayed him during the series that spanned

Charlie Chan, here played by Sidney Toler (left), in *The Chinese Cat*. Chan epitomized several stereotypes but is perhaps the most popular Asian character Hollywood has produced.

Source: © John Springer Collection/CORBIS.

six decades with the 1981 release of a Peter Ustinov version. Charlie Chan movies were rife with stereotypical affectations. Although Chan seemed the most cerebral of the characters involved in his movie escapades, there were also the "Oriental" traits with which American audiences could identify. Chan was mysterious in his crime-solving techniques; one never knew what thought processes or logic he was employing until the critical moment at the movie's end. White America's memories of the diabolical Asian were readily recalled when Chan offered this advice to one of his many sons: "Keep eyes, ears open. Keep mouth shut." His slow gait, drowsy manner, and halting speech suggested Chan might have spent private moments with an opium pipe. The character's immense popularity with American movie audiences throughout the 1930s and 1940s may have contributed to the pro-Chinese sentiment that existed then.

Ironically, the image of the Asian male had taken a somewhat positive twist with the appearance of the popular radio show "The Green Hornet" that first aired in 1936. Kato, the lead character's sidekick, was not only a dutiful servant but a martial arts master. *The Green Hornet* (1940) was brought to the movie screen and to comic books in the 1940s. But, with the onset of World War II, Hollywood revived and escalated its negative portrayals of the Japanese. Although the Chinese peasant image enjoyed favored status among Americans in the afterglow of Pearl Buck's *The Good Earth* novel and subsequent movie, Hollywood had little difficulty resurrecting the Yellow Peril theme against Japan, as it became a threat to both China and the United States. The Japanese attack on Pearl Harbor sealed their fate in American cinema for many years, and Japanese Americans who were shuttled to "relocation" camps during the war felt the sting of attitudes long since implanted in the mass psyche and nurtured in movie houses.

In films produced between 1942 and 1945, Hollywood dusted off the old images of Japanese duplicity, inhumanity, and lust for White women.

Sam Jaffe portrayed the title character in the 1939 movie adaptation of Rudyard Kipling's "Gunga Din" that glamorized British colonialism in India.

Source: © John Springer Collection/CORBIS.

Unlike the Germans, who were portrayed as a respectable but misguided people under the influence of the Nazi regime, the Japanese were seen in American theaters strafing Red Cross ships, bayoneting children, and delighting in applying torture techniques presumably handed down from centuries of malevolent practice. Examples can be found in *Wake Island* (1942), *Guadalcanal Diary* (1943), and *Objective, Burma!* (1945).

In 1939, when Rudyard Kipling's poem "Gunga Din" was adapted for the Hollywood screen, the era of British colonialism in India was glamorized. The notion of racial hierarchy was plainly evident as the title character was a water boy for the British soldiers who longed to become accepted into the military ranks of the colonial occupants of his country. Thus, although there was little or no presence of South Asian Indian residents in the United States at the time, the idea of their inferiority was introduced or reinforced for legions of Anglo American moviegoers across the country during Hollywood's heyday. Other literary works by Kipling (*The Jungle Book*, 1894) and Jules Verne (*Around the World in 80 Days*, 1873) were later adapted as popular American films and added to the stereotypical legacy of Asian Indians.

By the 1930s, Middle Eastern cultural stereotypes had been firmly entrenched in the post–silent movie era. Among the films that brought images of unsavory Arabs to the screen were *The Barbarian* (1933) and the 1939 version of *Beau Geste*. One of the earliest comedies of the era that disparaged Muslims was the 1931 Geste spoof *Beau Hunks*. In the film, slapstick stars Stan Laurel and Oliver Hardy save drastically outnumbered Legionnaires trapped in a fort. The Arab enemy suffers defeat (despite shouts of "Allah be with thee") as its forces storm the fort. The attack is thwarted when Laurel and Hardy spread tacks on the ground, rendering their barefoot foes unable to pursue the battle.

Comedic portrayals of Middle Eastern cultures continued into the World War II years with the release of *Lost in a Harem* (1944) where the comedy team of Bud Abbott and Lou Costello ply their trade among an array of stereotypical Arabs including sensual dancing women, lecherous sheiks, and a desert palace with secret passages and a dungeon. By the 1950s, a variety of Hollywood films had parlayed "Arabian Nights"–type escapades—complete with images of flying carpets and thieves in Baghdad including *The Magic Carpet* (1951) and *The Desert Song* (1953 version)—into the notion that Arab nations existed as fantasylands.

Post–World War II to the 21st Century

By the 1950s, Native American Indians were being used as metaphors by filmmakers seeking to make political or philosophical statements about other issues. For example, *Arrowhead* (1953) was seen by critics as an ultra-right-wing allegory of the McCarthy era while *Cheyenne Autumn* (1964) spoke strongly against German extermination camps as well as Indian persecution. Later, both *Soldier Blue* and *Little Big Man* (1970) made statements about American involvement in Vietnam. At the same time, White America (in the midst of the Black-inspired civil rights movement) experienced a guilt complex over the historical and persistent mistreatment of Native American Indians. The result was a series of Hollywood productions designed to purge that guilt including *Hombre* (1967), *Tell Them Willie Boy Is Here* (1969), and *Jeremiah Johnson* (1972). Taking matters further, Hollywood reversed itself on portrayals of two Indian tamers it had immortalized in earlier films. In *Little Big Man* (1970), General George A. Custer is characterized as meeting a just end at the Little Bighorn massacre as retribution for atrocities perpetrated against the Indians. Similarly, William Cody is portrayed as a mercenary eagerly exploiting Native Americans for the sake of showmanship in *Buffalo Bill and the Indians* (1976).

The 1970s can generally be viewed as the decade when movie portrayals became pro–Native American Indian. Although the image of the violent Indian remained into the 1980s, Hollywood tended to mitigate the violence by placing it in the context of survival, self-defense, or retribution. The 1990s brought more sympathetic, although idealized, portrayals of Native Americans to the big screen. Foremost were *Dances With Wolves* (1990) and *I Will Fight No More Forever* (1975), *The Last of the Mohicans* (1992), and *Geronimo* (1993). The animated feature *Pocahontas* (1995) continued the mythical "noble savage" portrayals of years past.

Meanwhile, Black Americans benefited from a shift in White attitudes following World War II when—under the prodding of the National Association for the Advancement of Colored People, other civil rights groups, and President Harry Truman's administration—Hollywood began to make films illustrating the folly and unfairness of racial discrimination against them. A catalyst in this movement was the manner in which Black military men had distinguished themselves during World War II. The practice of prejudice against Blacks was denunciated in *Pinky, Lost Boundaries,* and *Home of the Brave* (1949); *No Way Out* (1950); *Blackboard Jungle* (1955); and *The Defiant Ones* (1958).

The 1960s belonged to the imagery of the sophisticated Black who was heroic in proportions. Actor Sidney Poitier epitomized the intelligent, cool Black American who harnessed his hidden rage in tolerance to prejudice and ignorance found in Whites of lesser refinement in *Guess Who's Coming to Dinner* and *In the Heat of the Night* (1967). Poitier won the Oscar for "Best Actor" for his portrayal of a handyman who builds a chapel for White European nuns in a rural American community in *Lilies of the Field* (1963). Harry Belafonte and Sammy Davis Jr. were two other Black actors who starred in films of the period in roles that showed Blacks in nonthreatening circumstances.

Whoopi Goldberg is among the Black performers who moved from nightclub stand-up comedy ranks to movie stardom in the 1980s.

Source: Daniel Langer and Comic Relief, Inc.

The mid-1960s and early 1970s brought a definitely threatening Black image to the movies as the so-called blaxploitation movies featuring nearly all-Black casts cavorted on screen with the assumption of a militant posture. The civil rights movement led by Dr. Martin Luther King Jr. was at its zenith. Hollywood again purged its conscience as urban Blacks took revenge against Whites in such movies as *Sweet Sweetback's Baadasssss Song* (1971) and in two urban detective films featuring Richard Roundtree in *Shaft* (1971) and *Shaft's Big Score* (1972). Whites generally showed little box-office interest in blaxploitation movies, and the genre soon lost its financial luster.

The mid- to late 1980s, however, brought a resurgence of African American presence in cinema due largely to the popularity of two Black comics—Eddie Murphy and Whoopi Goldberg—who had made their marks in television and the stand-up comedy circuit. Murphy proved to have major racial crossover appeal at the box office following a string of movies including *Trading Places* (1983), *Beverly Hills Cop* and its sequel *Beverly Hills Cop II* (1984 and 1987), *Coming to America* (1988), and *Harlem Nights* (1989). Goldberg made her movie debut to critical acclaim in *The Color Purple* (1985) and followed it with *Jumpin' Jack Flash* (1986) and *Clara's Heart* (1988). In the 1990s, she starred in *Ghost* (1990), *Sarafina!* and *Sister Act* (1992), and *Sister Act 2* (1993), among others. Goldberg's roles ranged from purely whimsical and comedic to serious and sensitive portrayals of Black women.

Black films with a harsher edge depicting life in urban ghettos also appeared in the 1990s including *Boyz N the Hood, Jungle Fever,* and *New Jack City* (1991). These works coincided with the emergence of a group of Black film directors who were successful in getting Hollywood to bankroll their efforts. Among them were Spike Lee, John Singleton, and Matty Rich. By the 1990s, Denzel Washington (*Glory,* 1989; *Mo' Better Blues,* 1990; *Malcolm X,* 1992; *The Pelican Brief,* 1993) had replaced Sidney Poitier as the foremost Black male dramatic actor.

The immediate post–World War II period saw a continuation of the relationship established before the war between Latinos and Hollywood that was built on economic considerations. During the war, U.S. filmmakers could not distribute their wares to European markets. Latin American countries came to represent 20% of Hollywood's total foreign market business during the era resulting in the development of joint movie projects. Many movies were filmed in Latin American nations with writing and financing provided by Hollywood. Most of the supporting roles were played by Latino actors, and the alliance led to an overly positive image of Latino characters as evidenced by such films as *The Fugitive* (1948) and *Way of a Gaucho* (1952). In 1954, a precedent was established with the independent production of *Salt of the Earth* in which Latino or Latin American actors portrayed all of the major roles.

By the 1960s, the Latin American market withered for Hollywood because Latin American countries had developed their own film industries and screen personalities. The number of Hollywood movies utilizing Latino themes dropped drastically, and those that did reverted to old stereotypical form by reintroducing the "greaser" as an urban gang member. Puerto Ricans were singled out for updated "greaser" treatment in two 1961 films, *West Side Story* and *The Young Savages.* The emphasis was on gang violence in urban America. Hollywood continued the violent "greaser" trend with *Duck, You Sucker* (1972), *Bring Me the Head of Alfredo Garcia* (1974), *The Warriors* (1979), and *Boulevard Nights* (1979). A distorted view of the Mexican family was presented in *The Children of Sanchez* (1978), but the early 1980s included movies produced and directed by Chicanos (*Seguín*, 1981; *The Ballad of Gregorio Cortez*, 1982). The 1981 release of *Zoot Suit* followed the success of the play that began its run in 1978. In *Zoot Suit,* based on an actual incident, the Mexican American is realistically portrayed during a World War II–era race riot in Los Angeles.

A series of movies beginning in the 1970s featured the nonthreatening, comedic adventures of "Cheech and Chong" in the Mexican American urban barrio. These films, however, were criticized for their perceived glorification of the drug culture, sexist orientation, and nontraditional lifestyle of the featured characters. In general, Hollywood offerings did little to portray Latinos as part of the social mainstream in the United States during the first half of the 1980s other than in bit parts. A more positive portrayal appeared with the release of *Stand and Deliver* (1988) based on the true story of a Mexican American high school mathematics teacher. Also receiving critical acclaim were *La Bamba* (1987) and *The Milagro Beanfield War* (1988). Generally, however, the late 1980s and early 1990s found Latinos in the story line background as either street toughs or drug traffickers as in *Colors* (1988), *Tequila Sunrise* (1988), and *Carlito's Way* (1993). Better images resulted when veteran actors Jimmy Smits and Edward James Olmos were featured in *My Family/Mi Familia* in 1995, which told the story of three generations of a Latino immigrant family, and the film biography of "Tejano" singer *Selena* (1997) helped bring Latina singer/actress Jennifer Lopez to stardom.

Japanese portrayals continued to be very negative immediately following World War II as American audiences were offered more war movies. Japanese acts of cruelty and torture were seen in *Tokyo Joe* (1949) and *Three Came Home* (1950). An exception, perhaps inspired by guilt response to the Japanese relocation camps, was *Go for Broke!* (1951), a positive portrayal of the heroic Japanese American military units that fought in Europe. A major reversal would soon take place, however, between Japanese and Chinese imagery in the movies.

With the coming of the Korean War, the Cold War, and McCarthyism, the issue of communism became the focal point of American fears and anxieties. Synonymous with communism were the Soviet Union and China. China, whose people had been viewed so warmly by Americans only a decade earlier, was once again seen as home of the Yellow Peril. Japan, on the other hand, was virtually a U.S. satellite and close ally by the late 1950s. Popular movies reflected both attitudes. The Japanese were initially portrayed with much more sensitivity than at any time since the Immigration Act of 1924. *The Bridge on the River Kwai* (1957) and *Battle of the Coral Sea* (1959) are examples of the softer treatment given the Japanese by Hollywood. Even the touchy subject of Japanese Anglo romance was explored in *Sayonara* (1957) and *My Geisha* (1962). Although such romances did not have happy endings, they were nevertheless not treated as a basic violation of nature.

Meanwhile, China (by now commonly referred to as "Red China" or "Communist China") took on the movie depictions reminiscent of the early 1930s. The Chinese regime was seen as oppressive and exploitive of its own people in *Satan Never Sleeps* (1962) and as a devious threat to the American system in *The Manchurian Candidate* (1962). The year 1963 marked the release of *55 Days at Peking* followed in 1966 by *The Sand Pebbles*. The latter two films were set in early-20th-century China and reinforced the image of drug addiction, prostitution, inhumanity, and deceit as staples of Chinese life. From the mid-1970s, following the reopening of diplomatic and trade ties with China, the pendulum swung again in China's favor, and Hollywood curtailed its negative portrayals after several fantasy characterizations such as *Dr. No* (1962) and others in the James Bond spy thriller series. A surge of American interest in Oriental martial arts, however, spurred the creation of a series of films featuring almost nonstop violent action scenes showing villains and heroes employing kung fu, karate, and other combative techniques.

Chinese American actor Bruce Lee, an acrobatic master of the martial arts, became the catalyst for that motion picture genre that portrayed the Chinese as sadistically violent. Generally, however, his films depicted Chinese characters in both heroic and villainous roles. In terms of popularity with American audiences, Jackie Chan succeeded Lee as the martial arts master. Chan's roles, however, were comedic, and he teamed with Black comedian Chris Tucker in a series of movie escapades including *Rush Hour* (1998) that generally played to traditional stereotypes.

In the post–Vietnam War era, American film producers made the Vietnamese their next target of Asian stereotyping based on the same long-standing attitudes. These people were portrayed on screen as crafty, devious, guerilla warfare perpetrators of violence in *The Deer Hunter* (1978), *Apocalypse Now* (1979), and *Platoon* (1986), among other films into the 1980s. From the mid-1980s into the 1990s, White actors Chuck Norris and Jean-Claude Van Damme assumed the mantle as filmdom's leading martial arts masters, often vanquishing Asian foes in the process. Although the Japanese American community voiced concerns about stereotypical characterizations in *Rising Sun* (1993), more sensitive portrayals of Asian peoples surfaced occasionally during the period including *The Killing Fields* (1984) and *The Last Emperor* (1987). Perhaps the most insightful American film portrayal of Asians in many years was the screen adaptation of Amy Tan's novel, *The Joy Luck Club* (1993). The movie explored Chinese and Chinese American cultural nuances and resulting interpersonal conflicts through the eyes of three generations of Chinese women. A continuation of the trend toward a more esoteric view of Chinese culture was manifest in the special effects triumph of *Crouching Tiger, Hidden Dragon* (2000).

As U.S. forces fought conflicts in the Middle East in the mid-1990s and early 2000s, racial, cultural, and religious intolerance toward Arab, Muslim, and Islamic peoples brought forth a spate of new negative stereotypes to American movie screens. It was against this backdrop that the 1995 bombing of a federal office building in Oklahoma City—later determined to be perpetrated by a White disillusioned former U.S. soldier—initially set off public fears that Arab terrorists were responsible. By 1998 *The Siege,* a story about terrorism in New York City, featured a government roundup of Arab American citizens called "towel heads" by a character in the film.

Television Brings Stereotypes Home

Commercial television became a significant factor in American information and entertainment in 1948 when Milton Berle's network variety show *Texaco Star Theater* achieved nationwide popularity. The show spurred the purchase of TV sets in epidemic proportions. Little time was wasted in telecasting tried-and-true stereotypes of marginalized racial and cultural groups into America's homes. The Second World War had ended, and the old notions and images were seamlessly transferred to the new medium. Moreover, sponsors lined up to cash in on the new communications technology.

In short order, the "noble savage" was revisited. Among the first was Tonto, the Lone Ranger's "faithful" Indian companion played throughout the series's eight-year run by Jay Silverheels, an actor of Mohawk tribal heritage. *The Lone Ranger* first aired on television in 1949 but had begun

Jay Silverheels, an actor of Mohawk heritage, played the trusted sidekick of the masked Lone Ranger in the 1950s television series that began on radio in 1933.

Source: © Bettmann/CORBIS.

as a radio series in 1933. While the Lone Ranger's mask often made those he encountered in his Western adventures apprehensive, the fact he maintained a friendship with a Native American Indian made him even more suspect. Tonto's image, however, was otherwise positive because he fought for justice in the highest tradition of American folklore. His role as a Native American reflected the established stereotypes including the pinto pony, broken English dialect, fringed buckskin attire, and secondary status relative to the White hero.

In ensuing years, the historical portrayal of Native Americans on network television differed little from that experienced in Hollywood cinema. The list of prime-time TV series featuring positive, accurate representations of Native Americans is extremely brief as an examination of either past or present conditions. Perhaps the only attempt to do so was made in the 1955–1956 season when CBS aired *Brave Eagle*. The show sought to portray Native American Indians' viewpoint of the White expansionist movement into their territory during the latter part of the 19th century. The program did feature Native American cast members, but, ironically, a real Indian (Keena Nomkeena) played the foster son to White actor Keith Larsen who played a Cheyenne tribal chief. There was also an old sage who orally recited tribal history and events—a character also played by a White actor. *Brave Eagle* was followed by ABC's *Broken Arrow*, which appeared for five years (1956–1960). The series, however, featured an all-White cast, and the story line centered on Indian and White cooperation in fighting frontier injustice. During the 1960s when television was dominated by Westerns, Native American Indians were mostly relegated to their movie image, serving as either foils or backdrops to the stories of how the West was won.

This basic pattern continued into the 1990s. One example was *The Young Riders* offered by ABC from 1989 into the early 1990s. In the show Gregg Rainwater played the role of Running Buck Cross, who was half Kiowa Indian. The story line was about the Pony Express era, but television sensibilities of the 1980s and 1990s demanded revisionist history of the western frontier, so *The Young Riders* spent most of their time protecting the innocent and displaying kindness to any Native Americans who happened to wander into an episode. A different and unique twist came to Native American TV portrayals with the 1990 arrival of *Northern Exposure* on CBS. In it Elaine Miles portrayed Eskimo medical receptionist Marilyn Whirlwind, an unflappable and down-to-earth personality. The show was a ratings success and continued on prime time into the mid-1990s.

Black Americans composed the largest non-White racial presence on network television over the last 50 years of the 20th century. That fact, however, did not result in an altogether satisfactory TV portrayal of the realities of the diverse and complex Black experience in the United States. In variety programming, Blacks appeared frequently as guest performers almost from the inception of network commercial television. Ed Sullivan featured them as early as 1948 on his CBS *Toast of the Town* show (later called *The Ed Sullivan Show*) as did Steve Allen as host of NBC's *The Tonight Show* from 1954 to 1957. In 1950, three network shows went on the air featuring Blacks in their casts as regulars. They were *Beulah, The Jack Benny Program,* and *The Stu Erwin Show,* and each portrayed Blacks in subservient, domestic roles. The *Beulah* character was a maid and mammy figure in a White household; Eddie Anderson portrayed Jack Benny's valet "Rochester" on TV for 15 years; and Willie Best, who had played imitative Stepin Fetchit roles in numerous movies, brought the character to the *Erwin Show* as the family handyman.

The first show with an all-Black cast made its television debut in 1951, although it had been immensely popular as a radio series since 1929 with its White creators playing the major roles. *The Amos 'n Andy Show* was awaited with much anticipation across the nation because the show's creators, Freeman Gosden and Charles Correll, held a widely publicized four-year search for the Black actors who would bring the show to television. A special televised segment was arranged before a studio audience for Gosden and Correll to introduce the handpicked cast prior to the first show. In introducing the male actors, the creators occasionally referred to them as *boys*, a term long despised by Blacks as a relic of slavery in the United States. The original series lasted two years, but reruns continued into the mid-1960s, always in controversy over the images projected about Blacks. Although the show was based on characters with little intellectual capacities or otherwise lacking ethical values and employment, there were Black characters seen as attorneys, business owners, educators, and other professionals. Nevertheless, pressure from civil rights groups forced the program off the air entirely in 1966 when CBS withdrew it from sale. The advent of videocassette technology made *Amos 'n Andy* a brisk seller in the home entertainment market into the latter half of the 1990s.

Two other significant programs featuring Blacks prior to the civil rights movement of the 1960s starred male vocalists. In 1952, ABC's 15-minute *Billy Daniels Show* was the first national TV program with a Black host. It ran for only 13 weeks, one third of a season by industry standards of the time. A musical-variety show hosted by singer Nat "King" Cole, which aired for 59 consecutive weeks from 1956 to 1957, fared somewhat better. Many prominent entertainers, several sponsors, and NBC executives supported Cole and made considerable efforts to keep the show afloat despite poor ratings throughout its 13-month history. Although Cole was an extremely talented vocalist and successful recording star, his show could not win the ratings competition against the popular mainstream programs in its time slot.[1] From the mid-1960s into the mid-1980s, Blacks were seen on numerous TV series usually as comedy-variety show hosts or in situation comedies.

Many shows employed what were seen by critics as a single "token" Black character and from "Amos 'n' Andy" to the fall of 1984 there were only four other shows (all situation comedies) with predominantly Black casts that lasted more than one season in regular network television: *Sanford and Son* (1972), *Good Times* (1974), *The Jeffersons* (1975), and *What's Happening!!* (1976). Of course, the TV ratings epoch *Roots* aired as a prime-time "miniseries" special in 1977, and many believed it served as a catharsis of guilt for Whites over the historical treatment of Blacks in America. An estimated 100 million viewers watched the program over eight consecutive nights that began several trends in television programming.

Into the mid-1980s the primary roles for Blacks in prime-time network television were still in situation comedies rather than serious dramatic programs. Arguably, however, critics maintained that network television in the 1980s was almost all

Actress Diahann Carroll broke racial and cultural barriers in her nonstereotypical role as nurse Julia Baker in the weekly series *Julia,* which ran from 1968 to 1971 on NBC.

Source: © Bettmann/CORBIS.

Bill Cosby (right) starred in the nation's top-rated television program throughout much of the 1980s. His sitcom, *The Cosby Show,* featured an all-Black cast, including Malcolm-Jamal Warner, pictured here, who played his son.

Source: © Jacques M. Chenet/CORBIS.

situation comedies and prime-time "soap opera" serials. Actress Diahann Carroll, who became the first Black woman to star in a network comedy/dramatic series (*Julia,* 1968), made history again in 1984 when she joined the regular cast of ABC's prime-time soap opera *Dynasty.* That same year marked the opening season of NBC's *The Cosby Show,* which became television's number-one rated program throughout the mid-1980s, proving that a show with an all-Black cast could be an overwhelming commercial success. *The Cosby Show*'s success opened the way for numerous other Black-oriented sitcoms that flooded the airwaves into the early 2000s. Few of them, however, had the production and scriptwriting qualities that characterized the *Cosby* program.

The most significant Black comedy/variety show of the early and mid-1990s was the Fox network's *In Living Color,* which first aired in 1990. The fast-paced show resembled a hybrid of *Laugh-In* and *Saturday Night Live,* and its success was due primarily to its multitalented writer, producer, director, actor, and comedian, Keenen Ivory Wayans. By the mid-1990s, advertisers and their television network cohorts had awakened to the fact that Blacks watched more TV than any other racial group, and, in 1994, 25 programs were aired on the four networks either starring or featuring Blacks in major roles. Significantly, however, there were major differences in the viewing patterns of Blacks as compared to the general American audience. A listing of the most popular shows of the 1993 season revealed no programs made the top 10 on both lists.[2] A significant development of the late 1990s and early 2000s was the emergence of television's United Paramount Network (UPN), which seemed to target the African American audience with all-Black situation comedies such as *The Hughleys* and *The Parkers.*

Latinos were also brought to the small screen early in television history when the romantic figure of *The Cisco Kid* rode into American homes in 1950. The series aired for seven years but only in syndication to independent stations. In 1994, some 37 years after the original series ended, it was revived as a movie with Jimmy Smits in the lead role. *The Cisco Kid* was the first successful syndicated program and was among the first color filmed series. *The Cisco Kid* had been an entertainment fixture since the character's creation in the O'Henry short story, "The Caballero's Way." Cisco was originally a bandito-type character in O'Henry's story who preyed on the rich to help the poor, à la Robin Hood. The character was brought to the movies in several productions with various leading men including Duncan Renaldo, who brought the role to TV. Cisco and his sidekick Pancho delighted youngsters, who were the key to their popularity, as they enjoyed a jovial repartee while roaming the Southwest to fight injustice. Renaldo's portrayal was vintage "Latin lover" except he never got romantically involved with the love-stricken ladies given the fact his audience was primarily children. Pancho, played by Leo Carrillo, was a rotund, gregarious character who affected the stereotypical speech American audiences had come to expect from movie Mexicans who were not "Latin lovers." Often Pancho would urge his partner, "Hey Cees-ko, let's went!" The next Latino role appeared in 1951 when a White actor, Don Diamond, played El Toro, the Mexican sidekick to the lead in *The Adventures of Kit Carson.*

But the biggest Latino television personality of the early days of television was Desi Arnaz who was Lucille Ball's actual and theatrical husband in the long-running show, *I Love Lucy.* Although Arnaz played a respectable husband who was a bandleader, he also played the straight man to Lucy's zany schemes. His Latin temperament, which exploded into a torrent of Spanish diatribe when Lucy's ill-fated activities were revealed, was classic stereotyped imagery. The popular series came to television in 1951 and continued in original production until 1957. A swashbuckling adventure show, *Zorro,* debuted in 1957, and although set in early California, it concerned the political struggles of Spanish settlers. Mexicans, however, served only as villains, buffoons, or backdrops to the affairs of the more highly cultured Spanish aristocracy.

In the 1960s three television programs stood out for their Latino portrayals. In *The Real McCoys* (1957–1963), Tony Martinez played farmhand Pepino Garcia, a role consistent with audience expectations. A non-Latino carried the TV image of the simple-minded Mexican when *The Bill Dana Show* appeared in 1963 for a two-year run. Dana's opening line with a thick Mexican accent became a virtual national catchphrase because of his nightclub act and record sales: "My name, Jose Jimenez." In the show Jimenez worked as a hotel bellhop whose ineptness constantly got him into comedic situations. Perhaps the most unusual prime-time TV show centering on Latino characters was *The High Chaparral* (1967–1971). It was one of the numerous "adult Westerns" aired during the period and featured an interracial marriage between the daughter of a Mexican cattle baron and a wealthy White rancher. The characters portrayed by Latino actors, however, generally had roles as ranch hands.

Latino (Puerto Rican) actor Jimmy Smits became a prominent fixture in the cast of several network television shows beginning in the 1980s.

Source: ©istockphoto.com/EdStock.

In the 1970s, there were two network situation comedies based on the Mexican American barrio of East Los Angeles. Most recognized and criticized of the two was *Chico and the Man* starring Freddie Prinze Sr., which aired for five seasons on NBC beginning in 1974. Chico was a young streetwise character who used his savvy to drum up business for the auto repair garage where he worked. The racial "humor" and image portrayed by Chico was the subject of controversy throughout the show's network existence. In 1976, another "sitcom" was brought to ABC titled *Viva Valdez* about an East Los Angeles family. It lasted only four months. Two other series featuring Latino actors began in the 1970s and continued until 1983. NBC screened *CHiPs* for the first time in 1977 cofeaturing handsome Latino actor Erik Estrada as a California Highway Patrolman with romance on his mind. *Fantasy Island* (1977) starred Ricardo Montalban as the romantic figure host on an idyllic isle. Neither portrayal was very distant from the Latin lover roles that Hollywood had created decades earlier. In 1984, ABC made its second attempt at a sitcom centered on the life of an East Los Angeles barrio family with Paul Rodriguez in *a.k.a. Pablo*. Critics claimed the show was harmful because Rodriguez's jokes were seen as ridiculing Mexican American culture. The program lasted only six episodes and did not return in 1985. A Latino flavor was captured in NBC's *Miami Vice,* which aired from 1984 to 1990 with Edward James Olmos starring as Lt. Martin Castillo against a backdrop of various drug operatives, many of whom were Latino. A more positive portrayal came in 1986 with Jimmy Smits's role as lawyer Victor Sifuentes on NBC's *L.A. Law.* The show continued its run into 1994, a year in which Latinos filled only 11 of national television's 800 prime-time roles.

Although the multibillion-dollar Latino consumer market in the United States created an expanded presence for them in television, change was gradual. Some Latino actors such as Raquel Welch and Martin Sheen once took non-Latino roles and subverted their cultural identities to obtain steady employment. By the year 2000, they were "able to be ethnically present to the Latino audience but ethnically invisible to a majority audience," said Felix Sanchez, president of the National Hispanic Foundation for the Arts, in a *New York Times* article.[3] Sanchez added, "We need to move it beyond that to where our culture and identity are fully integrated in a character."[4]

Asian portrayals came to television in 1949 in an ABC crime show called *Mysteries of Chinatown* starring White actor Marvin Miller as Dr. Yat Fu. The show was set in San Francisco's Chinatown where Miller's character was in stereotype as owner of an herb and curio shop. The regular supporting cast was all White and, as evidenced by the show's title, was designed to exploit the old stereotype of the "mysterious" Asian. Next to surface was the TV version of *The Adventures of Dr. Fu Manchu* (1956), another crime drama with an all-White cast. The program was full of vintage "Yellow Peril" imagery with Dr. Fu sending his agents on various missions designed to subvert the cause of Western civilization. The nefarious and wily Dr. Fu was based in various cities in the Orient as the series dredged up the old Sax Rohmer stereotypes. In fact, the series was facilitated by Rohmer's sale of rights to his creation in 1955 to Republic Pictures. The show was a non-network syndicated production and aired for only one season. Ironically, the following year (1956) it was followed to television by the other venerable Chinese character, Charlie Chan. *The New Adventures of Charlie Chan* was also a syndicated series lasting only one year. J. Carrol Naish played Chan, but an Asian actor, James Hong, was cast in the role of Chan's "number-one son" Barry Chan. The series was produced in Great Britain, and the Chan character operated from London.

In the 1960s, ABC aired an adventure series, *Hong Kong,* which reinforced the Chinese image of intrigue, sexy women, smuggling, and drug peddling. At least two Asian actors were cast as series regulars during its single-year run (1960–1961). The same network brought *The Green Hornet* to prime-time TV for a one-year stay in 1966–1967. The significance of the series was the casting of Bruce Lee as the Green Hornet's sidekick Kato. Lee's weekly demonstration of martial arts skills as he fought crime helped launch the popularity of Oriental self-defense techniques in the U.S. Interestingly, *The Green Hornet* was the creation of George W. Trendle who also developed *The Lone Ranger.* In both concepts, a trusty ethnic minority sidekick, perhaps for the purpose of adding a fantasy appeal for the mass audience, supports the hero. Bruce Lee's influence sparked another ABC series, *Kung Fu*, a Western starring David Carradine and supporting Asian actors including Keye Luke and Philip Ahn. Lee was a consultant to those who developed the *Kung Fu* show and labored under the impression he was to be their choice for the lead role. When Carradine was selected for the part, Lee confided to friends that he had been the victim of racism. *Kung Fu's* producers told Lee they didn't believe a Chinese actor could be seen as a hero in the eyes of the American television audience.[5] The show became a throwback to the "mysterious" Asian stereotype. It aired from 1972 to 1975. With racism standing as a barrier to stardom in the United States, Bruce Lee went to Hong Kong where he achieved superstardom throughout Asia as a film star.

The greatest Asian presence in television began in the 1960s and featured an array of supporting police and criminal characters in the long-running CBS series *Hawaii Five-O* (1968–1980). At least three Asian actors appeared as regulars on the show, and lead character, Detective Steve McGarrett, pursued an archenemy Asian character, Wo Fat, periodically throughout its 12-year tenure. Generally, Asian portrayals in *Hawaii Five-O* were varied and diverse although definite stereotypes were projected. The show's vulnerability to stereotypical criticism was its portrayal of White superiority and leadership in a predominantly Asian environment.

There have been several prime-time shows throughout the history of American television that perpetuated the subservient, humble Asian image. Among them were *Bachelor Father* (1957–1962) with an Asian "houseboy" character played by Sammee Tong and *Bonanza* (1959–1972) with Chinese cook Hop Sing played by Victor Sen Yung. In *The Courtship of Eddie's Father* (1969–1972), Miyoshi Umeki played a housekeeper who was often befuddled by situations that arose in the household. Umeki's character was apparently married to an American because her role was that of "Mrs. Livingston" although her mannerisms and philosophy were clearly Japanese, as U.S. entertainment media have defined them over the years.

The early 1980s were characterized by a continuation of Asian supporting roles in various sitcoms and dramatic offerings. Two unique programs utilizing Asian themes came to network TV in 1980. A weeklong miniseries, *Shogun*, was based on the exploits of a White adventurer in feudal Japan. Although providing American audiences with some insight into Japanese culture, the program placed an emphasis upon the violence of samurai warriors and an aura of the sexual mysticism of Japanese women. The same year NBC brought a variety show called *Pink Lady* to its schedule featuring a Japanese singing duo of the same name. The two young ladies were attractive and spoke little English, so comic Jeff Altman served as facilitator. As an attempt to bring the demure, humble, and sexy image of the Japanese woman to network television, *Pink Lady* was a failure and was cancelled after less than two months on the air. That female image, however, returned to prominence in 1983 when actress Rosalind Chao took a costarring role in *After M.A.S.H.* In the CBS series, which aired until December 1984, Ms. Chao's role was as the Korean wife of a White ex-GI who had served in the Korean War. A different Asian female portrayal

Pat Morita, a Japanese American actor, was featured in the popular television series *Happy Days* and later starred in his own series, *Ohara*, in which he portrayed a police officer who used mystical Asian techniques to apprehend criminals.

Source: ABC Photo Archives/Contributor/Disney ABC Television Group/Getty Images.

came to television in 1994 with the ABC sitcom *All-American Girl* featuring Margaret Cho. Cho's character personified a quick-tongued modern Asian woman with a distinctly "American" attitude, but the show failed to convey a genuine sense of Asian America, as discussed further in a subsequent section of this chapter.

Japanese American actor Pat Morita, who had played the role of Arnold in the long-running (1974–1984) *Happy Days* on ABC, became the star of his own series on the same network. For two seasons in 1987–1988, Morita starred in *Ohara* as the title character, a Los Angeles police detective who preferred mystical Asian patience and persuasion to violence in dealing with criminals. Lt. Ohara usually didn't carry a gun but, true to stereotype, would resort to martial arts when necessary. A similar series using a Chinese actor in the lead role was *Martial Law* (1998) featuring corpulent Sammo Hung Kam-Bo as a Hong Kong detective on loan to the Los Angeles Police Department.

Television viewers of the 1950s through the 1990s found little original programming featuring Middle Eastern characters. In general, they saw television airings of movies that had been made decades earlier, thus providing new generations of Americans the "opportunity" to absorb old stereotypes from a bygone era. Unfortunately, there were plenty of films featuring Sinbad the Sailor, magic carpets, and an assortment of dubious sheiks. When fresh material featuring Muslim people and other persons from the Middle East made their way onto the small screen after the turn of the 21st century, the resulting programming was decidedly more disturbing.

And There's Sexism Too

For women of color, the lack of representation in the media is even bleaker. Not only do they face the obstacles of gender discrimination, but they must also overcome the hurdles of tokenism in an industry notorious for its lack of performance in achieving diversity goals. As was noted at a 2002 conference on Empowering Women of Color in the media:

> The universes of "media" and "women of color" have a strained relationship borne out of absence and misrepresentation. We may think of the tokenized Asian character in an otherwise completely white TV sitcom, of the newspaper articles that unequivocally state it is young Latina and African American girls that are predominantly unwed and uneducated mothers, or of the ongoing portrayals of Middle Eastern women as utterly oppressed and uneducated victims. It can seem that the face of mainstream media in the United States has, in some ways, changed very little; our articulate, authentic, and ever-evolving voices are simply unheard.[6]

Research data that specifically address women of color are limited, but the following discussion provides a broader overview of the status of women in the media, with an emphasis on minority women where data are available. The dearth of minority female perspectives in media management perpetuates stereotypical, sexist, and often classist images that continue to undermine the credibility and value of women in the larger society.

Breaking the Barrier

It was a historical night for African American performers when Halle Berry and Denzel Washington won Oscars for "Best Actress" and "Best Actor," respectively, at the 74th Academy Awards in 2002. Not only was it the first time that two African Americans won Hollywood's highest awards for acting, but Berry also became the first African American woman to win for Best Actress for her role in *Monster's Ball.* Three years earlier, she won an Emmy for her portrayal of Dorothy Dandridge, the first African American woman to receive an Oscar nomination for Best Actress for *Carmen Jones* in 1954. Upon receiving her award, an emotional Berry acknowledged the magnitude of the moment as she gushed: "This moment is so much bigger than me. This moment is for Dorothy Dandridge, Lena Horne, Diahann Carroll. It's for the women who stand beside me, Jada Pinkett, Angela Bassett, Vivica Fox, and the nameless, faceless women of color who now stand a chance tonight because the door has been opened."[7]

The groundbreaking evening trumpeted a new era in which women of color not only could break racial barriers, but also could play leads in nontraditional—though often stereotypical—female roles in mainstream films. While lead roles that featured African American women are still few and far between, such as Whitney Houston's role in *The Bodyguard* (1992), a number have been cast in high-profile supporting roles such as Whoopi Goldberg in *Ghost* (1990) and Beyoncé Knowles in *Austin Powers in*

Goldmember (2002). Indeed, African American women had come a long way since the days when they were cast as affable servants content to serve their White masters, as in *Gone With the Wind* (1939), or as subservient buffoons as in the 1950s ABC show *Beulah*, or even as a tough femme fatale that made Pam Grier the queen of blaxploitation in films like *Coffy* (1973), *Foxy Brown* (1974), and *Friday Foster* (1975).

Diahann Carroll broke down racial barriers in the 1960s with her television role as earnest nurse Julia Baker in NBC's *Julia* (1968–1971). In response to the social movements and racial reforms of the 1960s, television moved to present "respectable" images of Blacks that more closely reflected America's newfound sense of racial morality. Consequently, Carroll became the first African American actress who did not portray a servant to star in her own series.[8]

But the drawbacks to such "assimilationist" shows like *Julia* that featured African Americans in middle-class lifestyles unfortunately positioned them as tokens in a White world disconnected from the stark realities of a largely economically disadvantaged Black community. In contrast, during the 1970s, a series of Black-oriented sitcoms featuring African American women emerged on network television such as *Good Times* (CBS) and *The Jeffersons* (CBS) that exposed the gritty realities of inner-city and/or urban life—albeit sanitized with humor and comic relief. However, while the shows were firmly set in the Black world with Black characters, they were still developed by White writers and producers to appeal to the predominantly White television audience. In fact, some critics questioned whether the medium had actually regressed back to the buffoonish portrayals of the 1950s.[9]

African Americans have experienced the greatest success both on screen and behind the scenes. According to a study published by the UCLA Center for African American Studies (2002), both Black and White Americans were overrepresented on the screen in 2001, accounting for 76% of all characters, and 16% of all "featured" characters—or those who have speaking roles or who are explicitly highlighted by the words or actions of other "featured" actors. Combined, these two groups represented 92% of all prime-time characters, while composing only 82% of the nation's population.

In contrast, Latinos were grossly underrepresented in prime time, constituting only 2% of all characters, while Asian Americans approached appropriate representation at roughly 3% of all characters. Native Americans were the most underrepresented group, at 0% of all characters. When comparing genders, Black men significantly outnumber Black women on the screen 59% to 41%. The percentages are identical for White men and women.[10]

In the 2001–2002 and 2002–2003 television seasons, African American women enjoyed the greatest amount of exposure on their own prime-time shows—although essentially "ghettoized" on the two least-watched networks (UPN and WB) in a handful of Black-oriented sitcoms. In the

2002–2003 fall lineup, Tracee Ellis Ross, Golden Brooks, Persia White, and Jill Marie Jones reprised their roles in UPN's *Girlfriends.* Although there were no plans for singer/actress Brandy to return in UPN's *Moesha,* her show was responsible for spinning off *The Parkers,* featuring the popular actress Mo'Nique. And Rachel True, Essence Atkins, and Telma Hopkins were featured in UPN's 2002–2006 show, *Half & Half.*[11]

While television has been considered by many to be the most powerful medium, it has historically been resistant to diversifying the power at the top. However, a number of African American women have risen through the ranks to hold real power positions that influence projects and determine what we see and don't see on the small screen.

In 2001, Pamela Thomas-Graham was named president and CEO of CNBC, and took responsibility for overseeing the company's $500 million domestic operations—which include programming, advertising sales, and ensuring brand synergy across CNBC's TV and Internet platforms. Broadcast veteran Lana Corbi is president and CEO of Crown Media United States. Prior to becoming CEO, she was executive vice president and COO of the holding company, which owns the $114 million Hallmark Channel, and had held several top-level executive positions at Fox Broadcasting Company. In 2002, Christina Norman was named executive vice president and general manager of VH1, a subsidiary of Viacom that reaches more than 82 million U.S. households. At the time, she supervised VH1's sister channels, VH1 Classic, VH1 MegaHits (Brazil only), VH1 Soul, VH1 Country (now CMT Pure Country), and VH1 Uno (now mtvU). Paula Madison, who began her journalism career as a print reporter and moved to television news in 1984, was president and general manager of NBC 4 (KNBC), NBC's owned and operated station in Los Angeles, until 2011. She was the first African American woman to become general manager at a network-owned station in a top-five market.[12]

Arguably the most prominent, powerful woman of color in television is Oprah Winfrey, who is chairman and CEO of Harpo Productions and cofounder of Oxygen Media, which includes a women's cable network. She became a television icon when her television program, *The Oprah Winfrey Show,* debuted in 1986 and became an enormous success—attracting 26 million U.S. viewers. In fact, her influence was so far-reaching that when a book was featured on Oprah's Book Club, it instantly hit the best-seller list. Her development deals with ABC through Harpo Productions resulted in the award-winning TV movie, *Tuesdays with Morrie,* and she also starred in and produced the Oxygen Network show, *Use Your Life.*[13]

Sexism in Hollywood

Historically, Latina women have been portrayed in the media as either fiery, passionate, tempestuous sexpots or domestic help. Mexican film stars such as the glamorous Maria Felix, whose perfect beauty got her discovered as she was walking down the street and catapulted her to international stardom, portrayed a collection of fierce women over several decades in such films as *La Generala* (1970) and *Enamorada* (1946).[14]

One of the most recognizable Latina actresses is the former Raquel Tejada, better known as Raquel Welch. When Welch broke into movies in the mid-1960s with such early hits as *One Million Years B.C.* and *Fantastic Voyage*, the studios never promoted the fact that she had a Latino background. Today, she trumpets the fact, and has reinvented herself as a Latina actress who now boasts of her cultural roots. The PBS series, *American Family*, created by Gregory Nava (director of *Selena*), premiered in 2002 and was billed as the first drama series on broadcast TV featuring a Latino cast. The series about a Mexican American family deals with the serious— and often comedic—aspects of life in East Los Angeles.[15] Welch plays Aunt Dora, the drama queen of the family, who is a passionate, romantic woman who might have become a Hollywood star if she had vigorously pursued an acting career. As one television critic noted, Welch infused the role with her trademark sultriness and smoky voice.

As for getting beyond the role of the maid or sex kitten, actress Lupe Ontiveros's idea of a plum role that counters traditional media stereotypes was that of Hispanic heroine and union organizer Dolores Huerta, who founded the United Farm Workers, or the 17th-century Mexican poet and nun Sor Juana Inés de la Cruz—who is often viewed as the first feminist of the Americas.[16]

Despite the headway some Hispanic actresses have made by being cast in nonstereotypical roles, most Latinas are still portrayed by the media in ways that connote sex and sexuality. For instance, the Winter 2002 edition of *Sports Illustrated* featured bikini-clad model Yamila Diaz-Rahi on the cover with the subheading "Red Hot in Latin America . . . Yamila sizzles in Mexico." Even on the Spanish-language publication *TVyNovelas*, the cover had two Latina actresses posing in swimsuits—despite the fact that the issue has nothing to do with swimwear. In a *New York Times* article titled "Latino Style Is Cool. Oh, All Right: It's Hot," author Ruth La Ferla describes 17-year-old Lisa Forero of La Guardia High School of Performing Arts in Manhattan, perched on 4-inch platform boots, playing up her curves in a form-fitting gray spandex dress and sporting outsize gold hoop earrings with pink and cream airbrushed fingertips. Did she fret that her image—that of a saucy bombshell—bordered on self-parody? Not in the least. In fact, dressing up as a familiar stereotype was Ms. Forero's pointedly aggressive way of claiming her Latino heritage.[17]

In "Will the Real Latina Please Stand Up?" *Latina* magazine (July 2002) profiled three nonstereotypical Latina authors to show how, in reality, Hispanic women come packaged in many different shades and sizes. While the public may immediately conjure up images of Cameron Diaz (tall, blonde, blue-eyed), Salma Hayek (petite, brunette, olive-skinned), or Gina Torres (statuesque, curly haired, dark-skinned), the truth is that Latinas include a broad range of peoples from various ethnicities and nationalities. For example, profiled author Veronica Chambers hails from Panama and may look African American, but she cannot deny her Latin roots. When people see author Michele Serros's straight black hair, prominent nose, and flat face, they automatically assume she's Native American, but she is—as her Latina friends assert—"totally Mexican." For author Rosa Lowinger, her rapid-fire Spanish perplexes most people who'll ask, "What language is that?" When she replies it's Cuban, they look astounded and blurt, "How can you be Cuban with light hair and blue eyes?" She may explain that her grandparents were Eastern European Jews who emigrated to Cuba in the 1920s, but if she detects a racist or stereotypical attitude behind the question, she'll retort, "What, am I not dark enough to call myself *Cubana*?"[18]

Perhaps the most visible and successful Latina actress to emerge in the 1990s and transition into nontraditional, nonstereotypical roles is the multitalented Jennifer Lopez. She not only appeared in a string of box-office hits with some of Hollywood's leading men, but she also topped the music charts with her CDs *On the 6, J.Lo,* and *This Is Me . . . Then.* Born in the Bronx, New York, and of Puerto Rican descent, Lopez got her first big break in 1990 when she won a dance audition that landed her a spot as a Fly Girl on Keenen Ivory Wayans's Fox television series *In Living Color.* She went on to appear in the series *Second Chances* and *Hotel Malibu* (credited on both as Melinda Lopez), the short-lived *South Central,* and the television movie *Nurses on the Line: The Crash of Flight 7* (1993).

In 1995, Lopez made her big-screen debut in *The Money Train* opposite Wesley Snipes and Woody Harrelson, before working with director Gregory Nava in *My Family/Mi Familia* (1995). This led indirectly to the high-profile role of murdered Tejano star Selena Quintanilla in the 1997 biopic *Selena,* which garnered Lopez Golden Globe and MTV Movie Award nominations for "Best Actress." By 2002, Lopez became the first Latina actress to earn $12 million per film, and her long list of movie credits include *Jack* (1996), *Anaconda* (1997), *Out of Sight* (1998), *The Cell* (2000), *The Wedding Planner* (2001), *Angel Eyes* (2001), *Enough* (2002), and *Maid in Manhattan* (2002).[19]

Future roles for Latinas may be best illustrated by actress Salma Hayek, who moved to Los Angeles in 1991 to make movies after being Mexico's most popular soap opera star at age 21 on *Teresa.* After enrolling in a Shakespearean acting class to learn English, she soon found out she did not need it to play the parts she was being offered: extras and maids. Although she eventually landed a recurring role in 1993 as a neighbor on sitcom *The Sinbad Show,* work remained scarce. "I came here and had to start at the bottom," said Hayek. "There were no parts for Latinas. It was very painful, but the hardest part about staying was that I was constantly offered soaps in Mexico. The temptation to take the work was great. Then I got the part in *Desperado* [1995], and everything changed."[20]

After landing roles in such movies as *Fools Rush In* (1997), *Dogma* (1999), and *Wild Wild West* (1999), she founded her own production company, Ventanarosa (*Pink Window*), and starred in several films the company produced: *No One Writes to the Colonel* (1999), *In the Time of the Butterflies* (2001), and *Frida* (2002)—a film both Madonna and Jennifer Lopez tried to make about the life of the innovative Mexican artist and free thinker, Frida Kahlo, but that Hayek won out with pure passion after a seven-year struggle to produce and star in the film. Her performance in the film earned her an Academy Award nomination. Reflecting on her success, she said, "I used to be a whiner . . . Now, instead of whining that there are no parts for women, no parts for Latinas, I am creating them."[21]

From Geisha Girl to Woman Warrior

Over the past two decades there has been an unusual proliferation of Asian women news anchors in major markets, spurred by Hollywood's stereotypical images and the success enjoyed by such high-profile newscasters as Connie Chung. From portrayals of the submissive, subservient "geisha" girl in such 1950s movies as *Sayonara,* to the Asian woman as an exotic, sexual object in films like *The World of Suzie Wong,* Hollywood has created a favorable perception of the Asian woman as being beautiful, docile, and sensual to the American audience.

Nancy Kwan portrayed Chinese women in the early 1960s movies *The World of Suzie Wong* and *Flower Drum Song.*

Source: © John Springer Collection/CORBIS.

San Francisco news anchor Wendy Tokuda believes the profusion of Asian women newscasters reflects the fascination Americans have with the geisha girl—or Singapore Girl—and is rooted in the experiences U.S. servicemen had with Asian women while overseas in China, Japan, Korea, the Philippines, and Vietnam. The contact, however, was primarily with prostitutes, "a very select strata of the society overseas, and they bring those images home," says Tokuda. This, in turn, has contributed to—if not created—the "Suzie Wong syndrome," or distinct impressions about the exotic Asian female that still lingers today.[22]

This archetype of the Asian woman is vividly illustrated in a 1979 *Oakland Tribune* feature article titled "East Meets West," in which the author describes a 48-year-old divorcée who found the ultimate gift to the American male in a 23-year-old "Oriental" servant:

> She would be required to be a complete housekeeper. She would prepare meals on the evenings when he dines at home. She would do laundry. She would keep the apartment immaculate because he's a "nutsy clean." . . . Naturally, she would do the grocery shopping and the cooking from a marketing allowance of $90 a week.
>
> And the understanding went beyond that. He liked to be bathed. He told her all of his requirements in advance. And he would like on occasion more than just massage. She understood. And about every 10 days or so he would be entertaining. He likes to give dinner parties for three couples, and the young maid would be expected to prepare and serve, with no indication she was other than hired help. No twinges of jealousy were to cross her eyes; no hints to the lady he'd brought as his date to one of his dinner parties.
>
> "You couldn't believe," he said. "She's only 23, but with the wisdom of a woman much older. That's the Oriental mind. And she doesn't get demanding. She's grateful for what I've given her—her privacy when she wants to go into her own room and shut the door, her $100 a month which she can save, her uniforms which she seems proud to wear. It's working out very well."[23]

Asian actresses have also been typecast in roles that perpetuate the Asian mystique. In the 1957 film *Sayonara*, Miyoshi Umeki portrayed the stereotypical coy, subservient geisha, and Nancy Kwan defined the "Suzie Wong" sex-object image with long hair, long legs, and slit dress in the 1960 film *The World of Suzie Wong.* Later, Joan Chen perpetuated these images in her role as the sensual, submissive Asian Pacific woman in the 1986 movie *Tai-Pan.*

Comedienne Margaret Cho's prime-time network comedy, *All-American Girl* (1994), departed from the stereotypical portrayals of Asian females in earlier movies and programs, but her attempt to convey a genuine sense of Asian America within a U.S. television comedy framework was unsuccessful in

While Margaret Cho's sitcom, *All-American Girl*, was one of the first to feature a mostly Asian American cast, the show's portrayal of the culture was very stereotypical due to its mostly White crew.

Source: ©iStockphoto/EdStock.

the short-lived series. *All-American Girl* featured a predominantly Asian American cast, but its tone of hip-20-something-California-"Valley Girl"-meets-the-Borscht-Belt had mostly White writers and producers. In addition, her TV Asian family was largely parodied, wasting the talents of such accomplished actors as BD Wong. In short, the show revealed to America not an emerging subculture, but rather the watered-down stereotypes of Asian Americans. By 2002, no prime-time network television series with an Asian emphasis had aired since *All-American Girl* was cancelled.[24]

While Asian women have also historically been depicted as dragon ladies, domestic workers, gang molls, and hookers or in subservient, overexoticized images, more contemporary roles for Asian women have launched a new genre that typecasts them as "women warriors." Whether it's Zhang Ziyi performing gravity-defying stunts in the Academy Award–winning *Crouching Tiger, Hidden Dragon* (2000), Lucy Liu kickboxing as a femme fatale in the 2000 remake of *Charlie's Angels,* or Kelly Hu storming soldiers and tyrants in *The Scorpion King* (2002), a contemporary woman's strength and independence these days is measured by her ability to master her maneuvers in the martial arts. As film critic Leonard Maltin says, images of strong women in the more organic or cerebral sense of the word do not sell tickets; what young women in the audiences today want to see are women kicking butt on screen.[25]

A Shameful Legacy

Entertainment stereotypes of non-Whites in American mass media have historical roots in racist attitudes that existed for various social and political reasons against each of the groups prior to their inclusion in media. The stereotypes were based upon negative prejudicial characteristics that, when compared against the values of the majority White society, were deemed to be innately inferior traits. Because the economic success of mass entertainment media in the United States was predicated upon their ability to meet audience demands, mass support for negative and inferior portrayals of people of color indicates that producers satisfied consumer desires. The stereotypes, then, were representative of popular attitudes.

We have also seen that although wide cultural differences exist among the cultural and racial groups under consideration, their portrayals in American mass media have been remarkably similar and are the result of the attitudinal premise of White intellectual and moral supremacy. The fundamental concepts of racial stereotyping were applied consistently across all platforms of American mass entertainment media. Now, in the second decade of the new century, the technological evolution of media platforms for information and entertainment has broadened the challenge of media practitioners to apply better standards of ethics and accountability in providing content for a society that continues to become more racially and culturally diverse.

The record shows that the force of demographic change accompanied by the buying power of the diverse racial and cultural marketplace has brought about improvements in the inclusion of a wider array of Americans in media coverage and portrayals. Yet, there remains a lack of racial and gender sensitivity in the new media order that operates in context of what some describe as a social lack of civility in American discourse. That uncivility is too often expressed in terms that reflect racial and cultural intolerance and continues to spread racism across media outlets including blogs, politically charged talk radio, cable TV programs, and independent videos in addition to the "old" media platforms of newspapers, over-the-air commercial radio, television, and general-audience motion pictures. The shameful legacy of marginalization and stereotyping of peoples of color permeated the communications media industry in the United States at the beginning of the 21st century. How these media have reacted to the new multicultural milieu is the subject of the following chapter.

Notes

1. For a comprehensive review of the history of Black Americans as network television performers, see J. Fred MacDonald, *Blacks and White TV: African Americans in Television Since 1948* (Chicago: Nelson-Hall, 1992).

2. "A Television Trend: Audiences in Black and White," *Washington Post*, November 29, 1994, A1, A20.

3. Mireya Navarro, "Raquel Welch Is Reinvented As a Latina: A Familiar Actress Now Boasts Her Heritage," *New York Times*, June 11, 2002, B1, B3.

4. Ibid.

5. See the account of Bruce Lee's encounter with the producers of *Kung Fu* in Kareem Abdul-Jabbar and Peter Knobler, *Giant Steps: The Autobiography of Kareem Abdul-Jabbar* (New York: Bantam, 1983), 188–189.

6. Libby Lewis, "Racial Constructions and Visual Representations of Blacks in Television News Media," paper presented at the annual Empowering Women of Color Conference, Berkeley, CA, March 2, 2002.

7. Cited in Robert W. Welkos and Susan King, "Beautiful Historic Night," *Los Angeles Times*, March 25, 2002, A1, A15.

8. *The CAAS Research Report* 2(1), published by the UCLA Center for African American Studies (June 2002); "50 Sexiest Stars of All Time," *TV Guide*, September 28–October 4, 2002, 17–51.

9. *The CAAS Research Report* 1(1), published by the UCLA Center for African American Studies (June 2002).

10. *The CAAS Research Report* 1(1), published by the UCLA Center for African American Studies (June 2002).

11. "Fall TV Preview, "*Entertainment Weekly*, September 13, 2002, 29–108.

12. For more details on the most popular African Americans in television, see "10 Most Powerful Blacks in TV," *Ebony*, October 2000, 86–96.

13. "10 Most Powerful Blacks in TV," *Ebony*, October 2000, 86–96.

14. "Milestones Apr. 22, 2002," *Time*, April 22, 2002.

15. James Brady, "In Step With Raquel Welch," *Parade Magazine*, March 17, 2002, 26–27.

16. Mireya Navarro, "Trying to Get Beyond the Role of the Maid; Hispanic Actors Are Seen as Underrepresented, With the Exception of One Part," *New York Times*, May 16, 2002, accessed July 30, 2002, http://premium.news.yahoo.com.

17. Ruth LaFerla, "Latino Style Is Cool; Oh, All Right: It's Hot," *New York Times*, April 15, 2001, accessed July 30, 2002, http://premium.news.yahoo.com.

18. "Will the Real Latina Please Stand Up?," *Latina*, July 2002, 83.

19. *People*, December 30, 2002, 106–107. For more information on Jennifer Lopez see the following websites: www.jenniferlopez.com and www.jennifer lopezonline.com.

20. Gail Buchalter, "Now, I Have Found Real Challenges," *Parade Magazine*, September 22, 2001, 9–10.

21. Ibid., 9–10.

22. H. Chang, *Asian Americans in the News*, unpublished paper prepared for the honors colloquium at UC Berkeley, 1984.

23. Bill Fiset, "East Meets West," *Oakland Tribune*, May 2, 1919, 68.

24. *Asian Week* (June 2, 1995), in William Wong, ed., *Yellow Journalist: Dispatches From Asian America* (Philadelphia: Temple University Press, 2001), 233–239.

25. Glenn Whipp, "Brains or Brawn? In the Cinematic Battle of the Sexes, Which Weapon Should Women Wield?" *Pasadena Star News*, June 2, 2001, Section U, 4–6.

Race, Culture, and Gender in the New Media Age

5

On September 11, 2001, the terrorist suicide attacks by Islamic extremists against U.S. interests abroad visited the homeland in the form of devastating assaults on New York City's World Trade Center and the Pentagon in Washington, D.C., and an unsuccessful attempt that ended in the crash of a commercial airliner on a rural Pennsylvania field. From that date into the following decade, the American media image of Middle Eastern cultures—particularly those whose members profess the Islamic faith—took an abhorrent turn. The national response was quickly termed a "war on terrorism" as Islamic extremists waged a holy war or "jihad" against the United States and its allies around the world.

The events of the day that Americans now simply call "9/11" created a rush to learn more about the Islamic community. Unfortunately, however, intense media emphasis on the religious fanaticism of the protagonists resulted in stereotyping Americans of Middle Eastern heritage, and worse. Although the vast majority of Middle Eastern Americans are conventional practitioners of the Islamic faith—and share the national abhorrence to terrorism—general media reportage often failed to emphasize that distinction in public discourse. The result was that negative stereotypes across various media platforms in the first decade of the 21st century fostered an atmosphere that led to violence and other acts against fellow Americans who had the misfortune to be Muslim or descendants of Middle Eastern heritage.

During the first nine weeks following the September 2001 terrorist attacks, the American-Arab Anti-Discrimination Committee (ADC) recorded more than 700 violent incidents against Arab Americans, or those perceived to be members of that community. This phenomenon had its antecedent six years earlier when anti-Arab hysteria occurred following the bombing of an FBI building in Oklahoma City only to learn the perpetrator was a White male.

Meanwhile, despite subtle changes to accommodate what some called a postracial American society, racial stereotypes from the 19th and 20th centuries continued to find expression across various media platforms of the information age. The advent of 21st-century communication technologies helped spread vicious and indiscriminate stereotypes of what the media commonly called Arabs that ranged from motion picture and television screens to the new media platforms that pervaded popular culture in America. Stereotypical treatment of Middle Eastern people clearly moved beyond what Arab American media scholar Jack Shaheen termed the "three B syndrome"—bombers, belly dancers, and billionaires—of the earlier era into a more sinister imagery. Shaheen cited the popular film *Black Hawk Down* (2001) for its depiction of Somalian Muslims as if "they were gang members in Los Angeles defying the police department." In *Towelhead* (2007), an abusive Lebanese father severely beats his teenage daughter who is caught in a cultural dilemma when she undergoes sexual awakening in an American city where the social milieu differs greatly from that in Lebanon. Network television contributed to "Arab bashing" in the first decade of the new century in long-running series *NCIS* and *The Unit,* which began airing on CBS in 2003 and 2006, respectively.

American popular culture and media images often stereotype Middle Eastern people and practitioners of the Islamic faith. These women are wearing traditional veils called niqabs that are worn by the most conservative Muslim groups.

Source: Nitin Madhav (USAID).

A more benign yet equally offensive example can be found in the feature movie *Sex and the City 2* (2010) in which cultural insensitivities to Islamic tradition are blatantly apparent. Although the script called for a setting in the United Arab Emirates city of Abu Dhabi, the production had to be filmed in Morocco when UAE officials refused permission. Morocco allowed the movie—with its portrayals of suggestive sexuality and other cultural taboos—to be filmed in Marrakech only under the stipulation that the city not be identified.

Other critics, however, believe that attitudes toward Middle Eastern cultures and American Muslim practitioners actually began to soften after the September 2001 attacks because the idea of racial and religious tolerance implanted in the civil rights

Tyler Perry emerged in the first decade of the 21st century as a major filmmaker whose work attracted a large following among Black moviegoers. However, his portrayal in drag of a mammy-like character, Madea, drew criticism.

Source: AP Photo/Peter Kramer.

era began to influence hegemonic Anglo European attitudes. The films *Kingdom of Heaven* (2005) and *The Kite Runner* (2007) have been cited as examples of nuanced movies that offer more balanced portrayals of Middle Eastern Muslims. It is noteworthy that the movie *The Kite Runner* was based on a book authored by an Afghani writer.

If it is true that racial stereotypes in pop culture were entering a transition period at the dawn of the 21st century, the evolution nevertheless continued to reflect current political viewpoints, popular attitudes, and moods of the White majority audience. In 2002 Denzel Washington won the Oscar for "Best Actor" (*Training Day*, 2001) and Halle Berry won the award for "Best Actress" (*Monster's Ball*, 2001), marking the first sweep by performers of color in the top acting categories. Both played roles, however, that were reminiscent of long-standing stereotypes consistent with traditional sensibilities of White racial superiority. The awards to Washington and Berry began a spate of Oscars for Black actors throughout the decade. Jamie Foxx (*Ray,* 2004), Forest Whitaker (*The Last King of Scotland,* 2006), and Jennifer Hudson ("Best Supporting Actress," *Dreamgirls,* 2006) highlighted a feel-good era for African Americans in the industry.

Adding to the phenomena was the rise of African American filmmaker Tyler Perry who rose to prominence in the decade as an actor, director, and producer. Perry's films, including *Diary of a Mad Black Woman* (2002), *Madea Goes to Jail* (2006), and *Madea's Big Happy Family* (2011), were box-office successes. His films carried an underlying religious theme, and predominantly Black audiences filled theaters across the nation to see them. Critics, however, saw throwbacks to the stereotypical "mammy" character as Perry—in drag—portrayed Madea, the matriarchal head of a dysfunctional Black family in many of his films.

The year 2012 brought recognition to Black actresses when the 2011 film, *The Help,* swept the Screen Actors Guild Awards in three of the five top categories: "Best Leading Actress" (Viola Davis), "Best Female in a Supporting Role" (Octavia Spencer—who also went on to win the Golden Globe and Oscar in this category), and Best Cast in a Motion Picture. In accepting her award, Davis—who triumphed over Hollywood darling Meryl Streep—evoked civil rights issues tackled in the film when she proclaimed, "The stain of racism and sexism is not just for people of color or women. It's all our burden . . . I don't care how ordinary you feel, all of us can inspire change, every single one of us."[1] Although Latinos have the largest so-called "minority" group population in the United States, they have faired far worse than African Americans in capturing Oscar recognition since 2000. Benicio del Toro was "Best Supporting Actor" in *Traffic* (2000) and was a nominee in the same category for *21 Grams* (2003). Latinas earned two "Best Actress" nominations in the first decade of the 21st century: Salma Hayek (*Frida,* 2002) and Catalina Sandino Moreno (*Maria Full of Grace,* 2004).

Perhaps the 2011 release of *The Green Hornet* began a trend of reinventing the trusty culturally marginalized sidekick. That version gave Kato clear intellectual and creative prominence over his wealthy, but incompetent, Anglo European crime-fighting partner. The film, however, is a comedy, and general audiences have always accepted people of color in comedic roles throughout American history. Perhaps the humor is based in the role reversal of the characters.

Despite the inroads made in network television, Asian Americans face continued exclusion and discrimination on the big screen. In the article, "Hollywood Whitewash" (2010), writer Chris Lee recounted Hollywood's history of using White actors to play ethnic characters, including John Wayne as Genghis Khan in *The Conqueror* (1956), Peter Sellers as the bumbling Indian in *The Party* (1968), and, more notoriously, Mickey Rooney's stereotypical, bucktoothed Mr. Yunioshi in *Breakfast at Tiffany's* (1961). In 2007, *AsianWeek* ranked Rooney's character second on the list of "the 25 most infamous yellowface film performances"; third was the Charlie Chan series; and the top spot was claimed by the Fu Manchu series.[2] The proclivity for Hollywood to cast White actors as Asian characters remained well into the 21st century. "Although these portrayals took place decades ago, their legacy lives on," Lee wrote. "Even now, in the age of Obama—when the [2011] Miss USA Rima Fakih is Lebanese American, Will Smith is the biggest movie star in the world and Sonia Sotomayor became the first Latina to sit on the U.S. Supreme Court—movie industry decision-makers can still seem woefully behind the times when it comes to matters of race."[3] He pointed out that even in 2011, major studios like Disney still elected to have actor Jake Gyllenhaal and British actress Gemma Arterton, who are both White, portray Iranian characters in *Prince of Persia* (2010).[4]

Similarly, when Paramount Studios decided to turn the popular Nickelodeon television show *Avatar: The Last Airbender* (2005–2008) into a live-action feature film (*The Last Airbender,* 2010), it also managed to "whitewash" the entire cast—even blatantly promoting racial bias in its casting call for "Caucasian or any other ethnicity." While the television series exclusively featured Asian and Inuit characters and culture, the four lead roles of Aang, Katara, Sokka, and Zuko were eventually given to actors Noah Ringer, Nicola Peltz, Jackson Rathbone, and Jesse McCartney, respectively. Only when Jesse McCartney dropped out, following scheduling conflicts with his music tour, was the role of Zuko—a villain—given to *Slumdog Millionaire* actor Dev Patel, an artist of Asian Indian heritage.

Guy Aoki, founding president of Media Action Network for Asian Americans (MANAA), was quick to respond. "How can you, in good faith, say you are trying to honor the integrity of the television series by taking a story written with Asian themes, settings, characters, and populating it with white leads—especially when there are so few Asian roles available in Hollywood? You are continuing a generations-long practice of racial discrimination where the opportunity for actors of color to be heroes for a change is taken away (this time in the name of 'diversity')."[5] Aoki added: "Those character names again: Zuko, Aang and Sokka. Played by a Jesse, a Noah and a Jackson . . . And the Dev Patel character starts off being a bad guy. The three white people are heroes. It's confusing to us. They're supposed to

Octavia Spencer received the Oscar as "Best Supporting Actress" for her role in *The Help*, a film depicting the travails of Black domestic maids in the segregated South.

Source: ©istockphoto.com/EdStock2.

be leading a band of Asian- or Inuit-looking people." Casting director Dee Dee Ricketts dismissed the charges of blatant cultural insensitivity with the response that "the best actors were cast, and that was it."[6]

Some laid the blame on the director—M. Night Shyamalan—who claimed to have complete authority in the casting process. In defending his decisions in an interview on indiemoviesonline.com ("M. Night Shyamalan in His Own Words on *The Last Airbender* Race Controversy"), the director said, "I had to eventually make a decision about what nationality each of them are. What happened was, Noah Ringer walked in the door—and there was no other human being on the planet that could play Aang except for this kid. To me, he felt mixed race with an Asian quality to him. I made all the Air nomads mixed race—some of them are Hispanic, some of them are Korean . . .

"You're coming at me, the one Asian filmmaker who has the right to cast anybody I want, and I'm casting this entire movie in this color blind way where everyone is represented. I even had one section of the Earth kingdom as African American, which obviously isn't in the show, but I wanted to represent them, too! . . . So if you need to point the racist finger, point it at me."[7]

But coproducer Frank Marshall admitted the casting notice for "Caucasian or any other ethnicity" was both poorly worded and offensive, and in his article in the *Village Voice*, Michael Musto agreed that whitewashing is still a problem in Hollywood today. "One might have more sympathy for this kind of colorblind casting if Asians were more often given parts that weren't written as Asian. But it seems like only whites get that kind of privilege." Film critic Roger Ebert acknowledged the limited roles available to Asian actors when he said, "I suspect the American group most underrepresented in modern Hollywood is young Asian American males."[8]

Race and Representation in Prime-Time Television: More or Less?

From the mid-2000s forward, television brought numerous programs before national audiences as the demographic swell of multicultural Americans forced producers and advertisers to develop entertainment content to include representation of the exponentially growing markets. The shows were primarily situation comedies featuring Black and Latino characters. Dramatic shows featured people of color in supporting roles, often exhibiting multicultural casts. Among those offerings were *The Closer* (TNT) and *The Office* (NBC) that began their multiyear runs in 2005. South Asian Indian characters began to appear during this period including roles in *The Office*, *Royal Pains* (USA, 2009), *Parks and Recreation* (NBC, 2009), and *Outsourced* (NBC, 2010), a comedy set in Mumbai featuring several stereotypical Indian characters. *Outsourced* was a throwback to stereotypes of the past wherein a White character supervises Indian employees who appear as weird misfits within their own culture and social setting. Pacific Island Asian characters returned in a major way with the updated version of *Hawaii Five-0* on CBS in 2010.

The most significant Middle Eastern Arab presence on weekly television programming in the first decade of the 21st century was veteran Lebanese American actor Tony Shalhoub who starred as *Monk*, an eccentric detective on USA from 2002 to 2009. Shalhoub's character was not defined specifically as a person of Arab descent, and the series never focused on his ethnicity or cultural background.

The arrival of the 21st century saw the development of cable and satellite television into major entertainment forces competing with traditional over-the-air networks for viewers. Most Americans—including people of color—gained access to many more channels of programming. Moreover, in what is now called the "video age," visual entertainment also became available to con-

The Arabian background of Lebanese actor Tony Shalhoub was not emphasized in his lead role in *Monk*, a USA network show that ran for seven seasons.

Source: ©istockphoto.com/EdStock.

sumers using DVD technology at home and/or in portable computers and tablet devices. Executives and producers of video entertainment are using the expanded capacity to bring audiences specialized "niche" programming including television channels devoted exclusively to ethnic groups and to such diverse areas as vintage movies, sports, comedy, shopping, history, home gardening and décor, and so on. Subcategories of all the above appeared to meet virtually every area of human interest.

However, the exigencies of providing program content 24 hours a day, coupled with the high production costs of original programming, led many outlets to rely on "reruns" of material previously aired. Exceptions are occasional programs produced by pay cable television channels such as Home Box Office (HBO) and Showtime that carry some original movies featuring people of color and/or cultural themes. For example, in 2000 Showtime offered *Soul Food*, a Black series based on a theatrical film released a few years earlier, and *Resurrection Blvd.*, a Latino American dramatic series.

When the Multi-Ethnic Media Coalition released its 2009 Report Card on Television Diversity, Karen Narasaki, then chair of the Asian Pacific American Media Coalition, noted that in the 10 years since the four major networks—ABC, CBS, Fox, and NBC—announced a fall prime-time lineup of shows that were virtually devoid of minority characters, the coalitions have continued to work with the networks on initiatives to boost inclusion of minorities both in front of and behind the camera. "We believe increasing the number of APA [Asian Pacific American] and other minority writers and producers will help lead to the further development and quality of roles for APA and other minority characters. By now, each network should have a strong pipeline of minorities who are ready to become the next Shonda Rhimes (creator, executive producer, and head writer of *Grey's Anatomy* and *Private Practice*)."[9]

However, of the four major networks, only CBS improved its overall grade, from a C+ to a B–, while the other networks maintained their previous scores (B– for ABC and C+ for Fox and NBC). Opportunities for Asian American directors at three of the four networks increased from 2000 to 2010, but Asian Americans remain underrepresented as central characters on prime-time shows. Moreover, while many network and cable television shows that aired in the second decade of the 21st century have greater diversity in their ensemble casts—including Fox's *Glee*; TBS's *For Better or Worse*; TNT's *Leverage*; USA's *Psych* and *Suits*; CBS's *Hawaii 5-0*, *NCIS*, and *The Big Bang Theory*; NBC's *Law & Order* franchises; and ABC's *Modern Family*—people of color still constitute a relatively small percentage of supporting roles. There is vast room for improvement to increase diversity in programming across the television entertainment spectrum.[10]

Advocacy groups further note that networks continue to treat diversity as an afterthought, and essentially camouflage White shows with a token person of color. For example, *Better With You* features five White characters and one Latina, *Happy Endings* features five White characters and one Black male, and the cast of *Mr. Sunshine* includes four Whites and one Black male. One way to increase representation in network prime-time television is to offer more family-oriented shows that feature a predominantly ethnic cast, such as the *George Lopez* show, Tyler Perry's *House of Payne,* and 1994's *All-American Girl.* Although *George Lopez* centered on a Latino family, it appealed broadly to non-Latinos; similarly, *All-American Girl* didn't just appeal to Asian Americans. Producer Gail Berman—who later became president of Fox TV—noted that the show was actually more popular in Louisiana than in San Francisco.[11]

Meanwhile, situation comedies, dramas, and other programs produced in the 1960s, '70s, '80s, and '90s continued to be aired on cable and satellite television networks. Motion pictures from the advent of the sound movie era can still be seen on American television on any given day. In addition, retail sales of "old school" videos are consumed for repetitive viewing in homes across America. Therefore, it is easy to see why old racial stereotypes die hard. In essence, the technology of the video age has resulted in the continued conveyance of old stereotypes to new generations of viewers.

Old Problems Linger in the New Media Era

In the "new media era," the concepts of racial diversity and multiculturalism have become part of the fabric of American discourse. Consequently, as noted herein, the mass communications industry faces increased pressure from advocacy groups to better reflect the nation's demographic reality. If prime-time television is to truly reflect the America we live in, the networks must do more to invest in shows that feature diversity among their characters. Many observers of American popular culture believe television fare presented when children are most likely to be viewing is critical to advancing racial tolerance and diversity in the United States.

Racial, cultural, and gender self-esteem is developed during the childhood years, and television programming—aside from educational and public broadcasting venues—has generally failed to fulfill a socially responsible role in that regard. Children Now, a national children's advocacy organization, periodically conducts research on television programming and its impact on children. The group's 2004 prime-time diversity report found that although 40% of American youth (ages 19 and under) were children of color, their cultural heritages were woefully underrepresented on television. Despite the fact that television programming featured more ethnically diverse casts in the new century, disparities continue to exist between real-life racial and gender diversity experienced by youth and the world presented to them on prime-time television.

Nevertheless, a few improvements were reflected in the Children Now report. For example, the number of Latino characters on prime-time television increased to the extent that more than half of the shows included at least one Latino character. And in 2010, George Lopez was the first Latino to get his own late-night talk show (TBS) when he was bumped to a prime-time 10 p.m. slot after Conan O'Brien was given his former 11 p.m. airtime. Lopez's success, however, did not extend to all racial groups, as only one in seven Asian/Pacific Islander characters (14%) were featured in integral roles on prime-time television. These Asian groups were represented mostly as secondary and tertiary characters.

The most diverse programs on television were dramas, and multicultural casting was found in nearly half of such shows. In 2011, examples included top-rated dramas like the *Law & Order* and *CSI* franchises, *Grey's Anatomy, Hawaii 5-0,* and *Castle.* Even the plethora of unscripted reality shows began to show greater diversity with such programs as *The Real Housewives of Atlanta, Top Chef, Keeping Up With the Kardashians,* and

Khloe and Lamar where at least half of the casts feature people of color in starring roles.

However, the Children Now study also found many problematic areas in both representation and programming. For starters, nearly three fourths of all prime-time characters were White. Also, youth characters (18 and under) were less racially diverse than the overall sample (13%), and fewer racial groups were represented. Gains for Latinos were not reflected in youth roles as only 4% of all youth characters were Latino, and Asian/Pacific Islanders composed a mere 1% of the total youth population on prime time, with many appearing only as supporting characters.

Although youth are most likely to watch television during the 8 p.m. prime-time hour, it remained the least racially diverse segment with only one in five shows featuring a multicultural cast. On the other hand, the most racial diversity was found in the 10 p.m. shows where more than two thirds of the casts featured a mixture of races and ethnicities. During that time slot, however, youth are probably less likely to be watching television. Despite the fact that situation comedies are the most popular genre among youth, such programs continued to be the least diverse and most segregated shows on prime-time television as nearly three fourths featured all-White casts.

More than half of the African Americans with starring roles on prime-time television appeared in situation comedies, but Blacks were severely underrepresented (4%) on reality programs. Also, despite the progress Latinos have made in prime-time television, they still continue to be typecast in low-status occupations, and were four times more likely to be portrayed as domestic workers than other racial groups.

Other findings in the study show that Asian/Pacific Islanders were more than three times as likely to play supporting rather than starring roles, and Arab/Middle Eastern characters were most likely (46%) to be portrayed as criminals, compared to Asian/Pacific Islanders (15%), African Americans (10%), and Whites (5%). Not surprisingly, not a single Native American character was featured in any episode in the 2004 Children Now study.

Gender Inequities Abound

It would be wishful thinking to conclude the new millennium brought with it a steadfast stream of progress on matters of race, culture, and gender in the media. But the reality is much more of a mixed bag. On the positive side, 2011 proved to be a landmark year of firsts for minorities and women in sports and entertainment wherein they received extensive and nonstereotypical exposure in the media. For the first time, an African American man topped the list of biggest moneymakers in Hollywood with Tyler Perry claiming the top spot with $130 million. Although no women of color were among the top five wage earners in the motion picture industry in 2011, Jennifer Yuh Nelson, an Asian female, was chosen to direct the blockbuster sequel *Kung Fu Panda 2*, while British beauty Cheryl Cole was booted as a judge on Fox television's *The X Factor* and replaced by former Pussycat Dolls frontwoman Nicole Scherzinger, a native of Hawaii. As a result, half the judges on Simon Cowell's highly anticipated hit show were women of color!

Other unlikely firsts occurred at the 2011 summer movie box office. Walt Disney Studios' *The Help*—a period drama that daringly tackled the explosive race and class issues of the American South of the 1960s—outpaced the earnings of bigger bankrolled box-office competition for three consecutive weeks. But the extraordinary critical and commercial success of the film—a complex tale of White women in the South and their relationships with Black maids who cleaned their houses and cared for their children—wasn't without criticism from a host of prominent detractors. "Some critics carped about a white author writing in a black dialect for a pair of maids who serve as two of the book's three narrators. Others thought the White narrator—an idealistic college grad named Skeeter Phelan, who persuades the Black maids of Jackson, Miss., to tell their stories to her and causes a sensation when she publishes their tales anonymously—was too much of a savior."[12] This is a common critique of ensemble casts, where a White character traditionally takes on the "lead" role and is often positioned to "save" the other characters played by actors of color.

The Black actresses also had their share of challenges in combating criticism from their own community. Viola Davis, also an Oscar nominee for *Doubt* (2008), was understandably circumspect about agreeing to play the role of stoic house servant Aibileen: "There is huge responsibility within the African American community. I mean huge," said Davis. "There are entire blogs committed to saying that I'm a sellout just for playing a maid."[13]

But director Tate Taylor spent hours making Davis feel comfortable with the role and ensuring that *The Help* would not be "a watered-down portrayal of race relations in the 1960s South." And Davis added the significance of sharing this type of story was "Because we've never seen those kinds of relationships on screen, we bastardize it by saying that she's a 'great white hope' and she's 'just a mammy.' Who's written these kind of complicated relationships ever?"[14]

But before major accolades are bestowed on Hollywood for racial progress, it must be noted that three years earlier so few roles went to Latinas that the Imagen Awards—which honors positive portrayals of Latinos and Latino culture in entertainment—issued no awards for 2009 for either Best Actress or Best Supporting Actress in a feature film. Moreover, Hollywood continued to cast Latina actors, in particular, in stereotypical fashion. Whenever Emmy Award–winning actress Sofia Vergara, known more for her killer curves than her comic timing, is mentioned in the media, it is usually accompanied by a "Va-Va-Voom!" or "Muy Caliente!" Vergara recalled that before she got her big break in the ABC series *Modern Family,* she didn't fit the traditional stereotype of the sultry, raven-haired Latina vixen. "When I started auditioning for American acting roles, they didn't know where to put me. A blond Latina? In L.A. They're used to Latin women looking more Mexican. But if you go to Uruguay, Argentina, Colombia, everybody is blond."[15]

In her article titled "The Hypersexualization of Latinas in Television and Film," Eliana Grijalva-Rubio (2011) further lamented that, "twenty years ago, there were hardly any Latinas in any kind of mass media. Unfortunately, the price we're paying now to see ourselves represented is a set of exaggerated, overdone stereotypes that put the African-American bad boy and the bespectacled Asian math whiz to shame." As if these stereotypes aren't bad enough in mainstream television and films, Grijalva-Rubio added that the hypersexualized, vixenish bad-girl depictions where the miniskirts get shorter, the necklines get lower, and the heels get higher even extend into Spanish-language television where "the networks have sexualized women all the way to the news shows . . . and even the female anchors, women that should be considered professional, are wearing tiny skirts and scanty halter tops that, literally, let it all hang out."[16]

Dr. Brenda Risch, director of women's studies at the University of Texas at El Paso, believes that the best—if not only—way to combat these negative portrayals is for Latinas to create their own positive representations, much like Salma Hayek did by starting her own production company after being told to "go back to Mexico" because her accent would prohibit her from getting any roles other than servants or maids. When asked about how she thought the hypersexualized stereotype of Latinas was damaging to women, she replied that "these portrayals are damaging to a young woman's self-esteem because they confirm the old stereotype that a woman's main worth lies solely in her appearance, rather than on her creativity,

Salma Hayek engineered a movie career that took her from playing stereotypical Latina roles to producing films that portray a broader range of the rich and varied Hispanic culture.

Source: ©istockphoto.com/EdStock.

intelligence, emotional maturity, values, and so on."[17] Alicia Rascon, one of the founding editors of *Latinitas*, feels that the image of the hypersexualized Latina perpetuates not just a stereotypical—but also a simplistic— view of Latinas as a whole. "I think there's a big stereotype that Latinas are super-sexy and to me it's disturbing that that's the only way they look at us. Very often when we see a show on TV or a movie, we don't see a lot of Latina characters, and when we do, they're the really scantily clad Latinas that are going to steal your boyfriends. I think we're a lot more complex than that, so I think it's horrible that they're simplifying us."[18]

In retrospect it would seem that 2008 was a bad year for all women of color in prime time television. According to an article titled "The Rise and Fall and Rise Again of Black TV," Jennifer Armstrong (2011) observed that 2008 was the year broadcast television officially "got out of the African-American sitcom business" when it "canceled the long-running *Girlfriends*, and the following year it yanked both *Everybody Hates Chris* and the *Girlfriends* spin-off, *The Game*—also known as the last two successful black-centric shows on network television."[19]

While the broadcast networks have made some progress toward casting more diverse ensembles, the crop of new shows for the 2011–2012 season still lacked any series with a predominantly African American, Latino, or Asian American cast. "The world on television should look like the world I see when I walk outside my door," said *Grey's Anatomy* creator Shonda Rhimes. Rhimes pioneered color-blind casting for television and developed a show with a Black female lead, ABC's *Damage Control* (later retitled *Scandal*), starring Kerry Washington as a PR guru.[20] Queen Latifah, who has taken a more proactive stance to produce and promote greater diversity on prime-time television, argued that diverse ensembles in general—and African American series in particular—provide a way to represent a point of view sorely missing on television: "People live in bubbles, and they perpetuate racism and classism. There's still plenty of places they can go [on TV] that are as un-diverse as they could possibly be . . . it's just something that's going to be a continuing fight, to try to keep making these things happen."[21]

The African American audience, however, proved to be practically ravenous for these types of shows. In response to direct viewer demands, a resurgence occurred in Black television programming—thanks to cable stations BET, VH1, and TBS. In January 2011, BET revived *The Game* to a record-breaking 7.7 million viewers, three times the audience it got on the CW channel and twice the size of any show airing on the teen-oriented network. Its success spawned the network's additional development of *Reed Between the Lines*, and VH1 joined with Queen Latifah, who became executive producer, to bring the "dramedy" *Single Ladies* to the small screen. In addition, reruns of previously canceled series such as *My Wife and Kids* and *Everybody Hates Chris* remained popular among African American viewers. In an oblique message to the profit-centered television industry, actor Malcolm-Jamal Warner noted, "The black viewership is important. Black shows do make money. It seems like a no-brainer."[22]

The revival of African American scripted television programming can probably be traced to TBS's successful 2007 run of Tyler Perry's *House of Payne*—and his later shows *For Better or Worse* and an adaptation of his film, *Why Did I Get Married?* Jacque Edmonds Cofer, executive producer of *Let's Stay Together,* says "I've had plenty of people say to me that it's great to see something on TV that represents them," and "It's also important for people to see that every African-American woman is not a Real Housewife." And Jeff Olde, executive vice president of original programming for VH1, adds, "I think our shows should reflect the country that we're living in . . . we're thrilled that we have a large number of African-American women who watch us, and quite frankly, we're always looking for new stories to tell."[23]

When the second decade of the century unfolded the prime-time network lineup had yet to feature an Asian American female in a lead role—with the exception of Hawaii-born Maggie Q who starred in the CW series *Nikita.* ABC could have boosted the ranking of its diversity report card when two medical roles—one on *Body of Proof* and the other on *Off the Map*—were written for South Asian women, but instead were given to Jeri Ryan and Meryl Streep's daughter—both White women.[24] There were, however, a number of hit shows that featured an Asian male or female in supporting roles. They included *Glee* (Harry Shum Jr. and Jenna Ushkowitz), *Hawaii 5-0* (Daniel Dae Kim and Grace Park), *How I Met Your Mother* (Nazanin Boniadi and Kal Penn), *The Mentalist* (Tim Kang), *Grey's Anatomy* (Sandra Oh), and *The Big Bang Theory* (Kunal Nayyar).

In culturally insensitive Hollywood, however, the revamped version of *Hawaii 5-0* increased the diversity in its cast only following persistent urging of advocacy groups such as MANAA. Despite the state of Hawaii having a 60% majority Asian population, the show initially planned to feature only one Asian—or 25%—among its four lead characters. After persistent negotiations with CBS producers and casting directors, Daniel Dae Kim (*Lost*) was finally cast in the role of Chin Ho Kelly and Grace Park (*Battlestar Galactica*) was chosen to play Kono Kalakaua. The show premiered in September 2010 with 17.59 million views, making it the top-rated "new" show of the 2010–2011 television season.[25] However, in its second season, actress Lauren German joined the cast as agent Lori Weston, effectively replacing Grace Park—or Kono Kalakaua—as the lead female in the series, thus decreasing the 50/50 balance of minority characters to a 60/40 dominant cast of White characters.

Impact of Oprah Winfrey

Despite the vacillating inroads and pitfalls of expanding diversity on network and cable television and in film, perhaps no other media personality has had as much impact on shaping American popular cultural landscape as Oprah Winfrey. After launching her iconic talk show in 1986, Winfrey decided to end the program in 2011. Despite being a woman—and a woman of color—Winfrey shot to the top from talk show queen to media icon by interviewing celebrities, authors, and politicians and tackled topics that ranged from weight loss to race relations. In the process, she created a billion-dollar media empire. Most of Winfrey's viewers were White women, and according to University of Southern California Annenberg School for Communication faculty member David Craig, she defined the power of personal narrative that was a precursor to the surge in what became known as "reality" television programming. She was everybody's Black girlfriend, and she developed the Oprah brand that forever changed television and other forms of media.[26]

When her daily show ended, Winfrey devoted her energy to expanding her OWN (Oprah Winfrey Network) cable television channel. Despite facing formidable challenges to provide appealing and marketable programming on cable television to a broad audience, Winfrey brought to the effort a proven track record of adapting to changing realities. As Lena L. Kennedy, who served on President Barack Obama's National Finance Committee, aptly observed, "When you think of Oprah and her achievements, you think of the impact she's made in the talk show world, but it's so much greater . . . while it is always nice see someone who looks like you in the media . . . I think the impact she's made on women transcends beyond race."[27]

Despite Winfrey's contributions and success, gender inequities continued to persist in the television and film industries even as she closed her talk show. Male characters on prime-time television outnumbered female characters nearly two to one, and males were twice as likely to be older (in their 50s and 60s) compared to their female counterparts. According to the Media Report to Women (2010), in the 2009–2010 prime-time television season, women accounted for 27% of all creators, executive producers, producers, directors,

> Oprah Winfrey parlayed her appeal to a largely White female television audience and extraordinary skills as a businesswoman into a position among the wealthiest communications media operatives in the United States.

Source: ©istockphoto.com/EdStock.

writers, editors, and directors of photography working on sitcoms, dramas, and reality programs airing on the broadcast networks. In the feature film industry, women composed only 16% of all directors, executive producers, producers, writers, cinematographers, and editors working on the top 250 domestic grossing films in 2009. This actually represented a decline of 3% from 2001.[28]

Racial Gaffes on Radio and the Web

Although the days of popular radio dramas of the 1930s and 1940s had long since passed from the airwaves, syndicated radio programs featuring nationally known personalities drew large audiences in the first two decades of the new century. Network and cable television brought dramatic and comedy shows to the mass American audience with content that expanded the boundaries of social tastes in subject matter including breakage of sexual taboos and civil discourse. This new era ushered in more media content involving racial and cultural themes and frank dialogue that bordered on incivility.

In syndicated radio, the rise of political and sports talk shows often found racial issues as prime subject matter. One such controversial figure was Rush Limbaugh, a politically conservative radio commentator whose sharp tongue and brusque delivery led him to venture occasionally beyond politics into other realms of American life. Limbaugh began his radio career in the 1970s, and he also hosted several television programs. During a brief stint as a sports commentator on ESPN in 2003, Limbaugh was embroiled in racial controversy when he made comments about Black professional football player Donovan McNabb. Limbaugh told his audience that it was "absurd to say that the sports media haven't overrated Donovan McNabb because he's black." Limbaugh said McNabb held his quarterback position primarily because the National Football League desired to see a Black player succeed in the position. The following year McNabb led his team to the Super Bowl, and during his career with the Philadelphia Eagles he quarterbacked the team to four division titles.

Another syndicated radio performer, Don Imus, made racist and sexist comments in 2007 about members of the Rutgers University women's basketball team. Without provocation Imus called the Black female athletes "nappy headed hos" (whores) and "jigaboos" on his CBS broadcast. The ensuing uproar from civil and women's rights organizations and others resulted in his firing. Within a few months, however, Imus had apologized and returned to the airwaves with another syndicated radio deal.

In 2009 two KLBJ-AM radio personalities, Don Pryor and Todd Jeffries ("The Todd and Don Show"), offended many in their Austin, Texas, community when they used the term *wetbacks* more than 30 times during their one-hour show in reference to undocumented Latino workers. The men were suspended for two weeks after protests from various persons including the city's Mayor Pro Tem Mike Martinez.

Internet radio has also been a platform for racial slurs as evidenced by comments made by South Carolina State Senator Jake Knotts. In June 2011, Knotts accomplished a two-for-one slur when he said of Nikki Haley, then a candidate for governor, "We already got a raghead in the White House" and "We don't need another one in the governor's mansion." Knotts apologized but justified his remarks by equating the Internet radio program to the satirical NBC television show *Saturday Night Live.*

In 2006, syndicated radio host Adam Carolla mocked the Asian Excellence Awards by airing a skit featuring various people saying nothing but variations of "ching chong" on "The Adam Carolla Show." MANAA representative Guy Aoki later went on the show to confront the host and to promote the award show, and was even asked to be a call-in guest to talk about racial issues. But when the station Carolla broadcasted from, KLSX 97.1 Free FM, didn't improve its ratings enough to satisfy parent company CBS, the Top 40 format was dropped, and "The Adam Carolla Show" and everything on that frequency was cancelled. Two days before signing off in 2009, Carolla said when he went to a live podcast format that he wouldn't have to worry about "racist a-holes . . . like Guy Aoki who are gonna climb up my ass if I say anything about all the Asian people that he, evidently, represents. That's every single Asian person on the entire planet."[29]

Later, on his popular podcast, when Carolla talked to sidekick Teresa Strasser about the Dr. Laura (Schlessinger) controversy where she repeatedly used the "N-word" and decided to end her syndicated radio show, Carolla ranted:

Who was actually hurt, other than the watchdog groups that have to pretend that people were actually hurt? You know what I mean? Like who really, when all these watchdog groups just jump on this shit and it's all extortion deal anyway, and we all have dealt with it, anyone who's been in the media, been in radio for long enough have dealt with all these world class assholes out there, Jesse Jackson, Al Sharpton, there's a guy named Guy Aoki who speaks for every Asian culture when they're so diverse and there's so many of them on this planet. That he gets to be the mouthpiece for all of them sounds very racist to me. Like if I say, "I speak for all white people, you speak for all Jews, or you speak for all bald people with a tumor."[30]

Aoki responded by sending a letter to Carolla, stating, "On behalf of the entire Asian American community (which, as you know, I represent), congratulations on the success of our podcast." It was signed, "Your favorite asswipe, Guy Aoki."

The Web has also proven to be a source of trouble for teen Disney sensations Miley Cyrus and Joe Jonas when photos of them making racist gestures went viral on the Internet. In 2008, Miley Cyrus was caught slanting her eyes in a public photo with her girlfriend that offended the Asian

American community. She insisted she was only making "goofy faces" but issued two public statements—although she never fully acknowledged the significance of the hurtful and racially offensive gesture that was satisfactory to civil rights and media groups.

In early 2009, another Disney star, Joe Jonas—who was also part of the pop-rock boy band the Jonas Brothers—was caught on gossipteen.com in a photo showing him pulling back his eyes to look Asian. Although the photo may have been several years old, it surfaced on the Web and created an outcry among the Asian American community. An article titled "Joe Jonas Does the 'Asian Eyes'" by Gossip Gal asserts that "Miley Cyrus has done it and got into big trouble since everyone started saying she is a racist and mocking Asians. Joe Jonas did the 'Asian eyes' too. Now let's see if someone tries to sue him too!" MANAA demanded that Jonas issue an apology after the photo went viral and was widely seen in cyberspace, and felt that because he was such a popular star and role model, he could have turned an embarrassing situation into a positive learning experience for his fans.[31]

The aforementioned intolerant examples are indicative of relaxed standards of civility in public discourse that was an early-21st-century hallmark not only of American politics—where political parties were firmly entrenched in uncompromising ideological positions—but of the general "in your face" attitude that pervaded much of the content in communications media. That such attitudes would find expression in race relations was an inevitable consequence.

Video Games: One Step Forward, Two Steps Backward

With the 2011 Supreme Court ruling that declared it unconstitutional to ban the sale or rental of violent video games to children, the doors were left wide open for the gaming industry to take aim at its core demographic—young male gamers. Gone are the warm and fuzzy pet simulations and music games that flooded the market a few years before. The industry has shifted toward action and military games that cater to its most loyal and devoted core base.

Despite their efforts to expand their market to "casual" gamers such as women and older adults, those players were the first to curtail their spending on video games when the U.S. economy declined. The casual market tended to switch to less expensive or free games on Facebook and smartphones. However, "core" young male gamers remained a loyal consumer base and continued buying action titles like Activision's *Call of Duty: Modern Warfare* and *Black Ops* and Rockstar Games' *Grand Theft Auto*, which have sold many millions of copies. Consequently, other game publishers have launched a slew of new titles geared toward the young male audience, such as *Mass Effect 3, Saints Row: The Third, Gears of War 3,* and *Halo 4.*[32]

Meanwhile, as young males garner the marketing and creative attention of the gaming industry, women continue to be left on the sidelines of the video game revolution. A 2007 survey by *Game Developer* magazine found only 20% of the industry's workers were female, and only 3% were game programmers. In fact, Kathy Vrabeck, a top executive at one of the largest video game publishers, Electronic Arts Inc., often completes an entire workday without meeting with another woman.[33] Brenda Brathwaite, a game developer who teaches game design at the Savannah College of Art and Design in Georgia describes some of the video recruiting ads as screaming

Images depicting menacing warriors of undefined—but clearly non-White—ethnicity and scantily clad female combatants have brought racist and sexist stereotypes into the extremely popular video game industry.

Source: Fanafzar Game Studio, Dead Mage Inc.(left). Georges Seguin (right).

"college fraternity" and says "there are still companies that throw recruiting parties with strippers." However, to combat the pervasive sexist stereotypes—including the Electronic Entertainment Expo's infamous "booth babes"—the show banned appearances by scantily clad women in 2006."[34]

But the industry needs to go a step further. Simon Carless, publisher of *Game Developer* magazine, noted, "It's important for women to be involved creatively because we need to broaden the reach of games . . . They should be a universal art form." In short, the video game industry needs to "become more diverse if it's to break out of the young male market and into the mainstream."[35] The problem with a skewed video game market is that it tends to perpetuate racial and gender inequities and stereotypes. For example, in a Children Now study titled "Fair Play: Violence, Gender and Race in Video Games" (2001):

- Females were less likely to be player-controlled characters, which in turn means there were fewer characters with whom females could identify.

- Half of all female characters were props or bystanders while male characters were predominantly competitors and thus engaged in action.

- Male characters were more likely to engage in physical aggression (52% to 32%) while female characters were nearly twice as likely to use verbal aggression and ridicule and more than three times as likely to scream.

- Female characters were often hypersexualized or had unhealthy, unrealistic, and disproportionate body sizes, while the males were often hypermuscularized.

- Females were more than twice as likely to wear highly revealing clothing by either having their breasts partially or fully exposed, showing their bare midriffs, or having their buttocks exposed.

Concerning racial diversity and stereotyping, the study found that:

- More than half of all human characters were White, and nearly every video game hero was White. White female characters also outnumbered female characters of every other racial group.

- Games especially created for young children featured only White characters.

- Latinas and Native American characters were virtually nonexistent, while Latino characters only appeared in sports games and were almost always involved in physical harm and pain.

- There were few Asian/Pacific Islander characters, and they were rarely player-controlled, were usually wrestlers or fighters, and were often antagonists.

- Most of the African American males were portrayed as competitors, while most African American females were non-action characters. The females were also far more likely than any other group to be victims of violence.[36]

These data raise several questions and issues: What types of messages do such portrayals send to children and young adults? Do they perpetuate racial and gender stereotypes and social barriers? Does the lack of racial diversity and gender equity have the same impact in video games as it does in traditional forms of media? Do these images consciously—or subconsciously—inform young people that certain groups are valued differently by society?[37]

Notes

1. N. Sperling, "'Help' Wanted?" *Los Angeles Times*, Calendar Section, January 30, 2012, D1.

2. Media Action Network for Asian Americans, *Eyes & Ears* 18 (No. 1, Summer 2011).

3. C. Lee, "A Whitewash for 'Prince of Persia: The Sands of Time' and 'The Last Airbender,'" *Los Angeles Times*, May 23, 2011.

4. Media Action Network for Asian Americans, *Eyes & Ears* 18 (No. 1, Summer 2011).

5. Ibid., 26.

6. Ibid., 25.

7. Media Action Network for Asian Americans, *Eyes & Ears* 18 (No. 1, Summer 2011).

8. Ibid., 15.

9. Ibid., 20.

10. Ibid.

11. Ibid.

12. N. Sperling, "'Help Wanted?'" *Los Angeles Times*, Calendar Section, January 30, 2012, D1.

13. Ibid., D5.

14. Ibid.

15. J. Rader, *Parade*, July 24, 2011, 9.

16. E. Grijalva-Rubio, "The Hypersexualization of Latinas in Television and Film," April 17, 2011.

17. Ibid.

18. Ibid.

19. J. Armstrong, "The Rise and Fall and Rise Again of Black TV," *Entertainment Weekly*, May 20, 2011, 43.

20. Ibid.

21. Ibid.

22. Ibid., 44.

23. Ibid.

24. Media Action Network for Asian Americans, *Eyes & Ears* 18 (No. 1, Summer 2011).

25. Ibid.

26. B. Gazzar, "Saying Goodbye: Oprah Revolutionized the Talk Show Genre," *Pasadena Star News,* May 26, 2011, A1, A4.

27. Ibid., A4.

28. "Media Report to Women," August 2010, retrieved October 3, 2011, http://www.mediareporttowomen.com/statistics.htm.

29. Media Action Network for Asian Americans, *Eyes & Ears* 18 (No. 1, Summer 2011): 6.

30. Ibid., 6–7.

31. Media Action Network for Asian Americans, *Eyes & Ears* 17 (No. 1, Winter 2009): 30.

32. A. Pham and B. Fritz, "Video Games Rev Up Action," *Los Angeles Times,* Business Section, June 7, 2011, 1–3.

33. A. Pham, "Women Left on Sidelines of Video Game Revolution," *Los Angeles Times,* Business Section, October 31, 2008, 1–9.

34. Ibid.

35. Ibid.

36. *Fair Play? Violence, Gender and Race in Video Games* (Children Now, 2001).

37. G. L. Berry and J. K. Asamen, "Television, Children, and Multicultural Awareness," *Handbook of Children and Media,* ed. D. Singer and J. Singer (Thousand Oaks, CA: Sage, 2001), 359–373; *Fall Colors: 2003–04 Prime Time Diversity Report* (Children Now, 2004).

PART III

Racism and Sexism in Public Communications

6 The Press

Whose (News) Media Is It?

The first decade of the new millennium brought a mixture of news coverage that ranged from promoting diversity to perpetuating age-old stereotypes. Despite groundbreaking headlines heralding "Obama Elected First Black President" and "Gay Couples Line Up to Wed in New York," the news was nonetheless riddled with stories that reminded us that old stereotypes die hard. When Anders Behring Breivik launched his dual terrorist attacks in Norway to "purge the continent of Muslims and punish the 'indigenous Europeans' who had failed to protect their nations from 'cultural suicide,'" news media were quick to lay suspicions on Islamic extremists or possibly neo-Nazi groups. Although it was not immediately clear who was responsible for the attacks, speculation by European and U.S. news initially blamed Islamic militant groups and domestic right-wing extremists, alleging that "Al Qaeda previously has singled out Norway as an intended target, and a shadowy group affiliated with the terrorist network reportedly claimed responsibility."[1]

But beyond the major news media coverage was the impact of social media on disseminating rhetorical messages that lambasted diversity—especially as evidenced by Breivik's 1,500-page manifesto that was posted on the Internet and referred to "an American anti-Islamic website and to others who share his fears of what he called mutli-culturalism."[2] In the immediate wake of the Norway bombings, right-wing websites "quickly pointed the finger at 'jihadis,'" and Pamela Geller, publisher of the website Atlas Shrugs and executive director of Stop Islamization of America, posted, "You can ignore jihad, but you cannot avoid the consequences of ignoring jihad."[3]

Although Muslims felt a collective sigh of relief when the attacks were found not to be related to Islamic extremists, they nonetheless felt the sting of initially being targeted as scapegoats—much akin to the finger-pointing during the aftermath of the Oklahoma bombing by right-wing American extremists in 1995. "This is predictable and something that we have come to expect, but it is sad," said Safaa Zarzour, secretary general of the Islamic Society of North America. "For most Muslims, it is a confirmation of how they already feel, that they are guilty until proven innocent."[4]

Based on media depictions, Muslims and others of Middle Eastern heritage have also noted a double standard when it comes to labels and the use of the word *terrorism*, much like the news coverage of the Columbine, Colorado, shootings where the suburban high school shooters were described as "alienated" or "maladjusted" compared to inner-city urban youth who are portrayed as violent and predatory "gangbangers" and "cop killers."

"When attackers are not Muslim, the attack often is not given the 'terrorism' label . . . and people think, 'Oh well, it is an isolated incident, or it is a deranged gunman,'" said Farhana Khera, executive director of Muslim Advocates. Consequently, the impulse by the news media to blame Muslims only leads to further inflaming anti-Muslim sentiments and demonizing the Islamic community.[5] At the same time, the problem is exacerbated by the proclivity of many Americans to erroneously think that all people of Middle Eastern heritage are practitioners of the Islamic faith.

Social Function of News in Society

These issues raise an important question about the historical ideology and context wherein news is defined and presented. The notion of "news"—which Americans receive every day via general audience newspapers, radio, television, magazines, and online information services—represents a vital commodity. Researchers call news reporting in these media the "surveillance" function of mass communication, the task of surveying the trends and events occurring in society and reporting those that seem to be most important and consequential to its well-being. Without such information, people would be seriously hindered in their ability to participate in the political affairs of the republic or to make business, professional, and personal decisions. Obviously, tens of thousands of events and activities take place daily in the United States and throughout the world, but only a miniscule fraction of them are reported through the various national or local news media platforms.

The most important characteristic of news is "consequence" (importance).[6] In other words, those who make decisions about news media content first consider the importance of the event to the audience. This process is, of course, subjective, but the decision makers (theoretically, at least) stake their professional livelihood on their ability to provide the information most desired and needed by society.

Another, closely related, social role of news media is the "correlation" function, or the task of analyzing the selected news, offering analysis and opinion to the society concerning its potential impact, and/or suggesting what should be done about it. Often, opinion leaders formulate social policies with the assistance of news media as a forum.

Researchers have labeled the persons who are involved in the news selection process "gatekeepers" of information because they are in the position of either letting information pass through the system or stopping its progress. Performance of the gatekeeping function results in what some scholars have called "agenda setting" for the society. The process of filtering out huge volumes of information while allowing only a few items to reach the audience is an act that by itself adds credence and importance (consequence) to the surviving events and issues. The extent to which gatekeepers bear responsibility for the flow of news information and set the agenda in the United States is a topic of discussion among social scientists. It is clear, however, that gatekeepers are vitally influential in the process. The perspectives of American values, attitudes, and ambitions brought to society have largely been those of gatekeepers and others with access to media. The result of this racially and culturally flawed process leaves those without a role in its production to wonder whose news is being proffered in the name of a self-proclaimed representative American democracy.

Historically, and generally continuing into the 21st century, non-Whites and women have not been gatekeepers in American news media organizations. News coverage of people of color and women has been and remains a reflection of the attitudes held by gatekeepers and those who influence them. The frequency and the nature of the coverage of marginalized groups in news media, therefore, reveal the attitudes of the majority population throughout American history as much as do portrayals in entertainment media. News coverage may be more significant, however, because of its role and function in society: While entertainment is "make-believe," the news is "real." Since news content, in theory, reflects what is really important to society, the coverage of people of color in general audience news media provides insight into their social status. By their professional judgments, the gatekeepers of news reveal how consequential they regard non-Whites in American society by determining the ways in which they are interpreted to the general audience.

As noted in a subsequent chapter, by the early 1880s ethnic minority groups in the United States found a voice through their own networks of local newspapers and newsletters with stories about issues affecting their communities. In the 20th century, mainstream media doors were slammed shut to people of color until the social upheaval of the 1960s, when the need to cover civil unrest forced newsroom managers to find reporters who could access minority neighborhoods without being perceived as outsiders.

w/ goal to help white — still not serving poc

Discrimination in News: An Overview

News about people of color in White general audience news media has been characterized by developmental phases commonly experienced by each of the groups under consideration. Five stages can be identified historically: (1) exclusionary, (2) threatening issue, (3) confrontation, (4) stereotypical selection, and (5) multiracial coverage phases. The first four phases were so uniformly practiced by news media as to become virtually established as covert policy. In early-21st-century American newsrooms, the fifth phase has been met with grudging acceptance and uneven application of journalistic standards. Although there have been slight changes in the number of non-Whites on the news stage, the stages of coverage have remained the same.

When the Kerner Commission on civil disorders issued its report in 1968, it condemned this historical trend in news coverage by a press that "has too long basked in a White world, looking out of it, if at all, with White men's eyes and a White perspective."[7] More than four decades later and following major demographic shifts in the U.S. population, many marginalized citizens continue to ask the question: Whose news perspective dominates press reports across media platforms? The answer can be found in the news media's legacy of exclusion—a legacy that began in the American colonial era and has proven to be very difficult to overcome.

EXCLUSIONARY PHASE

Although in turn each non-White group had relationships with and contributed to the social-historic development of Anglo American society, none was initially included in the general reporting of news. Insofar as the gatekeepers of public information—and, by extension, their constituent audience—were concerned, people of color were not an important consideration in the conduct of social affairs. In the colonial era, this was made clear in such a sacrosanct document as the Declaration of Independence, wherein the phrase "all men are created equal" was understood to exclude Indians and Blacks. The point was so obvious that there was no need to insert the word *White* between *all* and *men*. Furthermore, the U.S. Constitution (Article 1, Section 2) specified that for purposes of determining the number of members in the House of Representatives, a state could not count the Indian population, and each slave counted as only three fifths of a person. Free Blacks were generally prevented from participating in political affairs by requirements of extensive property holdings as a qualification to vote.

Although the policy of virtual exclusion of people of color in news coverage may seem benign, it had a significant impact on the historical development of race relations in the United States. Its most immediate effect, as

in what world?

noted above, was to signal the status and role Whites accorded non-Whites in society. Lack of coverage of people of color in mainstream news media had the effect of asserting their lack of status, a powerful social psychological message delivered to Whites and non-Whites alike. Ultimately, exclusion from news media coverage signified exclusion from American society, because the function of news is to reflect social reality. For that reason, racial exclusion determined the course followed by the subsequent phases of the treatment of non-Whites in news. It is the basis of a legacy that permeates American news media into the 21st century.

THREATENING ISSUE PHASE

When non-White cultural groups first began to appear as subjects of news media reports, it is because they were perceived as a threat to the existing social well-being. Threat is grounded in fear. As may be expected, Native Americans were the first to attract the attention of the news media because of their uneasy relationship with White colonial settlers. The ambivalence manifested in the "noble savage" attitude of Whites toward Indians was the result of fear of Indian resistance to colonial expansion. Although the European settlers were intruders on the natives' soil, reporters for the colonial and early national press began to characterize their Native American hosts in the role of adversary with heavy use of the term *savages*. Newspapers, therefore, made it easy to justify the displacement of Indians by focusing coverage on acts of Indian violence to reinforce the savagery theme. "Civilized" Whites were made to seem heroic for any actions, however extreme, resulting in the overthrow of "uncivilized" savages. By the time the penny press era reached its zenith, the Indian wars of the West were in full hostilities.

Similarly, Blacks were the objects of fears that set the press awash in a flood of articles speculating on the aftermath of emancipation. In the far West, Chinese laborers became the focus of fears they would displace Whites from the labor market, and the *San Francisco Chronicle* led the press attack against them during the 1870s. In the 1950s, the same fear manifested itself in the California press, as headlines blared against Mexican immigrant workers the journalists labeled "wetbacks." The 1980s and 1990s saw the press indiscriminately use the terms *illegals* and *aliens* to depict Latinos, who argue that, when used as nouns, the labels are dehumanizing and inaccurate. A report by San Francisco State University's Center for Integration and Improvement of Journalism explained that "individuals can commit illegal acts . . . but how can a human being be deemed an 'illegal' person?" The report further noted that the term *alien* conjures up images of creatures who are invaders from another planet.[8] A 1990 article in New York City's *Downtown Express* newspaper characterized the expansion of the Lower East Side

Chinatown with a headline reading "There Goes the Neighborhood."[9] In 1991, *The Daily Breeze* in Torrance, California, headlined a front-page story about changing demographics in its circulation area as an "Asian Invasion"and rekindled White fears of a "Yellow Peril."[10]

In early-21st-century America, there remains increasing fear among media critics that oversimplifying news coverage of people of color contributes to racial polarization by making them scapegoats for the nation's problems and fueling White fears and hatred of other racial groups and lifestyles. Little has changed since a 1992 research study titled "The News as If All People Mattered," which reported that the media often reduce complex conflicts into simply one side versus another. The study concluded that "the media further stimulate polarization by such actions as treating subgroups within communities of interest differently, repeating

Demonstrators lined the sidewalk where an Islamic mosque was being constructed not far from New York City's "ground zero." The issue gained national news coverage because Muslims in America have become a classic example of a "threatening issue."

Source: David Shankbone.

inflammatory comments without challenge or balancing statements, omission of relevant news, disregard for certain communities, [and] quoting and referencing sources predominantly from one subgroup."[11]

In 2010, press coverage of a planned Islamic community center to be located within blocks of the site of the demolished Twin Towers in New York City helped inflame tensions and resentment toward the American Muslims who sought to build the facility. Although media outlets tried to "balance" reports on the issue, it was clear that many news consumers viewed the presence of fellow citizens who practiced the Islamic faith as a threat—a classic case of "threatening issue" coverage.

CONFRONTATION PHASE

When a non-White or cultural "other" group stimulates fear and apprehension in the general population, the response is inevitably a social confrontation. News media, having already brought the threat to society's attention and exacerbating racial polarization, then proceed to cover the response. The response is often violent in nature, such as the Indian wars of the westward expansion, the Mexican War, or the lynching of Blacks in the South, Mexicans in the Southwest, and Asians in the West. At other times the response culminates in legislative action, such as segregation laws, peace treaties, anti-immigration laws, or the creation of agencies such as the Bureau of Indian Affairs. On still other occasions, race riots dominate the news with a historical consistency that has involved almost every non-White racial group.

American news media generally approach confrontation coverage of race-related issues from the perspective of "us versus them." Again, this is a natural progression from the exclusionary phase: Newspeople think of non-Whites as outside the American system; thus, their actions must be reported as adversarial because they are seen as threats to the social order. Until the late 1960s, news headlines and text were filled with racial epithets in reporting on these social confrontations, thereby encouraging conflict instead of conciliation. More than during any other phase, it is during confrontation that news media have the opportunity to exhibit leadership in race relations; unfortunately, their historical track record has been poor and continues so into the 21st century.

In 2005, Hurricane Katrina devastated the city of New Orleans, Louisiana creating a classic news story of confrontation between humanity and Mother Nature. African Americans composed 60% of the city's population prior to the hurricane. A total of more than 130,000 residents were displaced as a result of the storm. In the midst of the catastrophic event that left thousands of victims without food and shelter for days, the attitudes of a racially insensitive press became evident. Reportage of White journalists included a racially biased Associated Press photo caption that described a Black person who rummaged through the flooded debris for food as "looting" while the same activity was captioned in an Agence France-Presse image of a White survivor as "finding" food.

Superficial and oversimplified news reporting of isolated and racially tinged events is often structured to conform to existing attitudes and perceptions of Whites and the hegemonic social system. This is evident in the confrontational arena of the American judicial system wherein African Americans and Latinos predominate as criminal defendants. Wallace L. Walker, a criminal attorney and former professional journalist, has noted that persons of color are routinely "overcharged" for their criminal conduct while the reverse is true for White defendants. In essence, defendants of color are charged with multiple infractions and counts to ensure that at least some

News coverage of the volatile issue of undocumented immigrants—particularly with respect to Latinos—has fueled some acts of violence against them and set the stage for numerous examples of confrontation phase journalism.

Source: Cesar Bojorquez.

of them will result in conviction. Walker notes that news media—many of which employ staff trained in law—could easily bring the disparity in prosecutors' charges to the attention of the American public. And, in most cases, journalists could report such stories without subjective commentary "as a legitimate point of difference that can be objectively noted." By doing so, Walker added, news organizations could shine "a ray of light on a possible form of institutional racism." Walker, a criminal lawyer for nearly 40 years, believes the legacy of racial exclusion in news media has parallels in the U.S. system of jurisprudence and may explain why mainstream journalists often parrot the decisions of prosecutors. "Prosecutors who charge defendants with crimes are overwhelmingly White." Walker concludes "their discretions about what criminal charges flow from unlawful conduct [are] unfettered and generally unquestioned" by news media.[12]

News stories depicting otherwise marginalized and neglected groups during their cultural events are examples of stereotypical selection coverage. Pictured is a celebration of Chinese New Year in Seattle.

Source: Joe Mabel.

STEREOTYPICAL SELECTION PHASE

After society has met the perceived threat of a non-White or culturally marginalized group via confrontation, the social order must be restored, and transition must be made into a postconflict period. Although conflicts between Whites and other racial groups have been numerous throughout American history, none of the conflict resolutions has resulted in the disappearance of non-Whites from the American social landscape. News media reportage, therefore, moves into another phase designed to neutralize the hegemonic apprehension of people of color while accommodating their presence. Information items that conform to existing Anglo American attitudes toward other groups are then selected for inclusion in news media and given repeated emphasis until they reach thematic proportions.

Examples include news stories that ostensibly appear to be favorable to non-Whites, as in the cases of "success stories," where a person has risen from the despair of (choose one) the reservation, the ghetto, the barrio, Chinatown, or Little Tokyo. These stories accomplish the two objectives of stereotypical selective reporting: (1) The general audience is reassured that non-Whites are still "in their place" (i.e., the reservation, ghetto, etc.), and (2) those who escape their designated place are not a threat to society because they manifest the same values and ambitions of the dominant culture and have overcome the "deficits" of their racial/cultural backgrounds. At such moments of significant personal achievement, the news media come forth to put persons of color "in their place" and thereby legitimize their accomplishments in the eyes of the Anglo American audience. At the same time, such stories tangentially give credit to the social system that tolerates or praises upward mobility of non-Whites without facilitating it.

In the years since the 1968 issuance of the Kerner Commission report, the news media have responded to the call for better reporting of non-White groups with imbalanced and thematic stereotypical selective coverage. People of color are more likely to pass the gatekeepers if they are involved in "hard news" events, such as those involving police action, or in the "colorful" soft news of holiday coverage, such as Chinese New Year, Cinco de Mayo, Native American festivals, Ramadan, and other holidays. Other reporting in recent years has emphasized non-Whites on "welfare" who live in crime-infested neighborhoods; lack educational opportunity, job skills, and basic language skills; and, in the circumstance of Latinos and Southeast Asians, are probably not documented as U.S. citizens.

Among the positive signs that the tide may be turning for the better are two Pulitzer Prize–winning newspaper series. As background, note a classic example of stereotypical selective reporting for which the *Washington Post* received the 1995 prize. "Rosa Lee's Story: Poverty and Survival in Washington" was a nine-part series focused on the life of a Black family matriarch who lived in an impoverished section of Washington, D.C. It was written by an African American reporter and was replete with the typical anecdotes that reaffirm every Black racial stereotype held and cultivated by White Americans over the past 300 years. A glance at some of the series headlines is instructive: "Stealing Became a Way of Life for Rosa Lee," "Rosa Lee Pays a Heavy Toll for Illiteracy," "She [Rosa Lee] Wrestles With Recovery in a Changing Drug Culture," and "A Grandson's Problems Start Early."[13]

In contrast, five years later, the 2000 Pulitzer Prize was awarded to the *New York Times* staff for a 10-part series titled "How Race Is Lived in America." The journalists were honored for an honest and probing series that explored racial experiences and attitudes across contemporary America and went beyond the superficial stereotypes usually written to assuage the consciences of Anglo Americans.[14] Such enlightened and progressive reporting, however, still remains the exception across the spectrum of American journalism. The old stereotypes of people of color as violent people who are too lazy to work and who indulge in drugs and sexual promiscuity remain prominent in 21st-century "news" reporting. In fact, the preponderance of such reporting has led some observers to say the news media have offered an image of non-Whites as "problem people," which means they are projected as people who either *have* problems or *cause* problems for society. The legacy of news exclusion thus leads the general audience to see people of color as a social burden or problem to solve—the "us versus them" syndrome carried to another dimension.

The 21st century brought two CNN documentary series that took in-depth looks at issues facing African Americans and Latino Americans. CNN's Soledad O'Brien, a biracial journalist, produced *Black in America* in 2008 and *Latino in America* the following year. Although no television program can fully explore every aspect of life for "minority" cultures in the United States, the two series brought nuanced information to American viewers. The historical legacy of news media exclusion of marginalized groups has created a deep chasm of understanding that will require many years to bridge.

MULTIRACIAL COVERAGE PHASE AND ITS OBSTACLES

Multiracial news coverage is the antithesis of exclusion. If it is to become the goal and policy of American news media, the last vestiges of prejudice and racism must be removed from the gatekeeper ranks. This phase is still largely a hopeful vision of the future, but it is within the grasp of a society determined to include all Americans in the quest for social equality. This means not that all news about non-Whites will be good news, but that non-Whites will be reflected in all types of news. News will be reported from the perspective that "us" represents all citizens. A major step in the process, of course, is the increased employment of non-Whites in news media professions. Equally important is an increased sensitivity among news media personnel to be attentive to untold stories from non-White communities and the cultivation of news sources there.

The result should be a functional information surveillance system that promotes social understanding and alleviates unwarranted fears based on racial, cultural, or gender prejudices. In the meantime, major changes must be made in the training of journalists and in applied news philosophy if reporting concerning non-White racial groups is to improve. The issue of more equitable employment of people of color in news media professions represents an obvious opportunity to effect more accurate reporting of their role in society and merits detailed discussion, which is provided elsewhere in this book. The challenge is magnified in an era of new and emerging information platforms that provide nonprofessional journalists and "ordinary" citizens with means to express themselves under the guise of journalistic commentary. For the moment, however, it is important to look at other factors currently working against the achievement of multicultural representative news reporting in the United States. Progress toward this phase depends on the ability to overcome two major obstacles that have become matters of entrenched journalistic policy. Overcoming the first requires a renewed commitment to the ideals espoused by media owners and editors from the inception of professional news reporting standards; overcoming the second necessitates a change in the basic "news values" journalists apply to their work.

SOME WOMEN JOURNALISTS WHO PAVED THE WAY

In the late 1800s at a time when women were fighting for their basic rights in American society, a handful of Black women were emerging as important voices in the Black press. One of the most prominent was Lucy Wilmot Smith, who eloquently commemorated her fellow Negro women writers in the following passage in the Indianapolis *Freeman* on February 23, 1889:

> The Negro woman's history is marvelously strange and pathetic. Unlike that of other races, her mental, moral, and physical status has not found a place in the archives of public libraries. From the womb of the future must come that poet or author to glorify her womanhood by idealizing the various phases of her character, by digging from the past examples of faithfulness and sympathy, endurance and self-sacrifice and displaying the achievements which were brightened by friction. Born and bred under both the hindrance of slavery and the limitations of her sex, the mothers of the race have kept pace with the fathers. They stand at the head of the cultured, educated families whose daughters clasp arms with the sons. The educated Negro woman occupies vantage found over the Caucasian woman of America, in that the former has had to contest with her brother every inch of the ground for recognition, the Negro man, having has his sister by his side on plantations and in rice swamps, keeps her there, now that he moves in other spheres. As she wins laurels he accords her the royal crown. This is especially true in journalism. Doors are opened before we knock, and as well equipped young women emerged from the class-room the brotherhood of the race, men whose energies have been repressed and distorted by the interposition of circumstances, give them opportunities to prove themselves; and right well are they doing this by voice and pen.[15]

Other notable Black women journalists include Ida B. Wells, a former slave and prominent African American journalist who spoke out against lynchings in the late 1800s; Lucile Bluford, editor and publisher of the *Kansas City Call,* an African American newspaper where she worked since her graduation from the University of Kansas in 1932; and Marvel Cooke, who worked for the *Amsterdam News,* a Black newspaper in New York in the 1930s, and who was the only African American and woman reporter on the staff of the *Compass,* a liberal New York daily where she worked from 1950 to 1952.[16]

In the early 1900s during a tumultuous time for Mexicans in Texas, Jovita Idar became a celebrated "Heroine of La Raza." As the Mexican Revolution was raging and the Texas Rangers, or "los rinches," were routinely lynching Mexican Americans and Mexican children, Idar wrote about the atrocities and the extreme discrimination against Mexican children in the public schools in her father's newspaper, *La Crónica.* She wrote about the lynching and hanging of a Mexican child in Thorndale, Texas, by the Texas Rangers and the brutal burning at the stake of 20-year-old Antonio Rodriguez in Rocksprings, Texas. Of Rodriguez she wrote, "The crowd cheered when the flames engulfed his contorted body. They did not even turn away at the smell of his burning flesh and I wondered if they even knew his name. There are so many dead that sometimes I can't remember all their names."[17]

In 1911, Idar became the first president of the League of Mexican Women to promote the education of poor Mexican children, and the organization also provided free food and clothing for the needy. In 1913, Idar caught the attention of the U.S. federal government and Texas Rangers when she began writing articles supporting the revolutionary forces of Francisco Villa of Mexico and crossed the border to serve as a nurse in the Cruz Blanca on the side of General Villa. When she returned to Laredo in 1914, she wrote an article criticizing Woodrow Wilson's deployment of troops on the border, and the Texas Rangers were dispatched to Laredo to destroy Idar's printing presses. Although she bravely fended off "los rinches" for a short while, they eventually returned and, in the stealth of night, broke open the doors with sledgehammers and destroyed the presses and Linotype machines. At that moment the voice of "La Raza" was silenced.

Although few other women journalists of color have led such a strong and effective campaign for political and social justice as Jovita Idar, some have made significant steps toward progress in the fight for greater equality and fairer representation in news coverage and employment. In 1965, after Peggy Peterman was hired by the *St. Petersburg Times* to write for the "Negro Page," she concluded that news about the Black community should not be segregated and fired off a 14-page memo stating why the page should be abolished. The editors agreed, and she was immediately transferred to the "Women's Page."

Sexism in the Newsroom

Although the days are gone when such blatant segregation of news content was routine, what remains is an acute perception of physical divisiveness.

With few women of color as role models or mentors, many women journalists of color sense a degree of hostility in their newsrooms. Consequently, many minority women journalists have developed a professional strategy for negotiating their careers. They stay focused on their goals, and do not approach every situation with the expectation of being harassed or discriminated against.[18]

The civil rights movement of the 1960s enabled women of color to successfully wedge into the broadcast industry—albeit slowly. News directors at stations with large ethnic markets sought minority anchors and reporters who reflected the shifting demographics of the local communities, and their changing attitudes toward racial and ethnic minorities.

Proportionately, Asian Americans have witnessed the greatest proliferation of on-air jobs compared to any other racial or ethnic group. In the early 1970s, there were only a small number of Asian American broadcast journalists, but a decade later there were more than 30 nationwide—a far higher percentage than their presence in the general population. With the exception of San Francisco, where the numbers of Asian American men and women on-air are roughly equal, women outnumbered men by a 2-to-1 ratio.[19] This gender imbalance reflects the residual effect of the stereotype created by the "Suzie Wong syndrome" where Asian women are subservient, sexual objects of fantasy. It is perhaps best explained by the following passage from the *Far Eastern Economic Review:*

> Such stereotypes have made life difficult for women who object to the manner in which Hollywood, pornography and popular fiction continue to stereotype the "Oriental doll" as a sexually submissive slave. The many Asian American women who are anchoring major national and local news programmes are among the most talented of their profession. But their disproportionately high representation probably reflects the tendency for yellow women to be more acceptable in highly visible jobs in a predominately white society where their ethnic brothers are seen as unattractive.[20]

In recent decades, it appears that television news directors and station managers have determined the least threatening anchor combination to be a White male with a White or Asian female. Often referred to as the "Connie Chung syndrome," the disproportionate suc-

CNN hoped to capitalize on news anchor personalities with audience recognition to boost its ratings when it launched Connie Chung's own—but short-lived—news program *Connie Chung Tonight* in June 2002.

Source: © Bettmann/CORBIS.

cess of Asian women newscasters has garnered them public accolades—but at a cost of driving a wedge between Asian American women and men.

Despite the success of Asian American women in broadcast news, they remain virtually invisible at the national level. Only Connie Chung, the most high-profile Asian American female news anchor, was offered a coveted—although unsuccessful—stint cohosting a network news program. She was paired with Dan Rather on the *CBS Evening News*. Her journalistic credentials are impressive: Since launching her career in 1969, she is one of the few women of color who has been a correspondent and anchor at three of the network news operations—CBS, NBC, and ABC—as well as a local anchor at Los Angeles's KCBS-TV for seven years.[21]

In 2002, Chung became CNN's biggest news hire, commanding a $2 million salary to host *Connie Chung Tonight*. Her salary was second only to that of Larry King, who raked in $7 million a year for his top-rated *Larry King Live*. Yet, despite Chung's proven credentials and on-air talent, a reporter from *People* magazine still found it appropriate to inquire about who made the suit and shoes she wore to the news conference announcing her jump to CNN from ABC.

Admired for her fighting determination, accomplishments, and concern for the role of women and minorities in television news, Carole Simpson is one of the few African American women to regularly anchor a network news program. In the late 1990s, she commuted from the ABC Washington bureau every Sunday morning to anchor *World News Tonight* in New York. As the only Black woman to graduate from the department of journalism at the University of Michigan in 1962—and the only one of the 60 graduates who was not offered a job—her road to success was an arduous one laden with battles against racism and sexism. At the peak of the civil rights movement, the head of the journalism department finally arranged an internship for her at Tuskegee Institute in Alabama. Simpson explains what it was like for a girl who grew up in Chicago to go south to a rural town of 5,000 people:

Carole Simpson served as weekend news anchor for the ABC network but, as an industry pioneer, experienced racism and sexism throughout her career.

Source: AP Photo/Joe Marquette.

I had to go to segregated things. I had to shop in Montgomery, Alabama. You could not try on clothes. You had to guess at things because black people were not allowed to try on clothes. You couldn't try on hats. I refused to use the water fountains in the bathrooms. I would just hold it rather than go to a colored washroom. But it was an amazing experience.[22]

In 1970, after five years of hard news reporting at WCFL radio in Chicago, and after having earned a master's degree at the University of Iowa, Simpson was hired as a television reporter at WMAQ in Chicago where she wanted to anchor. It wasn't long before she once again confronted the all-too-familiar attitudes of race and sex discrimination:

I was told that White people didn't want to hear news from a Black person . . . It was patently absurd because I'd always been told I had a good delivery. I had an authoritative delivery. I had the credentials. I had the education. I had the experience. How could somebody say that I would not be able to anchor? And then they said my enunciation was too perfect, that it was too clear and too precise. And I'm going, "Excuse me. Isn't this what this is all about?" Yet other Black reporters in Chicago were told they sounded too ethnic. So, it was all the discriminatory efforts to keep us from the higher paying jobs, the top jobs, the jobs with more visibility. We were kind of window dressing. It became quite clear that we'd been hired so they could say they had one. But that was it. You can come this far but no further. We'll let you report but you can't anchor. So at WMAQ, I fought and fought and fought to be able to anchor and I finally got a chance to anchor on the weekends. It was okay, White people could hear somebody Black give news on the weekend. It was 1972, the beginning of the women's movement. Now everybody's got to try to put a woman up there. Then I was a "two-for." I was Black and a woman so I became a double token. But my emphasis was always to show, "Look, you're not hiring me because of what color I am or what my gender is. It's because I'm good. I'm a good anchor."[23]

Elizabeth Vargas was among the first Latina newswomen to attain a major network position when she joined NBC in 1993. Among the indignities she suffered were letters from viewers urging her to "go back to Mexico." Vargas is of Puerto Rican descent.

Source: AP Photo/Kathy Willens.

Although Latinas may not have saturated the news media to the extent of Asian and African American women, one who successfully worked her way to the top is Emmy Award–winning reporter/anchor Elizabeth Vargas, who joined NBC in 1993 as one of the few Latina women in network news. Not only had she worked for many of the top-rated news programs on ABC—*20/20, World News Tonight, 20/20 Downtown,* and *Good Morning America*—and NBC—*Now With Tom*

Brokaw and Katie Couric, Dateline NBC, and *NBC Nightly News*—but she also had been at the center of our country's biggest news stories. She covered the Middle East conflict, Elian Gonzalez, the JonBenet Ramsey case, and the mauling death of Diane Whipple in San Francisco.

Born in Paterson, New Jersey, to a Spanish Italian father and Irish German Swedish mother, Vargas was keenly aware of the benefits and limitations of both her Hispanic heritage and her gender. According to Vargas, being a Hispanic journalist is as much a part of her as being a woman. She has always worked hard to be the best reporter in the newsroom. Although she serves as an inspiration to Hispanic women aspiring to television news careers, she has also been the target of racist attacks. Earlier in her career, she was taken aback when she received "rude letters" suggesting she "go back to Mexico." She replied, "And by the way, my family is from Puerto Rico."[24]

Very few women of color have delivered the news at the network level, and, in general, local stations have done better in employing on-air talent

Ann Curry (left) and Meredith Vieira—both of multicultural heritage—have managed to carve out successful careers in network television as women of color in an industry dominated by White males.

Source: AP Photo/Richard Drew.

more representative of the larger population. Viewers want to see people on the news who look like they do, and network executives should ensure the people who deliver the news are representative of the audiences watching them.

Newsroom Power and Practices: Perpetuating Inaccurate Portrayals

Despite hints of progress, it would be premature for women to start congratulating themselves for the inroads made in dictating news coverage of women's issues and stories. Studies of sex roles in the media continue to show that women are still far from being seen as a major influence either inside or outside the newsroom. The 2002 American Society of Newspaper Editors newsroom census found that only 37% of newspaper newsrooms employed women despite the fact that roughly 60% of students in college journalism programs were female. Minority women fared even worse: Only 2.99% of all women in newspaper newsrooms were women of color. And a 2001 survey conducted by the Radio-Television News Directors Association and Foundation showed that women account for less than one quarter (24%) of television news directors, and only one fifth (20%) of radio news directors.[25]

In his handbook, *Best Practices: The Art of Leadership in News Organizations* (2002), former *Los Angeles Times* editor Shelby Coffey III offers insights from the careers of 20 news executives. Only four of the interviewees (20%) are women, and of those only two (10%) are women of color. When addressing the issue of diversity in the newsroom over the past 25 years, Karen Jurgensen, then editor of *USA Today*, offered this account based on her own experience:

> The industry has failing grades in diversity. Originally, diversity meant a few African-Americans and women in the newsroom. It didn't mean pay much attention to them, it just meant get them in the newsroom. Now I think diversity means that you have to reflect the broad richness of the country, whether it is Latinos or African-Americans or Asian-Americans or whatever. And everyone has a part of the news decisions. Diversity is what the country is. So you have to reflect that in the newsroom or you are not producing something that speaks to a large chunk of the population or is accurate. At the same time, those people have to be in a position to make decisions about what is going into the paper or not going into the paper. You can't have (just) one of each. I remember there were times in my history at USA TODAY when I would run the daily news meeting. And it was me and 15 white guys . . . With all due respect to white guys, the world is not entirely populated by [them]. I would feel that I had to be the one voice for women at the table.[26]

In "Genderizing Latino News: An Analysis of a Local Newspaper's Coverage of Latino Current Affairs," Lucila Vargas (2002) studied the coverage of Latino news from 1992 to 1995 by *The News & Observer* in Raleigh, North Carolina, and found that certain newsroom practices, which she calls "genderization," enable a newspaper to operate as a technology of gender, race, and class—thus relegating Hispanic news as feminine and perpetuating the stereotype of Latinos as an underclass. Vargas asserts that news media are arenas of public speech, and who gets to speak in public spaces is determined by the way power is exercised and social relations are structured.

According to Vargas, the subtle techniques employed by today's journalists obscure the way sexism, racism, and classism are validated in journalistic practices. She argues that the genderization of journalistic products and texts occurs through the following editorial techniques practiced by reporters and editors: (1) privileging either men's or women's voices in a story or in the entire coverage of an issue, a realm, or a group; (2) foregrounding either men or women in photographs and other graphic displays; (3) writing either a "soft" feature or a "hard" news story on a given event or issue; (4) placing a news item in the Home or Business section; (5) highlighting characteristics of newsmakers that in Western culture have been traditionally considered either masculine or feminine; (6) positioning stories as subjective or feminine rather than as objective or masculine knowledge; and (7) covering those actions and events of a social group (e.g., Latinos, African Americans, Asians) pertaining to women's stereotypical domains (e.g., education, domestic violence), while neglecting the group's actions and events pertaining to men's traditional domains (e.g., politics, business).[27]

Feminist scholars contend that the genderizing of newsroom practices occurs within the ideological framework of patriarchy, and thus the distinction by sex connotes value judgments that have subtle—yet tremendous—impact on the public's perception of minority groups. Nancy Leys Stepan (1993) argues that the race-gender comparisons naturalize the subordination of both women and minority groups:

> In short, lower races represented the "female" type of the human species, and females the "lower race" of gender. . . . By analogy with the so-called lower races, women, the sexually deviate, the criminal, the urban poor, and the insane were in one way or another constructed as biological "races apart" whose differences from the white male, and likenesses to each other, "explained" their different and lower position in the social hierarchy.[28]

Because this analogy is embedded in Western ideology, journalists routinely use the race-gender comparison to represent social groups. Thus, by genderizing social or "ethnic" groups as feminine, reporters and editors essentially construct them as an "inferior" other. For women of color, this practice positions them at the bottom of the social order.

To illustrate: Over the past six decades, there were only a small number of national rape stories involving African American women. One was from 1959 about a "Negro coed" who was raped by four lower-class White boys, called the "Tobacco Roaders' Case"; another was the Tawana Brawley case of 1988; and a third and most recent was the rape of Desiree Washington by boxer Mike Tyson. On a smaller, more local level, the director of the rape crisis center in Buffalo, New York, indicated that 80% of women in the Black community there had been raped, yet to read, listen, or watch the news media you wouldn't know about any of them.

Third World women historically have received inadequate or biased media attention—unless they are the victims of some bizarre act or arrive in the United States in a dramatic way. When the *Golden Venture,* a ship carrying roughly 300 Chinese immigrants, ran aground off the coast of New York City in the summer of 1997, the media clamored for an interview with a Chinese illegal immigrant—preferably a woman who had survived the grueling trans-Atlantic ordeal. What the media apparently didn't want to adequately address was the living and working conditions of immigrant laborers. Consequently, no experiences of striking Chinese sweatshop workers ever made it onto the front page of a major newspaper or on the network evening news.[29]

When covering stories of Third World women, the media tend to portray them as oppressed victims who are bound by centuries of brutal and barbaric cultural practices. For example, during the height of the global conflict in Afghanistan in 2002, the *Los Angeles Times* reported a story about an 18-year-old woman who was ordered to be gang-raped by a tribunal council to punish—or shame—her family after her 11-year-old brother was seen walking unchaperoned with a girl from a higher-class tribe. According to the graphic news article, the woman said, "I touched their feet. I wept. I cried. I said I taught the holy Koran to children in the village, therefore don't punish me for a crime which was not committed by me. But [four council members] tore my clothes and raped me one by one . . . in a mud hut as hundreds of people stood outside laughing and cheering."[30] Interestingly, the accompanying photo in the *Los Angeles Times* did not even include a picture of the woman—the subject of the story—but rather showed pensive images of her father and younger brother provided by the Associated Press.

This type of problematic coverage might change if women—and particularly women of color—obtain decision-making roles in the newsroom. Their presence should alter the nature of traditional newsroom culture and add a vital perspective that has been absent or overlooked. It not only should widen the scope of news coverage, but also could help diminish gender and minority stereotyping in the news. Laura Flanders notes in her book, *Real Majority, Media Minority: The Cost of Sidelining Women in Reporting* (1997), that, as more women are hired to report the news, editors are finding that topics historically regarded as "women's news" such as health, family issues, child care, domestic violence, education, and child abuse have become stories of general interest to all readers.

News Coverage of Women: Vamps, Victims, and Violence

Helen Benedict, author of *Virgin or Vamp: How the Press Covers Sex Crimes* (1992), says women are more likely to get mainstream media coverage as crime victims than in any other role.[31] As one U.S.-based journalist explained, there is so little coverage of women outside of sensationalism that the media often disregard women as leaders and are more likely to portray them as individuals rather than groups, victims instead of heroines, and sexual figures as opposed to thinkers.

Flanders (1997) suggests that this point is perhaps best exemplified by the sensationalized story in 1993 when genital mutilation hit the headlines—not the kind that affects an entire class of 100 million women in parts of Africa, the Middle East, and Asia who are ritually mutilated prior to adolescence, but rather an isolated incident in the United States. The press reported in detail how Lorena Bobbitt hacked off her husband's penis in a fit of fury while he slept, and then—perplexed by what to do with it—drove off in her car and casually tossed it out of the window. News agencies across America picked up the sordid story, and the New York *Daily News* even printed a full-page headline that screamed, "It Really Hurt."

More often than not, media coverage of female victims is associated with sex. And when it comes to sex crime coverage, more is not necessarily better. Given that a woman is raped every five minutes in the United States, it is the duty of the press to cover stories of rape—from the angle not just of victims, but of perpetrators as well. Sex crime media coverage continues to be both genderized and racialized: The rape of a White woman by a Black man is the most commonly covered type of rape, while the rape of a Black woman by a Black man is the least commonly covered. This practice not only is statistically inaccurate—most rapes are committed by men of the same race and class of the victim—but also reflects and perpetuates the notion that White women are more valued and valuable than Black women.

Women receiving mainstream news coverage as sex crime victims are often categorized in one of two ways. They are presented either as "virgins" or "vamps." In "virgin" rape stories, media coverage suggests that a perverted man, usually of a lower class and darker complexion, has attacked a virtuous woman. Examples include beauty pageant winner Desiree Washington, who accused boxer Mike Tyson of rape, or the case of the

Central Park jogger where a White woman was allegedly attacked by non-White youths. The "vamp" approach suggests that a woman's physical appearance, dress, or behavior drove the perpetrator to commit rape. An example is the case of Patricia Bowman, who alleged that William Kennedy Smith raped her. Media coverage of the court trial emphasized the defense position that Bowman held questionable moral values and had a history of sexual promiscuity. It is interesting to note that Ms. Washington's case resulted in Tyson's conviction and Ms. Bowman's case resulted in acquittal for Smith. Framing rape stories in these two extremes not only reflects racism, classism, and sexism, but is grossly inaccurate. Such coverage ignores the fact that most rapists are of the same race and social class as their victims, usually know the victim, and have more normal psychological profiles than any other kind of criminal. Moreover, it makes news media guilty of perpetuating stereotypes and false notions about who rapes and who gets raped, and ignores the reality of rape as a crime. Media coverage tends to focus attention on the victims (women) rather than the criminals (men). News organizations should be looking at why rape is so persistent and prevalent in American society. Editors need to consider whether sexism is a factor in making decisions about such stories. This is unlikely to happen until more women—and women of color—are in decision-making positions and can exert greater influence on how sex crimes are reported.[32]

If news media reporting does expand to encompass wider representation, it will first have to rededicate itself to the principle that meeting the substantive communication needs of society is its first priority. The news media obligation to provide information and interpretation of issues and events to society is essential to the development and maintenance of an enlightened citizenry. A major barrier to more racially comprehensive news coverage has been preoccupation with profit incentive, as media "marketing" of the news has led to, among other questionable practices, an increased emphasis on information targeted to high-economic-profile audiences. Among some major metropolitan daily newspapers, increased circulation among affluent readers has become the primary objective, while broadcast media seek higher audience ratings to attract major advertisers. The decline of daily newspaper readership—and closing of some major dailies across the United States—is partially the result of their failure to have cultivated racial and cultural demographic shifts in their markets. Because people of color are vastly underrepresented in the upper-middle- to upper-class income economic categories, they have been shortchanged in news media coverage. This failed approach to news reporting has affected both the frequency and nature of their coverage and the economic fortunes of many newspapers. Although news media, operating under the free enterprise system, have every right to pursue profits, they should not do so at the expense of their social responsibility to serve the informational needs of society. The surveillance function of mass communication requires that news media inform society about the perspectives, aspirations, and contributions of all its components.

As noted earlier, the Kerner Commission provided insight into the nature of a major news media problem: the values applied to news judgment. The commission noted that news was determined from "a White perspective." In other words, priorities of importance were based solely upon an event's significance to the White majority. This notion was instilled in future journalists at the very earliest stages of their training in colleges and universities. In the late 1990s and early 2000s, journalism academic organizations increased efforts to make students aware of the importance of racial and cultural diversity in reporting. But historically, journalism students were taught that news—by definition—encompassed events of consequence to the majority population audience, which meant Anglo Americans. This concept was easily made practicable because the social system ensured that news sources (persons of authority and social standing in the fields of politics, business, education, law enforcement, the military, etc.) were White. Journalism educators taught their students that the essence of good news reporting is the attribution of facts gathered from authoritative sources. Those news sources, unfortunately, represented in disproportionate numbers White ideals and values held in common with the journalists and gatekeepers who reported on their activities. The perspective of non-Whites, therefore, was not "newsworthy." Even in reporting events about non-Whites, the news sources sought by reporters to interpret them were invariably White ones. This practice was a primary reason for the alienation and distrust of news media by citizens of color. Collegiate textbooks on newswriting and journalistic practice became more sensitive to these issues as the second decade of the 21st century approached.

Because America's non-White communities generally have not been reported on in the mainstream context by news media, their stories have not been told adequately. In the 1970s and early 1980s, news media began to make inroads via special newspaper series and broadcast documentaries on specific issues of concern to people of color. However, the task of integrating them into the news requires ongoing inclusion of their views regarding all major issues confronting society. Examples of attempts to forge a change began in the 1990s and included content audits of news topics and news sources by newspapers; guideline stylebooks for journalists on proper usage of terms and labels; a Multicultural Management Program at the University of Missouri School of Journalism; total community coverage programs of the Robert C. Maynard Institute for Journalism Education in Oakland, California; and the development of multicultural newsroom training workshops at the American Press Institute in Reston, Virginia.

As the effects of demographic change alter the racial makeup of America's opinion leaders, it has become imperative that new sources of information be tapped from non-White communities. Perhaps the 2008 election of Barack Obama, the nation's first African American president, reinforced the notion that opinion leaders previously unknown to them are worthy of editorial attention. To accomplish that objective, journalism educators and news professionals will need to redefine news values to include the perspectives of a wider spectrum of American citizens. One result may be a change in the composition and priorities of issues on the national agenda and better insight into national and global perspectives.

Newsroom Policy and Race

We have observed that the misrepresentation of people of color in news media is partly the result of long-standing policies concerning news values and economic incentive, another legacy of racial exclusion. Although the Kerner Commission report was the watershed of national recognition that news media were derelict in responsibility to people of color, change has come very slowly. Professional news organizations began to publicly address the issues of non-White training, employment, decision making, and coverage in 1968. The years since, however, have generally been characterized by an increase in stereotypical selection phase reporting, notable exceptions notwithstanding. The nearly five-decade struggle to improve matters suggests the difficulty of changing policy in news organizations. Thus, it is important to understand the fundamental workings of workplace policy in institutional newsrooms.

Sociologist Warren Breed in his work "Social Control in the Newsroom" set forth the nature of newsroom policy. Among the major findings in Breed's study of daily newspapers was that every paper has policies that are covert and that often contravene ethical standards of professional journalism, including issues of politics, business, and class consideration.

Because the policies are covert and, therefore, not written and codified for persons new to the staff, they must be learned by other means. Among the ways new reporters learn policy are by observing the content of the newspaper or news broadcasts, noting which material has been edited from one's work, conversing with staff members concerning the preferences and affiliations of superiors, and noting the priorities assigned to news story ideas discussed in planning conferences.

A common complaint of non-White reporters working in mainstream newsrooms is the pressure of unwritten policy applied to their stories and "news angle" ideas. This is the manifestation of news being defined in terms of the dominant cultural perspective. Both non-White and White reporters face sanctions when policy is violated. Sanctions include reprimand, loss of esteem among colleagues, and lessening of opportunity for upward mobility in the organization. A revealing look at how newsroom policy affects news coverage of people of color from the vantage point of a staff newcomer is presented below.

CONTENT OBSERVATION

A contemporary reporter intent upon analyzing the news editorial product issued by his or her organization would find reportage of non-Whites ranging from the threatening issue to confrontation to stereotypical selection phases, depending on the historical moment and ethnicity of the group involved. The absence of a fully multicultural approach to either individual reports or general coverage would be a strong indicator of organizational policy. Conversely, stories about non-Whites focusing on special occasions—such as Cinco de Mayo, Chinese New Year, or Dr. Martin Luther King Jr.'s birthday—to the exclusion of more substantive reporting are likewise indicative of policy. Observation of multiracial views being included in reporting environmental issues, alternative energy sources, foreign policy, or the national economy would signal the newcomer that such efforts on his or her part would be welcome.

An extreme example of how unwritten policy concerning racial issues was manifest in February 2009 when the politically conservative *New York Post* ran an editorial cartoon that seemingly depicted President Barack Obama as a monkey. In the drawing by cartoonist Sean Delonas, the author of the economic stimulus bill (the President) is depicted as a dead monkey after having been shot by policemen. The cartoon is captioned, "They'll have to find someone else to write the next stimulus bill." The cartoon drew the ire not only of African Americans but also of many journalists and news commentators of various racial backgrounds. It was, however, strongly defended by senior officials of the *Post*. It must be assumed that the presence of a culturally diverse editorial leadership would have prevented publication of the cartoon with its historically racially charged characterization of a person of color as a monkey.

Past performance, therefore, becomes a policy statement as strong as any written or orally expressed edict, perhaps stronger. In certain contexts it is easier to challenge formal policies, because they are often accompanied by a procedure for making changes to them. It is difficult for the newcomer to counter the explanation that conditions exist "because that's the way we do things around here." It is more likely, however, that the force of content observation will not elicit inquiry from a newcomer anxious to accommodate him- or herself to the work environment. The compelling instinct is to conform in order to survive.

EDITING BY SUPERIORS

A more direct means of conveying policy is the editing process. Newsroom editors are gatekeepers and enjoy professional superiority over staff reporters. The journalist who produces newspaper or broadcast material that is inconsistent with policy will be edited, either by alteration or by deletion of offending work. As such editing relates to news about non-Whites, the professional explanation—if any is given—is that the item lacks "newsworthiness" or that lack of space or time prevents its inclusion. Since it is the reporter's job to get work into print or on the air, the inability to achieve those objectives reflects upon professional competence. Editing is not necessarily a sanction against the newcomer, but it often denotes a policy infringement, and one or two applications are usually enough to complete indoctrination.

INFORMAL CONVERSATION

When staff members gather around the water cooler or have lunch together, their conversations often provide insight into policy. Mention of political and/or civil affiliations and preferences maintained by executive superiors suggests to the astute newcomer which issues and topics to emphasize or avoid. Attitudes held by peers toward other racial groups are evidenced by their informal conversation and comments about race-related news stories. Policy facilitates a newsroom atmosphere, and when consensus is apparent, whatever the issue may be, newcomers quickly get the message.

The informal conversation of newsroom colleagues, however, need not be supportive of the views and attitudes of superiors. For the newcomer's purposes, even negative conversation regarding the attitudes of superiors is sufficient to convey policy. Staff members are obliged not to agree with policy, only to adhere to it.

NEWS PLANNING CONFERENCES

Journalists who become privy to news story planning meetings can observe the hidden force of policy in action. The priority ranking of news events, activities, and ideas for future reporting assignments reflects the thinking of executives and editorial gatekeepers. The reception and "play" given to race-related news as opposed to other comparable items reveals policy clearly. It is here where the relative consideration of values is weighed, where the perception of social consequence is manifest. Even the decision to do a special series on one racial group or another only highlights the ongoing neglect of established policy to provide the general audience with a complete surveillance of the social landscape. The news perspective is askew, but the newcomer accepts it as "standard operating procedure."

SANCTIONS FOR POLICY VIOLATIONS

Although organizational policy works subtly but effectively as a barrier to multiracial news coverage, the sanctions for policy violations are equally subtle. There are four major sanctions that are self-motivated and psychologically self-imposed, but nonetheless real. An important reason for newsroom conformity to policy is the reporter's desire to hold the esteem of peers. Few journalists, apart from those who attain national prestige, gain consistent recognition for performance. In the absence of letters, phone calls, or e-mails from the public, perhaps the greatest job satisfaction is the acknowledgment from fellow staff members of a job well done. Newcomers to a staff arrive with the desire to demonstrate quickly their right to "belong" by earning the respect of colleagues. Any violation of policy would cast the newcomer as incompetent or, worse, as a rebel.

As is true of most American professionals, journalists seek the rewards of career advancement. The fear of not getting the challenging assignments that lead to promotions and recognition by superiors is a strong motivation to learn and conform to policy. Conversely, as was the case of the Black writer of the *Washington Post*'s "Rosa Lee's Story," the possible Pulitzer Prize award apparently precluded any concern that the story was consistent with Black stereotypes. Because policy virtually defines the parameters of news value, breaches severely handicap a staff member competing with several peers for promotion.

A third major sanction is the desire of journalists to please superiors who have afforded them opportunity for employment. With that desire is a feeling of obligation to submit to policies and procedures (published or otherwise) established by management.

Finally, there is the ever-present possibility of job loss if policy is violated. Although it is rare for a reporter to be fired over misinterpretation policy, journalists who violate policy may become subject to scrutiny. It is not difficult for an editor or a management superior to find other reasons to terminate policy transgressors or to make them feel "uncomfortable" on the job. One example of the latter is the continued assignment of routine work that offers no prospect for personal satisfaction or peer recognition except to denote one's status "in the doghouse."

It must be understood that newsroom policies and sanctions work against change in news coverage of non-Whites without regard for the racial heritage of reporters. Non-White journalists lament the newsroom atmosphere that forces them to see their profession from a White perspective. They complain that colleagues and superiors—not overtly racist but insensitive or ignorant—evaluate their performance on culturally biased news criteria. To focus too heavily on race-related issues jeopardizes peer esteem, and work on such issues rarely results in the kind of recognition that leads to promotion. Given the nature of the various factors supporting traditional newsroom policy, the slow progress made toward more equitable and accurate news reporting concerning racial groups in American media becomes understandable although not excusable.

American society will not achieve the goal of multicultural news coverage that accurately reflects an image of it until the concept of news is redefined to include non-White perspectives. The consequences of failure to do so will result in a nation that falls short of its own vision and purpose for existence. Much of the responsibility for change must come from news media organizations where dedicated, conscientious efforts must be made to examine whether outmoded and counterproductive policies are preventing progress toward multicultural reporting.

Moving into the 21st century, there are signs that the news industry is acknowledging how vital the issues of multicultural diversity are to its future and credibility. The Society of Professional Journalists revised its Code of Ethics to reflect that concern and noted in its trade journal "journalists must avoid the stereotyping and limited vision that corrupt accuracy."[33] It also joined a number of other professional news groups in providing a "diversity source book" as a reference tool to assist reporters in identifying non-White news sources that may be utilized to gain broader perspectives for their stories. These efforts are examples of the commitment required by news organizations to overcome the legacy of exclusion that began in colonial America.

Notes

1. Henry Chu, "Twin Attacks Rock Norway, At Least 87 Dead," *Los Angeles Times*, July 22, 2011.

2. "Norway and Us: Hate Is Losing," *San Bernardino Sun*, July 29, 2011, A15.

3. Quoted in Raja Abdulrahim, "Muslims Feel Sting of Initial Blame," *Los Angeles Times*, July 24, 2011, A8.

4. Ibid.

5. Ibid.

6. For a discussion of the definition of news and news values, see any of several basic news writing texts, including Curtis MacDougall, *Interpretative*

Reporting (Macmillan, 1982), and William Metz, *Newswriting* (Prentice Hall, 1985).

7. Kerner Commission, *Report of the National Advisory Commission on Civil Disorders* (Bantam, 1968), 389.

8. Center for Integration and Improvement of Journalism, *News Watch: A Critical Look at Coverage of People of Color* (San Francisco State University, 1994), 44.

9. Cited in *Project Zinger: The Good, the Bad and the Ugly* (Center for Integration and Improvement of Journalism, San Francisco State University, and Asian American Journalists Association, August 1991), 4.

10. "Asian Invasion: South Bay's Chinese, Japanese, Korean Populations Swell," *Daily Breeze* (Torrance, CA), March 24, 1991, 1.

11. M. J. Bridge, "The News as If All People Mattered," cited by Debra Gersh, "Promulgating Polarization," *Editor and Publisher,* October 10, 1992, 30.

12. Wallace L. Walker, Esq., personal correspondence to Clint Wilson, June 25, 2002.

13. The series appeared in the *Washington Post* from September 18 through September 25, 1994.

14. The series was published intermittently in the *New York Times* from June 4 through June 29, 2000.

15. Lucy Wilmot Smith, "Some Female Writers of the Negro Race," *Indianapolis Freeman,* February 23, 1889.

16. Maurine H. Beasley and Sheila J. Gibbons, *Taking Their Place: A Documentary History of Women and Journalism* (Washington, D.C.: The American University Press in cooperation with the Women's Institute for Freedom of the Press, 1993).

17. "Jovita Idar: 1885–1946: Por La Raza y Para La Raza," *La Voz de Aztlan* I(5), February 27, 2000, retrieved July 3, 2002, http://aztlan.net.

18. In *Women Journalists of Color: Present Without Power* (International Women's Media Foundation, September 1999).

19. H. Chang, *Asian Americans in the News,* unpublished paper prepared for the honors colloquium at University of California, Berkeley, 1984.

20. *Far East Economic Review* (1983, December 8), 51, cited in H. Chang, *Asian Americans in the News,* unpublished paper prepared for the honors colloquium at University of California, Berkeley, 1984.

21. Elizabeth Jensen, "CNN's New Star Format Put to the Test," *Los Angeles Times,* June 24, 2012, F1, F12.

22. Quoted in Judity Marlene, *Women in Television News Revisited: Into the Twenty-First Century* (Austin: University of Texas Press, 1999), 98.

23. Ibid.

24. Elinor J. Brecher, "Elizabeth Vargas: Tuning In at the Top," *Hispanic* 15 (No. 6, June 2002): 24–25.

25. *WENews* (May 28, 2002). Directory: http://www.womensnews.org. World Wide Web: http://nytimes.com. Retrieved June 4, 2002, from aol.com.

26. Shelby Coffey III, *Best Practices: The Art of Leadership in News Organizations* (Arlington, VA: Freedom Forum, 2002).

27. Lucila Vargas, "Genderizing Latino News: An Analysis of a Local Newspaper's Coverage of Latino Current Affairs," *Critical Studies in Mass Communication* 17 (No. 3, September 2002): 261–293.

28. Cited in Lucila Vargas, "Genderizing Latino News: An Analysis of a Local Newspaper's Coverage of Latino Current Affairs," *Critical Studies in Mass Communication* 17 (No. 3, September 2002): 266.

29. Laura Flanders, *Real Majority, Media Minority: The Cost of Sidelining Women in Reporting* (Monroe, ME: Common Courage Press, 1997).

30. Associated Press, "Pakistan Investigating Rape Ordered by Tribal Council," *Los Angeles Times,* July 4, 2002, A4.

31. In Laura Flanders, *Real Majority, Media Minority: The Cost of Sidelining Women in Reporting* (Monroe, ME: Common Courage Press, 1997), 58.

32. Ibid.

33. "Source Book to Launch This Month," *Quill* (June 2002): 59.

7

Marketing and Advertising
The Media's Not-So-Silent Partners

In the late autumn of 2011, The Learning Channel (TLC) on cable television hoped to build multicultural understanding when it launched a new reality series *All-American Muslim*. The series promised to follow the daily lives of five American Muslim families in Dearborn, Michigan, and offer an "intimate look at customs and celebrations, as well as misconceptions, conflicts, and differences these families face outside and within their own community." Rather than focus on how these families were different from other Americans, the network said the series would reveal "how these individuals negotiate universal family issues" such as marriage, juggling busy careers, and raising a family. In fact, the network said the series would show that, although the family members shared the same religion, "the families of *All-American Muslim* lead different lives."[1]

The lineup of real-life characters in the program reflected both reality and diversity. It included two sisters, one who wore the traditional head scarf and prayed daily and another decorated with piercings and tattoos who had married an Irish Catholic who was converting to Islam. Others in the program were the head football coach of a local high school team, a deputy chief sheriff, an automotive marketing coordinator, and the businesswoman owner of Dearborn's premier wedding and banquet hall. All were involved with aspects of life common to all Americans and wanted to move into life in the United States without losing touch with their religion. The *Hollywood Reporter* review of the story called the series "a heartfelt story of immigration and assimilation that is as American as apple pie."[2]

Although Muslims are members of the Islam religion and are not a race or an ethnicity, the media's portrayal of Muslims has been racialized by focusing on Muslims who are Arabs, Middle Easterners, and South Asians.

But most Muslims in the United States are not Arabs or from the Middle East. In fact, Muslims are the most racially diverse and inclusive religion in the United States. A 2009 study by the Gallup Center for Muslim Studies revealed that 28% of U.S. Muslims classified themselves as White, 35% were African American, 18% considered themselves Asian, and 18% claimed other race or ethnicity. In comparison, most other religions were predominantly White: Jews, 93%; Mormons, 91%; Protestants, 88%; and Catholics, 76%.[3] The families profiled in *All-American Muslim* all origi-nated in Lebanon, which conformed to the image of Muslims as being from the Middle East, a region in which the United States was engaged in conflicts when the series was broadcast.

The program's approach of showing these Muslims as adapting to tra-ditional aspects of American life was attacked by groups such as the Florida Family Association, which opposed what it called the "Islamization of America" and protested those "who are hostile toward Christianity and traditional American values."[4] The Florida Family Association's website criticized the program for "attempting to manipulate Americans into ignoring the threat of jihad" and hiding "the Islamic agenda's clear and present danger to American liberties and traditional values." By focusing on American Muslims living lifestyles shared by many Americans, the show excluded "many Islamic believers whose agenda poses a clear and present danger to liberties and traditional values that the majority of Americans cherish," the organization charged.

"Most Americans aren't suspicious of Muslims who are trying to get married, open clubs, and play football. Americans are suspicious of Muslims who are trying to blow up American buildings, subvert American free-doms, and assert the primacy of Islamic law over American law," wrote Robert Spencer, director of Jihad Watch, in an article reprinted on the Florida Family Association's *All-American Muslim* webpage.[5]

In protesting the show's portrayal of Muslims, the organization tar-geted not the TLC network, the program's producers, or the families featured in the series. Instead, the Florida Family Association launched a national campaign targeting companies whose advertising appeared next to *All-American Muslim* shows. The group sent six e-mail alerts encouraging those opposing the program to e-mail "the companies that advertised during the first six weeks that the program aired." After receiving the protests and calls for a boycott of its home improvement stores, the giant retail chain Lowe's pulled its advertisements from *All-American Muslim*. The Lowe's decision triggered criticism of the chain by those who felt the company should not have pulled away from the program. In a statement explaining its decision, Lowe's called the *All-American Muslim* reality series "a lightning rod" for many "individuals and groups [who] have strong political and societal views on this topic."[6]

"As a result we did pull our advertising on this program. We believe it is best to respectfully defer to communities, individuals and groups to discuss and consider such issues," the North Carolina-based company continued. In reaction to the Lowe's decision, others accused the chain of endorsing hate by pulling its advertisements and organized a petition drive urging other advertisers to stay with the program.

Both the role of the TLC network to try to show Muslims as adapting to life in the United States and the role of the Florida Family Association targeting advertisers to influence media content are central to the themes of this book. The focus of this chapter is the key role and pervasive influence of advertisers in shaping what the media show or do not show about people who historically have not been fully or accurately covered or portrayed. Though coverage of Arabs, Muslims, Middle Easterners, and South Asians is relatively new to the media scene, the relationships between advertising, media content, and audience reaction are not new.

Advertising and Media in the Land of Plenty

In 1950, historian David Potter was invited by the Walgreen Foundation to prepare six lectures at Harvard University on the American character and the impact of economic abundance on shaping the character of people in the United States. In the lectures, later published in revised form in the 1954 book *People of Plenty,* Potter identified advertising as the "institution of abundance," a unique part of the society "brought into being by abundance, without previous existence in any form, and, moreover, an institution which is peculiarly identified with American abundance."[7] He also noted that media scholars up to the middle of the 20th century had not recognized the central role advertising played in shaping and developing media in the United States. Advertising had been seen as a sideshow to the media's main content. But Potter saw advertising as the main message of the media, with the news and entertainment content being the sideshow.

As Potter and later scholars have noted, the development of advertising as a revenue source for print and, later, broadcast media required managers of media to develop news and entertainment content that would be bait to attract the largest possible number of people. This gave birth to the term *mass media,* which described the ability of the media to attract a large audience to which advertisers could direct their commercial messages through relatively few channels. *Class media* targeted to special audiences such as women, people of color, or people with special interests attracted fewer people and often advertisers offering products or services targeting the distinctive tastes of their audiences, such as food, entertainment, or travel to the mother country. The audience circulation for print media and rating figures for broadcasters became the bread and butter of the media, since they translated to increased advertising insertions and higher advertising rates. The larger the audience, the more money the media could charge advertisers.

Potter emphasized that, far from being an appendage to the mass media, advertising is a force that dictates the editorial and entertainment content of media that depend on advertising dollars for their revenues. The mass media charge artificially low subscription fees to boost their circulation, which forces the media to depend on advertisers even more for their revenues. This, in turn, is accompanied by editorial or programming philosophies that placed a priority on attracting the largest possible audience. News and entertainment content are nothing more than the bait to attract the audience and hold its attention between the commercial messages.[8]

> What this means, in functional terms, it seems to me, is that the newspaper feature, the magazine article, the radio program, do not attain the dignity of being ends in themselves; They are rather means to an end: that end, of course, is to catch the reader's attention so that he [or she] will then read the advertisement or hear the commercial, and to hold his [or her] interest until these essential messages have been delivered. The program or the article becomes a kind of advertisement in itself—becomes the "pitch," in the telling language of the circus barker. Its function is to induce people to accept the commercial, just as the commercial's function is to induce them to accept the product.[9]

As was shown by the experience of *All-American Muslim* and the Lowe's advertising pullout in 2011, Potter's description of media content as bait for the mass audience means that the mass media include material that attracts the most people and, at the same time, delete material that could offend and alienate potential members of the audience. The portrayal of Muslims in the program offended some potential customers who Lowe's wanted in its stores. Potter described the limits this relationship puts on media that depend on advertising.

First, a message must not deal with subjects of special or out-of-the-way interest, since such subjects by definition have no appeal for the majority of the audience. Second, it must not deal with any subject at a high level of maturity, since many people are immature, chronologically or otherwise, and a mature level is one that, by definition, leaves such people out. Third, it must not deal with matters that are controversial or even unpleasant or distressing, since such matters may, by definition, antagonize or offend some members of the audience.[10]

The *All-American Muslim* series qualifies on all three counts described by Potter. First, it dealt with a subject of special interest that had not been well covered by the media. Second, it presented complex portrayals and roles of Muslims that would cause viewers to rethink their understanding of Muslims in the United States. Third, it was seen as controversial and antagonized some members of the audience valued by at least one advertiser.

The targeting of advertisers by those opposed to *All-American Muslim* was a 21st-century example of the influence that some members of the audience have tried to exert on media content for decades. The social and legal restrictions historically placed on racial minorities in the United States and the desire of the media to cater to the perceived views of the mass audience had several important racial and ethnic implications that have made people of color especially vulnerable to such pressures. With few exceptions and until legally challenged in the late 1960s, the mass media were characterized by entertainment and news content that largely (1) ignored people of color, (2) treated them stereotypically when they were featured, and (3) avoided tough issues such as racial segregation, discriminatory immigration laws, land rights, and other issues that affected people of color more than they did the White majority. The entertainment and editorial portrayal of non-Whites is amply analyzed in other chapters of this book. Those portrayals were, to a large extent, supported by racial and ethnic advertising images that catered to the perceived attitudes and prejudices of the White majority.

Race and Ethnicity in Advertising

For years, advertisers reflected the place of non-Whites in the social fabric of the nation by either ignoring them or, when including them in advertisements for the mass audience, presenting them as palatable salespersons for the products being advertised. These portrayals in the media largely sharpened the focus of the lens through which many in the White majority saw non-Whites. Advertisers used familiar racial images and symbols that triggered stereotypes in the minds of the readers, viewers, and listeners to manufacture images of people of color featured in advertising that paralleled and reinforced their entertainment and news images. Though there is some truth in every symbol and stereotype, the constant and consistent images and portrayals of people of color in advertising, entertainment, and news provided an out-of-focus view of the people portrayed.

The history of advertising in the United States is replete with characterizations that responded to and reinforced the preconceived image that many White Americans apparently had of Blacks, Arabs, Latinos, Asians, and Native Americans. Over the years, advertisers have employed Mexican bandits like the mustachioed Frito Bandito, Black mammies like Aunt Jemima, Chinese laundry workers, and noble savages like the Santa Fe Railroad's Chief to pitch products to a predominantly White mass audience of consumers.

In 1984, the Balch Institute for Ethnic Studies in Philadelphia sponsored an exhibit of more than 300 examples of racial and ethnic images used by corporations in magazines, posters, trading cards, and storyboards. In an interview with the advertising trade magazine *Advertising Age*, Balch Institute director Mark Stolarik quoted the exhibit catalog, which recalled the evolution of advertising images of people of color.

"Some of these advertisements were based on stereotypes of various ethnic groups. In the early years, they were usually crude and condescending images that appealed to largely Anglo-American audiences who found it difficult to reconcile their own visions of beauty, order and behavior with that of non-Anglo-Americans. Later, these images were softened because of complaints from the ethnic groups involved and the growing sophistication of the advertising industry," Stolarik said.[11]

The advertising examples in the exhibit included positive White ethnic stereotypes, such as the wholesome and pure image of Quakers in an early Quaker Oats advertisement and the cleanliness of the Dutch in a 1900-era advertisement for Colgate soap. But other White ethnics were not treated as kindly. The exhibit featured a late-19th-century advertisement showing an Irish matron threatening to hit her husband over the head with a rolling pin because he didn't smoke the right brand of tobacco. Some products, such as Rosarita Mexican food and Red Man chewing tobacco, went beyond advertising to incorporate racial or ethnic images in the product name or label.

"Lawsee! Folks sho' whoops with joy over AUNT JEMIMA PANCAKES," shouted a bandanna-wearing Black mammy in an advertisement for Aunt Jemima pancake

Pigtailed Chinese laundrymen are frightened by a salesman selling "Celluloid Waterproof Collars, Cuffs & Shirt Bosoms" that threaten their business in this 1880s advertising trading card featuring popular Chinese images of the era.

Source: Donaldson Brothers, Five Points, NY.

mix. A plump Aunt Jemima was featured on the box.[12] Marilyn Kern-Foxworth, who studied African American images in advertising, describes how Aunt Jemima has lost weight and her bandanna over the years. But although the image has changed, her legacy continues. A neatly coiffed Black woman wearing pearl earrings is still featured on every Aunt Jemima box. Similarly, boxes of Uncle Ben's rice products still feature a well-groomed Black servant. Although "Aunt Jemima" and "Uncle Ben" represent Black slaves and servants who may have lived with the people they served, they were not really considered members of the families for whom the products and advertising were created.

Images of Blacks as friendly servants were for a long time pervasive in the national promotion of products. Early advertisements for Cream of Wheat featured Rastus, the Black servant whose picture is still on the box, in a series of magazine pictures with a group of cute, but ill-dressed, Black children. Some of the advertising ridiculed Blacks, such as an ad in which a Black schoolteacher, standing behind a makeshift lectern made out of a boldly lettered Cream of Wheat box, asks the class, "How do you spell Cream of Wheat?" Others appeared to promote racial integration, such as an advertisement captioned "Putting it down in Black and White," which showed Rastus serving bowls of breakfast cereal to Black and White youngsters sitting at the same table.[13]

Earlier images of Blacks in servitude were not designed to promote racial equality, and, in some, Black slaves were the property and product being bought and sold in advertising in both Southern and Northern newspapers. An 1855 Lexington, Kentucky, advertisement featuring a picture of a Black man on the move with his belongings on his back was placed by a slave trader offering to pay "$1200 TO 1250 DOLLARS FOR NEGROES!!" Another newspaper advertised "CASH FOR 500 NEGROES," and, on September 7, 1835, a Washington, D.C., newspaper, the *Washington Globe*, offered "FIFTY DOLLARS REWARD" for the return of the "runaway Dennis," a slave.

Racial imagery also influenced the naming and advertising of passenger routes by the Santa Fe Railroad. It named its passenger lines the Chief, Super Chief, and El Capitan and featured highly detailed portraits of noble

In the 1950s advertisements for Aunt Jemima Pancake Mix featured romanticized images of relations between Black slaves and their White owners. Closer to reality were the first images of people of color in American advertising, such as these 1784 newspaper advertisements offering slaves for sale.

Negroes for Sale.

A Cargo of very fine ftout Men and Women, in good order and fit for immediate fervice, juft imported from the Windward Coaft of Africa, in the Ship Two Brothers.—
Conditions are one half Cafh or Produce, the other half payable the firft of January next, giving Bond and Security if required.
The Sale to be opened at 10 o'Clock each Day, in Mr. Bourdeaux's Yard, at No. 48, on the Bay.
May 19, 1784.   JOHN MITCHELL.

Thirty Seafoned Negroes
To be Sold for Credit, at Private Sale.

A MONGST which is a Carpenter, none of whom are known to be difhoneft.
Alfo, to be fold for Cafh, a regular bred young Negroe Man-Cook, born in this Country, who ferved feveral Years under an exceeding good French Cook abroad, and his Wife a middle aged Wafher-Woman, (both very honeft) and their two Children. Likewife, a young Man a Carpenter.
For Terms apply to the Printer.

Source: © CORBIS (right).

Indians in promoting its service through the Southwest. In other advertisements, the railroad featured cartoons of cute Native American children to show the service and sights passengers could expect when riding the Santa Fe line.

These and other portrayals catered to the mass audience mentality by either neutralizing or making fun of the negative perceptions that many Whites may have had of racial minorities. The advertising images, rather than showing people of color as they really were, portrayed them as filtered through Anglo eyes for the mass audience. This presented an out-of-focus image of racial minorities, but one that was acceptable, and even persuasive, to the White majority to which it was directed. These symbolic images of people of color in advertising were designed to trigger stereotypical thoughts in the minds of readers, viewers, and listeners that promoted purchase of the products being advertised.

Looking Back: Advertising Images, Protests, and Progress

In the mid-1960s, Black civil rights groups targeted the advertising industry for special attention, protesting both the lack of integrated advertisements including Blacks and the stereotyped images that the advertisers continued to use. The effort, accompanied by pressure from federal officials, resulted in the overnight inclusion of Blacks in nonstereotypical roles in television advertising during the 1967–1968 television season and a downplaying of the images many Blacks found objectionable. In 1968, the *New York Times* reported, "Black America is becoming visible in America's biggest national advertising medium. Not in a big way yet, but it is a beginning and men in high places give assurances that there will be a lot more visibility."[14]

But the advertising industry did not apply the concerns of Blacks, or the changes made in response to them, to other people of color. Some Black issues were being addressed with integrated advertising in the late 1960s and early 1970s. But other groups were still ignored or experienced continued stereotyped treatment in commercials such as those featuring the Frito Bandito, a sneaky Mexican bandit who stole "cronchy" corn chips from unsuspecting homemakers. Although the Frito Bandito campaign was highly effective, it was withdrawn in the early 1970s after being targeted by Latinos and others who found the bandito image and behavior offensive.

Among the Latino advertising stereotypes cited in a 1969 article by scholar Tomás Martínez were commercials for Granny Goose potato chips featuring fat, gun-toting Mexicans; an advertisement for Arrid underarm deodorant showing a dusty Mexican bandito spraying his underarms as the announcer intoned, "If it works for him it will work for you"; and a magazine photo of a Mexican sleeping under his sombrero against a Philco television set. Especially offensive to Martínez was a Liggett & Myers

Latino activists in the late 1960s protested the Mexican bandit imagery of Frito-Lay's Frito Bandito advertising campaign, illustrated by this 1968 wanted poster using both visual and language stereotypes. The campaign was withdrawn in the early 1970s after protests intensified.

commercial for L&M cigarettes, which featured Paco, a lazy Latino who never "feenishes" anything, not even the revolution he is supposed to be fighting. In response to a letter complaining about the commercial, the director of public relations for the tobacco firm defended the commercial.[15]

"'Paco' is a warm, sympathetic and lovable character with whom most of us can identify because he has a little of all of us in him, that is, our tendency to procrastinate at times," wrote the Liggett & Myers executive. "He seeks to escape the violence of war and to enjoy the pleasure of the moment, in this case, the good flavor of an L&M cigarette."[16] Although the company spokesman claimed that the character had been tested without negative reactions from Latinos, Martínez roundly criticized the advertising images and contrasted them with nonstereotypical images of Blacks that were clear evidence of the breakthroughs Blacks were making in advertising in the late 1960s.

"Today, no major advertiser would attempt to display a black man or woman over the media in a prejudiced, stereotyped fashion," Martínez wrote in 1969. "Complaints would be forthcoming from black associations and perhaps the FCC. Yet, these same advertisers, who dare not show 'step'n fetch it' characters, uninhibitedly depict a Mexican counterpart, with additional traits of stinking and stealing. Perhaps the white hatred for blacks, which cannot find adequate expression in today's ads, is being transferred upon their brown brothers."[17]

A 1971 Brown position paper prepared by Latino media activists Domingo Nick Reyes and Armando Rendón charged that the media had transferred the negative stereotypes they once reserved for Blacks to Latinos, who needed to fight their own battles to gain racial justice for Latinos in advertising portrayals.[18] The protests of Latinos soon made the nation's advertisers more conscious of the images that Latinos found offensive.

It took protests on the part of offended members of the groups portrayed for advertisers to understand the potential harm embedded in the racial and ethnic advertising stereotypes others found so appealing. National advertisers had withdrawn much of the advertising that negatively stereotyped Blacks and Latinos by the end of the 1970s, but they sometimes replaced the ads with images of affluent, successful people of color that were as far away from reality as the negative portrayals of the past. The advances made by those groups were not extended to Asian Americans and Native Americans until they launched their own protests.

Native Americans have all but disappeared from broadcast commercials and print advertising. The major exceptions to this exclusion are the SUVs, pickup trucks, and motor homes that bear the names of indigenous people, such as Cherokee, Winnebago, Dakota, and Navajo, to evoke a rugged, outdoors, woodsy image. To show their toughness, some professional teams and schools still used Native American racial mascots in the 21st century. The Kansas City Chiefs, Washington Redskins, Florida State University Seminoles, University of North Dakota Fighting Sioux, Atlanta Braves, and Cleveland Indians are names that play on 19th-century stereotypes and images of the First Americans. Other 19th-century images include Land O'Lakes dairy products, which show the purity and wholesomeness of their goods by featuring an Indian maiden on the label.

The Santa Fe Railroad attached Native American names and images to trains carrying passengers across Midwestern and Southwestern regions that native people once dominated. This 1940s advertisement for the Santa Fe Chief reinforced the image of Native Americans as a people whose proudest era was in the past.

the **Chief**

Famous All-Pullman Streamliner to and from California
Roomy comfort • Smooth-riding speed • Fred Harvey cuisine

The de luxe, extra-fare Santa Fe *Chief* provides daily service between Chicago and Los Angeles, and San Diego; also between Chicago and Phoenix. And in conjunction with the *20th Century Limited*, *Broadway Limited*, and *Capitol Limited*, daily through sleeping-car service is provided between New York and Los Angeles, and Washington and Los Angeles.

For full details, just consult the nearest Santa Fe ticket office or any travel bureau.

SANTA FE SYSTEM LINES
Serving the West and Southwest
T. B. Gallaher, General Passenger Traffic Manager, Chicago 4

Santa Fe

After more than 40 years of protests, some schools have dropped the stereotypical images, although most professional teams have held onto their mascots. In the early 1970s, Stanford University dropped its Indians mascot after criticisms of its racist implications were raised. In 2002, the

Massachusetts College of Liberal Arts dropped the Mohawks mascot and stern warrior image after a Mohawk tribal officer told college officials the name given to his people by Europeans translates to "maneater" and did not honor them. San Diego State University retired the stereotypical Monty Montezuma and replaced him with Montezuma II, a more historically accurate figure who told schoolchildren about the achievements of Mexico's Aztec people.[19] Native Americans and others have long protested the marketing of these racial team names and images, as well as the pseudo-pageantry and souvenirs that accompany many of them. The prospects for change improved early in the 21st century as governmental groups, such as the U.S. Commission on Civil Rights and some state education agencies, took positions against the Indian mascots.

Advertisers have also used images of Asian Pacific Americans that cater to the fears and stereotypes of White America. As with Blacks and Latinos, it took organized action by Asian Americans for corporations and advertising agencies to get the message. Following protests in the mid-1970s, a Southern California supermarket chain agreed to remove a television campaign in which a young Asian karate-chopped his way down the store's aisles cutting prices.

Nationally, several firms hard hit by Japanese imports fought back in the 1980s through commercials, if not in the quality or prices of their products. One automobile company featured an Asian American family carefully looking over a new car and commenting on its attributes in heavily accented English. Only after they bought it did they learn that it was made in the United States, not Asia. Another automobile company, which markets cars with an English name that are manufactured in Japan, showed a parking lot attendant opening the doors of the car to find the car speaking to him in Japanese. Sylvania television ran a commercial in which the announcer boasted that its picture had repeatedly been selected over competing brands, while an off-screen voice with a Japanese accent repeatedly asked, "What about Sony?" When the announcer responded that the Sylvania picture had been selected over Sony's, the off-screen voice trailed off shouting what sounded like a string of Japanese expletives. In 1982, *Newsweek* reported that "attacking Japan has become something of a fashion in corporate ads" because of resentment over Japanese trade policies and sales of Japanese products in the United States. Motorola's advertising manager was quoted as saying, "We've been as careful as we can be" not to be racially offensive.[20]

Many of the television and print advertisements in the 1980s with Asians featured themes that were racially insensitive, if not offensive. And these advertisements were for real. One commercial featured a Chinese family laundry that used an "ancient Chinese laundry secret" to get customers' clothes clean. Naturally, the secret turned out to be the packaged product paying for the advertisement. Companies pitching everything from pantyhose to air travel featured women coiffed and costumed as seductive China dolls or scantily clad Polynesian maidens to promote their products, some of them cast in exotic settings and others attentively caring for the needs of Whites. One airline boasted that those flying with them would be under the care of the Singapore Girl.

Asian Pacific women had an exotic, tropical Pacific Islands look, complete with flowers in their hair, a sarong or grass skirt, and a shell ornament. Asian Pacific men in advertising were often beefy and muscular, with an aptitude for surfing or martial arts. Asian women in commercials were often featured as China dolls—with small, darkened eyes; straight hair with bangs; and a narrow, slit skirt. Asian American women who hoped to become models sometimes found that they must conform to these stereotypes or lose assignments. Leslie Kawai, the first Asian American Tournament of Roses Queen, was told to cut her hair into a style with stereotypical bangs when she auditioned for a beer advertisement. When she refused, the beer company hired a model with bangs.[21]

Martial arts themes have long been used in some advertising featuring Asians and Asian Pacific Americans, such as this 21st-century "Got Milk?" advertisement showing actress Zhang Ziyi slicing through a milk bottle with her hand.

9 essential nutrients in every easy-to-open bottle.

got milk?

The lack of a sizable Asian Pacific American community, or market, in the United States was earlier cited as the reason that members of the group were still stereotyped in advertising and, except for children's advertising, rarely presented in integrated settings. However, their population and income growth rate in the United States from the 1980s into the 21st century made clear their potential to overcome such stereotyping and their lack of visibility in advertising. By the mid-1980s, there were signs that advertising was beginning to integrate Asian Pacific Americans into crossover advertisements designed to have a broad appeal. In one commercial, actor Robert Ito said that he loved to call relatives in Japan because the calls made them think he was rich and successful in the United States. Of course, he added, it was because the rates of his long distance carrier were so low that he was able to call so often.

Integration in Advertising

By the end of the 1970s, mass audience advertising in the United States had become more racially integrated than it had been at any time in the nation's history. Blacks, and to a much lesser extent Latinos and Asians, could be seen in television commercials and major magazines. In fact, the advertisements on network television often were more integrated than the television programs they supported. Like television advertising, general circulation magazine advertising showed an increase in the appearance of Blacks, although studies of both media showed that most of the percentage increase had come by the early 1970s.[22] At that time, the percentage of prime-time television commercials featuring Blacks had apparently leveled off at about 10%. Blacks were featured in only between 2% and 3% of magazine advertisements as late as 1978. That percentage, however small, was a sharp increase from the 0.06% of news magazine advertisements featuring Blacks reported in 1960.

The advertising breakthroughs were socially significant at the time, since they demonstrated that Blacks could be successfully integrated into advertisements. But some worried that Blacks in advertising might trigger a backlash among potential customers in the White majority. This spurred research to study the reaction among Blacks and Whites as the advertising breakthroughs took place. Both sales figures and research conducted in the late 1960s and early 1970s showed that the integration of Black models into television and print advertising did not adversely affect sales or the image of the product. In fact, while integrated advertisements triggered no adverse effects among Whites, such ads helped draw Black consumers, who responded favorably to positive Black role models in print advertisements.[23]

Studies conducted in the early 1970s also showed that Whites did not respond negatively to advertising featuring Black models.[24] However, one 1972 study examining White backlash did show that an advertisement prominently featuring

As the United States has become more racially diverse, companies are featuring celebrities of color with "crossover appeal" to sell products to people of all races, as in this Smartwater advertisement featuring award-winning actor Idris Elba. The ad ran in magazines targeting African Americans and also magazines geared to more general audiences.

smartwater.
smart because it's made that way

smart because
simplicity inspires

darker-skinned Blacks was less acceptable to Whites than one featuring lighter-skinned Blacks as background models.[25] Perhaps such findings help explain why later research revealed that, for the most part, Blacks appearing in magazine and television advertisements in the 1970s were often featured as part of an integrated group.[26] In the 1970s and 1980s, people of color who appeared in general audience advertising often played token roles in upscale integrated settings, which the Balch Institute's Stolarik criticized as taking advertising "too far in the other direction and creat[ing] stereotypes of 'successful' ethnic group members that are as unrealistic as those of the past."[27]

Having established that featuring African Americans would not offend potential White customers, corporations and advertising agencies turned their attention to ways to maximize their profits among all racial segments of society in the 1980s. But still unanswered at that time was how much and how often they would feature non-White models in their advertising. Once again, the answer would come down to dollars and cents.

"If it is believed that the presence of Black models in advertisements decreases the effectiveness of advertising messages, only token numbers of Black models will be used," wrote Lawrence Soley in 1983. "Given the consistency of the research findings, more Blacks should be portrayed in advertisements. If Blacks continue to be underrepresented in advertising portrayals, it can be said that this is an indication of prejudice on the part of the advertising industry, not consumers."[28]

Decades later, more Asian Pacific Americans, Blacks, and Latinos were featured in mass audience advertising. But their numbers were still below reflecting the growth of these groups in the nation's population. And it was this sharp growth that had captured the attention of advertisers.

Multicultural Marketing: Courting Consumers of Color

While Soley stopped short of accusing corporate executives of racial prejudice, he contended that a "counter pressure" to full integration of Blacks into portrayals in mainstream media was that "advertising professionals are businessmen first and moralists second."[29] Thus it was the business sense of marketing executives that led to increasingly aggressive advertising and marketing campaigns to capture people of color as consumers—particularly Blacks and Latinos in the 1970s and 1980s and Asian Pacific Americans in the 1990s.

Long depicted as low-end consumers with little money to spend, Black and Latino customers became more important to those national and regional advertisers of mainstream goods who took a close look at the size, composition, and projected growth of the groups. Although Asian Pacific Americans experienced a sharp percentage growth in the 1970s and were generally more affluent than Blacks and Latinos, they were not targeted to the same extent as those groups, probably because of their relatively small numbers and the differences in national languages in the group. And, except in regions in which they composed a sizable portion of the population, Native Americans were still ignored as consumers of mainstream products through the 20th century, and Muslims were not identified as a potential market until the 21st century. A 2003 *American Demographics* article on race, ethnicity, and marketing in the United States included data and charts on Blacks, Whites, Hispanics, and Asians but not on Native Americans or Muslims.[30]

The first major breakthroughs in the advertising industry's courtship of Blacks and Latinos grew out of the civil rights movements of the 1950s and 1960s, in which consumer boycotts challenged racial segregation and helped unionize farmworkers. In the 1960s, Black ministers organized the Philadelphia Selective Patronage Program, in which Blacks did business with companies that supported their goal of more jobs for Blacks. In the same era, Cesar Chavez and the United Farm Workers of America effectively organized a nationwide boycott of California table grapes until growers recognized the rights of their largely Mexican and Filipino workers to form a labor union. After labor contracts were signed in 1970, the union asked supporters to buy table grapes. This philosophy of consumers using their purchases to patronize the corporations that recognized the importance of minority communities and causes was replicated elsewhere. It was often accompanied by slick advertising campaigns directed at minority consumers. In 1984, the same line of thinking led to the Coors brewery attempting to end disputes with Blacks and Latinos by signing controversial agreements with the National Association for the Advancement of Colored People (NAACP) and five national Latino groups. The agreements committed the brewery to increase its financial support of the organizations as Blacks and Latinos drank more Coors beer.

The second, and perhaps more influential, element of the courtship was the hard selling job of advertising agencies and media targeting Blacks and Spanish-speaking Latinos. Spurred by Black advertising executive D. Parke Gibson's 1968 book *The $30 Billion Negro* and a steady stream of articles on Black and Latino consumers in media trade publications, national advertisers in the 1960s began to see these groups as potential purchasers of a wide range of products, not just ethnic foods and cosmetics. Advertisers were persuaded that the inattention Latinos and Blacks had previously received from mainstream products made them loyal to companies that courted them through neighborhood billboards and in their publications and broadcast stations. Once advertisers saw people of color as potential product purchasers, their negative images declined or disappeared from advertisements, and they were courted through more positive appeals.

The third, and most important, element in advertising's courtship of Latinos and Blacks was a fundamental change in the thinking of marketing and advertising executives. Witnessing the success they had in advertising on radio stations and in magazines targeted to specific audience segments

The United States' growing racial and language diversity has led to more 21st-century advertising appealing to different groups with images and language tailored to reflect them, as illustrated by these nearly identical Walt Disney World advertisements in magazines targeting Latinos (left) and African Americans (right).

following the advent of television as the dominant mass audience medium in the 1950s, advertising agencies advised clients to target potential customers classified by smaller market segments rather than the larger mass audience. Advertisers found that classifications of race, like differences in sex, residence, education, and age, were easy to use in targeted advertising appeals through segmented class media directed toward these audiences. As the advertisers moved from *mass media* to *class media*, Black and Latino media produced studies to show their effectiveness in reaching and delivering the desired segments of the mass audience. They also focused on the rapidly growing purchasing power of people of color.

"In 2009, the combined buying power of African Americans, Asians and Native Americans will be $1.5 trillion—65 percent more than its 2000 level of $898 billion—which amounts to a gain of $586 billion," the University of Georgia Selig Center for Economic Growth reported in 2009. Looking ahead, the Georgia center predicted that the three groups' combined purchases would total $1.9 trillion by 2014, nearly 15% of the country's buying power. In addition, the purchasing power of Hispanics, who can be of any race, increased from $489 billion in 2000 to $978 billion in 2009. The purchasing budgets of these groups of people of color also grew at a faster rate than those of Whites, whose increase was 46% from 2000 to 2009. In the same period, the buying power increased by 100% for Hispanics, by 89% for Asian Americans, by 65% for Native Americans, and by 54% for African Americans. Muslims, who can be of any race, were estimated to represent a $200 billion market in the United States in 2011, with the population expected to double by 2030. These figures set the scene for continued growth in corporations marketing and advertising their products and services to people of color and accelerated changes that had been in the works for decades.

THE BLACK MARKET

In a 1984 article in the advertising trade magazine *Madison Avenue,* Caroline Jones, executive vice president of Mingo-Jones Advertising, wrote,

> It is a basic tenet of marketing that you go after markets with rifles, not shotguns. It is foolhardy—and idealistic in the worst way—to try to sell the same thing to everyone in the same way. Good marketing involves breaking down potential markets into homogeneous segments; targeting the most desirable segments; and developing creative programs, tailored for each segment, that make your messages look different from your competitors. All of that should be done with the guidance of thorough research on characteristics, beliefs and preferences of the people in the targeted markets.[31]

Jones, whose agency focused on reaching Black consumers, advised advertising professionals to target Black consumers because "there's money in it." Among the factors she cited in 1984 as making Blacks desirable customers was the group's disposable income, a "high propensity for brand names and indulgence items," a strong sense of "brand loyalty," a young and growing population, improved education and income, population centers in the nation's largest 25 cities, and "its own growing media network."[32]

Although the population growth rate of Blacks since 1980 has not been as steep as that of Latinos and Asian Pacific Americans, Blacks have continued to grow as an important segment for marketers and advertisers through the early 21st century. With African Americans' purchasing power projected to increase to $1.1 trillion and accounting for nearly 9 cents of every consumer dollar spent by 2014, they constitute a significant portion of the U.S. audience. Black-targeted advertising has certainly increased, but it still needs to be approached strategically and carefully through a wide variety of print, broadcast, and digital media. Some appeals to this market have backfired, such as two Toyota ads—one featuring an African

American with an SUV etched in gold on one tooth and another in Black-targeted *Jet* magazine promising about the car that, "unlike your last boyfriend, it goes to work in the morning." Both advertisements were reportedly pulled by Toyota after protests.[33]

SPANISH GOLD

The promise of untapped profits also motivated marketers to target advertising to Latinos, who by the 1960s had become a target too good to pass up. A 1965 article in the trade magazine *Sponsor* called Latinos "America's Spanish Treasure," a 1971 *Sales Management* article proclaimed that "Brown Is Richer Than Black," and in 1972 *Television/Radio Age* told readers, "The Spanish Market: Its Size, Income and Loyalties Make It a Rich Marketing Mine."[34] Latinos were depicted as having the characteristics that made Blacks an attractive market and as being especially vulnerable because their use of Spanish supposedly cut them off from English-language advertising. Advertisers were advised to use the Spanish language, culture, and media most familiar to their target audience to give their messages the greatest delivery and impact.

"U.S. Hispanics are most receptive to media content in the Spanish language," wrote Antonio Guernica in his 1982 book *Reaching the Hispanic Market Effectively.*[35] Guernica and others counseled advertisers to package their commercial messages in settings that reflect Latino culture and traditions. These appeals link the product being advertised with the language, heritage, and social system that Latinos are most comfortable with, thus creating an illusion that the product belongs in the Latino home. The cultural and language preferences of Latinos were important to marketers and advertisers. But even more important was their sharp population purchasing power growth in the United States.

By 2014, one out of six persons living in the United States was projected to be of Hispanic origin, the University of Georgia study reported in 2009. Along with that growth came more Latino spending dollars. The study predicted the annual Latino purchasing power would reach $1.3 trillion by 2014, up from $212 billion in 1990 and more than double the 2000 figure of $978 billion. As the Latino population grew in numbers, it also became more diverse, including more people from a wider variety of nations, as well as generational, gender, and regional differences.[36] Latinos, once a single market segment, were split into more subgroups, each with its own characteristics and vulnerabilities. One conference, titled "Marketing to U.S. Hispanic Youth," featured panels on such topics as "Marketing to Hispanic Girls and Boys (Ages 2–12)," "Entertainment Tie-ins: Advertising and Promotional Opportunities to Reach Hispanic Youth," and "Taking Cultural Differences Into Account: Regional Segmentation in Your Marketing Campaign." Another conference featured sessions on "Marketing to the Hispanic Female Head of Household," "Got Hispanics? Applying the

'Got Milk?' Campaign to Ethnic Marketing," and "How Miller Brewing Company Appeals to the Hispanic Market with Music."[37]

ASIAN AND PACIFIC TREASURES

Constituting about 5% of the U.S. population and just under 15 million people in the United States in 2009, Asian Americans represent the portion of the population that is growing at the fastest rate, up from 3% of the population in 1990. Marketing and advertising figures for this group often combine Native Hawaiians and other Pacific Islanders with people whose roots are on mainland Asia and use the term *Asian Pacific Americans* to designate the consumer group. On a percentage basis, this is the nation's fastest growing racial group, but was long undervalued because of its relatively small size and different languages. However, in the 21st century, it grew in significance as a market with growth in both its overall numbers and the size of its various nationality groups, such as Koreans, Filipinos, and Asian Indians.

The combined purchasing power of Asian Pacific Americans posted an 89% gain from $269 billion in 2000 to $509 billion in 2009 and was projected to reach $697 billion in 2014 by the Selig Center in Georgia. Much of the Asian Pacific population growth is fueled by strong immigration, and the trend is expected to continue. Asian Pacific Americans became more attractive to marketers and advertisers as their share of the nation's purchases grew, up from 2.7% in 1990 to 4.7% in 2009, and they reached higher educational, employment, and income levels. As a result, the group spent nearly 22% more than average U.S. households on homes, furniture, clothing, footwear, vehicle purchases, education, and groceries. The Selig Center also reported that Asian Pacific Americans live in households with more people than national averages and have more wage earners per household, indicating that the purchases made are benefiting a larger number of people than average. Along with differences between themselves and other racial/ethnic groups in the United States, Asian Pacific Americans are also a very diverse group among themselves.

Noting the different national origins in this group, some marketers and advertisers have asked whether Vietnamese, Chinese, Koreans, Filipinos, Japanese, and other Asian Pacific Americans have anything in common "beyond rice" and have been advised to be careful to avoid cultural conflicts. For instance, it was reported that for Filipinos white is the color of weddings and happiness, but for Japanese white with black is the color of mourning.[38] The diversity within the group was further reflected in the Census Bureau's combining people from more than 15 distinct ethnic groups and nations under the Asian and Pacific Islander label in 2000. Still, marketers noted that 88% of those so labeled were found in just 6 of the 15 groups. In order of size, these are Chinese, Filipino, Asian Indian, Vietnamese, Korean, and Japanese— many of them living "highly concentrated in tight ethnic communities."[39]

This makes members of the group easily targeted through advertising in print and broadcast media reaching those communities. "The fact that Asian Americans predominantly speak their native languages yields incredibly high ratings and shares for Asian-language media," wrote Jon Yasuda, president of Southern California Asian format television station KSCI in 2002. He advised marketers to "utilize Asian language media to best influence Asian Americans to make wise and educated purchasing decisions" and noted that "Asian media provides sophisticated marketing tools for advertisers."[40]

Like many Hispanics, many Asian Pacific Americans are newcomers to the United States who prefer media in their home country language, which is what advertisers use to reach them. And, like Blacks, they also share physical characteristics that distinguish them from Whites in advertising appeals. Long-term effectiveness in reaching this increasingly important market segment will depend on advertisers becoming acquainted with Asian Pacific Americans on their own terms, not in the way they have long been seen by Whites or as offshoots of the Black or Hispanic market.

NATIVE AMERICAN GROWTH

Though smaller in number than the other groups already mentioned, Native Americans are growing at a fast rate. Their 17.2% growth rate from 2000 to 2009 outpaced the 10.2% gain for Blacks and the 7% gain for Whites, Georgia's Selig Center reported. The group's younger median age of 32.1 years, compared to 39.2 years for Whites, meant that more Native Americans would be available for work and raising families in the future.

However, the small population base of about 1% of the U.S. population means that Native Americans have much less purchasing power in the marketplace than the other groups. In 2009, they were estimated to account for 0.6% of all U.S. purchases, about $64.7 billion in disposable income. This was projected to grow to $82.7 billion by 2014. Though the percentage gains in Native American purchasing power, up 65% from 2000 to 2009, outpaced those of Whites (45%), the overall population (49%), and Blacks (54%), the lower number of dollars being spent in comparison to other groups made Native Americans less attractive to national advertisers.

The relatively low purchasing power and population numbers of Native Americans in comparison to those of other racial and ethnic groups that have become desirable targets for marketers and advertisers have made it more difficult for companies to look for cost-effective ways to reach Native American people. Perhaps another blocking to their vision and understanding of Native Americans is the persistence of stereotypical sports team mascots such as the Cleveland Indians, Atlanta Braves, and Washington Redskins. These warlike and comical images feature Native Americans as frozen in the 19th century and obscure the reality of what Native Americans were then and are today. They also come at a time when today's Native Americans are exercising increasing economic clout as business leaders and employers through casinos and investments made in other businesses from casino revenues.

REACHING OUT TO THE "HALAL MARKET"

Although Muslims can be of any race and Islam is the most racially diverse of any major religious group in the United States, Muslims' identity and image are often racialized by their portrayal as being primarily Arabs, South Asians, or from the Middle East. Marketers and advertisers have sometimes classified them as a potentially important ethnic market. The *2011–2012 Source Book of Multicultural Experts* by Multicultural Marketing Resources lists Muslim American along with African American, Asian American, and Hispanic among its "key cultural and niche markets." The Muslim Ad Network in 2011 quoted articles from *The Economist, The New York Times, Entrepreneur,* and other media portraying American Muslims as a potentially rich market for advertisers.

"Muslim Americans spend about $170 billion on consumer products, JWT estimates; this figure is expected to grow rapidly as the population expands and younger Muslims build careers," *The New York Times* reported in 2007.[41] The story was based on a JWT study on the Muslim market in the United States and how companies could tap into it through advertising. Because the U.S. Census does not ask people to report their religion, marketers and advertisers do not have a hard number on the size of the potential market. However, the *New York Times* article reported some advertising executives felt that "ignoring this group—estimated to be about five million to eight million people, and growing fast—would be like missing the Hispanic market in the 1990s."

The Muslims surveyed by JWT said they felt left out of general audience advertising and wanted companies to recognize the holidays and customs associated with their religion. A young woman interviewed for the story reported turning away from media "after seeing too many negative stereotypes of Muslims." The negative view that some consumers have of Muslims was also identified as a possible factor keeping some companies away from including Muslims in their advertisements and in their marketing plans.

"United States companies don't want to risk alienating their domestic consumers," said Nasser Beydoun, who was working with IKEA, Walmart, and Comcast to find ways to reach Muslim customers, whose different races, national backgrounds, and languages sometimes make them difficult to reach. Some marketers have tried using religion as part of their strategies for reaching the $2.1 trillion worldwide "Halal Market," which refers to what is permitted under Islamic law. In 2010, Ogilvy Noor was launched as the first Islamic branding agency to help companies build brands appealing to Muslims around the world. The following year

Marketing Daily ran an article on the American Muslim market headlined "Reach Muslim Consumers During Ramadan" with tips on how to "court Muslims while the market is still mostly untapped."

Mining Multicultural Markets

With the United States growing more diverse by all measures, marketers and advertisers have intensified their search for ways to ride multicultural images and ethnic media into the hearts and minds of people of color.[42] For both Blacks and Latinos, the slick advertising directed to them often has meant that advertisers were trying to sell high-priced, prestige products to people who do not fully share in the wealth of the country in which they live. Blacks and Latinos, who have median household incomes well below national averages, have nonetheless been targeted as consumers for premium brands in all product lines, particularly alcohol and tobacco. In response, Black and Latino community groups and health organizations have protested the aggressive targeting of alcohol and tobacco products to their communities and, in some cases, forced outdoor advertising companies to restrict the number of such billboards in their communities.

Alcohol and tobacco companies have long targeted Latinos and Blacks through ethnic media with the goal of increasing smoking and drinking in these groups as other segments of the population become more aware of the health hazards linked to these substances. A 1968 Philip Morris internal memo boasted of "a series of newspaper ads that will appear in the Negro press in an attempt to capture a larger share of the market for Benson & Hedges 100s Menthol in this sizable segment of the trade."[43]

The influx of advertising dollars has also made some ethnic media financially dependent on alcohol and tobacco companies. "Tobacco and alcohol advertising revenues are substantial for Hispanic publications," Tino Duran, president of the National Association of Hispanic Publications, told a congressional subcommittee on hazardous materials in 1990. "For some Hispanic publishers, tobacco and alcohol advertising can sometimes make the difference between staying afloat or going under."[44]

Demographics and Psychographics

Marketers and advertisers reach out to potential customers identified by Census Bureau *demographic* identifiers: race, ethnicity, age, gender, education, and other terms that define target audiences. But they often make their sales pitch based on *psychographics,* which is who consumers want to be or want others to think they are.

Through advertising, corporations making and marketing products from beer to diapers try to show people of color that consumption of their goods is part of the good life in America. It may not be a life that they know in the ghetto, the barrio, Chinatown, a reservation, or another country. It may not even be a life that they or their children will achieve in the United States, but it is a lifestyle they can share by purchasing the same products used by the rich and famous.

Psychographic prestige appeals are used in advertising to all audiences, not just to people of color. But they have a special impact on members of racial and ethnic groups looking for ways to show that they are advancing up the socioeconomic ladder. These consumers are especially hungry for anything that will add status or happiness to their lives and help them show others that they are "making it." They are more vulnerable than Whites to advertising that associates buying a product with a quick way to living the good life.

In 1984, advertising executive Caroline R. Jones wrote in *Madison Avenue* that, "in the light of life's uncertainties, Blacks also seek instant gratification more than do Whites, who can enjoy 'the good life' earlier and longer." These advertisements promote conspicuous consumption, rather than education, hard work, and saving money, as the key to the good life. She continued,

> The Black consumer is not unlike other consumers when it comes to the basic necessities of life—food, clothing and shelter. There is a difference, nevertheless, in the priority the Black consumer adopts in the pursuit of happiness; in other words, in how he [or she] structures the *quality* of his [or her] life. Some differences are by choice. And some differences are because of *lack* of choice. The Black consumer must often react to what he [or she] has *not* been able to enjoy or choose, or what he [or she] must choose from among products that have not overtly invited him [or her] to use them . . . in general the Black consumer all too often has learned to live with his [or her] feelings of being ignored altogether or excluded psychologically.[45]

Asian Pacific Americans and Latinos, particularly recent immigrants or those who have moved up from the economic level of their parents, share with Blacks the ambition of making it in American society. In addition, they also have language preferences that cut them away from appeals in English and make them more receptive to advertising in their own language and in the media directed toward their communities. For people of color, marketing and advertising campaigns targeted to them are corporate America's welcome mat, the Happy Face that lets them know that they are important and recognized. Some marketing and advertising campaigns provided long overdue recognition of Asian Pacific, Black, and Latino cultures and heritages as they also prominently displayed the corporate symbols of their sponsors during Black History Month, the Lunar New Year, and National Hispanic Heritage Month.

Increased advertising by local and national businesses targeting people in diverse racial and language groups has spurred a growth of ethnic television stations and networks, as in these commercials on stations directed to Asian American and Latino audiences.

Ethnic marketing professionals stress that, in the long run, such blatant overtures making marketing commodities out of cultural symbols and historical events must be replaced by advertising focused on the quality and price of the product. If not, people of color will see that the racial and ethnic welcome mat did not open the door to good value for their dollars and will turn to products offering more than a cultural fix.

Marketing and Advertising Ethics

Since the goal of advertising is to promote the sales and consumption of products, advertising agencies serve no moral code other than to advocate products so that people will buy them. Print and broadcast media that reach the audiences advertisers wish to cultivate have benefited from increased advertising budgets for media targeting Blacks, Latinos, and, more recently, Asian Pacific Americans. Most surveys show that Blacks and Latinos depend on radio and television for information and entertainment more than they do print media, a fact probably related more to their lower median level of education and the wide availability of Black and Spanish-language broadcasting than to any innate racial preferences. Accordingly, most of the millions of dollars that national advertisers spend to reach these audiences are spent on broadcast media. Although their share of broadcasting has grown, Asians and Pacific Islanders in the United States have long been reached by print media that are local editions of mother-country media chains, such as the *Korea Times,* the Hong Kong-based *Sing Tao* newspaper chain, and the Taiwan-based *World Journal.*

But the people of color reached by some of these media are less valued than those reached by general audience media. The viewers, listeners, and readers reached by media targeting Blacks or Latinos yield fewer advertising dollars per audience member than the general audience media. In 2001, several Black and Latino organizations challenged the practice of advertising agencies paying broadcasters less for advertising on stations for Blacks and Hispanics than for their general audience counterparts reaching the same sized audience. It was charged some advertisers had a "no urban/no Hispanic" policy in deciding which stations would get their advertising dollars and that *urban* was a code word for Blacks. A 1996 study of 3,745 radio stations for the Federal Communications Commission found that stations targeting listeners of color earned less money per listener than general audience stations and that stations owned by people of color earned less per listener than those owned by Whites.[46]

Advertising is the lifeblood of print, broadcast, and some online media in the United States. But as website advertising, direct mail, telemarketing, and promotional events have become more important in targeting desired audiences, it is no longer necessary for corporations to put their messages on print pages or broadcast airwaves to pitch their products to the people they want to reach. They can reach people in target markets in other ways, and, if these new avenues prove to be profitable, the print and broadcast media reaching those audiences will suffer a revenue loss.

Advertising's Double-Edged Sword

Ethnic publications and broadcasters and other class media have benefited from the increased emphasis on market segmentation by promoting to advertisers the purchasing patterns of the audiences they reach and their own effectiveness in delivering persuasive commercial messages to their readers, listeners, and viewers. But advertising is a double-edged sword: It expects to take more money out of a market segment than it invests in that segment. Thus media that focus on Blacks, Latinos, and Asian Pacific Americans will benefit from the advertising dollars of national corporations only as long as they are the most cost-effective way for advertisers to persuade their targeted audience to use the advertised products.

This situation places the racial and ethnic media in an exploitative relationship with the members of their audience, who because of language, educational, and economic differences sometimes are exposed to a narrower range of media than are Whites. Marketers will support delivery of their messages in places that deliver the audience with the best consumer profile at the lowest cost, not necessarily in the media that best meet the information and entertainment needs of their audience. And, given increased competition from digital, telemarketing, direct mail, and other advertising delivery systems, they may not put their messages into advertising-supported media at all.

The slick, upscale lifestyle portrayed by national advertisers is more dream than reality for most Blacks, Asian Pacific Americans, and Latinos. It is achieved through education, hard work, and equal opportunity for employment and housing. Rather than encouraging people to save money to meet long-term goals, advertisers promote their products as the shortcut to happiness and the good life, a quick fix for low-income consumers. The message to people of color is clear: You may not be able to live in the best neighborhoods, have the best educational opportunities, or work at the best job, but you can drink the same liquor, smoke the same cigarettes, and drive the same car as those who do. At the same time, advertising appeals that play on the cultural heritage of people of color make the products appear to be "at home" in those communities.

Recognizing the importance of national holidays and peoples' history, advertisers have actually helped bring recognition to important dates, events, and people in the lives of people of color. But advertisers also make culture a commercial commodity by piggybacking their advertising on the recognition of such events, leaders, and heroes. People or actions that in their time represented protests against slavery, oppression, and discrimination are now used to sell products.

Advertising is an extractive industry. European and American companies went into Africa, Asia, the Middle East, the Pacific Islands, and Latin America to cut timber, mine minerals, drill oil wells, and exploit other natural resources to produce profits. Along the same lines, advertising's

Happy Face enters the ghetto, Chinatown, and the barrio to persuade people to transfer money from their pockets to the merchants selling advertised products and services. Advertisers' subsidizing of print, broadcast, and online media is only a by-product of their primary purpose of selling their products, and it is possibly decreasing in importance due to the recent proliferation of advertising delivery systems.

With the advent of social media and other digital forms of communication, the role of advertising in subsidizing the production of news and entertainment content to serve as bait to attract the audience to the advertising messages has lessened somewhat. Some digital sites carry no advertising, and many have content that is developed by the users themselves. Often the users share their demographic information and interests when registering to use a site for free. The companies then direct advertising and other messages to people based on their demographic categories and interests. It is not clear how digital advertising will develop or whether the racial and ethnic experiences of the past will be applied in the new media. An early study of race and ethnicity in digital advertising indicated that the lessons of the past may have been lost and not learned as media and advertisers moved into the multimedia/multicultural age.

"Ethnic Groups Don't See Themselves in Advertising, Digital Content": *eMarketer* headlined a 2011 story reporting a survey that showed "brands that want to reach ethnic minorities online are not doing a very good job . . . according to Hispanics, blacks and Asian-Americans digital advertising does not engage them." Seventy-two percent of the Asian Pacific Islanders and Blacks surveyed and 70% of the Hispanics said ads should show "a larger diversity of people." In contrast, 49% of the Whites agreed with that statement, showing a deep divide in the way that Whites and people of color perceive the importance and impact of advertising as marketing goes digital.[47]

Notes

1. *All-American Muslim,* accessed January 5, 2012, http://tlc.howstuffworks.com/tv/all-americanmuslim/all-american-muslim/about-all-american-muslim.htm.

2. David Knowles, "All-American Muslim: TV Review," *The Hollywood Reporter,* November 8, 2011, accessed January 5, 2012, http://hollywoodreporter.com/review/all-american-muslim-tv-review-258770.

3. Mohamed Younis, "Muslim Americans Exemplify Diversity, Potential," March 2, 2009, accessed January 5, 2012, http://www.gallup.com/poll/116260/Muslim-Americans-Exemplify-Diversity-Potential.

4. "Defending American Values," Florida Family Association, accessed January 5, 2012, http://floridafamily.org/full_article.php?article_no=58.

5. "All-American Muslim Show Loses 96% (or 101 Out of 105) Advertisers," Florida Family Association, accessed January 5, 2012, http://floridafamily.org/full-article.php?article_no=108.

6. "Lowe's Pulls Ads From TV Show About U.S. Muslims," *Los Angeles Times*, December 12, 2012, accessed January 4, 2012, http://www.latimes.com/business/la-fi-1212-lowes-muslims-20111212,0,7712626.

7. David M. Potter, *People of Plenty: Economic Abundance and the American Character* (Chicago: University of Chicago Press, 1954), 166.

8. Ibid., 166.

9. Ibid., 181–182.

10. Ibid., 184–185.

11. "Using Ethnic Images—An Advertising Retrospective," *Advertising Age*, June 14, 1984, 9.

12. Ibid.

13. For a comprehensive study of African American images in advertising, see M. Kern-Foxworth, *Aunt Jemima, Uncle Ben and Rastus: Blacks in Advertising, Yesterday, Today and Tomorrow* (Westport, CT: Greenwood, 1994).

14. Cited in Philip H. Dougherty, "Frequency of Blacks in TV Ads," *New York Times*, May 27, 1982, D19.

15. Tomas Martínez, "How Advertisers Promote Racism," *Civil Rights Digest*, Fall 1969, 10.

16. Ibid., 11.

17. Ibid., 9–10.

18. Domingo Nick Reyes and Armando Rendón, *Chicanos and the Mass Media* (Washington, DC: National Mexican American Anti-Defamation Committee, 1971).

19. For a case study of two efforts to change Native American mascots, see V. S. Holden, W. Holden, and G. Davis, "The Sports Team Nickname Controversy: A Study in Community and Race Relations," *Facing Difference: Race, Gender and Mass Media*, ed. S. Biagi and M. Kern-Foxworth (Thousand Oaks, CA: Pine Forge, 1997), 69–75.

20. Joseph Treen, "Madison Ave. vs. Japan, Inc.," *Newsweek*, April 12, 1982, 69.

21. Ada Kan, *Asian Models in the Media*, unpublished term paper, Journalism 466: Minority and the Media, University of Southern California, December 14, 1983, 5.

22. Studies on increase of Blacks in magazine and television commercials cited in James D. Culley and Rex Bennett, "Selling Blacks, Selling Women," *Journal of Communication* 26 (No. 4, Autumn 1976): 160–174; Lawrence Soley, "The Effect of Black Models on Magazine Ad Readership," *Journalism Quarterly* 60 (No. 4, Winter 1983): 686; and Leonard N. Reid and Bruce G. Vanden Bergh, "Blacks in Introductory Ads," *Journalism Quarterly* 57 (No. 3, Autumn 1980): 485–486.

23. Cited in D. Parke Gibson, *$70 Billion in the Black* (New York: Macmillan, 1979), 83–84.

24. Laboratory studies on White reactions to Blacks in advertising cited in Soley, "The Effect of Black Models," 585–587.

25. Carl E. Block, "White Backlash to Negro Ads: Fact or Fantasy?" *Journalism Quarterly* 49 (No. 2, Autumn 1980): 258–262.

26. Culley and Bennett, "Selling Blacks, Selling Women."

27. "Using Ethnic Images," 9.

28. Soley, *The Effect of Black Models*, 690.

29. Ibid.

30. For historical, current, and projected purchasing power of Whites, Blacks, Asian Americans, American Indians, and Hispanics see "The Multicultural

Economy" periodic reports issued by The University of Georgia Selig Center for Economic Growth.

31. Caroline R. Jones, "Advertising in Black and White," *Madison Avenue* (May 1984): 53.

32. Ibid., 54.

33. B. White, "Ads for Minorities Take Tact," July 29, 2001, Cox News Service. For a deeper analysis, see Chapter 7 "Selling Marginality: The Business of Culture," in *Latinos Inc.: The Marketing and Making of a People,* by Arlene M. Dávila (Berkeley: University of California Press, 2001).

34. Félix Frank Gutiérrez, *Spanish-Language Radio and Chicano Internal Colonialism,* doctoral dissertation, Stanford University, 1976, 312–314.

35. Antonio Guernica, *Reaching the Hispanic Market Effectively* (New York: McGraw-Hill, 1982), 5.

36. Eduardo Porter, "All Agree the Latin Market Is Hot, But Solid Statistics Are Hard to Find," *Wall Street Journal,* October 13, 2000.

37. US Hispanic Marketing 2002, Brochure, April 30–May 1, 2002. International Quality and Productivity Center conference, US Hispanic Marketing 2002, Los Angeles.

38. Arlene M. Dávila, *Latinos Inc.: The Marketing and Making of a People* (Berkeley: University of California Press, 2001).

39. Saul Gitlin, "The Asian American Market: An Untapped Opportunity for America's Marketers," *The Source Book of Multicultural Experts 2002–2003* (New York: Multicultural Marketing Resources, 2002).

40. J. Yasuda, "Asian Language Media Works!" *The Source Book of Multicultural Experts 2002–2003.* (New York: Multicultural Marketing Resources, 2002).

41. Louise Story, "Advertisers Rewrite the Rules on Reaching Muslims," *The New York Times,* April 28, 2007, C1.

42. For additional readings on multicultural marketing and advertising, see *Multicultural Marketing: Selling to the New America,* by A. L. Schreiber, (New York: McGraw-Hill, 2000), and *Marketing and Consumer Identity in Multicultural America,* by M. C. Tharp, (Thousand Oaks, CA: Sage, 2001). For current reports, see the bimonthly newsletter *Multicultural Marketing News* from the Multicultural Marketing Resources website: http://www.multicultural.com.

43. Quoted in E. L. Cohen, M. J. Cody, & S. T. Murphy, *Industry Watch: Targeting African American Smokers.* (Los Angeles: School of Communication, Annenberg School for Communication, University of Southern California, 2001), 4.

44. This is from a statement made by Tino Duran, as president of the National Association of Hispanic Publications, before the Subcommittee on Transportation and Hazardous Materials, Committee on Energy and Commerce, U.S. House of Representatives, in Washington, DC, on March 2, 1990, p. 3.

45. Jones, "Advertising in Black and White," p. 56.

46. Kofi Asiedu Ofori, *"When Being No. 1 Is Not Enough,"* paper submitted to the Office of Communication Business Opportunities, Federal Communications Commission, Washington, D.C., Civil Rights Forum on Communications Policy, 1996.

47. "Ethnic Groups Don't See Themselves in Advertising, Digital Content," *eMarketer,* December 22, 2011.

Public Relations 8

An Opportunity to Influence the Media

In 1992, the Public Relations Society of America (PRSA) chose "At the Crossroads" as the theme for its annual conference. As public relations professionals and educators met in Kansas City in October of that year, it was noted that the conference theme could well be the theme of their discussions on multiculturalism in public relations as well. This is because 1992 and much of the 1990s were years of discussion, dialogue, and debate on issues of race, diversity, and multiculturalism. Both public relations educators and professionals found themselves "at the crossroads" as they met to discuss and map out their own diversity plan for the industry.

The case for the diversity agenda in public relations education involves more than social justice and demography. It involves more than urging others to "do the right thing"; as former Newspaper Association of America President Cathie Black said, it involves urging others to "do the thing right." And it should go beyond simply mimicking the efforts of the print, broadcast, and advertising industries to become racially and culturally inclusive. It is an initiative that could be driven by the very essence of this nation's professed democratic ideals: freedom of speech.

Print journalists and journalism educators are quick to package their work in the wrappings of the First Amendment and rightfully proclaim their right to a free press. Similarly, advertisers present arguments for the right of commercial free speech, and broadcasters warn against the threats to free press and free speech that they believe are posed by government regulation. The case for the sometimes competing First Amendment rights of print media, broadcasters, advertisers, and new media technologies is most often fashioned and focused by public relations professionals.

But where is the public relations profession in this turf battle for the First Amendment high ground? On many campuses, its place in the mass communication curriculum is affected by the "last hired, first fired" mentality that people of color also have faced for many years. Public relations is sometimes seen as an adjunct to other media training, not a profession that can or should exist on its own. Its place on campus is often argued within and among educators both in and out of schools of journalism and mass communication. Administrators eagerly accept the large public relations enrollment numbers, but many question the value of the curriculum.

When it comes to the importance of a diversity agenda, however, multiculturalism in public relations should be a primary objective. If public relations practitioners and educators were to wrap themselves in the First Amendment rights of freedom of expression, the free marketplace of ideas, and the right to both send and receive information, they would find their case parallels the need for diversity raised by other media professions.

In many ways, the practice of public relations is like the practice of law. Public relations professionals believe in the free marketplace of ideas, just as lawyers believe in the legal system. Just as attorneys believe that everyone deserves his or her day in court, public relations practitioners believe, or should believe, that every viewpoint deserves to have its best case made in the court of public opinion. Just as attorneys learn to craft legal arguments before court, public relations professionals are skilled in shaping the public presentation of the viewpoints of those whom they represent to the media and the public. The message is important, but most important is the right of a message to be expressed and received. Less important is the messenger.

Public Relations' Influence on the News Media

This is a lesson two of the authors of this book learned in the 1960s when, finding themselves with a journalism education but no real opportunity to enter the nearly all-White newsrooms of Southern California general circulation newspapers, they did public relations for the Black Student Union and United Mexican American Students, community organizations, and antipoverty agencies to present the issues of Chicanos and Blacks to the news media. Much of this work involved gaining coverage for pickets, protests, demonstrations, marches, and all the other activism associated with the 1960s. But it also focused on gaining coverage and understanding of the need for youth job training, community credit unions, neighborhood beautification efforts, and drug diversion programs.

In the authors' efforts, two important lessons were learned that had not been taught in the process of earning their journalism degrees. For one, they learned that public relations workers are critical to the selection and presentation of the day's news. Second, they learned that journalists too often file inaccurate stories about non-Whites because they are influenced by biases and misconceptions about other racial and cultural groups. At the very least, this results in a lack of proper perspective in news reporting.

In the 1960s, this meant that news professionals often portrayed stories from the Black and Latino communities in terms of conflict, activism, and militancy. Too often they covered public demonstrations for civil rights by focusing on the demonstrators instead of the issues that necessitated the demonstration. In the 21st century, journalists too often focus on people of color as "problem people," either beset by problems or causing them for the larger society, and as "zoo stories," focusing on these communities during colorful observances of Chinese New Year, Kwanzaa, Mexican Independence Day, or Native American powwows. Once again, journalists still often see these communities through a lens that filters out certain elements of the story while allowing others to pass through to the audience.

Racial diversity in public relations can help sensitize journalism students and news professionals. Public relations expertise and experience are needed to forcefully, effectively, and accurately present the reality of the diverse cultural groups that now make up our nation to the news and information media. Public relations professionals are also needed to help journalists overcome their misunderstandings of racially and culturally diverse communities if they are to accurately report on those communities.

The need for multiculturalism in public relations is no less strong today than it was in the 1960s. With increased racial diversity in the United States—coupled with the proliferation of targeted, segmented, and micro media—the need for people of color to learn and practice public relations is more important than ever. Similarly, public relations students of all races and cultural backgrounds must learn to appreciate and understand cross-cultural communication if they are eventually to be effective in the profession. These skills will be even more important over the next generation as more persons from racially diverse backgrounds assume positions in public communications endeavors.

Diversity in Public Relations: The Need to Reflect Demographic Growth and Changes

A Public Relations Student Society of America (PRSSA) diversity report issued in December 2011 that, as future public relations specialists, students seeking careers in the field need to understand how people with differences can work together to communicate effectively. The Commission on Public Relations Education also notes that successful managers in all types of organizations now recognize that a diverse employee workforce "recruited, trained and retained" can deliver valuable insights and performance with regard to marketing, strategic planning, human resources, and management issues. Furthermore, it is currently recognized in higher education that a "culture of inclusion" has been encouraged—if not mandated—with new standards for accreditation of schools of journalism/mass communication and certification programs in public relations. Moreover, trade associations, research foundations, and professional societies in public relations now emphasize the need for diversity and offer training and workshops to promote diversity in the field.[1]

The Commission on Public Relations Education's 2006 report asserted that public relations practitioners, educators, and students need to develop an introspective awareness of their own individual cultures, socialization, and privileges, and must recognize the pitfalls of being ethnocentric in their thoughts and approaches to managing public relations projects and teams.[2] As Michael Palenchar, a public relations professor at the University of Tennessee, notes, "Like society as a whole, the PR field finds itself struggling with the role of diversity," and he believes that "at the core of PR scholarship should be the concepts of mutual respect, collaboration, appreciation for a wide range of perspectives and the creation of a platform for the open and transparent engagement of the marketplace of ideas." He adds that diversity should encompass much more than gender or ethnicity, and also include intellectual, experiential, and workplace diversity.[3]

The Commission on Public Relations Education subscribes to this notion, and asserts that diversity in public relations generally takes two forms: intercultural/multicultural communication and diversity management. The growing reach of our global economy into all corners of the world supports this need for today's public relations practitioners to learn how to navigate multicultural and multiethnic environments and understand how diverse populations play a role in each aspect of a public relations project from research and planning to communication and evaluation. Equally important is the ability to hire, manage, and retain diverse teams, which will enhance the development of "best practices" campaigns and solutions that are both innovative and effective.[4]

In 1990, the U.S. Census Bureau counted 167,000 persons working as public relations specialists. Of these, 14% were people of color: 7% Black, 4.3% Hispanic, 1.7% Asian/Pacific Islander, and 0.3% Native American/Eskimo/Aleut.[5] This is about the same percentage as those in broadcast newsrooms at the time.

By 2010, the number of public relations practitioners nearly doubled to 311,000, and these professionals now compose roughly 10% of all occupations in the United States. However, while the number of public relations practitioners nearly doubled, the percentage comprising people of color essentially remained stagnant at 14.1%. The number of African Americans in the field actually declined while Asians saw only a modest increase among public relations practitioners. It is interesting to note, however, that Bureau of Labor Statistics data showed that by 2010 the number of Latinos in the field nearly doubled to 8.7% of public relations specialists and 9.7%

of advertising and promotions managers. In the public relations manager category, Latinos experienced a more modest increase of 5.2%.

On the other hand, the number of African American public relations specialists fell to 2.8% in 2010, and they composed only a mere 0.8% of advertising and promotions managers and 4.4% of all public relations managers. Asians composed only 2.6% of public relations practitioners, 2.3% of advertising and promotions managers, and 4.6% of all public relations managers in the field.[6]

With Latinos now the largest ethnic group and one of the fastest growing minority groups—along with Asians—in the United States, it is imperative for organizations to diversify the public relations workforce to better understand and serve their increasingly diverse target audiences. U.S. Census Bureau figures from 2010 indicate that, between 2000 and 2010, the Latino population grew by 43%—rising to 50.5 million—while the Asian population showed the fastest growth and increased by 43% to 14.7 million in 2010. Latinos now compose 16% of the total U.S. population—but only half that percentage is reflected in the number of current public relations practitioners.[7]

Publicist Simone Smalls is founder and president of Simone Smalls Public Relations Inc., a New York–based full-service public relations and strategic marketing agency launched in 2008 that specializes in entertainment, sports, and celebrity public relations and marketing.

Source: Joe Corrigan/Stringer/Getty Images Entertainment/Getty Images.

The Importance of Minority Publics

The increase in money spent by African American, Latino, Asian and Pacific Islander, and Native American consumers has made them more attractive as targets for advertising and the media that advertisers support. If current trends continue, these markets will soon compose about 30% of the American population. These figures made people of color attractive as consumers and advertising targets during much of the 1980s and 1990s. But the diversity message need not stop there. Instead, it should be extended to include the positive values that a diversified workforce brings to an organization's ability to understand and communicate to audiences of different races, cultures, languages, and nationalities. This is a point that was made by Marilyn Kern-Foxworth, a scholar who analyzed multicultural trends in public relations. She noted, "Public relations and marketing executives should realize what an asset they have in their own employees of fellow officers who are African American, Native American, Latin American or Asian American. Members of these communities are also valuable assets when companies attempt to communicate and market to other countries . . . by bridging cultural and communication gaps."[8]

As far back as the late 1980s, Gloster and Cherrie (1987) found that companies realized they must reach all of the racial and ethnic groups in their markets and in their communities in order to be successful. That increasing awareness has led to greater opportunities in the form of growing numbers of minority-owned advertising and public relations firms and in the form of aggressive recruiting of Black, Hispanic, Asian American, and Native American professionals by other firms.[9]

However, according to the Ford and Appelbaum (2005) survey of multicultural public relations, about 57% percent of the non-White practitioner sample perceived the industry to be only somewhat successful in retaining a diverse workforce. Roughly 60% of the sample responded that multicultural practitioners were put on slow-moving tracks in their jobs, and about 63% reported that they had to be more qualified than Whites. Moreover, about 55% reported not being afforded the same opportunities as Whites, 53% said that some employers didn't want diverse practitioners working for them, and 54% reported experiencing subtle discrimination by their employers and coworkers.[10]

Even with the Census Bureau's admitted undercounting of people of color in mind, it should be clear that public relations has a long way to go to narrow the gap between the estimated 14% that minorities make up of the public relations workforce and their overall population that approaches 30%. Until positive steps are taken in that direction, the public relations profession will continue to encounter difficulties in capitalizing on the multicultural and multinational opportunities described by Kern-Foxworth and others.

Diversity in Public Relations: Good Business

According to PRowl Public Relations, the student-run PR firm at Temple University, the importance of diversity-driven planning in today's business world is essential to success, and it asserts that the public relations profession must play a crucial role in developing diversity awareness to achieve their company's objectives.[11] Jaya Bohlmann, public relations vice president for Sodexo Inc., said that diversity is important because "the job of any good PR professional is to fully understand their client to achieve their client's overall objectives" and, "without recognizing diversity, the PR department could not do its job, because they would not fully understand their client's perspective." Gorki De Los Santos, communications manager for Coca-Cola, adds that "diversity, both in the marketplace and work-place, is critical to the company's sustainability" and that "diversity is crucial for a business' survival in today's competitive market."[12]

PRSA, the industry trade association, has proclaimed that the profession "should reflect the great diversity that exists" and that all practitioners "have a role to play in ensuring public relations is representative of the diverse publics it serves." However, according to a 2009 *PRWeek* survey, more than 85% of respondents either "strongly" or "somewhat" agreed that the industry "has a problem recruiting ethnically diverse professionals," and 69% said the industry "has a problem retaining ethnically diverse professionals."[13]

This notion was confirmed when *PRWeek* released its 2011 "Power List" of the top 50 PR professionals and did not include a single African American PR practitioner. Sakita Holley, CEO of House of Success, told *PRNewser* that the list made it seem as though there were no African Americans making progress in the industry, which she said was not true. In response, *PRWeek* editor-in-chief Steve Barrett issued a response stating that individuals on the list were chosen not because of the color of their skin, their gender, or their sexual orientation, but rather by the power and influence they wield. But Kim Hunter, president and CEO of Lagrant Communications, may have summed it best when he said, "Your refusal to acknowledge the significant contributions of African Americans in our industry is one of the primary reasons so many people of color do not find our industry welcoming or a viable career option." Rosanna M. Fiske, chair and CEO of PRSA, weighed in with a statement that noted, "Any list that attempts to rank the industry's most powerful or influential players should reflect the great diversity that exists within the profession as well as the diverse meanings of power and influence . . . to do so successfully, an organization's communications must represent the diverse range of voices and demographics that it attempts to reach."[14]

Women of Color in Public Relations

Although women now compose the majority of students majoring in public relations in colleges across the United States as well as in the profession, women of color are still woefully underrepresented in the public relations practice. While women in the profession compose 58.6% of all public relations specialists, 61.1% of advertising and promotions managers, and 60% of public relations managers, it is unclear how many are women of color. Grunig and Toth (2006) found that of the 60%–70% of public relations practitioners who are women, the majority undisputedly consists of White females.[15] Moreover, females now compose the majority of PR students today—and on some campuses they outnumber males by as much as 10 to

1. However, with males composing only about 20% of PR programs across the nation, they nevertheless appear to enter the field at higher levels or are promoted at a faster rate since 40% are in management positions.[16]

Dr. Amanda Gallagher at Texas Tech University believes that PR is facing issues of diversity that are shaping how the field is developing. "A large part of the PR work force is made up of women . . . among PR students today, 70–80 percent of them are women."[17] Consequently, PR students need to be educated concerning this demographic shift in the workforce.

Similarly, Dr. Lynne Sallot at the University of Georgia believes that PR is an excellent career choice for women. Having taught and worked with an eclectic range of students, peers, and supervisors, she said that she has "gained from their diversity of thought and perspective, as much as their diversity of gender and ethnicity," and that they "will have very prestigious and power career opportunities in management that women in other professions do not yet enjoy."[18]

Although determining the numbers of minority women working in public relations is difficult, Pompper (2004) estimated that only 4.5% of management public relations jobs were held by African American women, while 39% were held by White women and 48.3% by White men. Pompper also reported that focus groups of African American women who considered themselves valuable employees said "their organizations consistently discriminated against them, rendered them voiceless, excluded them, and poorly compensated them."[19]

In addition, women of color in the public relations profession typically play markedly different roles in the workplace, which in turn may hinder their potential career advancement. An earlier study by Len-Rios (1998) found that there are also distinct gender differences in perceived and actual discrimination. In her sample of 13 African American, Asian American, and

Yvette Noel-Schure (right), former senior vice president of Columbia Records, best known for her work with Beyoncé, was featured at the African American Public Relations Collective's "Conversation with Yvette Noel-Schure: How Music Publicists Help Artists Sizzle!"

Source: J. Merritt/Contributor/FilmMagic/Getty Images.

Hispanic American practitioners, she found that men recalled more instances of overt racism than did women. To explain this, she suggested three possible reasons: First, managers may not feel as threatened by women in the workplace, and consequently may be less likely to openly discriminate against them. Second, she surmised that women of color perceive less discrimination than do men of color because they are used to accommodating to and rationalizing the behavior of others. Third, she proposed that women may feel more disadvantaged by their gender than by their race.[20]

Minority practitioners are often further disadvantaged by being pigeon-holed in nonprofit or government jobs. They are commonly hired to fill quotas or serve in "show positions" with little significant input into policymaking and limited access to upward mobility or the higher-paying corporate jobs. Finally, it is not uncommon for minority practitioners to be hired primarily to communicate with minority audiences. According to a 1993 study by Kern-Foxworth, about one third of Black practitioners surveyed indicated that they direct their efforts to minority "markets."[21]

When minority practitioners exclusively handle minority issues, they tend to bear the burden of being the race representative, much like the token woman who is expected to serve as the voice for *all* women. Often Black practitioners in mainstream organizations find themselves the sole member of their race in an entire public relations department. They consequently are consulted on issues related to African American publics, and have to interpret—whether directly or indirectly—their culture for non-African Americans.[22]

Those in the field have mixed, though somewhat positive, feelings about their professional field. Gilliam's qualitative study of 10 Black women who are public relations managers mentioned the importance to target Black women as heads of households, the need for successful Black women to share their experiences, and that the Black participants more than Whites felt that Whites were uncomfortable working with Blacks. The study cited an Atlanta survey showing that, although women outnumbered men two to one in public relations, their earnings were lower, and that Black women earned less than White women.[23]

As the fastest growing ethnic minority population, Hispanic women are making significant strides in the public relations profession. In 2002, Rosanna M. Fiske received the D. Parke Gibson Pioneer Award—named after the pioneer in multicultural public relations who authored two books on African American consumerism. Fiske was the first Hispanic woman named president of the PRSA Miami Chapter, and was director of account service for JGR & Associates, Florida's largest Hispanic PR agency, where she led all of the agency's public relations efforts for the general, U.S. Hispanic, and Latin American markets. She was recognized for her multicultural understanding and expertise, and development of successful bilingual programs for local, national, and international clients such as Charles Schwab, American Airlines, Wells Fargo, and MCI.[24]

Building a Multicultural Foundation for Public Relations

Diversity of the population is continuing to translate into diversity of messages and messengers and create multiple opportunities for public relations practitioners and educators. As far back as the early 1990s, PR firm Ketchum's senior vice president and director of media services, Jonathan Schenker, cited increased demographic diversity as one of 10 key media trends, noting that demographics will have a huge influence on the PR industry and that people of color will be featured as matters of fact, not as exceptions to the rule.

"Consider these audiences when creating press kits, and hiring spokespeople," Schenker wrote. "Multiple spokespeople might be necessary for some national campaigns." Schenker forecast continued diversity and demassification on the media side as well, predicting a continuation of the trend of narrowcasting and media targeting to special audiences. He noted, "Expect more of these [targeted] publications and an equal, if not higher, number of them to fail."[25]

Many cited perceived discrimination based on race in terms of either promotions, access to a project, access to a public relations position, or salary increases. A moderate relationship was perceived between leaving the field and perceived discrimination. High satisfaction level indicates public relations professionals of color have developed coping mechanisms to endure what they perceive as a hostile environment.[26]

Kern-Foxworth's earlier survey of 196 non-White public relations professionals found the typical respondent to be a Black female, age 38, who had worked for nine years in public relations and attained a middle-level position, earning $38,337 per year. More than half had degrees in journalism, public relations, or communications. Having a journalism degree was more important than degrees in other areas in determining role. Those with journalism degrees were more likely to be responsible for writing, editing, and producing material to present management's position, but were less likely to guide management through step-by-step planning and programming: "The analysis supports the assumption that larger organizations do not allow minorities the opportunity to advance in their careers. The more people employed in the organization for which minorities work, the lower their salaries and the less chance they have to become expert prescribers."

Kern-Foxworth also found a gap between the role that minorities assign to themselves (middle-level management) and the role that they actually fulfill (communication technician, not problem solver). "The misconception indicates that what they perceive perhaps is not the reality of the situation."[27]

No doubt their skills are increasingly needed in developing management strategies and media messages. Kern-Foxworth asserted that one of the reasons R.J. Reynolds' $10 million African American–targeted venture in Uptown cigarettes went up in smoke is because the company did not use a Black agency to research and assess community and opinion-leader reactions in the targeted community.[28]

Diversity Practices in Public Relations Education

Public relations educators have both an excellent opportunity for advancement and a clear agenda of needs to be addressed. Some of the obstacles to overcome:

1. Too few non-White students are oriented toward journalism once they reach college. They know little about journalism, and other professions are better known to them. Educators and high school and college counselors should identify and reinforce the high achievers with the motivation and drive to be successful.

2. Professors should use racially and culturally inclusive textbooks and classroom materials in their teaching. There has been little research on inclusiveness of textbooks, which have a great influence in portraying the field, its practice, and its practitioners to aspirants and students of the field.

3. People of color are not newcomers to the profession, nor are their newspaper histories separate from their public relations history. The first Black, Native American, and Asian American newspapers in this country were all founded as public relations or public advocacy vehicles: *El Misisipí* to rail against Napoleon's takeover of Spain, *Freedom's Journal* "to plead our own cause," the *Cherokee Phoenix* to advocate a tribal identity and disseminate tribal news to the Cherokees and the native viewpoint to a wider audience, and *The Golden Hills' News* to Christianize the Chinese and to gain respect for them among the 49ers in the California gold rush.

A Public Relations Education Diversity Agenda

By explaining to their students the economic advantages of working in a corporate environment and stressing the opportunities for community service as part of public relations, professors can help students understand the unique opportunities in public relations. Community involvement is encouraged, not discouraged, on the public relations side of the communications profession.

In its ongoing commitment to diversity, PRSA is now represented by PRSSA chapters at 13 historically Black colleges and 27 schools that have been accredited by the Hispanic Association of Colleges and Universities. PRSSA has also created its own pathways to diversity by offering internship opportunities and scholarships to its minority members.[29]

The other media professional associations, such as the American Society of News Editors, offer models of multicultural programs that public relations faculty and professionals can replicate, emulate, and improve upon. Similarly, non-White professional associations can also help to establish links for internships, mentors, part-time faculty, and campus speakers. The Los Angeles–based Hispanic Public Relations Association's 80 to 100 members annually raise $10,000 in scholarships and look for contacts on campus.

Mentoring programs with professionals, internships, early tracking, and a national competition to select, train, place, and track students will help to attract and keep the best students in public relations. Contacts with historically Black colleges, schools that are members of the Hispanic Association of Colleges and Universities, and campuses with large minority student enrollment will also help identify and nurture public relations faculty and students. Such contacts should be seen as a two-way street. Public relations agencies and educators who have only focused on general audiences can learn from the students and faculty at predominantly non-White campuses as they work with them.

In a world of "demassified" society and media, those who are aware and able to function in more than one culture and to work in more than one medium will be the most advantaged. Public relations students and professionals must know how to communicate with people of all cultures and to use all the media at their disposal. Therefore, it is crucial that they gain an understanding of the crossover skills necessary to effectively communicate with diverse audiences through diverse media.

A Public Relations Professional Diversity Agenda

Though specialized public relations agencies were among the first to make corporate America and government agencies aware of effective ways to reach communities of color through targeted campaigns dating back to the early 20th century, PRSA did not start its own Multicultural Communications Section until 1997, as an outgrowth of its National Multicultural Affairs Committee, which began in 1980.

"From its inception, the Section has been dedicated to championing multiculturalism and nurturing the careers of ethnically diverse public relations practitioners," said chair Rhonda Welsh at a 2003 teleconference on U.S. Hispanics sponsored by the Multicultural Communications Section. Citing the Census Bureau's projection that by 2040 nearly half of all Americans will be what are now called "minorities," she added that "the numbers suggest that our organizations in general and our practice specifically must realize the importance of building relationships with all of our publics."[30]

Some public relations firms, such as internationally renowned Fleishman-Hillard and Lagrant Communications, have recognized the need to diversify their workforce to meet the shifting demographics of target audiences by offering minority scholarship and training programs. In the mid-1990s, Fleishman-Hillard's Los Angeles office created a minority internship training program whereby the firm recruited qualified minority juniors and seniors from regional colleges and universities who were interested in pursuing careers in the public relations field. One candidate, an African American female selected in the second year of the program, said she was the only person of color in the entire office. She was subsequently hired full-time and transferred to the firm's office in Chicago.[31]

The 2003 PRSA Multicultural Communications Section conducted several national programs to fulfill its vision to serve "as a link between multicultural issues, practitioners and the society." Activities included multicultural events at the PRSA convention, multicultural scholarships for promising students, a quarterly newsletter and increased outreach to leaders of ethnic public relations associations, other professional societies, and PRSA accreditation training for ethnic public relations associations.

Partnering with ethnic public relations associations, such as the Hispanic Public Relations Association and Hispanic Marketing and Communication Association, PRSA's teleseminar cosponsors, has helped general market public relations associations and agencies link with the nation's growing racial and ethnic groups and the media that serve them. In so doing, the ethnic professional organizations and PR agencies have been able to go beyond translating press releases into other languages and putting a racial happy face on an already established campaign. Instead, they contribute their creative expertise and knowledge of different racial and ethnic communities to influence the content and focus of these campaigns so they will be more effective.

The task for increasing diversity in the public relations profession is twofold: It must start with university public relations curricula and programs as well as become an integral part of the corporate model and business agenda. PRSA recognized this need to expand diversity both in PR programs and in the profession when it established a national Diversity Committee in 2003. Its objective was to develop a more inclusive professional society by reaching and involving members who represent diverse genders, ethnicities, races, and sexual orientations, and by providing them with dedicated professional development opportunities and support to help them succeed in public relations. It also instituted a Chapter Diversity Award as a way to recognize PRSA chapters that are embracing diversity and inclusion. However, PRSA still has a way to go to achieve equity in diversity, since 87% of its members are White. The organization reported only a 6% increase in minority membership between 2005 and 2011.[32]

PRSA is also attempting to accomplish greater diversity by providing a "PR Planning Toolkit" that provides a comprehensive list of multicultural/diversity contact names and organizations for reaching African American, Arab American, Asian American, Disabled American, LGBTQ, Hispanic/Latino, and Native American organizations. Other practical guidelines offer tips on how to communicate with diverse publics for each phase of the public relations planning process. These guidelines explain how practitioners can choose effective communication strategies with regard to rhetorical styles, tone, language, and spokespersons in the research, strategy, tactics, and evaluation stages to create a "best practices" approach to working with diverse audiences.[33]

Some corporate organizations—such as Coca-Cola, Xerox, and American Express—are also committed to enhancing diversity in their workforce by offering education and training programs, by encouraging minority and female-based businesses as suppliers, and by communicating company initiatives through guest speakers, programs, and networks, both within and outside of the company. As Chief Diversity Officer Kerrie Peraino of American Express noted, diversity is important because it "creates a culture of inclusion" and "drives business success," and PR departments can help diversity initiatives by communicating both to their employees and to their customer base about how the company values diversity and what programs it has to maintain diversity—not only when managing within the company, but also when catering to the needs of its clientele.[34]

The multicultural/multilingual understanding and skills that men and women of color bring into the public relations profession are important in effectively communicating to and with all American communities. As they become more valued by the public relations profession, people of all races and ethnicities who have these skills will also become more valuable to the corporations, nonprofit agencies, and public relations organizations and governments that employ them.

Notes

1. Commission on Public Relations Education, "Public Relations Education for the 21st Century: The Professional Bond," November 2006, accessed May 18, 2012, www.commpred.org/_uploads/report2-full.pdf.

2. Ibid.

3. Miranda Yow, "Diversity: A Challenge Worth Welcoming," accessed December 28, 2011, http://www.platformmagazine.com.

4. Commission on Public Relations Education, "Public Relations Education for the 21st Century: The Professional Bond," November 2006, accessed May 18, 2012, www.commpred.org/_uploads/report2-full.pdf.

5. U.S. Bureau of the Census, "1990 Census of the Population Special Report 1–1," *Detailed Occupation and Other Characteristics from the EEO File for the United States,* 3.

6. Bureau of Labor Statistics, U.S. Department of Labor, 2010, accessed January 15, 2012, http://www.bls.gov.cps.

7. "2010 Census Shows America's Diversity: Hispanic and Asian Populations Grew Fastest During the Decade," accessed January 8, 2012, http://www.census.gov/newsroom/releases/archives/2010_census.

8. Marilyn Kern-Foxworth, "Black, Brown, Red and Yellow Markets Equal Green Power," *Public Relations Quarterly* (Spring 1991): 30.

9. D. Gloster and J. Cherrie, "Communication Careers: Advertising or Public Relations May Mean Opportunity," *Equal Opportunity* (Spring 1987): 36–39, as cited in Marilyn Kern-Foxworth, "Status and Roles of Minority PR Practitioners," *Public Relations Review* (Fall 1989): 40.

10. Rochelle L. Ford and Lynn Appelbaum, "Multicultural Survey of PR Practitioners," accessed March 20, 2012, http://www.ccny.cuny.edu/prsurvey/index.html.

11. PRowl Public Relations, "PR Blogs Worth Reading (And More!)," December 31, 2010, accessed May 19, 2012, http://prowlpublicrelations.blogspot.com/2010.

12. Ibid.

13. Kevin Allen, "PRSA: Industry Lists Should 'Reflect the Great Diversity . . . of the Profession,'" *PR Daily,* July 19, 2011, accessed December 28, 2011, www.prdaily.com.

14. Ibid.

15. J. E. Grunig and E. L. Toth, "The Ethics of Communicating With and About Difference in a Changing Society," *Ethics in Public Relations: Responsible Advocacy,* ed. K. Fitzpatrick and C. Bronstein (Thousand Oaks, CA: Sage, 2006), 41–42. Cited in Michael Cherenson, "Public Relations' Diversity Problem," Public Relations Society of America, February 10, 2009, accessed December 28, 2011, http://prsay.prsa.org/index.php/2009/02/10/public-relations-diversity-problem.

16. Cherenson, op. cit., accessed December 28, 2011, http://prsay.prsa.org/index.php/2009/02/10/public-relations-diversity-problem.

17. Miranda Yow, "Diversity: A Challenge Worth Welcoming," accessed December 28, 2011, http://www.platformmagazine.com.

18. Ibid.

19. Donalynn Pompper, "Linking Ethnic Diversity and Two-Way Symmetry: Modeling Female African-American Practitioners' Roles," *Journal of Public Relations Research* 16(3) (2004): 285.

20. M. E. Len-Rios, "Minority Public Relations Practitioner Perceptions," *Public Relations Review* 24(4) (1998): 535–555. Cited in L. A. Grunig, E. L. Toth, and L. C. Hon, *Women in Public Relations: How Gender Influences Practice* (New York: Guilford Press, 2001).

21. M. Kern-Foxworth, "Minority Practitioners' Perceptions of Racial Bias in Public Relations and Implications for the Year 2000," *Diversity in Public Relations Education: Issues, Implications and Opportunities: A Collection of Essays* (Florida International University, North Miami, and University of South Carolina, Columbia: Diversity Committee, Educators Section, Public Relations Society of America, 1993),

35–51. Cited in L. A. Grunig, E. L. Toth, and L. C. Hon, *Women in Public Relations: How Gender Influences Practice* (New York: Guilford Press, 2001).

22. For more details, see W. A. Mallett, *African Americans in Public Relations: Pigeonholed Practitioners or Cultural Interpreters?*, unpublished master's thesis, University of Maryland, College Park, 1995. Cited in L. A. Grunig, E. L. Toth, and L. C. Hon, *Women in Public Relations: How Gender Influences Practice* (New York: Guilford Press, 2001).

23. J. N. Gilliam, *Black Women in Public Relations: Climbing to the Top*, master's thesis, Graduate School of the University of Maryland, 1992.

24. Public Relations Society of America, November 11, 2002, Directory: http://www.prsa.org/_News/press/pr111102a.asp, accessed February, 19, 2003, pacbell .net.

25. *How New Media Trends Affect PR Activities* (J. R. O'Dwyer Co. Inc., PR Services, April 1992).

26. Eugenia Zerbinos and Gail Alice Clanton, "Minority Public Relations Practitioners: Career Influences, Job Satisfaction, and Discrimination," Top Faculty Paper (Minorities and Communications Division, Association for Education in Journalism and Mass Communication, Montreal, August 1992).

27. Marilyn Kern-Foxworth, "Status and Roles of Minority PR Practitioners," *Public Relations Review* (Fall 1989): 42–44.

28. Marilyn Kern-Foxworth, "Advertising and Public Relations: An Educator's Perspective," *Black Issues in Higher Education* (June 6, 1991).

29. Cherenson, op. cit., accessed December 28, 2011, http://prsay.prsa.org/index.php/2009/02/10/public-relations-diversity-problem.

30. Public Relations Society of America, February 5, 2003, Directory: http://www.prsa.org/_Networking/mc/index.asp?ident=mc1, accessed February 19, 2003, pacbell.net.

31. Coauthor, L. M. Chao nominated students from California State University, Los Angeles to interview for the program. Two African American female students in the four years CSULA was informed of the program were selected from a competitive process, each receiving a $5,000 scholarship and a full-time summer internship with Fleishman-Hillard's Los Angeles–based office.

32. Michael Cherenson, "Public Relations' Diversity Problem," Public Relations Society of America, February 10, 2009, accessed December 28, 2011, http://prsay.prsa.org/index.php/2009/02/10/public-relations-diversity-problem.

33. Elizabeth Toth, "Diversity and Public Relations Practice," April 9, 2009, accessed December 28, 2011, http://institutforpr.org/topics/diversityand-pr-practice.

34. PRowl Public Relations, "PR Blogs Worth Reading (And More!)," December 31, 2010, accessed May 19, 2012, http://prowlpublicrelations.blogspot .com/2010.

PART IV

Overcoming Race and Gender Insensitive Media

9

Advocacy

Keeping Their Feet to the Fire

The year was 1827, and the words appeared in the premier issue of *Freedom's Journal,* the first newspaper published by Black Americans:

> The peculiarities of this Journal, renders it important that we should advertise to the world our motives by which we are actuated, and the objects which we contemplate . . . We wish to plead our own cause . . . Too long has the publick been deceived by misrepresentations, in things which concern us dearly . . . From the press and the pulpit we have suffered much by being incorrectly represented.[1]

Thus, from the beginning it was obvious that one of the primary objectives of the Black press was to protest and counter the negative and false reportage of the White press. We shall see that Blacks were not alone in exercising the option of "advocacy" for their own cause as a response to White media and, furthermore, that media advocacy by people of color has long-standing historical roots.

But first, let us put the issue in perspective. We have established in previous chapters the nature of White-owned media and their treatment of racial and cultural minority groups. The social and cultural imperative that people of color communicate en masse is an issue of survival. As noted previously in this volume, marginalized ethnic and cultural groups in the United States have three methods or coping strategies by which to address Anglocentric media tainted by racism and insensitivity to their needs: (1) They may develop and maintain their own alternative communications media; (2) they may seek access to mainstream media through employment and effect change from within; and (3) they may advocate for change in mainstream media content by applying pressure techniques of various forms.

Some students and media activists have simplified the approaches by referring to them as the "three As," meaning advocacy, access, and alternative (media). The methods are related and have been utilized both independently and in combination with each other. For example, people of color who have obtained professional employment in hegemonic media often form organizations that work to change their portrayals or news coverage in the media industries. Or, a medium owned by people of color may protest inequities it finds in general audience media, as was the case with *Freedom's Journal*. In this chapter, we shall look at the advocacy option and complete the circle of media activism by the subject groups.

Nearly a century after the appearance of *Freedom's Journal*, the Black press was still publicly defending its constituency against the denigrating reporting of the White press. In 1919, the Black weekly *Wichita Protest* complained about the racial coverage of the Associated Press:

Every newspaper editor of our group in the country knows that the Associated Press, the leading news distributing service of the country, has carried on a policy of discrimination in favor of the whites and against the blacks, and is doing it daily now. The Associated Negro Press is in receipt of correspondence from editors in various sections of the country decrying the way in which the Associated Press writes its stories of happenings where Colored people are affected.[2]

Even renowned Black spokesman Booker T. Washington spoke frequently of the poor coverage his speeches received from the White press. A Black journalist reported in 1916 Washington's lament that his successful speeches before large crowds, normally expected to receive front-page attention in the White press, would be relegated to the last page and given an inch or so of space. Instead, the front page would invariably be given to considerable reporting of a Black person involved in a minor criminal offense.[3]

There was advocacy for change from the earliest days of the motion picture industry. In 1911, the Spanish-language

Booker T. Washington was a leading early-20th-century advocate for fair press coverage of the issues and perspectives of African Americans by the White general audience news media.

Source: Cheynes Studio, Hampton, VA.

weekly *La Crónica* of Laredo, Texas, launched a campaign against the numerous movies shown throughout the state that denigrated both Mexicans and Native American Indians. The period marked the beginning of the heyday of Western movies. Movie screens were filled with images of "greasers" and "savage" Indians who were brought to justice by White cowboy heroes. Several prominent members of the Native American community wrote protest letters to the Bureau of Indian Affairs in Washington, D.C., over the images such movies projected of their people. *La Crónica* wrote:

> We are not surprised about the complaint of the North American Indians . . . because the Mexicans can make the same complaint . . . and other Latin races, who are generally the only and most defamed in these sensational American movies (such as are seen on the Texas border) . . . that serve only to show the level of culture of the learned makers of films, who have no more ingenuity except to think of scenes with many bullets, horses, "cowboys" and then it's over.[4]

La Crónica proceeded to call for support from other Texas Mexican newspapers in urging an end to the offensive movies. Earlier the paper had addressed the negative effects such movies had upon its community.

> We judge these with much indignation and condemn them with all our energy . . . all exhibitions that make ridicule of the Mexican . . . because the showing of these facts are indelibly recorded in the minds of the children and this contributes very much to the development of the dislike with which other races see the Mexican race, who the film company has chosen to make fun of.[5]

In addition, the paper sought to persuade Texas theater owners not to acquire and show the films and to follow the lead of two Latinos who wrote letters to filmmakers to cancel further shipments to their theaters. *La Crónica* wrote that Latino families often reacted to negative stereotypes by leaving the theaters when they saw such portrayals and roles that "in reality [don't] fit us."[6] The paper noted that it would "with pleasure" publish the names of film companies that rejected movies denigrating to Mexicans.

The first generation of Chinese immigrants who settled primarily in California were, for the most part, unsophisticated laborers whose immediate concern was survival in a new and hostile Anglo-Saxon world. Because they were not made to feel a part of American culture and because most were from the uneducated working class in China, aside from relatively mild protestations in *The Golden Hills' News* they did not often express displeasure of their treatment by Whites in written form. As small "Chinatown" enclaves developed in settlements in California and the Far West, the Chinese immigrants sought internal refuge and protection from the ravages of racism. They dared not, given their small numbers and immigrant status, publicly protest too vociferously against their hosts whose image of them as inferior precluded tolerance of criticism.

However, the second wave of Chinese immigrants included a number of representatives from China's upper classes. These people were educated and were not affected by the anti-Chinese immigration laws passed prior to 1900. They were diplomats, scholars, and prosperous merchants, and despite their interest in promoting closer economic and political ties with the United States, some expressed disapproval of White racism against them in writing. One such writer was Wu Tingfang, a Chinese diplomat who lived in America for nearly a decade. Wu wrote his book *America Through the Spectacles of an Oriental Diplomat* in 1914. By that time, Sax Rohmer's fictional and diabolical Chinese character, Dr. Fu Manchu, was four years old, and the negative stereotype had found White Americans eager to adopt his imagery to existing racial prejudices against Chinese people. Ever the diplomat, Wu asked forgiveness if his "impartial and candid observations" should offend American readers:

> American readers will forgive me if they find some opinions they cannot endure. I assure them they were not formed hastily or unkindly. Indeed, I should not be a sincere friend were I to picture their country as a perfect paradise, or were I to gloss over what seem to me to be their defects.[7]

Despite this early warning in his book, Wu's criticisms were generally innocuous. He made it clear, however, that he opposed the racism against Blacks and Chinese he had observed in America. He tried to appeal to rationality among his White readers by arguing that they could not be racially superior to the Chinese whose rich culture and intellectual history merited respect throughout the rest of the world.

There are numerous other incidents throughout American history in which people of color expressed their disfavor with White media as a means of advocating change in their treatment by them. Such activity has included every non-White cultural group and every form of mass communication media. The methods of advocacy have ranged from boycotts to letter-writing campaigns and from monitoring hegemonic media content to seeking legal redress of grievances as well as other techniques.

Civil Rights Organizations

As people of color began to organize against racism and discriminatory practices and for equality in the areas of employment, housing, education, and other basic rights of American citizenship, the indignities of maltreatment in and by media industries were never far from their consciousness. Following are a few of the representative groups that have respectively taken up the cause of media fairness over the years.

* The National Association for the Advancement of Colored People (NAACP) was founded in 1909 and led the opposition to such media atrocities as the motion picture *The Birth of a Nation* and the imagery of the "Amos 'n' Andy" radio show.

* The League of United Latin American Citizens (LULAC), founded in 1929, has used radio and television messages to fight Latino discrimination in media and other areas of life in the United States. Since the 1960s, another Latino organization, the National Council of La Raza (NCLR), has advocated for nonstereotypical media portrayals and initiated the ALMA Awards, the first prime-time television network Latino awards show.

* The Indian American Leadership Council (IALC) was formed in the early 1990s "to promote civic awareness and protect the civil rights" of Indian American and South Asian residents. Among the group's objectives is to support community action through education and advocacy.

* The Council on American-Islamic Relations (CAIR) was founded in 1994 as an "organization that challenges stereotypes of Islam and Muslims." CAIR frequently provides media outlets with the Islamic perspective on issues related to its constituency.

Advocacy activists received a major boost when the Civil Rights Act was enacted in 1964. For the first time, the weight of law added clout to media activists who sought change via employment in the media. Interestingly, it was often difficult to convince people of color that necessary changes could be made in media institutions by pursuing legal channels. The period of the late 1960s through the mid-1970s was marked by sit-in demonstrations, street rallies, marches, and picket lines. Many of those techniques had proven effective. The legal establishment, which included law enforcement agencies, prosecutors, lawyers, and judges, was seen by many people of color as a major contributor to the problems they were addressing. Thus, the suggestion that working through the legal system would result in the changes they sought was a difficult proposition to sell. Ultimately, however, the legal system paved the way for success in addressing concerns about the media.

As we have noted elsewhere in this book, people of color initially were able to effect changes much more rapidly in broadcasting because Federal Communications Commission (FCC) employment guidelines for broadcast licensees were more stringent than those of the Equal Employment Opportunity Commission (EEOC), the federal body to which newspapers are answerable. In addition, other social, economic, and political forces began to bear upon mass media institutions. Although he was referring to the political process, futurist John Naisbitt captured the essence of why people of color were able to exert considerable leverage in the effort to improve their lot in media. The issue is related to racial pluralism and the trend toward decentralization in the United States. According to Naisbitt in his book *Megatrends*:

> The key to decentralization of political power in the United States today is local action. Localized political power is not delegated from the federal level to the state, municipal, or neighborhood levels. Rather, it stems from the initiatives taken by the state or neighborhood in the absence of an effective top-down solution . . . Successful initiatives hammered out at the local level have staying power. Local solutions are resistant to top-down intervention and become models for others still grappling with the problems.[8]

How decentralization through technology and economics is generally affecting mass media in America is more thoroughly discussed elsewhere in this book. Here, we shall examine how multicultural advocates, working at the local level and using the force of law, began making an impact on mass media in the late 1960s. In some respects, their successes are reminiscent of how the populist movement of the 1830s drastically altered communications media and entertainment in the United States, with the exception that meaningful change often had to be won in hard-fought courtroom battles. Despite advances occasioned by legal actions, the greater challenges of social tolerance and attitudinal change remain. As Pluria Marshall Sr., long-term chairman of the National Black Media Coalition (NBMC), once said, it is the role of advocacy activists to constantly serve as media watchdogs to keep offenders' "feet to the fire" to obtain fairness and equitable treatment.

Challenging Bias in Broadcasting and Electronic Media

Perhaps the legal advocacy story for people of color in broadcasting and electronic media began with the United Church of Christ's Office of Communication. The United Church of Christ (UCC) has had a long-standing interest in civil rights, freedom of religion, and other forms of expression. It has committed its resources to such efforts in the United States and in various other nations. Generally the organization, a coalition of Protestant denominations, has dedicated itself to the proposition that the communications media should operate under Judeo-Christian principles. It considers mass media to be a missionary sphere of interest. UCC's Office of Communication was the organizational entity assigned to the task of media advocacy. It was responsible for landmark legal decisions that changed the American broadcasting industry and its regulatory agency, the FCC, in ways even beyond the scope of racial concerns.

The first major race-related case involved radio station WLBT in Jackson, Mississippi, in the 1960s. WLBT had incurred the wrath of Jackson's Black community for a number of years because of its discriminatory racial practices, which included on-air references to Black people as "niggers" and refusal to carry a network show on race relations by airing a sign that read "Sorry, Cable Trouble" during the scheduled time slot. The station openly advocated racial segregation in a region where Black people composed some 45% of the station's service area. UCC became involved, among other reasons, because it had a congregation in nearby Tougaloo, Mississippi, and Blacks composed a significant portion of its membership. When WLBT began to attack local civil rights activity in which church members were involved, UCC took up the legal challenge.

UCC filed a petition to deny renewal of WLBT's FCC license in 1964. Under the social, political, and economic conditions of the time, local Blacks faced reprisal and likely violence had they attempted to challenge WLBT strictly as a local effort. The crux of the legal case was the FCC requirement (established by the Communications Act of 1934) that all licensees broadcast "in the public interest, convenience and necessity." On the surface, it appeared that Black residents of Jackson and the UCC would have little trouble preventing WLBT from retaining its license assuming their well-documented case was adequately presented. Unfortunately, although FCC rules allowed for license challenges, only a miniscule fraction of license challenges had ever been successfully upheld since the agency's inception. As subsequent legal developments made clear, the FCC had evolved into a protector of broadcasters instead of the public's rights. When the UCC and representatives of Jackson's Black community appeared before the FCC, the agency denied them "standing" to even present their petition on grounds they had no "interest" (financial) in the license renewal procedure.

When WLBT's license was renewed, the UCC filed suit in the U.S. Court of Appeals, which granted standing to the complainants and ordered the FCC to hold a full hearing of their case. The court maintained that members of WLBT's audience most certainly had standing because as consumers they had an interest in local broadcasting content over public airwaves. In fact, the court's position was that the FCC could not do its job without the assistance of the public in determining public interest. Despite participation in the hearing process, the UCC was distressed when the FCC granted a license renewal to WLBT on a one-year probationary status.

Believing the FCC decision to be improper and unfair, the UCC once again took the issue to the Court of Appeals and found relief. In harsh language that took the FCC to task for its shoddy treatment of the petitioners, the court took matters into its own hands and denied the license to WLBT. Significant also was the court's ruling that public petitioners should not bear the burden of proof in such cases but rather the licensee must be able to show it handled its license privilege in a responsible manner. Moreover, the court ordered the denial on the grounds that the Fairness Doctrine had been violated and that WLBT practiced racial discrimination in programming and hiring—all extremely important issues for marginalized racial groups. Another important right, the right of standing in FCC license hearings, was also won in the initial phase of the case.

The UCC was also instrumental in a case involving Native Americans in Rosebud, South Dakota.[9] Rosebud is a Sioux reservation whose inhabitants undertook a legal action against two South Dakota television stations, KELO and KPLO, that reached a combined 90% of the broadcast audience in the state during the 1950s and 1960s. KPLO became a virtual satellite of KELO and by the mid-1960s was originating little or no local programming to serve the interests and needs of the Rosebud Sioux. The UCC assisted in filing a petition to deny a license to KELO, which resulted in the negotiation of agreements with both stations. The agreements called for program changes and the employment of five Native Americans to full-time positions in broadcasting.

The concept of advocacy groups and potential broadcast licensees reaching negotiated settlement on matters of nondiscrimination in employment and program content set the stage for the last major UCC-inspired milestone we shall consider. In a 1968 case involving local citizens' groups in Texarkana, Texas, with support from the UCC, the license of KTAL television was challenged by a petition to deny its renewal. The station's owners negotiated a settlement that resulted in withdrawal of the petition. Part of the agreement called for reimbursement of legal expenses to the UCC incurred during the process. The FCC, however, refused payment of the reimbursement citing the possibility of encouraging frivolous lawsuits in the future and the potential for overpayment of such expenses. The FCC also feared the public-interest merits of petition-to-deny cases could be overshadowed by the financial ramifications. Again, the UCC took the issue before the appeals court and was granted a ruling, which held negotiated reimbursements to be valid in instances where the petition-to-deny case is bona fide and the public interest has been served. The ruling gave advocacy groups added bargaining power (broadcasters have more at stake if they choose to draw out a proceeding in hope the citizens would exhaust their funds) and encouraged challenged licensees to negotiate settlements more quickly to avoid the more lengthy and expensive process of a fully litigated case.

A capsule review of the typical multicultural advocacy group (or other local citizens' group) procedure for prompting change in broadcasting was basically as follows. If it could be shown that racial discrimination existed in programming, employment, or other areas detrimental to the public interest, a "petition to deny" the station's license renewal would be filed with the FCC. If the petition reached a hearing at the FCC, the licensee bore the burden of showing how its practices were, indeed, in the best interests of the community it served. That was because local citizens' groups had "standing" as interested parties to the license renewal process. If the citizens' advocacy group challenge was upheld, the broadcaster faced loss of its license, or an arrangement could be made to ensure that the wrongs were rectified. If, however, the challenging group and the licensee negotiated a settlement prior to a hearing before the FCC, the challengers could withdraw the petition-to-deny action and seek reimbursement of legal expenses incurred. By the mid-1980s, more than 100 such actions had been initiated, including some by other groups benefiting from precedents established by people of color.

However, during the late 1980s and throughout the 1990s, government "deregulation" policies eroded the ability of advocacy groups to challenge broadcasting licenses. With deregulation came relaxation of enforcement, and the tactic became much less of a factor in advocacy efforts. This circumstance led to the 1986 creation of the Minority Media and Telecommunications Council (MMTC). Nevertheless, some gains were made during the period. FCC data revealed that in 1978 people of color owned about 0.5% of all commercial broadcast stations in the United States, but by 1994 the figure had increased to 3%. That trend, however, was short-lived.

David Honig, who has served as MMTC director since its inception, notes a severe decline in minority and women ownership since 2000. As a collective group, persons of color owned only 7% of the full-power radio stations in the United States in 2009, and women of all racial categories owned 6% of commercial radio stations and 5% of television stations. African Americans, for example, owned 23 television stations in the United States at the peak year 1992. By 2012, however, they owned only 8.

Thus, since 2002, much of the MMTC's work has centered on preventing further erosion of gains made

David Honig, executive director of the Minority Media and Telecommunications Council, spearheaded legal challenges against racial inequities in commercial broadcasting for more than two decades.

Source: David Honig.

in previous decades. These efforts became increasingly important in the wake of a 2001 District of Columbia U.S. Court of Appeals ruling that struck down equal employment opportunity rules established by the FCC a year earlier as unconstitutional.

Into the second decade of the 21st century, the MMTC declared its mission as "promoting and preserving equal opportunity and civil rights in the mass media, telecommunications and broadband industries and closing the digital divide." The group's efforts have been particularly important as media convergence and corporate mergers decreased opportunities for minority ownership and employment representation in the industry. In 2012, slightly more than 1 in 10 persons of color in the United States were served by a commercial radio or television station owned by a member of their racial or cultural group.

Multicultural Efforts in the Newspaper Industry

Although newspapers, as private enterprises, operate under difficult-to-enforce equal employment opportunity guidelines and their response to grievances by people of color has been relatively slow, advocacy activists have managed to make inroads. However, some of the progress can be attributed to advocacy efforts directed toward broadcasting stations because many of them are owned by large corporations with media holdings that are subject to FCC regulation such as broadcasting, satellite, or cable television. In 1980, for example, the Times-Mirror Company (then owner of the *Los Angeles Times, Dallas Times Herald,* and *Newsday,* among other newspapers) reached a negotiated settlement with the NBMC over the purchase of several broadcasting stations. The settlement not only addressed rectification of employment discrimination and programming shortcomings existing in the broadcast operations Times-Mirror was purchasing, but included the appointment of a Black and a Latino to the company's board of directors. The company also agreed to provide scholarships for journalism and broadcasting students attending predominantly Black colleges located near the newly acquired broadcast stations. In addition, several other employment and training programs were funded as a result of the agreement. (The agreement was made possible because citizen advocacy groups could also intervene when broadcast licenses were transferred—as in a change of ownership—as well as when licenses were considered for renewal.)

In the early 1980s, two major events signaled the beginning of a more committed effort to increase multiculturalism in American newspaper staffs. Legal actions brought against the *New York Times* and the Associated Press forced the two news organizations to hire more people of color in the hope that more culturally sensitive coverage in the newspaper press would follow. That hope was founded on the premise that successful legal action—particularly when large, respected institutions were involved— would spur others because of the fear they, too, may be vulnerable to similar legal actions.

Individual activists also have aimed their efforts directly at newspapers and achieved some success in keeping the issue before the industry. Among the leaders who emerged in the mid-1970s to mid-1980s were Robert Maynard and his wife Nancy Hicks Maynard (instrumental in founding the Institute for Journalism Education, now known as the Robert C. Maynard Institute for Journalism Education, among other efforts); Jay T. Harris (who conducted demographic studies of employment in newspapers for the American Society of Newspaper Editors from 1978 to 1983); and Gerald Garcia (an executive with Gannett Company).

Perhaps most influential of all was a White executive, Gerald M. Sass of the Frank E. Gannett Newspaper Foundation (now Freedom Forum), who was instrumental in the expenditure of more than $4 million in grants for multicultural programs in the newspaper industry between 1975 and 1985. Through the foundation, Sass helped provide financial support to the Institute for Journalism Education, the California Chicano News Media Association, the Asian American Journalists Association, the Native American Journalists Association, the National Association of Black Journalists, and the National Association of Hispanic Journalists, among others.

The efforts of these and other advocates for multiculturalism in American daily newspapers were responsible for most of the progress that was made in the 1980s. They prompted the American Society of Newspaper Editors (ASNE) to adopt in 1978 the goal to have the nation's non-White newsroom population equal in percentage to the non-White U.S. population by the year 2000. Although that goal was not met and was revised to the year 2025 (see Chapter 10), ASNE has maintained an active institutional commitment to multiculturalism since 1977 through regional job fairs and an annual survey of newsroom employment. From the mid-1990s into the 21st century, the Newspaper Association of America (NAA) and the Associated Press Managing Editors (APME, known since 2011 as the Associated Press Media Editors) have been among the professional media trade associations that maintain a profile of involvement in the move to multiculturalism and "diversity." The Dow Jones News Fund, known until 2010 as the Dow Jones Newspaper Fund, has several programs for aspiring journalists of color including efforts aimed at high school students. It is among several corporate or private foundation-sponsored endeavors focusing on various aspects of the issue on behalf of the newspaper industry.

Contributions of Minority Media Professional Associations

A significant advocacy movement of the 1980s involved the resource of racial and cultural minority professionals who had personally succeeded in mainstream newspapers or electronic broadcast media but who were aware of, and keenly affected by, the biases that non-Whites encounter on the job. At the same time, they maintained a commitment to see other people of color join them in the profession. The result was the formation of national professional associations for journalists of color with membership categories open to practitioners in print and electronic media as well as related fields. Among them were the National Association of Black Journalists (NABJ), the National Association of Hispanic Journalists (NAHJ), the Asian American Journalists Association (AAJA), and the Native American Journalists Association (NAJA). Each works separately but cooperatively to improve working conditions, increase job opportunities, and sponsor scholarships for promising students.

The organizations hold national and regional conventions where seminars and workshops are presented on issues relevant to news professionals of color. In 1994, the groups cosponsored the first national "Unity" conference in Atlanta, Georgia, where more than 5,000 multicultural journalists convened to assess progress and strategize plans for the future as it relates to the role of people of color in communications media. The conference was covered nationally by the mainstream press throughout its five-day span and was a visible demonstration of the positive impact multicultural advocates had made on media industries over the previous two decades. An outgrowth of that event was the formation of Unity, an association representing all of the minority professional journalism advocacy organizations.

Women of color are also among the ranks of organizations that work to advance the cause of gender equality. Among those organizations are the American Women in Radio and Television (AWRT), which changed its name in 2010 to the Alliance for Women in Media; the Association for Women in Communications (AWC); the Emma L. Bowen Foundation for Minority Interests in Media; and the International Women's Media Foundation (IWMF).

Advocacy in the Entertainment Industry

As documented in previous chapters, anyone critically looking at film and television portrayals of people of color in the early 21st century would find there is still ample need for change. Notwithstanding the unprecedented fact that Denzel Washington and Halle Berry swept the

"Best Actor and Actress" Oscars in 2002, the employment of people of color in the various trades and crafts responsible for movies and entertainment television remains low. The number of strong, meaningful character roles and script plots is sporadic. However, that state of affairs is not for lack of multicultural activism among those who are part of the industry. Over the years, people of color have organized caucuses in the Directors Guild, the Writers Guild, and the Screen Actors Guild. Professional actors and other artisans speak out frequently on the plight of artists of color. Among the groups historically addressing these issues on the West Coast where they could apply direct pressure to Hollywood were the Media Forum, Nosotros, and Asian Americans for Fair Media. The question is whether conditions would be worse were it not for the efforts of those who speak out for multicultural inclusion and sensitivity in entertainment.

As technology brings new forms of communication into use, there will be a continuing need for advocacy voices in public policy to ensure that people of color—particularly those in lower income categories—are active participants in and have access to new information delivery systems.

Advocacy in Media Communications Education

The Association for Education in Journalism and Mass Communication (AEJMC) is the primary organization representing college and university journalism and mass communication education in the United States. Nationally, some 90% of all full-time academic instructors in the discipline are White. In 1968, under the prodding of the late Lionel C. Barrow Jr. (who had written an "open letter" to the organization's convention urging the journalism education establishment to end its de facto segregation against non-Whites), an ad hoc committee was formed by resolution to bring "minority group members into [the AEJ] pipeline."[10] A comprehensive set of multicultural-related goals was established by the AEJMC (the Association for Education in Journalism until 1982). Goals included fund-raising for 500 non-White student scholarships for 1969–1970 and the development of curriculum changes to reflect the contributions of non-White groups in America and media reporting of those contributions.

In 1971, the association's Minorities and Communication (MAC) division was created. Barrow, who later became dean of the school of communications at Howard University, was the division's first head. MAC's membership came to reflect multiculturalism and included a number of active White members. Increasingly over the years the division has become the conscience of the larger body, and the ideals and goals under which MAC was founded have become distant memories. The ambitious goals were never achieved, but the attitude of the association paralleled that of American society once the initial rush of the civil rights movement had passed. In general, the association's members responded as if it were MAC's job alone to handle multicultural affairs.

In 1978, 10 years after the creation of the ad hoc committee that led to MAC's birth, the AEJMC enacted another "Resolution on Minorities," but by 1985 much of its promise, too, was unfulfilled. In 1991, the AEJMC elected its first non-White president when Tony Atwater of Rutgers University assumed the leadership mantle for a year. That same year, perhaps in recognition of the unremarkable progress of multiculturalism in the journalism and mass communications academy, the AEJMC established a Commission on the Status of Minorities to place additional emphasis on the issue. Meanwhile, the Minorities and Communication division continued to press for a greater multicultural presence in journalism and mass communication education through curriculum revision, expanded research, and the maintenance and development of service programs.

Dr. Lionel C. Barrow Jr., former dean of the Howard University School of Communications, was the leading advocate for inclusion of diverse cultural groups in journalism and in journalism education. He founded the Minorities and Communications division of the AEJMC.

Source: Howard University.

In 2000, a fellowship program initiated by Marilyn Kern-Foxworth (the AEJMC's first African American woman president) and Shirley Staples Carter (a Black woman, then director of the Wichita State University communications school) was created to groom persons of color and women for journalism education leadership positions. The Journalism and Mass Communication Leadership Institute for Diversity (JLID) was a joint effort of the AEJMC and the Association of Schools of Journalism and Mass Communication (ASJMC) to bring underrepresented groups into the ranks of college department chairs and deans.

In the mid-1980s, partly spurred by publication of the first edition of this book, a significant number of journalism and mass communication academic units began offering courses on the role of racial minority groups in communications history and response to their treatment in the general audience media. Over the past three decades, other instructional materials, including textbooks, textbook supplements, and audiovisual presentations, have been developed to meet the increased interest in the subject. In the second decade of the 21st century, increased interest in scholarly research and course offerings have broadened the scope of diversity in journalism and mass media education to include works on gender and other areas of media inadequacy of representation.

The Accrediting Council on Education in Journalism and Mass Communications (ACEJMC) incorporated recognition of multicultural inclusion in faculty hiring (1982) and curriculum (1992) as part of accrediting standards. Despite the fact that the American journalism academy remained at least 90% White into the 21st century, there is no record of any college or university having lost its accreditation for lack of multicultural or gender representation on its faculty. A few, however, have been afforded one-year provisional accreditation to improve their record at risk of losing accreditation. The number of non-White doctoral graduates in journalism and mass communication in the early 2000s remained less than a trickle for the new faculty "pipeline" mentioned in AEJ's 1968 "minorities" resolution, although at the graduate school level there was discernable increase in students of color from foreign countries.[11] By 2009, the annual survey of journalism and mass communications students published by the University of Georgia found only 9.4% of doctoral graduates were African American, and Latinos composed only 2% of the total.

Overview: Confronting the Status Quo Toward Multiculturalism

Throughout their experiences in American society, peoples of color have expressed their discontent with the treatment they received from Anglocentric media industries. Persons of color believed it was necessary to protect themselves from the harmful effects of the distorted portrayals and negative news reporting of American mass media. Their responses took several forms, but the object was the same—they wanted to change the status quo that had offended and disturbed them. Each group developed advocates who fought for changes and reform of hegemonic media. With the passage of the Civil Rights Act in 1964, legal avenues were opened along which the advocacy activists could drive their point. Through the leverage provided by federal regulation of the broadcasting industry, major legal victories were won, and some of the worst offenders were driven off the air. Meanwhile, the American free-enterprise philosophy that encouraged multiple business ownership and the development of conglomerates ushered in the concept of cross-media ownership. Where broadcast licensees and newspaper groups shared common ownership, multicultural advocates had opportunities to affect the slow-to-integrate newspaper industry.

Individual professional activists stimulated major mainstream media organizations and trade associations to fund newspaper integration efforts. They served to keep the industry's "feet to the fire" on the issues of multicultural hiring, training, and coverage. Meanwhile, professional journalists of color, who had benefited from the activists' efforts to open doors to employment, began forming their own organizations on the local, regional, and national levels, which, in turn, became empowered institutional advocates for the entire communications spectrum. Although the film and entertainment television industries have multicultural advocacy groups as well as articulate spokespersons among Hollywood actors, little visible progress is apparent when the end products are considered. Technological innovations that may create new outlets for racial and cultural minority expression and the trend toward specialized audience media may force changes in the industry as people of color continue to be desirable target audiences for economic reasons.

Meanwhile, college and university educators, responsible for the training and ethical development of young mass media professionals, have been slow to meet the challenge of multiculturalism for an increasingly pluralistic American society. But, spurred by the efforts of internal advocates, the AEJMC has increased its efforts to racially diversify the higher education academy. While the professorate in American colleges remained virtually all White and male, course offerings began to reflect some progress toward multicultural inclusion in the curriculum. Hopefully, the inclusion of multicultural requirements as criteria for the accreditation of journalism and mass communication programs will lead to improvement of racial sensitivity and inclusiveness in professional media practitioners and their work.

Notes

1. "To Our Patrons," *Freedom's Journal,* March 16, 1827, 1.
2. Frederick G. Detweiler, *The Negro Press in the United States* (University of Chicago Press, 1922), 149.
3. Ibid., 150.
4. Translation from Spanish cited in José E. Limon, "Stereotyping and Chicano Resistance: An Historical Dimension," *Aztlán* 4 (No. 2, Fall 1973): 263.

5. Ibid.

6. Ibid.

7. Cited in Elaine H. Kim, *Asian American Literature* (Temple University Press, 1982), 31.

8. John Naisbitt, *Megatrends* (Warner Books, 1982), 112.

9. Emil Ward, "Advocating the Minority Interest: Actors and Cases," *Small Voices and Great Triumphs,* ed. Bernard Rubin (Praeger, 1980), 250.

10. Lionel C. Barrow Jr., *The Minorities and Communication Division—The Beginning,* a paper delivered before the Minorities and Communication Division, Association for Education in Journalism, at the 63rd Annual AEJ Conference, Boston University, August 1980.

11. See L. Becker, G. Kosicki, W. Lowery, J. Prine, and A. Punathambekar, "Undergrad Enrollments Level Off, Graduate Education Declines," *Journalism and Mass Communication Educator* 55 (No. 3, 2000): 68–80.

Access

10

Equitable Hiring Principles Elude Media Employers

In 1968, the Kerner Commission criticized news media and—by extension—other American mass communications industries for the lack of cultural diversity in their workforces. The commission's report noted that employment discrimination was a major reason for the stereotypical and often exclusionary practices that created a divided society and a large number of angry and disaffected citizens of color. The intervening years have seen the industries make limited and uneven progress toward a more balanced cultural representation in staffing and executive levels.

Media images in popular culture that are fashioned only through the eyes of Anglo European male creators and decision makers result in socially dysfunctional messages. The Kerner report recommended that hiring a culturally diverse workforce would result in more representative news content to the benefit of American society. Historically, people of color and women had already been very aware of discriminatory hiring practices in media professions and industries for generations. The effects of their historical exclusion as determinants of whether and how they were portrayed created in them attitudes ranging from futility to indifference to hostility.

Very little hegemonic attention was focused on minority group employment in media prior to the civil rights movement in the 1960s. By the late 1960s, U.S. governmental agencies had been formed to address the question of fair employment practices in American business and labor. Among those agencies were the Equal Employment Opportunity Commission (EEOC) and the U.S. Commission on Civil Rights. Upon publication of the Kerner Commission's strong indictment of mass media culpability in perpetuating racial discrimination, both the EEOC and the Commission on Civil Rights turned their attention to media hiring practices. The Kerner report stimulated some news media professional associations into assessing their hiring records. These efforts can be summarized by looking at racial employment patterns in the two major mass media categories of entertainment and news.

Background: Film and Television Entertainment Industries to 2000

Previous chapters in this book have discussed racial, cultural, and gender portrayals in Hollywood movies and television and the roles in which the actors were employed. Here we discover the nature of the participation of people of color in behind-the-scenes crafts and in production management roles. In 1969, the EEOC held hearings in Los Angeles on minority employment in the film industry. At that time, there was no assessment of employment of South Asian Indians or persons of Middle Eastern heritage. The commission found Hollywood's non-White employment rates were well below the average for other industries, which, themselves, had poor hiring records. Furthermore, the film industry data revealed discriminatory hiring practices in nearly every occupational category whether white collar or blue collar.

The EEOC concluded:

> The motion picture industry reports approximately 19,000 employees, 13,000 of whom are white collar workers. But it is not the raw numbers of people employed that is significant, it is the fact that the industry plays a critical role in influencing public opinion and creating this country's image of itself. In order to portray accurately the nation's minority groups, the industry must employ minority personnel at all levels . . .
>
> The Equal Employment Opportunity Commission's analysis indicates that this is not happening.[1]

At that time, a studio official who testified before the commission said that of 81 management level personnel only three were people of color. Two were Latino, the single Black manager headed the janitorial department, and there were no Asian or Native American managers. The studio executive also testified that his organization employed 184 workers classified as technicians. Of that number, only five were non-Whites, three Latinos, one Black, and one Asian. Generally, in the late 1960s, the non-White employment percentage among other industries in the Los Angeles metropolitan statistical area was twice that of the movie industry where non-Whites

composed approximately 40% of the Los Angeles metropolitan area population but made up only 3% of the movie industry labor force.

In 1977, the U.S. Commission on Civil Rights conducted its investigation of the television entertainment industry and also convened a hearing
in Los Angeles. Among those called to testify were officials of the various
unions representing producers, directors, and writers as well as non-White
craftsmen in the several theatrical trades. One witness, a member of the
Cherokee Nation, testified about how a trade union "lost" the job application of a highly skilled Native American worker. When a union official was
confronted about the incident, he replied, "No one tells us who we have to
hire or anything of that matter. We decide that."[2] Other testimony revealed
a union scheme to systematically phase out Blacks who attained union
membership by seeking their suspension without due process hearings.
Additionally, experienced union members of color were overlooked for
job promotion while young Whites, who were sons of union journeymen,
obtained superior status directly out of high school without job experience. These examples of systematic discrimination and nepotism in the
television industry were not countermanded by either network executives
or union officials. The civil rights commission noted the television entertainment industry had not assumed equal employment opportunity
responsibilities in hiring practices.

Data were compiled over a three-year period (1974–1976) on union
rosters representing the workers who produced the movies, situation comedies, and variety programs televised to millions of American viewers.
Crafts represented in the trade union data included makeup artists, pro-
jectionists, prop workers, set designers, script supervisors, story analysts,
and camera operators, among others. Keeping in mind that eight years had
elapsed since the EEOC had investigated the movie industry, the television
trade union data presented at the 1977 hearing showed an average of only
8% non-White employment for the period. More revealing was the fact
that not even one person of color obtained work during the three years as
either a script supervisor or a story analyst according to data supplied to
the U.S. Commission on Civil Rights. Although the industry was (as was
American society in general) experiencing the waning years of emphasis
on affirmative action, only 50% of non-Whites who applied for union
rosters achieved their goal. Meanwhile, 62% of the White applicants were
successful during the same period.

In August 1977, the civil rights commission published its findings on
racial and female employment in television.[3] For historical perspective, it
must be noted that in 1969 the Federal Communications Commission
(FCC) had adopted equal employment opportunity guidelines prohibiting
job discrimination by broadcast licensees. The implied penalty was loss of
license. It was during this period that the term *twofer* became part of the
lexicon of American broadcasting. A twofer was any woman employed in
broadcasting who happened to also be non-White. Broadcast executives

were able to list such women in their hiring statistics twice, once under the gender category and again under the ethnic category—a "two-for-one" employee. The tabulated result padded the actual affirmative action employment total. The use of twofers and other manipulative measures created some unusual employment data reported by American broadcasters. In an attempt to make the hiring and placement of people of color in upper-level job categories seem more equitable, the industry reported an astonishing 45% increase in ethnic managers between 1971 and 1975. At the same time, however, the proportion of all employees in those job categories increased by only 13%. A close look at the broadcasters' figures also revealed a dramatic decline in the number of clerical and service jobs listed. These data prompted a public interest group to ask, "Do more executives need fewer clerks to serve them? Do larger staffs need less janitorial service?"[4] It was obvious that broadcasters had merely reclassified their non-White employees into upper job categories while keeping them on the same old jobs with the same low salaries. Most of these "managers," particularly in television, held jobs with such titles as "Community Relations Director" or "Manager of Community Affairs." Almost without exception even those persons (who were far removed from day-to-day programming decisions) reported to a White male department head.

Among the significant conclusions drawn in 1977 by the U.S. Commission on Civil Rights regarding the employment of non-Whites in television were:

— An underlying assumption by television executives that realistic representation of non-Whites would diminish the medium's ability to attract the largest possible audience.

— Broadcasters misrepresented to the FCC the actual employment status of non-Whites and women via reports on FCC Form 395.

— People of color were not fully utilized at all levels of station management or at all levels of local station operations.

— White males held the overwhelming majority of decision-making positions.

— Non-Whites held subsidiary positions.

— Increased multicultural visibility as on-air talent belied the lack of minority representation in managerial and other jobs off camera; in other words, people of color were merely "window dressing."

Employment conditions changed little in the 1980s. FCC statistics released in 1982 showed that non-Whites held about 17% of all jobs in broadcast television and about 14% in cable TV. Although the FCC reported the number of non-White "officials and managers" to be 9%, it still included in that category low authoritative positions such as promotion directors and research directors, jobs most frequently held by people of color.[5] Those figures included the small and slowly growing number of TV stations that are owned by people of color and have largely non-White management staffs.

Another round of hearings descended upon Hollywood and the television industry on June 1, 1983, when the House Subcommittee on Telecommunications, Consumer Protection, and Finance heard from a group of Black actors led by Sidney Poitier. Poitier, the first Black to win an Oscar for "Best Actor," urged the committee to instigate a full-scale investigation of the "flagrant unfairness in the hiring practices of producers, the studios and the networks." Poitier's words seemed to echo the testimony of other witnesses who had appeared nearly 15 years earlier before another federal committee.

But, by the 1990s, EEOC employment data revealed that people of color had made significant strides in terms of overall share in the industry workforce. In 1969, non-Whites composed only 3% of the motion picture industry labor force but grew to more than 24% by 1991. Over the next decade, people

Oscar-winning actor Sidney Poitier spearheaded congressional hearing testimony about employment in the motion picture industry in 1983. He called the industry's discriminatory hiring practices "flagrant."

Source: ©iStockphoto.com/EdStock.

of color experienced only a very modest increase to 27% (see Table 10.1), according to EEOC data collected in the Hollywood region (Los Angeles/ Long Beach, California, statistical area). It should be noted, however, that non-Whites composed more than half of the resident population in the area. In a reflection of general demographic trends, Blacks had the largest "minority" share of industry jobs in 1991 (11%), but by 2000 their percentage had been surpassed by both Latino and Asian Americans. Significantly, during the same time period, the total percentage of persons of color holding jobs in the white-collar category of "officials and managers" dropped from 11% to under 6%.

The lack of significant progress in the entertainment industry was perhaps most revealed in 1999. Just before the turn of the new century, the major television networks announced their prime-time fall program lineups. Of the 26 new shows, none starred an African American in a leading role, and few even featured actors of color in secondary roles. Activist groups supporting underrepresented Americans were stunned. A major Latino organization, the National Council of La Raza, spearheaded a protest called the "National Brownout" and urged television viewers to turn off their sets for the entire week of September 12 that year. Kweisi Mfume, then head of the National Association for the Advancement of Colored People (NAACP), also called for a boycott and threatened legal action against the networks' FCC licenses. By November, a series of hearings was convened in Los Angeles in which each network's chief executive was invited to testify. Among the CEOs, only Leslie Moonves of CBS attended and spoke at the hearing. Lower-level executives from the other three networks (ABC, NBC, and Fox) attended but were not allowed to speak. Eventually, all of the networks agreed to develop minority hiring initiatives in acting, directing, writing, and producing program content. CBS soon launched a predominantly Black drama series (*City of Angels*), but it lasted only two seasons. A Latino family drama (*American Family*) was also developed for CBS for the 2000–2001 programming year, but the network did not include the show in its schedule.

Table 10.1   Minority Employment in Motion Picture Labor Force, 2000

	Percent of Total	Percent Officials/Mgrs.	Percent White Collar	Percent Blue Collar
Blacks	6.6	1.5	4.4	0.7
Latinos	10.9	2.0	6.0	2.8
Asians	9.3	2.3	6.4	0.6
Native Amer.	0.5	0.1	0.2	0.1
	27.3	5.9	17.0	4.2

Source: U.S. Equal Employment Opportunity Commission.

Film and Television Entertainment Employment in the New Century

If there was any momentum in the employment of underrepresented cultural groups going forward from the protests of the latter 20th century, it was soon lost when the calendar turned to the new millennium. By the middle of the first decade, Hollywood and the television industry had clearly returned to their old patterns. Hollywood critic Nikki Finke reacted strongly in her "Deadline" blog to the old corporate media refrain regarding minority hiring inertia, "I can't find anyone qualified." Finke posted (June 21, 2006) in response to a *Los Angeles Times* article by Patrick Goldstein complaining that Hollywood's lack of more racial and cultural diversity was not for a lack of interest or desire. Goldstein quoted 20th Century Fox executive Jim Gianopulos as saying "we're constantly searching for creative [people of color]. But it's a really difficult question and we haven't found an answer yet." Finke noted, however, that Gianopulos failed to attend his studio's "diversity" dinner event that had been arranged by the company's diversity department for the purpose of meeting and cultivating contacts with talented professionals of color. There were 50 or 60 Black, Latino, and Asian executives and producers in attendance. One attendee reported disappointment in the event when several of Gianopulos's staff members moved about the room in "speed dating" fashion introducing themselves. The eventual result was that none of the persons of color were considered or hired for any studio production jobs that likely would have provided 20th Century Fox with more culturally and racially nuanced theatrical movies.

In 2010, sociologist Darnell Hunt discussed his research on the employment of people of color in Hollywood during a hearing on the then-proposed merger of Comcast and NBCUniversal. Hunt has served on the U.S. Commission on Civil Rights and conducted studies on the minority hiring issue for the Screen Actors Guild and the Writers Guild of America. In his testimony, Hunt said that the Hollywood entertainment industry was "profoundly insular" and was one that "white males have traditionally dominated." He concluded that "employment opportunities rest squarely on personal networks largely defined by race and gender."

Sadly, the Hollywood employment data that Hunt gathered for the Writers Guild of America do not require illustrative tables, graphs, or bar charts to convey his findings. In the motion picture industry, minority employment was only 6% for the years 2005 through 2008, and in 2009 it dipped to just 5%. In the television entertainment industry, minority employment for the years 2005 through 2009 was at 10%, except for 2007 when it dipped to 9%. It is important to keep in mind that the underrepresented groups under consideration composed about one third of the U.S. population during those years. Hunt described the relationship between people of color and the motion picture and television industries in America as a circular chain of five components: (1) the display of insensitive and offensive portrayals, (2) public outrage and/or pressure, (3) the release of "depressing" statistics about minority exclusion from and underemployment in the industry, (4) token or symbolic industry response designed to appease critics, and (5) a return to business-as-usual practices that perpetuate the dominance of White males over the industry.

Background: Print and Broadcast News Media to 2000

Employment opportunities for people of color in professional journalism progressed at a pace similar to that of the motion picture entertainment industry over the last 30 years of the 20th century following the 1968 Kerner Commission report. A 1992 study of journalists working for all forms of news organizations (daily and weekly newspapers, news services, magazines, radio and television stations) found non-Whites to compose only 8.2% of the journalistic workforce.[7] The daily newspaper industry began to assess the racial composition of its labor force in the early 1970s. The American Society of Newspaper Editors—now the American Society of News Editors (ASNE)—reported that only 1.6% of daily newspaper professionals were members of underrepresented racial groups in 1972.

Interestingly, in the same year (1972), a Radio-Television News Directors Association (RTNDA) survey found that non-Whites held 14% of commercial television news jobs and 10% of those in radio news, figures that remained basically constant until the late 1980s. In 1988, RTNDA research revealed that television news hiring for non-Whites had increased to 16%, but radio had slipped to only 8%. By 1992, the percentage of non-Whites in the television news workforce had grown to 18.5%, and radio had reversed its decline with 11%. Nevertheless, the broadcasting industry moved much more quickly on the issue of multicultural hiring in news because radio and television frequencies are licensed by a governmental agency, the FCC, which has a regulatory mandate to ensure its licensees adhere to equal opportunity employment practices. Newspapers, on the other hand, are private enterprises that must be motivated by conscience, economics, or social pressure to improve their employment practices. Given that circumstance, there is little mystery why some daily newspapers have been slow to embrace racial diversity. Some editors have been hostile to the idea of hiring non-White staff members and publicly expressed their attitudes on the issue. The editor of one of the largest dailies in the Midwest once responded on the ASNE minority hiring survey that, "generally, hiring minorities means reducing standards temporarily. Except for one reporter and one news editor, every minority person we've hired in 10 years was less qualified than a concurrently available White."[8]

The discussion about qualifications of people of color to perform as journalists has been a sensitive one on a number of fronts. Even the Kerner report noted that news media officials complained that too few "qualified" minorities were available for hire. The implications raised the ire of some who observed that people of color have found success in fields ranging from medicine to engineering to law and the arts, and so on, but somehow are not "qualified" to be writers, reporters, and editors for news media. On that issue, one White newspaper editor agreed. "The business isn't magic. Mostly, it's trial-and-error training. If the word skills are adequate, any minority can be trained to do any newsroom task that any non-minority can do."[9]

In 1982, the *Columbia Journalism Review* reported that an angry exchange on the issue took place during a press coverage forum in New York City. In a confrontation reminiscent of Breed's study of newsroom policy (Chapter 6), WNBC-TV news correspondent Gabe Pressman responded to the charge of professional racism by invoking the importance of traditional standards of quality in reporting. J. J. Gonzalez, then a reporter for WCBS-TV, rose from the audience to proclaim, "Who passes . . . judgment on competency? Come on, now! Don't tell me 'competency' . . . When you get the competent person in, he is not allowed [to do the job.] So stop your bull!"[10]

Conservative media critic William McGowan joined the debate in support of the notion that a multicultural workforce in American newsrooms contributed to a "decline" in the quality of journalism. In his 2003 book *Coloring the News,* McGowan asserted that efforts to culturally diversify the journalism profession "corrupts" news media. Generally—notwithstanding McGowan's view—the debate over whether minority newspersons were less qualified than White journalists subsided after 2000 in view of the overwhelming professional successes they had attained in print and broadcasting venues nationwide.

Meanwhile, the emphasis turned instead to whether newsroom and other mass media efforts at multicultural inclusiveness were "politically correct" in a time when the terms *quota* and *affirmative action* were deemed passé. In 2001, R. D. Volkman, publisher of the *North Sioux City Times* in South Dakota, wrote in a trade journal, "We do not hire minorities merely to achieve a racial mix in our office. We tend not to hire any American-born and schooled minorities." Volkman continued, "We actually practice 'red lining' against graduates of certain colleges . . . we advise our newspaper brethren to do as we do, and to even divest themselves of overly [politically correct] staff members." The publisher concluded that "America . . . is tired of affirmative action" and that hiring minorities "is dangerous for newspapers who plan for a long future."[11]

That same year, an incident reported in the RTNDA newsletter highlighted another aspect of racial insensitivity among newspaper editors. The article described an entertainment event at the ASNE convention in Washington: "On stage was a white man donning a black wig and Coke-bottle glasses, gesturing wildly and shouting 'ching, ching, chong, chong' in a satirical commentary on Chinese-American relations in the aftermath of the U.S. spy plane incident. The audience of mostly white newspaper editors howled." The article noted that "the issue wasn't simply that white people were using negative stereotypes in an attempt to be funny . . . [but] that hundreds of newspaper editors . . . were hysterical with laughter as the skit went on. By all reports, no one stood up to protest, no one from ASNE ever apologized for the insensitivity of the mostly white editors." A student intern who witnessed the incident asked on ASNE's website, "Did they think the Chinese American community would have found that skit amusing? Would they have laughed at a white man in blackface if the crisis concerned an African country?"[12]

In summarizing minority hiring during the last two decades of the 20th century, research data show that in 1980 non-Whites represented only 4.9% of journalists working for the nearly 1,750 daily newspapers in the nation. The newspaper industry experienced a multicultural employment growth rate of less than 1% between 1980 and 1985 according to ASNE research data. Economic reversals decreased the number of daily newspapers to about 1,550 in 1995, and multiracial hiring did not exceed the 10% level until that year (see Table 10.2). Yet, 1995 was also a year in which only about half of all daily newspapers in the United States still had no journalists of color on their staffs. In 1998, ASNE revised its goal—established in 1978—that the racial composition of America's newsrooms would reach parity with the nation's population demographics by 2000. But, when the millennium year arrived, non-Whites were only 11.8% of the daily newspaper editorial workforce. The ASNE leadership then established a new diversity goal to achieve "by or before 2025."

In the broadcasting and newspaper industries, the gains that have been made must also be considered in view of the sagging U.S. economic fortunes of the early 1990s, and again in 2010 and 2011, that forced staff layoffs and resulted in the closing of many newspapers and network television news bureaus. In 1998, the Radio-Television News Directors Association adopted cultural diversity as one of its "core values" by proclaiming one of its purposes was "to diversify the nation's newsrooms and improve the quality of electronic journalism through meaningful coverage of communities and through the advancement of minority journalists to key decision-making and top management positions." (To better reflect the technological changes in its industry, the Radio-Television News Directors Association [RTNDA] changed its name to the Radio Television Digital

Table 10.2   Minority Employment Rate at 5-Year Intervals in Daily Newspapers, 1980–2000

Year	Minority Percentage	Percentage Increase
1980	4.9	—
1985	5.8	0.9
1990	7.9	2.1
1995	10.9	3.0
2000	11.8	0.9

Source: Based on research data compiled by the American Society of News Editors.

News Association [RTDNA] in 2010.) A tenet of RTDNA's mission statement is "encouraging diversity in news organizations and in news coverage," and for many years the organization has annually sponsored research on the status of women and minorities in the electronic news and information industry.

Retaining Media Professionals of Color

Whereas the industry rationale for the dearth of non-Whites in the workforce had been "we can't find any qualified," a companion issue emerged before the 21st century began: "We can't keep the qualified minorities we hire." The titles of the following studies and reports issued since 1990 are instructive: "Why Asian-American Journalists Leave Journalism and Why They Stay" (Asian American Journalists Association, 1990), "Employee Departure Patterns in the Newspaper Industry" (Task Force on Minorities in the Newspaper Business, 1991), and "The Newsroom Barometer: Job Satisfaction and the Impact of Racial Diversity at U.S. Daily Newspapers" (Ted Pease and J. Frazier Smith, Ohio University, 1991). In addition, a 1992 study of *The American Journalist in the 1990s* by Indiana University professors David Weaver and G. Cleveland Wilhoit revealed "a serious problem of retention may be just over the horizon" and that "more than 20 percent of those [journalists] surveyed said they plan to leave the field in five years, double the figure of 1982–83."[13] That prediction came true as the percentage of non-White newspaper journalists treadmilled because their departure rate from the profession matched or exceeded the number of those being hired. An ASNE survey found that although newspapers hired 600 entry-level non-White journalists in 2001, 698 left the profession that year.

The study by Pease and Smith revealed the reasons underlying the exodus of minorities from newspaper staffs:

— 71% of non-White journalists said their papers cover issues of concern to their racial constituency marginally or poorly; 50% of White journalists agreed.

— Journalists of color (63%) were twice as likely as their White colleagues (31%) to believe that race plays a role in newsroom assignments, promotions, and advancement.

— 72% of non-Whites and 35% of Whites said newsroom managers and supervisors doubt the ability of journalists of color to perform their jobs adequately.

Pease and Smith concluded, "These results paint a picture of newsrooms in which journalists of color feel themselves besieged because of their race.

It's a picture few whites are aware of."[14] The issue of retention of non-White journalists was not confined to newspapers. Randy Daniels, a Black journalist, left his job as a CBS correspondent in the 1980s after nearly 10 years because he saw no career advancement opportunities in the network: "I met with every level of management at CBS News . . . over issues that specifically relate to Blacks and other minorities . . . When it became clear to me that such meetings accomplished nothing, I chose to leave and work where my ideas were wanted and needed . . . I have found my race an impediment to being assigned major stories across the entire spectrum of news."[15] More than 20 years later in 2002, David Honig, executive director of the Minority Media and Telecommunications Council, reported that of 837 job listings posted on the Internet websites of broadcasters from 35 states, 348 (42%) did not contain equal employment opportunity notices. The omission signaled a failure to maintain even the pretense that broadcasting employers were committed to fair employment policies.

Newsroom Employment in the New Media Era

In the latter half of the first decade of the 21st century, major changes in communications technology transformed the media landscape, and new platforms for the delivery of news and public information emerged. Minority professionals were impacted heavily as traditional newspapers and broadcast news outlets scrambled to remain relevant in the wake of new social media platforms and electronic devices such as smartphones and tablets. The U.S. Congressional Research Service reported that between 2008 and 2010 eight major daily newspaper chains declared bankruptcy, although most survived through reorganizations and mergers. Meanwhile, between 2007 and 2010 the industry lost 13,500 jobs. In times of employment upheaval, people of color brace themselves for the realization of an old adage "last hired, first fired." Some found outlets for their services in online news services, blogs, or newly created websites developed by traditional print and broadcast media designed specifically to reach minority audiences. Hiring data reflected these trends, and minority employment percentages declined accordingly, as shown in Table 10.3.

RTDNA research data for the television news industry reveals that although minorities have their largest presence among the major organizations responsible for America's news and public information, there was nearly a 3.5% decline in minority journalists in 2010 from 2008 (see Table 10.4). This was during a period that saw significant news stories originate from parts of the world where the cultural interpretation of journalists of color could greatly contribute to a better-informed U.S. citizenry. Examples include such news events as immigration of persons from Mexico and Central America, the religious conflicts and wars in the

Table 10.3 Minority Employment Rate at 2-Year Intervals in Daily Newspapers, 2006–2010

Year	Minority Percentage	Percentage Change
2006	13.7	—
2008	13.5	– 0.2
2010	13.3	– 0.2

Source: Based on research data compiled by the American Society of News Editors.

Table 10.4 Minority Employment Rate at 2-Year Intervals in Television News, 2006–2010

Year	Minority Percentage	Percentage Change
2006	22.2	—
2008	23.6	1.4
2010	20.2	– 3.4

Source: Based on research data compiled by RTDNA/Hofstra University.

Middle East, and the continuing emergence of China and India as world economic powers. By the middle of the decade, the major cable and network news operations had begun to expand their reporting and commentary staffs to include journalists who could bring both reporting and cultural expertise to American audiences.

The hiring and staffing of minorities in radio news operations took a steep decline of more than 50% over the two-year period between 2008 and 2010 (see Table 10.5). The industry experienced contraction and consolidation throughout the decade as only a few national commercial radio syndicates controlled the airwaves. Although the percentages of minority news personnel shrunk, the industry continued to show increases in the employment of women as reporters and news executives.

Table 10.6 provides an overview of minority employment distribution among the major American news media platforms for the year 2010. Black television news personnel have the largest representation of any minority group. No comparable data are available for South Asian Indians or newspersons of Middle Eastern descent.

The decline in the number of minority journalists over the 10-year period 2000–2010 was startling. For example, ASNE data for 2010 showed there were 929 fewer Black journalists in American newsrooms than were recorded in 2001, a 31.5% decline.

Table 10.5   Minority Employment Rate at 2-Year Intervals in Radio News, 2006–2010

Year	Minority Percentage	Percentage Change
2006	7.4	—
2008	11.8	4.4
2010	5.1	– 6.7

Source: Based on research data compiled by RTDNA/Hofstra University.

Table 10.6   Minority Newsroom Employment in General Audience English-Language Media, 2010

	% Black	% Latino	% Asian	% Native American
Television	11.5	5.8	2.3	0.5
Radio	2.9	0.7	0.4	1.1
Daily Newspaper	4.9	4.6	3.3	0.5
Total	**19.3**	**11.1**	**6.0**	**2.1**

Source: Based on research data compiled by RTDNA/Hofstra University and ASNE.

Education and Training

Another major issue in the quest to improve racial diversity in news media is the preparation and training of future journalists of color. This is the juncture where the nation's secondary schools, colleges, and universities assume the spotlight. Educational institutions were asked by the Kerner Commission to develop training programs as early as the high school level with efforts to be "intensified at colleges." There have been obstacles, however, facing educators. For example, the small number of non-White students enrolled in journalism education programs partly reflects the historic discrimination against them in the news professions. As noted elsewhere in this book, the often negative and sporadic coverage of the non-White racial groups in American media has created a distrust and lack of media credibility among them. The result was lessened interest in the field among college-bound high school students of color when compared to the interest of their White counterparts.

In 1992, non-White students composed about 14% of the staffs of accredited college and university campus media, excluding those at historically Black institutions and the University of Hawaii where the student body is predominantly Asian.[16] This exceeded the percentage of non-Whites on professional newspaper staffs that year and remained larger than the figure attained by the professional industry a decade later. A survey released in 2000 projected about 23% of undergraduate students enrolled in journalism and mass communications programs nationally were non-White. They were categorized as 10.4% Black, 6.6% Latino, 2.8% Asian, and 1.3% Native American.[17] A decade later, the survey of collegiate journalism and mass communications programs reported that ethnic minority students composed 29.6% of undergraduates categorized as 14.5% Black, 10.4% Latino, 4% Asian, and 0.7% Native American.[18] In 2000, some 62.8% of undergraduate students were female with the number increasing slightly to 63.5% in 2010.

In 1978, the major academic journalism organization, the Association for Education in Journalism (now the Association for Education in Journalism and Mass Communication), adopted a "Resolution on Minorities." Eight years earlier, the AEJMC had created a Minorities and Communication division with a multiracial membership base, but by the time the resolution was adopted the division's membership was almost entirely composed of academicians of color.

In the 1990s, attendance at convention meetings of the Minorities and Communication (MAC) division led to the formation of a Commission on the Status of Minorities. Efforts of both the MAC division and the commission have focused on improving the cultural diversity of the journalism and mass communications curriculum and encouragement of research by and about people of color and their relationship to media.

Meanwhile, the organization charged with setting standards and certifying college journalism education programs is the Accrediting Council on Education in Journalism and Mass Communications (ACEJMC). The ACEJMC developed 12 criteria—called standards—to measure the quality of a program. The most controversial of the criteria was Standard 12, the one that addressed issues of cultural and gender diversity. Standard 12 required accredited academic journalism units to develop and follow a plan for ensuring racial and gender inclusiveness. In 2002, there were 105 journalism programs accredited by the ACEJMC. Over the years, Standard 12 sparked controversy because many units received accreditation despite not "being in compliance" with the criteria for hiring non-White faculty or enrolling students of color or for including multicultural issues in various courses in the curriculum. In 1998, 11.4% of the AEJMC membership was reported to be people of color.[19] In 2003, the ACEJMC scrapped Standard 12 in a revision of its accreditation requirements and effective with the 2004 academic year incorporated its principles within Standard 3, "Diversity and Inclusiveness."

Other Training Programs

Following the 1968 Kerner report, a number of training programs were established by media organizations and professional groups to augment the journalism education establishment in preparing marginalized groups for entry into the workforce. Perhaps most well known was the Summer Program for Minority Journalists. The program's history paralleled the interest level and commitment afforded the issue of multiracial inclusiveness by major media corporations and other interested parties. In the wake of the Kerner report, the Ford Foundation supported creation of a training program at Columbia University briefly known as the Michele Clark Program for Minority Journalists. The project trained and placed 70 newspeople of color in print and broadcasting jobs from 1968 to 1974. By the time it lost its funding support in 1974, the program had been responsible for 20% of all journalists of color employed in daily newspapers nationally. Although the program was effective, the loss of financial support reflected the short-term commitment of the nation to the cause of news media integration. Fortunately, with seed money from the Gannett Foundation (now Freedom Forum), the program was revived in Berkeley, California, as a newspaper-only training project under the auspices of the Institute for Journalism Education (IJE). IJE was formed by a dedicated interracial group of professionals to continue the struggle for racial parity in journalism. In 1978, IJE began a similar program to train minority editors at the University of Arizona also utilizing professionals as instructors. In 1993, IJE was renamed the Robert C. Maynard Institute for Journalism Education in memory of one of its founders, a Black journalist, editor, and publisher, who died earlier that year.

Acting on the belief that the issue of non-White employment is one of "supply and demand," a few newspaper organizations instituted and maintained "in-house" training programs for aspiring journalists of color to buttress what they considered to be an inadequate pool of job candidates. However, researchers at the University of Georgia say an analysis of data collected in 2001 refutes the notion that qualified non-White college journalism graduates were in short supply. "The inescapable conclusion from data we have gathered is that large numbers of minorities graduate from journalism programs, large numbers seek media jobs, and large numbers have the basic skills needed for media jobs."[20] Moreover, they noted that, had U.S. daily newspapers hired all the college minority graduates who sought jobs with them in 2001, the industry would have added more than 2,500 journalists of color to their staffs. The result would have raised the ASNE-reported percentage of such journalists in the industry by about 3%. Thus, the researchers concluded, "The problem isn't supply . . . The problem is that there is not a suitable link between supply and demand."

21st-Century Discrimination Against . . . Whom?

In summary, the hiring records of the motion picture and television entertainment industries in hiring non-Whites were found to be unacceptable by federal agencies that conducted investigations from the late 1960s through the mid-1980s. But by the 1990s the number of non-White employees had increased substantially to nearly approximate their percentage in the general population. Broadcasters, particularly in television, were the first to react to federal pressures because of the licensing power of the FCC. But, although their hiring rate initially exceeded those of companion media industries, broadcasters were caught cheating in reporting racial hiring statistics. One example was the ploy of counting non-White female employees twice, so-called twofers, in an effort to pad hiring figures. Generally, broadcast industry hiring of journalists of color took a back seat to that of women in the late 1970s and 1980s.

Coincidentally, as hiring of non-Whites slowed, White women were making rapid progress in assuming positions in both management and other job categories. In television, people of color were found primarily in visible "on-air" positions but were not generally found in decision-making management jobs. Perhaps the most significant indicator of the broadcast news industry's true commitment to cultural diversity is that when legal challenges eliminated FCC equal employment guidelines, hiring of non-Whites declined dramatically. Juan Gonzalez, then president of the National Association of Hispanic Journalists, noted that in 2001 Latino employment in the industry declined by more than 20% from the previous year. "It's deeply troubling to see this kind of backsliding after years of talk from industry leaders about the importance of diversity and the changing face of America," said Gonzalez, a columnist for the New York *Daily News*.[21]

Power and Positions: Gender and the Evening News

The absence of women in prominent news media roles is perhaps no more blatant than in the television network evening news anchor positions—an all-male bastion until 2006 when Katie Couric began her five-year stint as anchor of the *CBS Evening News*. As this is written, no other women or people of color have been chosen to fill the anchor chairs on a permanent basis although Connie Chung served as co-anchor of the *NBC Nightly News* from 1995 to 1995 with Dan Rather.

In the early 1980s, audience researchers found that viewers—both men and women—believed women lacked the necessary authority and reliability to fill the coveted evening anchor slots. Some network executives acknowledged that despite the gains women have made since Barbara Walters appeared on NBC's *Today* show in 1961, many television viewers still

Katie Couric became the first woman to anchor a network evening news program when she assumed the position for CBS from 2006 to 2011. No woman of color had yet attained that role by summer of 2012.

Source: Photograph by Joella Marano.

want the evening news delivered by a patriarchal figure. Erik Sorenson, president of MSNBC, who was executive producer of the failed CBS newscast that paired Connie Chung with Dan Rather, said in 2002 the American culture was not yet ready to embrace a woman in that role because of a perceived lack of gravitas, or credibility. That breakthrough attempt abruptly ended when ratings dropped and personalities clashed. The pairing of Walters and Harry Reasoner had met a similar fate 19 years earlier.

With lead anchor posts virtually closed to them, the top female personalities in the news media—Diane Sawyer of ABC's *Good Morning America* and Couric of NBC's *Today*—have moved to morning and prime-time positions on such "infotainment" shows as ABC's *20/20*. Although morning programs lack the "hard news" image, these slots have ironically become a bigger cash cow than the evening news, reaping millions of dollars more in revenue. In fact, with a $15 million-per-year contract, Ms. Couric was the highest-paid newsperson in television in 2002.

Some network news executives like David Westin, former president of ABC News, believe that audiences do not mind if the evening anchor position is filled by a man or a woman, as long as it's the right person for the job. In particular, he praised ABC anchor Elizabeth Vargas, a Latina, who occasionally substituted for the late Peter Jennings. When asked whether Vargas could ever be chosen to become an evening news anchor, he said the network would never put anyone on as a substitute who was not capable of doing the job. As some researchers suggest, most important to audiences is that lead anchors have deep experience. However, because of past bias in the workforce, there are simply more men who qualify in that regard than do women.

Other aspects of the news industry sadly match the shortage of women anchoring television newscasts. Results from a study reported in 2002 by the White House Project showed that women accounted for only 11% of all guest appearances on Sunday talk shows in 2000 and 2001. Their voices have remained virtually unheard on such major public policy issues of the 1990s as the North American Free Trade Agreement (NAFTA) or welfare reform—or even on issues deemed "women's affairs" such as abortion and family leave.[22]

When the *New York Times* ran a story on a massive protest against U.S. and United Nations actions in Somalia, the accompanying picture featured a woman at the head of the demonstration. Yet, despite the protest comprising mostly women and children, all of the sources named in the article were male. As Flanders (1997) recounts, the women's faces were seen, but their voices not heard.[23]

Power, Perceptions, and Promotion: Dealing With Double Jeopardy

Women of color who work in the U.S. media industry must often confront—or overcome—the dual challenges of both sexism *and* racism. Findings from a 1999 report by the International Women's Media Foundation (IWMF) summarize results from recent studies on women and minorities in the news media:

- Minorities compose 26% of the U.S. population, but only 12% of the U.S. newsroom workforce.

- Minority staff averages 20% in television, 16% in radio, and only 11% at newspapers.

- At the management level, the numbers drop to 9% in print and 8% in the broadcast media.

- In local television news, although women constitute 37% of the workforce, only 14% have achieved news director status.

- Compared to all U.S. businesses, newspapers hire proportionally fewer women at the management and executive levels.

A 2002 Radio-Television News Directors Association (RTNDA) survey found that the new millennium brought a *reduction* in minority employment progress in the newsroom. The RTNDA survey noted that the sharp decline in the percentage of minority journalists working at radio stations started with the elimination of the FCC's equal employment opportunity regulations.[24]

Over the years, the common thread among women journalists of color is that they "succeeded in spite of" obstacles, barriers, and outright exclusion, and these hurdles are not a thing of the past. In the 1980s, a prospective editor asked aspiring journalist Vicki Torres how it would feel to "leave (her) roots behind" as she advanced in her career. She responded by saying that as a fourth-generation Mexican American, she could trace her roots back to *Leave It to Beaver* episodes. Similarly, when Joaquin Estus was hired as the first Native American reporter by a Midwestern public radio station in 1995, her colleagues rebuked her qualifications and claimed she had only been hired because she was a minority. In her experiences, people felt free to come up to her and complain about Native Americans with complete disregard that it might be offensive to her. All they ever talked about around her was Native American issues, and she could never get them to really see her for who she was. As a result, Estus challenged herself to work even harder to get ahead.[25]

In a 2002 presentation on "Racial Constructions and Visual Representations of Blacks in Television News Media," former CBS and NBC television news anchor Libby Lewis explored how racialized perceptions of beauty, such as skin color or hair texture, shape the hiring practices within the television news industry. She discussed how racially constructed images continue to resonate within the television news media—particularly with regard to selecting in-house anchors and field reporters—and how these images both influence and undermine the broader perceptions of Black identity. As a news anchor and reporter, she found that station management would enforce hair and dress codes that would essentially mute her African American heritage. When she wore her hair naturally, she was told it was "unprofessional" and that she needed to "Anglicize" her hair. No ethnic clothing was allowed. She was astounded when a viewer actually called in to complain about her eyebrows, and that led to a big discussion with her producer about the shape of her eyebrows. She was finally forced to go to an image consultant to avoid further critique of her hair, eyebrows, or particular choice of sweater.[26]

According to an IWMF study (1999), the majority of Native American, Hispanic, African American, and Asian American women working in the media today do not feel they have to overcome insurmountable obstacles based on gender or race. However, while there are now more women of color working in the U.S. news media than ever before, the unfortunate reality is that few women journalists of color are positioned in the management hierarchy to make decisions about what becomes news. Consequently, while they may have greater numbers in the newsroom, they have little influence over news content or product. They are present without power, and without a voice in the gatekeeping process to prevent racist or sexist content in some news stories.

The majority of women of color working for the media say lingering racial stereotypes and subtle discrimination, particularly in terms of promotion opportunities, hinder their professional progress. Women journalists of color often feel they must work "twice as hard" to be perceived as being "half as good" as their White male counterparts in order to get ahead in the industry. In fact, the majority (61%) say they face barriers to professional advancement their White and male colleagues do not face. For these women, it's a catch-22: On the one hand, they often refuse to assimilate into the White male corporate culture; on the other hand, they continue to face stereotypes about their abilities and the perception that they merely got the job as an affirmative action hire. However, the major reason why women journalists of color may face barriers to opportunities is explained in the following rationale:

> Continued concentrations of power [are] in white male hands on a daily basis and throughout the organization. These informal power groupings decide what the paper looks like each day, who get the key assignments, how stories are played and who gets a "hand up" in the organization. No matter how many times our newsroom is reorganized and the systems revamped, those informal power groupings seem to survive and thrive.[27]

Other obstacles to professional advancement include not having a mentor, the lack of role models of the same race or ethnic group, and the lack of access to high-visibility assignments.

In addition, there is an enormous disparity in how managers and women journalists of color perceive cultural diversity in the newsroom and in the news product. While the vast majority of managers (82%) said that management respects cultural differences, only 32% of the minority women journalists agreed. When it comes to the news produced reflecting the diversity of the markets it serves, 69% of managers believe it does, while only 25% of minority women journalists concur.

Despite such formidable obstacles and disparities in the newsroom, some younger women journalists of color have enjoyed tremendous success in media careers. For example, Jemele Hill was the first woman—and woman of color—to cover Michigan State University football and basketball for a Michigan newspaper. Hill said she was fully aware of the "double whammy" she posed in both the newsroom and the locker room, but learned to accept those attitudes. Hill believed that as an African American woman in sports, it worked to her advantage, and helped her to be conscious of the responsibilities inherent in her position. Although she saw White males who were given opportunities more easily than she had been, she claimed that's all part of the game and didn't let it discourage her or keep her down.[28]

Creating a productive work environment in which men and women from various racial and ethnic backgrounds can perform their tasks comfortably is a challenge for any manager. Most newsroom managers are clearly aware that diversity plays a critical role in the news media's future and progress, and admitted that women journalists of color contribute the following to the news-gathering process:

- They are more able to bridge communities.
- They challenge assumptions.
- They cover angles that otherwise might be overlooked.

- They talk to people who too often are overlooked.
- They remind us of cultural institutions of which others are unaware.
- They understand cultural differences and their impact on daily life.

To ensure a more equitable work environment in the news media that reflects the diversity of the community it serves, mechanisms need to be developed to allow for more open dialogue between managers and women journalists of color. In addition, better training opportunities, diversity programs, and mentoring relationships need to be implemented that will not only maximize minority female journalists' potential, but also prepare them for crucial decision-making positions that will enable them to exercise their voice within the media organization.

"Reverse" Discrimination?

But, despite television news's disproportionate employment statistics and the protestations of equal rights proponents, some believe people of color gained an unfair advantage in hiring practices. Among them was former Philadelphia television news anchor Rich Noonan who claimed in 2002 that his contract with the local Fox news station was not renewed because he is White.[29] He filed a formal complaint seeking more than $300,000 in compensatory and punitive damages with the Pennsylvania Human Relations Commission. Noonan had been a member of the 10 p.m. news team comprising three White males and one White female. When his contract expired, Noonan was replaced by a Black male, resulting in a news team with only one non-White anchor. Although people of color compose a significant percentage of Philadelphia's population, Noonan believed Fox practiced racial discrimination by not renewing his contract and not maintaining an all-White news anchor team. He offered no challenge to his successor's professional qualifications as a television news anchor.

Meanwhile, the nation's daily newspapers have been the most grudging employers of people of color and maintained the lowest non-White employment rate of any media industry segment. In 1970 less than 1% of newspaper journalists were non-Whites, and in 1985 the industry was still short of 6% and losing ground. Perhaps indicative of why daily newspapers lagged in this regard was the openly expressed attitude by some editors that they had neither the desire nor the responsibility to diversify the profession.

In the early 2000s, the collegiate journalism education establishment, media organizations, well-intentioned individual practitioners, and others interested in accurate news content were still seeking to increase minority hiring into news media professions. But employers were not aggressively tapping the existing culturally diverse talent pool available to them. The executive summary of the 2010 Annual Survey of Journalism and Mass Communication Graduates reported the grim reality that "minorities continue to have much more difficulty finding work than those who are not classified as racial or ethnic minorities." The slow rate of news media integration—with little penetration into power management levels—was a precursor to the attrition of cultural diversity in the workforce.[30] Disillusioned journalists of color began to leave the profession, citing the lack of diverse perspectives in news coverage and charging their superiors with a lack of respect for their skills. Predictably, the result is a news media product that continues to distort the reality of the multiracial society in the United States.

Into the second decade of the 21st century, diversity and cultural inclusion remain a challenge for communications media industries as they grapple with changing technologies and new media platforms. There is evidence that some have hardened their stance against cultural diversity in hiring practices. In January 2011, an online news service—*The Huffington Post*—was among the news organizations that refused to disclose diversity data on its organization. A second attempt in April of that year by ASNE to gather the information resulted in a refusal to cooperate. But *The Huffington Post* was not alone as other online news organizations similarly declined to participate. These included Bloomberg, Politico, and Yahoo. This lack of transparency has led to the conclusion among critics that the new media journalistic operations—much like their "old" media predecessors—are falling short of ASNE diversity employment goals. This is reminiscent of the old adage "The more things change, the more they stay the same."

Notes

1. U.S. Equal Employment Opportunity Commission, *Hearings Before the Equal Employment Opportunity Commission on Utilization of Minority and Women Workers in Certain Major Industries* (Los Angeles, March 12–14, 1969), 352.

2. U.S. Commission on Civil Rights, *Hearing Before the United States Commission on Civil Rights* (Los Angeles, March 16, 1977).

3. U.S. Commission on Civil Rights, *Window Dressing on the Set: Women and Minorities in Television* (August 1977).

4. Ralph M. Jennings and Veronica M. Jefferson, *Television Station Employment Practices: The Status of Minorities and Women, 1974* (New York: United Church of Christ, Office of Communications, December 1975), 11.

5. Cynthia Alperowitz, *Fighting TV Stereotypes: An ACT Handbook* (Newtonville, MA: Action for Children's Television, 1983).

6. "Roles for Minority Actors Declined in 2001," accessed July 1, 2002, diversityinc.com.

7. David Weaver and G. Cleveland Wilhoit, *The American Journalist in the 1990s* (Arlington, VA: Freedom Forum, November 1992).

8. American Society of Newspaper Editors, *Minorities and Newspapers: A Report by the Committee on Minorities* (May 1982), 34.

9. Ibid., 35.

10. Michael Massing, "Blackout in Television," *Columbia Journalism Review* (November/December 1982): 38.

11. "Don't Hire Minorities Merely for Diversity, Political Correctness," *Publishers Auxiliary* (National Newspaper Association, September 2001).

12. Bob Papper and Michael Gerhard, *RTNDA Communicator* (July/August 2001).

13. Weaver and Wilhoit, op. cit.

14. Ted Pease and J. Frazier Smith, "The Newsroom Barometer: Job Satisfaction and the Impact of Racial Diversity at U.S. Daily Newspapers," *Ohio Journalism Monographs* 1 (No. 1, 1991): 40.

15. Massing, op. cit., 39.

16. Kent State University School of Journalism and Mass Communication, *Third Census of Minorities in College Media* (1993).

17. L. Becker, G. Kosicki, W. Lowrey, J. Prine, and A. Punathambckar, "Undergrad Enrollments Level Off, Graduate Education Declines," *Journalism and Mass Communication Educator* 55 (No. 3, 2000): 68–80.

18. T. Vlad, L. Becker, P. Desnoes, W. Kazragis, and C. Toledo, *Annual Survey of Journalism and Mass Communications Enrollments* (Cox Center, University of Georgia, 2010).

19. D. Riffe, K. Salomone, and G. Stempel, "Characteristics, Responsibilities and Concerns of Teaching Faculty: A Survey of AEJMC Members," *Journalism and Mass Communication Educator* 53 (1998): 102–119.

20. L. Becker, G. Daniels, J. Huh, and T. Vlad, *Diversity in Hiring: Supply Is There. Is Demand?* (James M. Cox Jr. Center for International Mass Communication Training and Research, University of Georgia, September 12, 2002).

21. National Association of Hispanic Journalists, press release, July 17, 2002.

22. *WENews* (May 28, 2002). Directory: http://www.womensnews.org. World Wide Web: http://nytimes.com. Accessed June 4, 2002, aol.com.

23. L. Flanders, *Real Majority, Media Minority: The Cost of Sidelining Women in Reporting* (Monroe, ME: Common Courage, 1997).

24. National Association of Hispanic Journalists, accessed July 30, 2002, http://www.nahj.org.

25. International Women's Media Foundation, *Women Journalists of Color: Present Without Power* (September 1999).

26. L. Lewis, *Racial Constructions & Visual Representations of Blacks in Television News Media,* presentation at the annual Empowering Women of Color Conference, Berkeley, California, March 2, 2002.

27. International Women's Media Foundation, *Women Journalists of Color: Present Without Power* (September 1999).

28. Ibid.

29. Stu Bykofsky, "Noonan: Fox Didn't Want 'Lily White' Cast," *Philadelphia Daily News,* August 28, 2002, A3.

30. L. Becker, T. Vlad, P. Desnoes, W. Kazragis, and C. Toledo, *Survey of Doctoral Programs in Communication: Updated Report for 2008–2009 Graduates* (Cox Center, University of Georgia, 2010).

Alternative Media 11

Everyone everywhere communicates. People of all races and cultures in all parts of the world have developed ways to share news, thoughts, and ideas with each other. But when people think about the roots of the media in the United States, they too often look through Europe for the beginnings of both the print technology and the political and economic systems that spurred the development of media. The history of journalism in the United States too often emphasizes the contributions of the general audience mass media and bypasses the contributions of targeted class media for audience segments, such as people of color. As helpful as these two approaches are, looking at the history of media through only two lenses results in an incomplete view of how the media in this country developed.

Communication Before the Europeans

Edwin and Michael Emery (1996) described some of the earliest forms of communication around the world.[1]

> Around 3500 B.C. the Sumerians of the Middle East devised a system of preserving records by inscribing signs and symbols in wet clay tablets using cylinder seals and then baking them in the sun. They also devised a cuneiform system of writing, using bones to mark signs in wet clay.... Pictographs or ideographs—drawing of animals, commonly recognized objects, and humans—were popular in the Mediterranean area, China, India, what is now Mexico, and Egypt, where they became known as hieroglyphs. There is evidence that a system of movable type was devised in Asia Minor prior to 1700 B.C., the date of a flat clay disk found in Crete. The disk contained forty-five different signs that had been carved on individual pieces of type and then pressed into the clay.[2]

The Phoenicians created an alphabet in 1500 B.C.E. and used colored fluids to outline its symbols to produce pictographs. About 1,000 years later,

243

the Egyptians began using reeds from the Nile River to make papyrus and had a god named Thoth, who was said to record information. Scribes, using brushes or quills, marked the papyrus with hieroglyphic images. The different sheets of papyrus were then joined to form scrolls, which were stored in centers of learning. Sometime close to 100 C.E., parchment made from animal skins was used for special manuscripts or scrolls.

But it was the Chinese who made the two greatest advances leading to modern communication: paper and printing.

> At about this same time (A.D. 100) the Chinese invented a smooth, white paper from wood pulp and fibres and also discovered a way to transfer an ideograph from stone to paper after inking the surface. . . . Wang Chieh published what is considered the world's oldest preserved book from wood blocks in A.D. 868. Large blocks could be carved so that one sheet of paper, printed on both sides, could be folded into thirty-two pages of booksize. Feng Tao printed the Confucian classics between 932 and 953 and in about 1045 the artisan Pi Sheng was inspired to devise a set of movable clay carvings—a sort of earthen ware "type"—that could be reused.[3]

Woodblock printing was not introduced in Europe until 200 years later when Marco Polo returned from China in 1295. Still the Asian printing advances sped ahead. Emery and Emery wrote that movable metal type of copper or bronze came into use in Korea in 1241, more than two centuries before Germany's Johannes Gutenberg introduced printing with movable metal type in Europe.

Black Africans south of the Sahara Desert, who were divided into three major groups and many tribes, also developed elaborate systems for recording and communicating information. Like the natives of North America, they used "talking drums" to communicate between villages and transferred information between tribes and with other parts of the world along land and water trade routes. Rock painting was a key activity for the ancient residents of the Kalahari Desert in southern Africa, as well as in the Sahara in the north.

Literature, often in the form of folktales performed with elaborate music and dancing, passed stories and news of important events from generation to generation. In some African tribes, special persons known as *griots* memorized tribal history and taught it to younger members of the tribe, as well as to future *griots* who would continue the telling of stories of important tribal leaders and developments to the next generation.

In what was to become Latin America, record keeping and communication were important long before Christopher Columbus arrived in 1492. The native Inca, Mexica (Aztec), and Maya all had elaborate systems of recording, transferring, and storing records, including the work of scribes who wrote on bark tablets and artisans who recorded information and pictures on stone carvings. The Incas, who governed a territory that rose precipitously from the ocean to the mountains, used an elaborate network of runners to transmit messages of importance throughout their empire including what is now Peru. The Mexica apparently used an early form of mass communication by hanging colored banners on the main public square of their capital city of Tenochtitlán, now Mexico City.

"No one should question now that Native Indians, prior to Columbus, built an information environment as vibrant as the overseas literary centers of the Middle Ages," wrote communication scholar Leonardo Ferreira, who researched pre-Columbian record keeping and communication in the Americas. Though not intended for mass communication to the public, "a pre-Columbian scribe had the skill to chronicle an array of events, from information on wars and victories, laws, legends, and prominent people or places to transcendental rites and ceremonies, such as childbirths, marriages, sacrifices and funerals."[4]

After the Spanish conquistadores invaded following Columbus's arrival in 1492, the Europeans translated the indigenous people's symbols and records into Spanish to build on the communication system of the people they sought to conquer. In 1571, the Spanish in Mexico City published a *vocabulario*, or bilingual dictionary, translating the native words into Spanish.[5]

Further north, the native people in what became the United States and Canada also developed complex communication systems before Europeans arrived. Hollywood movies have popularized the image of Indians communicating through tom-toms and smoke signals, but the Native Americans' actual communication systems were much more sophisticated

Indigenous people developed elaborate methods of recording and reporting their activities before Europeans arrived in America. Newspaper Rock in southeastern Utah contains petroglyphs made by Anasazi, Ute, Navajo, and other Native American people beginning about 1,000 years before Columbus landed in Santo Domingo.

Source: Luigi Anzivino.

and systematic. A network of trails and footpaths spanned the continent and was traversed by special couriers authorized to carry messages between tribes. James and Sharon Murphy (1981) wrote that

> a complex system of native communications covered most of North America before white contact. . . . It was a unique network of trails and footpaths that crisscrossed the continent, passing through dense forests, over rivers and streams, across mountains and meadows. Traversing these trails were Indian runners, known as tribal messengers, who were officially recognized by governing systems such as those of the Iroquois in the East, the Cherokees in the South and Southeast, the Yuroks in the Northwest, and the Eskimos in present-day Alaska. Other tribes, having less complex tribal governing structures, named and trained young men, and sometimes young women, to act as messenger communicators carrying news from tribe to tribe. Their extraordinary strength and endurance, their fleetness of foot, and their intimate knowledge of the land amazed early European immigrants.[6]

"Newspaper Rock" is the name given to carvings of figures along one wall in the Navajo's Cañon de Chelly and at other sites in Utah and Arizona, thus recognizing the communication role rock carvings, or petroglyphs, may have played. Utah's Newspaper Rock is described as "a four-thousand-year-old 'bulletin board'" in one guidebook.[7] Anasazi, Navajo, Hopi, and other early people developed petroglyphs and elaborate wall paintings, called pictographs, in what is now the Four Corners area of Arizona, New Mexico, Utah, and Colorado. Many images are still visible. One petroglyph in western New Mexico depicts native people driving a buffalo into a huge net trap surrounded by other hunters. Another in Cañon de Chelly in Arizona was made after the arrival of Europeans and shows Spanish soldiers riding into battle with the Navajo people.

Early Printing in America

Like the history of communication and printing in the world, the history of print media in America started with a group most historians have overlooked—in this case, the Spanish colonists. The first printing press in America was sent by Spain to Mexico City in 1535 or 1536, more than a century before the English colonists' first printing press in 1638. The earliest American printing, which was licensed by the Spanish crown to printer Juan Cromberger of Seville, was built on the European languages and the languages of native people. Spain saw the main use of the press as printing government notices and proclamations, as well as catechisms used to convert indigenous people to Catholicism. The first booklets printed were bilingual, using a European language such as Spanish or Latin in one column next to text translating the words into the sounds of the native language, such as Nahuatl or Tarascan, in the next column.

The first printed journalism in America was also produced by the Cromberger press. In 1541, a terrible storm and earthquake struck Guatemala City, south of Mexico City. After the storm, notary public Juan Rodríguez wrote what became the first printed news report in America. Rodríguez's story of the storm and the destruction of Guatemala City was taken to Mexico City, where it was printed as an eight-page booklet by Juan Pablos, the operator of Cromberger's printing house; pressman Gil Barbero; and a Black slave whose name is not known.

Giving readers a foretaste of news media to follow, the front page of the news booklet began with an attention-getting headline in large type: "Report of the Terrifying Earthquake Which Has Reoccurred in the Indies in a City Called Guatemala." The article continued, "It is an event of great astonishment

The first printed journalism in America was this 1541 report of an earthquake and storm that destroyed Guatemala City. It was written by Juan Rodríguez and published by Juan Pablos as a news booklet to be distributed in Mexico City.

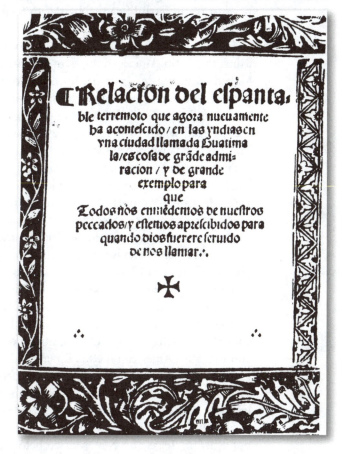

and great example so that we all repent from our sins and so that we will be ready when God calls us." A "summary of what happened in Guatemala" began on an inside page with a Guatemala dateline and the story.[8]

Rodríguez's news booklet was distributed in Mexico City and was the forerunner of a popular form of news reporting in New Spain, as the Spanish colonies were then called. Based on a European model, the news booklets known as *hojas volantes* (flying pages) or *relaciones* (reports) were issued when major news occurred, the government had a major announcement, or ships with news of world events docked at Veracruz.[9] As more presses arrived in New Spain, more printers printed and sold the irregularly issued news booklets. Mexican historian Julio Jiménez Rueda wrote that it was through the *hojas volantes* that "people knew of the death and coronation of kings, wars in Europe, earthquakes and calamities" (cited in Acevedo, 1965, p. 79; authors' translation).[10]

By 1600, nearly 40 years before a printing press even arrived in the English colonies, the presses of New Spain had produced at least 174 books. An additional 60 books have been identified without dates or verification.[11] In 1693, the news booklet format was used in America's first news periodical, the four volumes of the *Mercurio Volante* published by Carlos de Sigüenza y Góngora in Mexico City. One *Mercurio Volante* issue carried news of unsuccessful Spanish battles to reconquer and colonize the native people of what is now New Mexico.

Like the communication advances of Asians, Africans, and Native Americans, the Latin American roots of the American media have been overlooked or minimized by many historians of the United States, even though accurate information has long been available. In 1810, the first history of American journalism, Isaiah Thomas's *History of Printing in America,* correctly began with a 10-page chapter on Spanish America. However, when Thomas's book was reprinted in 1874 and in later editions, the first chapter— the chapter on Spanish American printing—was deleted. In 1941, journalism historian Frank Luther Mott relegated America's first printed news, the 1541 Mexico City report of Guatemala City's destruction, to a mere footnote and conveyed the false impression that "no regularly published newspaper on the continent antedated the earliest Boston papers."[12]

In the 1970s, journalism historians began paying overdue recognition to the contributions of Latinos and other groups in laying the foundations of American journalism. In its Summer 1977 and Autumn 1979 issues, *Journalism History* devoted the cover and several articles to the contributions of Latinos and the Latino press to news media in America. In the same era, editor Tom Reilly devoted other editions of the journal to the Black press and to Native American media. Emery and Emery in the 1980s revised the first pages of their comprehensive history book, *The Press and America,* to include early non-European contributions and a section on the Spanish influence in American journalism, including a picture of the 1541 news booklet.[13] The Latin American press traditions were linked to newspapers published in Texas and New Mexico before those Mexican territories were taken by the United States in 1848 after it declared war against Mexico.

The focus of this book is people of color and communication media in the United States. Although the general audience mass media have long overlooked news in these communities, each group has long had its own class media focused on the needs and interests of its communities in this country. Spurred by population changes, these racial and ethnic media are growing at a faster rate and are more important than ever. The remainder of this chapter describes how the first U.S. newspapers for Asians, Blacks, Latinos, and Native Americans began and explores the experiences these groups shared.

The first newspapers for people of color were preceded by class media targeted to other ethnic groups and began in a 50-year period around the first half of the 19th century, as the U.S. mass media system was developing. In chronological order, the first four are the first Latino newspaper, *El Misisipi,* founded in New Orleans in 1808; the first Black newspaper, *Freedom's Journal,* founded in New York City in 1827; the first Native American newspaper, the *Cherokee Phoenix,* founded in New Echota, Georgia, in 1828; and the first Asian Pacific American newspaper, *Kim-Shan Jit San-Luk, The Golden Hills' News,* founded in San Francisco in 1854. These first four newspapers all have something more important in common: Each one started as a response to a special crisis its readers faced.

The First Latino Newspaper: *El Misisipí* in 1808

El Misisipí was founded in the midst of the Napoleonic Wars in Europe in the early 1800s, when France had conquered much of the European continent, including parts of Spain, and claimed the extensive Spanish holdings in the Caribbean and America. New Orleans, a sea and river port built where the Mississippi River flows into the Gulf of Mexico, was a major transit point for people traveling between the United States and Europe, as well as to and from the Spanish colonies in the Caribbean, Central America, and South America. It was both the southern tip of the United States and the northern tip of the Caribbean and Latin America.

Named after the river that drew ships to New Orleans, *El Misisipí* was a four-page publication printed primarily in Spanish, but with English translations of many articles and almost all the advertising. It was started by William H. Johnson and Company and was printed on the press of the *Louisiana Gazette.* Not much is known about its founders, and apparently only two archived copies remain from its two-year run.[14]

News stories in the one copy in the United States reveal the crisis under which the newspaper's readers were living: Napoleon Bonaparte's conquest of most European nations and claim on their colonies. It was a newspaper for and about people who were exiles from the turmoil in Spain and sought to use U.S. press freedom to advocate freedom in their homeland. With Napoleon's French forces conquering most of Europe and establishing a puppet government in Spain, *El Misisipí* is filled with war reports from other newspapers and war news conveyed by sea captains, including a story on the uprising of Madrid citizens against Napoleon's occupation troops. The newspaper also speculated on the possibility of England ending hostilities with Russia and entering the war on the side of Spain against France.

All the news stories in *El Misisipí* came from outside of New Orleans, and almost all covered the war in Europe, including a long commentary on the events. Most of the stories came from newspapers or reports that were several months old and at times contradicted each other. In a separate column, the editor commented on the reports and their possible implications for Spain. The strident newspaper was distinctly pro-Spanish royalty, and its denigrating of Napoleon's puppet regime in Spain was carried by newspapers on the East Coast and Europe.

El Misisipí (1808) in New Orleans was the first Latino newspaper in the United States, publishing news of the Napoleonic Wars and advertising in both English and Spanish.

Source: Wisconsin Historical Society, WHI-49256.

"We do not think it worth while to publish the New Constitution of Spain, because it appears too ridiculous to hear scoundrels taking about equity, usurpers about justice, tyrants about clemency and liars about truth," wrote *El Misisipí*'s editor in an article reprinted in New York's *American Citizen* in 1809. "We shall publish in lieu of the constitution, an account of the glorious battles which the patriots of Spain have fought and won, and should they continue to be successful . . . this celebrated constitution may be returned to the 'pigeon hole' from which it was probably taken, whilst regenerated Spain, with the religion and laws of her ancestors will again take her high rank among the independent nations of the world covered with fame and glory."

El Misisipí, like other newspapers of the time, relied on news printed in other newspapers and reports from sea captains and sailors arriving from foreign ports, and the anti-Napoleon stories were carried to cities far from New Orleans. Among the articles in the October 12, 1808, issue were articles from the *Boston Chronicle* and a newspaper identified as the *Diario de New York* (*New York Daily*). The front page carried the report of the Madrid uprising in all three of its columns, adding only a brief notice of its publication schedule (Wednesdays and Saturdays), its subscription rates ($8 a year, half payable in advance), and its advertising language policy ("in both languages or in the one wanted"), as well as a bilingual advertisement for Don Juan Rodríguez, Abogado (lawyer), in Spanish with an English translation below it.

El Misisipí's second page offered the report "of a correspondent" on the problem of separating out the facts in the accounts in newspapers, official news, private reports, and rumors coming from war-torn Europe. *El Misisipí* summarized what its editors felt was the latest factual information and called the *Bayonne Gazette* "an official organ of the usurpers of the thrones of France and Spain." *El Misisipí* then engaged in some interpretation of its own: "Madrid has long been in the possession of the French and the patriots of Spain are not to be duped by the mockeries of Bonaparte, however solemnized by a recreant minister of religion." Citing uprisings against the French in Spain and Portugal, the paper continued that "we think therefore that nothing has yet appeared to discourage the friends of freedom. To hold their own ground is much for the patriots at the commencement of the struggle. Their armies will increase and improve in a far greater degree than those of the enemy."

The fourth page was devoted entirely to advertising, almost all in a bilingual format, Spanish above English. Everything from ships to hardwood to supplies for sailors was advertised in the two languages. The advertisements reveal the nature of commerce in the port of New Orleans, which the United States acquired from Napoleon's France five years earlier in the Louisiana Purchase. One company, A. & J. M'Ilvain, Grocers, No. 43, on the Levee, offered sugar, coffee, tea, and a "general assortment of groceries" along with "2500 lbs. James River Chewing Tobacco, 1000 bushels Indian Corn, 2000 feet Walnut plank." The firm advised ships' captains preparing to sail "SEA STORES Put up at the shortest notice." Another advertisement announced, "Five or six gentlemen may be accomodated with Genteel Boarding in a private family, at the rate of 20 Dollars per month."

The largest advertisements, taking up nearly all of the second and third columns, were for Mrs. Zacharie, who offered "a handsome assortment of DRY GOODS," and La Rionda, a dealer selling two brigantines, the *Sophia* and the *Minerve*, each "with all her tackle"; two houses on St. Phillip Street; and a long list of goods such as 800 tons of Campeachy Logwood, 40 bales of sarsaparilla, and 22 trunks of "Callicoes."

As the first Latino newspaper in the United States, *El Misisipí* exhibited many characteristics found in later media. For one, it served Spanish-speaking readers who came to the United States to escape warfare and political turmoil at home and also used U.S. press freedom to advocate homeland freedom to readers beyond the United States, a consistent theme in immigration from Latin America. Second, it was bilingual, recognizing the importance of both English and Spanish. Third, its news was heavily influenced by events elsewhere, just as much of the news and many programs in Latino media over the years have come from Spain and Latin America. And, fourth, like many Latino publications that followed, *El Misisipí* apparently was a business venture, devoting one fourth of its space to advertising.

The First Black Newspaper: *Freedom's Journal* in 1827

Freedom's Journal (1827) in New York City was the first Black newspaper in the United States, publishing general news of interest to African Americans, strident opposition to slavery, and advocacy of equal rights for free Blacks in northern states.

Source: Freedom's Journal, March 30, 1827.

A different kind of crisis triggered the founding of *Freedom's Journal*, the first Black newspaper, on March 16, 1827, by the Reverend Samuel E. Cornish and John Brown Russwurm. The crisis was the fight to end slavery, in which Blacks were kept as property in much of the United States. White abolitionists wanted to abolish slavery and campaigned against it by printing stories of slave life by freed Black slaves. But the abolitionists were divided on what should become of former slaves once they gained their freedom. Some argued they should go back to Africa. Others felt they should be allowed to remain in the United States as citizens. Still others advocated less than equal rights for freed Blacks staying in the United States. Of course, anti-abolitionists, who favored slavery, felt slaves should not be freed at all.

After an attack on abolitionists and Black leaders in the *New York Enquirer*, Cornish and Russwurm (the third Black person to graduate from a college in the United States[15]) decided that it was time for Blacks to speak through their own newspaper. In the first edition of the four-page weekly, the editors wrote,

We wish to plead our own cause. Too long have others spoken for us. Too long has the public been deceived by misrepresentation in things which concern us dearly, though in the estimation of some mere trifles; for although there are many in society who exercise toward us benevolent feelings, still (with some sorrow we confess it) there are others who enlarge upon that which tends to discredit any person of color.[16] (Daniel, 1982, p. 184)

Freedom's Journal is often described as an aggressive newspaper that agitated forcefully against slavery and for the rights of free Blacks in the North.[17] All of that is true, but the newspaper was also much more. It built a new consciousness in and community among Blacks and identified their struggle with the struggles of other people of color in America. It was able to do this because the newspaper reflected the broad interests of Blacks, which went beyond slavery, abolition, and freedom. In addition to abolitionist news and hard-hitting editorials, the newspaper offered information, features, culture, and entertainment.

Its first issue reflected the broad interests of its editors and readers, carrying news from Haiti and Sierra Leone; the first part of a serial on Captain Paul Cuffee, a Black Boston shipper; a poem titled "The African Chief"; and advertising for the B. F. Hughes School for Coloured Children of Both Sexes. In its two years, *Freedom's Journal* ran regular columns titled "People of Colour," "Foreign News," "Domestic News," and "Summary." Some of these columns were based on news from other newspapers and were highly sensational. The "Summary" column especially exploited the staples of sensational reporting: blood and sex.[18]

Freedom's Journal strongly opposed slavery and advocated the rights of free Blacks. The newspaper also attacked racism in the White media and reinforced the importance of the alternative viewpoint it presented on African American issues. Walter Daniel (1982) wrote that *Freedom's Journal* attacked the editor of the *New York Enquirer* as one "whose object is to keep alive the prejudice of the whites against the coloured communities of New York City." Other articles disagreed with the platform of the American Colonization Society, which advocated returning Afro Americans to Africa and reported on lynching. Russwurm believed in universal education as a critical need for Blacks who would be respected by White Americans.[19]

Russwurm left *Freedom's Journal* in 1828 to become an editor and official in Liberia, a part of Africa some abolitionists established for freed slaves. The newspaper continued to be published by Cornish under the title *Rights of All* until 1829. Lionel Barrow wrote in a 1977 *Journalism History* issue devoted to Black press history that

> *Freedom's Journal* gave Blacks a voice of their own and an opportunity not only to answer the attacks printed in the White press but to read articles on Black accomplishments, marriages, deaths that the White press of the day ignored. Slavery is no longer here, but its vestiges are and today's reporters and publishers—Black and White—could do well to study the *Journal,* adopt its objectives and emulate its content. Blacks still need to "plead our own causes," and will need to do so for sometime to come.[20]

Like many Black newspapers and other racial and ethnic newspapers that followed it, *Freedom's Journal* filled an important void. It did more than take issue with the coverage and editorial positions that were found in the mass audience White press. It presented a class media alternative by reporting events of interest to Blacks with dignity and pride, demonstrating that its Black readers, though targets of slavery and racism, were doing more than was reported in the White press and also wanted to know more about themselves and others.

Along these lines, *Freedom's Journal* linked the struggle of Blacks with the struggles of other people of color fighting for equal rights. The April 27, 1827, issue ran a story in its "Summary" section of attempts by Alabama authorities to extend state laws over "territory owned and inhabited by the Indian nations." The editors asked rhetorically, "Is this treating them as they are acknowledged to be an independent nation?" Another story, in the paper's "Varieties" section, was headlined "Indian Observation" and referred to Native Americans as "our red brethren of the west."

A week earlier, the April 20 issue of *Freedom's Journal* reprinted from the *New York Observer* an article headlined "The Revolt in Texas." The newspapers reported the troubles of "certain slaveholders from the United States" who took slaves to Texas, which was then part of Mexico, "with the expectation of amassing great fortunes by means of the sinews and traffic of slaves." But after Mexico gained its independence from Spain, it adopted a law prohibiting the importation of slaves, which had the potential to end slavery altogether. So the slave owners "set up a government of their own, which they called the Republic of Fredonia." They hoped that nearby Indians would help them enforce slavery, but the Indians "readily took sides with the Mexicans." Unable to hold off the Mexican troops sent to restore order, the article stated, "Those advocates for the liberty of enslaving others found plenty of business upon their hands, and are at length either captured or dispersed." The article praised the new Latin American republics for abolishing slavery or "lightening the bar which for centuries had oppressed the poor Indians."

For more than 175 years, Black media have continued to fulfill multiple roles. They have raised the concerns and protests of Blacks when confronted with slavery, segregation, lynching, violation of voting rights, and discrimination—in education, employment, and housing—and other forms of unequal treatment. They have reported on the organizational, social, religious, and other activities and interests within Black communities that have too often been ignored by the White media. And they have built bridges of understanding among all racial groups.

The First Native American Newspaper: The *Cherokee Phoenix* in 1828

Like the first Latino and Black newspapers, the first Native American newspaper was born out of a crisis, in this case the federal government's efforts to displace the people of the Cherokee Nation from the millions of acres of land they held across what are now several states, including North Carolina, Georgia, and Tennessee. During this crisis, the *Cherokee Phoenix* was born to unify and express the opinions of the Cherokee people and counter the portrayal of Native Americans in the White press (LaCourse, 1979).[21]

The *Cherokee Phoenix* was established by the Cherokee Nation in New Echota, near the current site of Calhoun, Georgia, and printed its first edition on February 21, 1828. It appeared weekly, with a few gaps, for 6 years—until 1834. Like *El Misisipí*, it was bilingual, using both English and the 86-character Cherokee written language introduced by Sequoyah (who was also known as George Gist) in 1821 after 12 years of work.[22] James and Sharon Murphy (1981) wrote that the newspaper was started out of two needs: the desire of missionaries to spread Christianity among the Cherokees and the desire of Cherokee Nation leaders to unify Cherokees and others in support of the fight to keep their homelands.[23]

The first editor of the *Cherokee Phoenix* was Cherokee schoolteacher Elias Boudinot (also known as Buck Oowatie), who also was clerk of the Cherokee National Council. To raise funds for the new newspaper, he traveled along the East Coast speaking to philanthropic and religious groups. Financial assistance for the newspaper came both from the Cherokee Nation, which approved the building of a newspaper office in 1826 and allocated $1,500 for a printing press in 1827, and from the American Board of Commissioners for Foreign Missions in New England, a Protestant group that helped finance the casting of Sequoyah's Cherokee syllabary into metal type needed to print the newspaper. Samuel Worcester, a missionary working among the Cherokees, requested the foreign mission support. The Cherokee Nation later repaid the mission board for its help.

Boudinot's vision, like that of the editors of *Freedom's Journal*, was of a newspaper to counter the biased accounts in White newspapers by accurately reflecting the lives of his people and mobilizing public opinion in support of their cause. In an

The *Cherokee Phoenix* (1828) in New Echota, Georgia, was the first Native American newspaper in the United States, publishing articles in both English and the Cherokee syllabary developed by Sequoyah.

Source: Cherokee Phoenix, March 13, 1828.

1826 "Address to the Whites" at the First Presbyterian Church in Philadelphia, he proposed a newspaper "comprising a summary of religious and political events, etc., on the one hand; and on the other, exhibiting the feelings, dispositions, improvements, and prospects of the Indians: their traditions, their true character, as it once was, as it now is, and the ways and means most likely to throw the mantle of civilization over all tribes; and such other matters as will tend to diffuse proper and correct impressions in regard to their condition—such a paper could not fail to create much interest in the American Community, favorable to the aboriginies, and to have a powerful influence on the advancement of the Indians themselves."[24]

In its first issue, the *Cherokee Phoenix* reprinted a prospectus prepared by Worcester that promised the newspaper would cover local happenings, Cherokee laws and customs, and the Cherokees' progress in education, religion, and culture. It would also print news about other tribes and "interesting articles calculated to promote Literature, Civilization, and Religion among the Cherokees."[25]

Subscriptions came from as far away as Germany. The newspaper was circulated through Cherokee villages—stretching from present-day North Carolina to Texas—to build the identity of the villages and their inhabitants as part of the Cherokee Nation, even though sometimes only one copy was allocated per village. In the fourth issue, the newspaper carried the first written laws of the Cherokees, with Boudinot's hopes that "our readers will perhaps be gratified to see the first commencement of written laws among the Cherokees."[26] Although the newspaper printed articles in two languages, only rarely was the same article published in both English and Cherokee. There were generally three columns in English for every two in Cherokee, because the structure of Sequoyah's written language devised single characters for whole syllables and it took less space to write in Cherokee than in English.

Boudinot has been credited with building the *Cherokee Phoenix* "into a strong and loud voice of the Cherokee people as they struggled against increasingly insurmountable government opposition."[27] But his voice was not always strident. In the first issue, he promised that the paper would "not return railing for railing, but consult mildness."[28] He made it clear that the newspaper would advocate Cherokee positions on issues that brought them into conflict with the encroaching Whites and their governments. Boudinot wrote in the first issue that

> in regard to the controversy with Georgia, and the present policy of the Central Government, in removing, and concentrating the Indians, out of the limits of any state, which, by the way, appears to be gaining strength, we will invariably and faithfully state the feelings of the majority of our people. Our views, as a people, on this subject, have been most sadly misrepresented. These views we do not wish to conceal, but are willing that the public should know what we think of this policy, which, in our opinion, if carried into effect, will prove pernicious to us.[29]

Boudinot concluded the editorial by attacking negative symbols and stereotypes often used by Whites and their newspapers when covering Native Americans.[30]

> We would now commit our feeble efforts to the good will and indulgence of the public, praying that God will attend them with his blessings, and hoping for that happy period, when all the Indian tribes of America shall rise, Phoenix like, from their ashes, and when the terms "Indian depredation," "war whoop," "scalping knife" and the like, shall become obsolete, and for ever be "buried deep underground."[31]

In subsequent issues, Boudinot used the paper to protest attempts by the state of Georgia to include the Cherokee Nation in its criminal laws and to fight against federal appropriations to remove the Cherokees from their mineral-laden lands. But, like *Freedom's Journal*, it is unfair to describe the *Cherokee Phoenix* as a newspaper that was concerned solely with the struggles of its audience. The newspaper carried advertising for merchants, a boarding school, and other businesses catering to the needs of its readers. The newspaper also campaigned against alcoholism and argued against the slavery in which Blacks were held, although Cherokee law permitted slaves. The newspaper sent mixed messages on slavery by running advertising by owners seeking return of runaway slaves and occasional anecdotes in Black dialect.[32]

In 1829, the newspaper enlarged its title and became the *Cherokee Phoenix and Indian Advocate*, which reflected its broadened coverage of issues faced by other tribes. Over the years, the editor and staff continued to protest the encroachment of Cherokees' legal and civil rights by Whites, including Georgia officials' threats, harassment, and arrests of the newspaper's staff. When the Cherokees came under intense pressure to move from their ancestral lands, the leaders of the nation were divided on the issue. Boudinot resigned the editorship in 1832, after he had been ordered by Cherokee Principal Chief John Ross not to publish news reports of the division among the leaders. The new editor was Ross's brother-in-law, John Hicks, who continued to fight against the harassment and land grabbing confronting the Cherokees. The newspaper appeared less regularly and ceased its first run of publication on May 31, 1834.

But, like its namesake, the mythical phoenix bird who died a fiery death and grew out of its own ashes, the *Cherokee Phoenix* rose again. The Cherokees were soon forcibly relocated by the U.S. government in a journey known as the Trail of Tears to reservation lands in the present state of Oklahoma, where the newspaper was later resurrected by the Cherokee Nation. The *Cherokee Phoenix* has gone on to publish both print and digital editions and in 2003 marked its 175th birthday.

The *Cherokee Phoenix* and other Native American newspapers that followed found the bilingual format to be an effective way to communicate with both its Native American and European immigrant audiences. Although the bilingual format is diminishing in print today, it is still used by Native American radio stations that broadcast programs in both English and their native languages. Some are published by tribal governments, and others are privately published by Native Americans to cover news and reach readers that cross tribal lines. Like the *Cherokee Phoenix*, many newspapers have devoted most of their space to news of specific interest to Native Americans. Tribally affiliated newspapers have had the longest publication runs. But tribal newspaper editors often have clashed, as did Elias Boudinot, with tribal government leaders who seek to limit their editorial freedom.[33]

The First Asian Pacific American Newspaper: *The Golden Hills' News* in 1854

As with the first Latino, Black, and Native American newspapers, the nation's first Asian Pacific American newspaper, *The Golden Hills' News*, was born during a crisis in the lives of its readers. The era was the California Gold Rush, which drew gold seekers from around the world to what became the Golden State. Among the new arrivals were the Chinese, who crossed the Pacific Ocean to California, which they called Gold Mountain. Although the first Chinese arrivals were welcomed, the Chinese who arrived in San Francisco shortly thereafter were targets of racial prejudice and discrimination. In 1853, a racist Foreign Miners Tax reduced their incomes in the Sierra Nevada gold fields.[34]

Asians and Pacific Islanders had long been traveling to what became the United States. There are documented, though disputed, reports of Hui Shên, a Chinese Buddhist priest, sailing down what is now the California coast from what is now British Columbia, Canada, in 458 C.E.—more than a thousand years before Christopher Columbus landed in America. Spanish explorers found the wreck of a ship believed to be of Asian construction on the California coast in 1774, and Filipinos worked on Spanish ships sailing to America, including some whose descendants, called Manilamen, settled in Louisiana in the 1760s.[35] People from Asia have been reported steadily, but infrequently, in the United States since at least 1785, when several Chinese sailors were stranded in Baltimore. The first enumeration of Chinese in a U.S. census was in 1820.[36]

But it was the need for inexpensive, hardworking labor in the California Gold Rush that brought the first large groups of Asian immigrants to the United States. Almost immediately they drew the attention of San Francisco's White press, although the coverage did little to foster better understanding between San Franciscans and the new immigrants.[37] A leading San Francisco newspaper, the *Alta California*, made what one scholar called "editorial humor" of the Chinese, including its own "Chinese letters" to ridicule Chinese writing. Where there was a profit to be made, English-language newspapers used lithography to insert Chinese characters into advertisements. Chinese characters also appeared in reports on the inscriptions on Chinese graves.[38]

In 1854, Methodist missionaries in San Francisco's growing Chinatown founded *Kim-Shan Jit San-Luk, The Golden Hills' News,* to reach the Chinese in San Francisco and foster a better understanding of them among Whites. The newspaper took its title from the name that the Chinese adopted for California during the Gold Rush—golden hills. Although some sources report that *The Golden Hills' News* began in 1851,[39] pioneer California editor Edward Kemble[40] cited a founding date of 1854, a date accepted by Karl Lo and Him Mark Lai in their 1977 book on Chinese newspapers in North America.[41] The 1854 date is also supported by the newspaper's own issue numbers.[42]

The Golden Hills' News (1854) in San Francisco was the first Asian Pacific American newspaper in the United States, publishing both news for Chinese immigrant readers and English-language editorials calling for fair treatment of Chinese coming to the California Gold Rush.

Source: California Historical Society, San Francisco.

Like the other newspapers discussed in this chapter, *The Golden Hills' News* was born at a time of crisis for its readers. The Chinese people had left their homeland, crossed an ocean, and come to the United States with hopes of making their fortune in the gold fields. They found a country vastly different from their own in race, language, and culture. Upon arrival, they often were forced into the most undesirable labor, at little or no pay, to repay the cost of their passage. Many of the newly arrived females were poor girls who were sold as slaves into prostitution.[43]

The Chinese people were treated as outcasts by the White world; they were targeted for legal, economic, and social discrimination in a California newly populated by European immigrants seeking to become rich. *The Golden Hills' News* was founded by Protestant churches with missionaries in China and outposts in San Francisco's developing Chinatown. The churches offered help to Chinese immigrants in the hostile land, hoping to convert them to Christianity in the process.

In his history of the Chinese in the United States from 1850 to 1870, Gunther Barth (1971) notes that the first issue of *The Golden Hills' News*, in April 1854, promised that the paper would appear twice weekly.[44] It was published by William Howard, with Chinese characters lithographed by F. Kuhl. The day after the first edition appeared, the *San Francisco Herald* poked fun at the newspaper and its language by comparing the newspaper's Chinese characters to the tracks of a spider crawling out of an ink bottle and onto a white sheet of paper.

"Chinese merchants leave their family and travel eight million miles to here. They make a living by themselves in severe conditions. They have to bear the unfairness and harshness but cannot express their feelings freely," *The Golden Hills' News'* Howard wrote in a Chinese-language front-page article in its first edition. "I am in sympathy with Chinese' bitterness, so I open a special daily in Chinatown to help them. The paper reports the latest news about ships, cargos and government affairs relevant to Chinese every day. It is written in the Chinese language and published every Saturday to inform Chinese merchants."

The paper sold for 25 cents a copy, with a monthly subscription costing 75 cents. Charges for advertising were $1 for less than 25 characters, $2 for between 25 and 50 characters, and 3 cents apiece for more than 50 characters. Barth (1971) describes most of the content of the paper as being in colloquial Cantonese, with much of the news coming from California.[45] By June of that first year, the newspaper had scaled back to weekly publication "until the Chinese generally adopt it, when it will be published semiweekly." In the June 24 issue, the advertisements of Hudson & Co., California Stage Company, Steam Navigation Company, and Miner's Exchange Bank and the want ads filled a full page of advertising targeting Chinese people.

Like *El Misisipí* and the *Cherokee Phoenix*, the newspaper was bilingual, although articles were not translated from one language to the other. The front page of the May 27, 1854, edition featured Cantonese characters on about two thirds of the page on the left-hand side, with an English-language column addressed to the Whites on the right. The Cantonese characters reported commercial news and other community notices of interest to Chinese readers. The English-language column was an editorial directed toward Whites and argued for better treatment of Chinese people in California and linked the mission of the missionaries' Chinatown chapel with the newspaper in assisting the Chinese. The editorial noted that while the eastern United States was welcoming European immigrants, Chinese coming to California were greeted with discrimination.

The "Eastern States" have their Irish exodus, their German exodus, and hordes of Saxons, Danes, Celts, Gauls and Scandanavians, but we have **all** of these, and the most wonderful of all a CHINESE EXODUS! The great wonder of the century is the astonishing flight of the hitherto immobile Chinamen across the Pacific ocean, to seek refuge and liberty in the bosom of "The Golden Hills."[46]

The writer quoted missionaries in Shanghai who wrote that Americans could "wander unmolested" 40 miles into the Chinese interior and claimed that Chinese who saw Americans would "look up to them with profound respect." That behavior was compared with the racism that Chinese immigrants found in California.

"No Chinaman sneers at you in the streets; there is no hindrance whatever to your study of their character and habits; they always look at you with an expression of good will," says Bayard Taylor. "Is it too much to ask of a Christian population 'to do unto them,' at least what it seems 'they do to us,' in their own land?"[47]

On July 1, 1854, an English-language editorial in *The Golden Hills' News,* "The Government, Press, Public and Chinese," noted that Chinese coming to the United States were "treated with the most rooted prejudice, hatred, and injustice." The newspaper urged that laws be translated and published so that Chinese people could learn the ways of the United States. The editorial stated that

at present each poor Chinese on emerging in our country with Asiatic habits and language is left to himself—a straggler in a strange land—a being, whose efforts are often repulsed—whose chance of employ are limited, and whose conduct is only watched or cared for by Policemen when they are likely to be mischievous to others! They are held responsible for taxes and other duties, but the State or County is responsible for no duties to them in return.[48]

Biased treatment of the Chinese by U.S. newspapers was a special target of *The Golden Hills' News* English-language editorials. On June 10, 1854, an editorial headlined "The Chinese and the Times" charged "our Conductors of the Press describe them as 'Apes,' 'Brutes,' and 'social lice'! Lower than the Negro-race."[49] An editorial in the July 29 issue, "American Preachings Versus Practice," argued that the "hypocrisy" of American democracy was "well illustrated in the infamous treatment of the Chinese in this country," especially in newspapers that supported racist practices against Chinese people. The editorial continued, "The Press almost unanimously have spoken against them with bitter contempt, and has excited an aggressive prejudice against them in the public mind."[50]

An editorial in the June 24 issue was particularly severe in its criticism of press treatment of Chinese in their new homeland. It was titled "Is There No help for the Chinese in California?" and charged that

the Press has stained its pages with filthy abuse usque ad nauseam—hot has been the indignation against their habits; fierce the denunciation against their labor—and fearful the vengeance against their offences. These facts stand recorded in our history and no editorial effrontery can efface it—no "theory of race"-sophistry can wrench it out of its place—that our Press, Legislature, Senate and Municipalities, have done their best, actively or passively, to shut out from the Chinese the light of knowledge of our Institutions and laws, and to stuff bigotry and prejudice against them into every chink of private benevolence or sympathy, which might be shone in upon them.[51]

Other English-language editorials advocated equal rights for the Chinese in America and cited their willingness to participate in the traditions of their new country. Barth (1971) wrote that the English-language editorials set a precedent that was followed by later Chinese newspapers in California.[52] The English-language columns were directed to White readers and were primarily concerned with discrimination and other civil rights violations against the Chinese as well as with pointing to evidence of Chinese adapting to the ways of the United States. The Chinese columns, on the other hand, were filled with commercial notices and other business-related news.[53] By all accounts, *The Golden Hills' News* did not publish for a lengthy period. Writing in 1858, Kemble concluded his three-line paragraph on the newspaper with the sentence "It did not live long."[54]

But Asian Studies bibliographer Kuei Chiu (1996) noted that what *The Golden Hills' News* achieved is more important than the length of its existence: "Although this paper was short-lived, it marked the beginning of the Asian language journalism in America."[55] Like the other newspapers discussed in this chapter, *The Golden Hills' News* established precedents followed by later media directed to its audience. One such precedent was the use of a bilingual format, which continues to be used in Asian Pacific American media today. Another precedent was a column directed to English-speaking readers that argues for fairer treatment of the Chinese while pointing to the contributions of the Chinese to society. A third precedent was coverage of news from Asia. A fourth precedent was the inclusion of advertising by White firms targeting Chinese readers. Finally, a fifth precedent set by *The Golden Hills' News* was its founding in San Francisco, which was also the birthplace of the first U.S. newspapers for people from Japan (*Shinonome [Dawn]* in 1886) and Korea (*Konglip Sinbo [Public News or United Korean]* in 1905).

Similarities in the First Newspapers of People of Color

Identifying the first Latino, Black, Native American, and Asian American newspapers in the United States is important for reasons that extend beyond establishing a chronology for the sake of historical accuracy. As important as the founding of the first printed communication medium for each group was, even more vital are the similarities among the newspapers begun for different groups at different times in different places. All the newspapers were founded, as we have already established, in the half-century when American mass circulation newspapers were becoming influential and at a time when each group was facing a crisis that was not being experienced by White people. In addition, the founders of each newspaper were men, reflecting the lower status of women across all groups. Three of the newspapers, *El Misisipí*, the *Cherokee Phoenix,* and *The Golden Hills' News,* were bilingual and used both their native language and English. Three of the newspapers had religious roots: The *Cherokee Phoenix* and *The Golden Hills' News* were founded with support of missionaries, and *Freedom's Journal* was cofounded by a minister.

All the newspapers were attuned to the news and information needs of their target audience and, like media for these communities today, offered news that was not well covered by the other newspapers. For example, two newspapers, *Freedom's Journal* and the *Cherokee Phoenix,* were established to provide an alternative voice, and a third, *The Golden Hills' News,* appeared when White media were actively ridiculing and disparaging the Chinese. These three newspapers also appeared when the members of their audience were victims of legal discrimination, social subjugation, and violent oppression, and the papers actively took issue with the negative way their people were seen by Whites and portrayed in their press.

Today's newspapers, magazines, broadcast stations, and digital media targeted to communities of color are growing rapidly in the United States as class communication becomes more important. Although in most of these media the content has become increasingly commercial and the voice less fiery than in their first predecessors, they continue to provide news, entertainment, and information alternatives to the general audience mass media. There is a long-standing need for people of color to have an alternative to general audience media—a need triggered by the behavior of the first mass circulation newspaper, the *New York Sun.*

In the 1840s, Willis A. Hodges, a Black man, took exception to editorials in the *Sun* that opposed voting rights for Blacks. The slogan of the *Sun* was "It Shines for ALL." So he first tried the access approach and wrote a reply to one of the editorials, which the newspaper printed for $15. However, when the newspaper published his message, it had been modified and was carried as advertising. When Hodges protested, he was told that "the *Sun* shines for all White men but not for Colored men." So he started his own Black newspaper, *The Ram's Horn,* in 1847.[56] As long as all people may produce their own newspapers, magazines, videos, and websites, members of all races will be able to follow Hodges and the founding editors of the first Latino, Black, Native American, and Asian Pacific American newspapers by launching media that reflect their own views and represent their communities.

The Future of Media By, For, and About People of Color

The class media targeting people of color grew at a steady pace into the 21st century. New America Media's ethnic media directory grew from 400 print, broadcast, and online media in 2001 to 2,500 media outlets reaching an estimated more than 60 million Americans in 2012. New America Media (NAM), a collaboration and advocacy organization serving ethnic media across the country, strengthened the reach and impact of media serving racial and ethnic audiences by translating and syndicating news stories to ethnic media via the NAM News Service, publishing the NAM Weekly Newsletter, organizing Newsmaker Briefings for ethnic media to meet with elected officials, offering professional development training for people working in ethnic media across the country, and conducting multilingual polling in many languages to gauge the pulse of racial and ethnic groups in the United States. NAM also conducted the National Ethnic Media Awards honoring outstanding news reporting in print, broadcast, or digital media serving racial and ethnic audiences.

Oftentimes these ethnic media cover a different angle than the general audience mass media reporting the same story. For instance, as possible changes in the nation's immigration laws were being considered in the early 21st century, the mass audience media covered the contentious debates between politicians, labor unions, human rights groups, and business leaders. The ethnic media focused more on how proposed immigration law changes might affect their audience's ability to get a job, visit relatives in their home country, get their children to and through college, or receive a pension or Social Security benefits. The mass media treated the issue as a spectator sport, reporting what the different players were saying and doing. The class media told their readers, viewers, and listeners how possible changes in the law could affect them and their families.

By covering issues and events close to people of color, the racial and ethnic media add more understanding of the United States as a multiracial, multicultural, multilingual, and multimedia stew pot, not a melting pot. In 2012, *Voices of NY*, a weekly compilation of stories produced by New York City's ethnic media, shared a story headlined "A Maggi-cal Sauce, Beloved Around the World" about Maggi, a common "seasoning sauce that's fundamental to cuisines around the world." Other stories ran under the headlines "Desi Comics Bring Joke Diplomacy to India," "Heroes of Past and Present Profiled for Black History Month," "Chinese Community Hit by Crackdown on Medicaid Fraud," and "Brooklyn Mother Hopes to Close Gap Between Arab Parents and Children."

At the same time ethnic media are growing, more people of color have been able to amplify their visions and voices by expressing themselves to others through their own websites, blogs, desktop publishing, DVDs, and other digital media of the era. They reached millions by posting messages on YouTube, Facebook, Twitter, and other electronic platforms that disseminate print, audio, video, and graphic material through computers, laptops, cell phones, newsletters, and other media applications. The rapid growth of these social media not only allowed more people of color to produce and send messages around the world; it also allowed them to express their own visions in their own voices.

In 2011, the most widely watched videos on YouTube included performances breaking through the stereotypical images of Asian Americans in predictable mass media roles as model minorities who are passive, super smart, and successful warriors. The popular videos were posted by young Asian Americans showing a wide range of talents as artists, dancers, musicians, and singers with performances not shown on commercial media. With names like Happy Slip, J.R.A., Kevjumba, David Choi, and J.Reyez, these Asian American performers were able to express themselves, show their talents, and draw an audience. Without the new technologies, they would not have been able to do any of these things.[57]

Notes

1. For earlier descriptions of communication in non-European cultures, see Leonard William Doob, *Communication in Africa* (New Haven, CT: Yale University Press, 1961); Irene Nicholson, *Mexican and Central American Mythology* (London: Paul Hamlyn Limited, 1967); Robert Tarbell Oliver, *Communication and Culture in Ancient India and China* (Syracuse, NY: Syracuse University Press, 1971); and Jacques Soustelle, *Daily Life of the Aztecs* (Stanford, CA: Stanford University Press, 1961).

2. Michael Emery and Edwin Emery, *The Press and America* (Boston: Allyn & Bacon, 1996), 3.

3. Ibid.

4. Leonardo Ferreira, *Centuries of Silence: The Story of Latin American Journalism* (Westport, CT: Praeger Publishers, 2006), 9–11.

5. Félix Gutiérrez, *Voices for Justice: 200 Years of Latino Newspapers in the United States,* CD-ROM (Los Angeles: University of Southern California Annenberg School for Communication and Journalism, 2010), panel 1.

6. James E. Murphy and Sharon M. Murphy, *Let My People Know* (Norman: University of Oklahoma Press, 1981), v.

7. Gregory Schaaf, "Newspaper Rock and Canyonlands National Park," *Ancient Ancestors of the Southwest,* eds. Lewis Kemper and Gregory Schaaf (Portland, OR: Graphic Arts Center, 1996), 53–54. More description and a picture of Utah's Newspaper Rock can be found in "Newspaper Rock," *Ancient Ruins of the Southwest: An Archeological Guide,* ed. David Grant Noble (Menomonie, WI: Northland, 2000), 176–178. For more on southwestern petroglyphs, see F. A. Barnes, *Canyon Country Prehistoric Rock Art* (Thompson Springs, UT: Arch Hunter Books, 2000), which includes information on and pictures of the Petrified Forest

National Park's Newspaper Rock (pp. 258–262) and Utah's Newspaper Rock State Historical Monument (pp. 244–249).

8. Félix Gutiérrez and Ernesto Ballesteros, "The 1541 Earthquake: Dawn of Latin American Journalism," *Journalism History* 6 (No. 3, Autumn 1979). See also Michael Emery and Edwin Emery, *The Press and America* (Boston: Allyn & Bacon, 1996), 5–7, and Al Hester, "Newspapers and Newspaper Prototypes in Spanish America, 1541–1750," *Journalism History* 6 (No. 3, Autumn 1979).

9. For a description of *relaciones* in Spain, see Henry F. Schulte, *The Spanish Press 1470–1966* (Champaign: University of Illinois Press, 1968), 72.

10. Julio Jiménez Rueda, *Historia de la Cultura en México, el Virriento* (Mexico City: Editorial Cultura, 1950), 222, as quoted by Carlos Alvear Acevedo, *Breve historia del periodism* (Mexico City: Editorial Jus, 1965), 79; author's translation.

11. Carlos Alvear Acevedo, *Breve historia del periodism* (Mexico City: Editorial Jus, 1965), 75.

12. Cited in Michael Emery and Edwin Emery, *The Press and America* (Boston: Allyn & Bacon, 1996), 615.

13. For an earlier Eurocentric account of America's journalism heritage, see Edwin Emery and Michael Emery, *The Press and America*, 4th ed. (Englewood Cliffs, NJ: Prentice Hall, 1978), 3–27, and for the later, more accurate approach, see Edwin Emery and Michael Emery, *The Press in America*, 6th ed. (Englewood Cliffs, NJ: Prentice Hall, 1988), 1–6.

14. Unless otherwise noted, all quotes are from *El Misisipí*, October 12, 1808, 1–4. For a more complete translation of the issue, see Félix Gutiérrez, "Spanish Language Media in the U.S.," *Caminos*, January 1984, 10–12. See also Félix Gutiérrez, "Spanish-Language Media in America: Background Resources, History," *Journalism History* 4 (No. 2, Summer 1977): 37, and Raymond MacCurdy, *A History and Bibliography of Spanish Language Newspapers and Magazines in Louisiana, 1808–1949* (Albuquerque: University of New Mexico Press, 1951), 8–9. *El Misisipí* quote in the *American Citizen*, New York, February 11, 1809, 3, was accessed by microfilm at Special Collections, Louisiana State University Library. For a comprehensive overview and listing of U.S. Latino periodicals through 1960, see Nicolas Kanellos with Helvetia Martell, *Hispanic Periodicals in the United States, Origins to 1960* (Houston, TX: Arte Público Press, 2000).

15. Armistead Scott Pride and Clint C. Wilson, *A History of the Black Press* (Washington, DC: Howard University Press, 1997), 12.

16. Walter C. Daniel, *Black Journals of the United States* (Westport, CT: Greenwood, 1982), 184.

17. For more recent and comprehensive accounts of *Freedom's Journal*, other Black publications, and their editors, see Armistead Scott Pride and Clint C. Wilson, *A History of the Black Press* (Washington, DC: Howard University Press, 1997); Frankie Hutton, *The Early Black Press in America, 1827–1860* (Westport, CT: Greenwood, 1993); and Clint C. Wilson, *Black Journalists in Paradox* (Westport, CT: Greenwood, 1991).

18. Walter C. Daniel, *Black Journals of the United States* (Westport, CT: Greenwood, 1982), and Kenneth D. Nordin, "In Search of Black Unity: An Interpretation of the Content and Function of 'Freedom's Journal,'" *Journalism History* 4 (No. 4, Winter 1977–1978): 123–124.

19. Walter C. Daniel, *Black Journals of the United States* (Westport, CT: Greenwood, 1982), 185.

20. Lionel C. Barrow, "'Our Own Cause': 'Freedom's Journal' and the Beginnings of the Black Press," *Journalism History* 4 (No. 4, Winter 1977–1978), 22; see also Henk La Brie III, "Black Newspapers: The Roots Are Deep," *Journalism History* 4 (No. 4, Winter 1977–1978), and Kenneth D. Nordin, "In Search of Black Unity: An Interpretation of the Content and Function of 'Freedom's Journal,'" *Journalism History* 4 (No. 4, Winter 1977–1978).

21. See Richard LaCourse, "An Indian Perspective—Native American Journalism: An Overview," *Journalism History* 6 (No. 2, 1979): 34–35, an issue of the journal devoted to Native American journalism.

22. For descriptions of the *Cherokee Phoenix* and Elias Boudinot, see James E. Murphy and Sharon M. Murphy, *Let My People Know* (Norman: University of Oklahoma Press, 1981), 21–23. See also Larry Worthy, "The Cherokee Phoenix (and Indian Advocate)" and "Elias Boudinot, a North Georgia Notable," in *About North Georgia,* Golden Ink, http://ngeorgia.com/history/phoenix.html. In addition, see Barbara F. Luebke, "Elias Boudinott, Indian Editor: Editorial Columns from *Cherokee Phoenix,*" *Journalism History* 6 (No. 2, Summer 1979): 48–53, and Sam G. Riley, "A Note of Caution—The Indian's Own Prejudice, as Mirrored in the First Native American Newspaper," *Journalism History* 6 (No. 2, Summer 1979): 44–47. Elias Boudinot apparently shortened the spelling of his last name to *Boudinot* from *Boudinott* early in his career, but he is referred to with his name spelled both ways in writings of the period and in subsequent scholarly works.

23. James E. Murphy and Sharon M. Murphy, *Let My People Know* (Norman: University of Oklahoma Press, 1981).

24. Cited in James E. Murphy and Sharon M. Murphy, *Let My People Know* (Norman: University of Oklahoma Press, 1981), 25. For more of Elias Boudinot's writings, see Theda Perdue, ed., *Cherokee Editor: The Writings of Elias Boudinot* (Athens: University of Georgia Press, 1996).

25. Cited in James E. Murphy and Sharon M. Murphy, *Let My People Know* (Norman: University of Oklahoma Press, 1981), 25.

26. "Cherokee Laws," *Cherokee Phoenix,* March 13, 1828, 1. Reprinted in *Journalism History* 6 (No. 2, Summer 1979): 46.

27. Barbara F. Luebke, "Elias Boudinott, Indian Editor: Editorial Columns From *Cherokee Phoenix,*" *Journalism History* 6 (No. 2, Summer 1979): 48.

28. Ibid.

29. *Cherokee Phoenix,* February 1, 1828, 3. Also cited in Barbara F. Luebke, "Elias Boudinott, Indian Editor: Editorial Columns From *Cherokee Phoenix,*" *Journalism History* 6 (No. 2, Summer 1979): 51.

30. For a more comprehensive account of portrayals of Native Americans in the 19th-century White press, see John M. Coward, *The Newspaper Indian: Native American Identity in the Press, 1820–90* (Champaign: University of Illinois Press, 1999).

31. *Cherokee Phoenix,* February 1, 1828, 3. Also cited in Barbara F. Luebke, "Elias Boudinott, Indian Editor: Editorial Columns From *Cherokee Phoenix,*" *Journalism History* 6 (No. 2, Summer 1979): 51.

32. Sam G. Riley, "A Note of Caution—The Indian's Own Prejudice, as Mirrored in the First Native American Newspaper," *Journalism History* 6 (No. 2, Summer 1979): 45.

33. For more on conflicts with tribal governments over editorial freedom and on Native American journalists, see Mark N. Trahant, *Pictures of Our Nobler Selves: A History of Native American Contributions to News Media* (Nashville, TN: The Freedom Forum First Amendment Center, 1995).

34. Ronald Takaki, *Strangers From a Different Shore: A History of Asian Americans* (Boston: Little, Brown, 1989), cited in Helen Zia, *Asian American Dreams: The Emergence of an American People* (New York: Farrar, Straus & Giroux, 2000), 25–27.

35. Sucheng Chan, *Asian Americans: An Interpretive History* (Washington, DC: Twain, 1991), 25; Gladys C. Hansen and William F. Heintz, *The Chinese in California: A Brief Bibliographic History* (San Francisco: Richard Abel, 1970), 7–8.

36. Jack Chen, *The Chinese of America* (New York: Harper & Row, 1971), 3.

37. For images of the Chinese in California gold rush popular culture, see Robert G. Lee, "The 'Heathen Chinee' on God's Free Soil," *Orientals: Asian Americans in Popular Culture* (Philadelphia: Temple University Press, 1999), 15–50. For later descriptions and pictures of the Chinese in the media, see Philip P. Choy, Lorraine Dong, and Marlon K. Hom, *The Coming Man: 19th Century American Perceptions of the Chinese* (Seattle: University of Washington Press, 1994).

38. Gunther Barth, *Bitter Strength* (Cambridge, MA: Harvard University Press, 1971), 174.

39. Emerson Daggett, ed., *History of Foreign Journalism in San Francisco* (Works Project Administration, 1939), as cited in Gladys C. Hansen and William F. Heintz, *The Chinese in California: A Brief Bibliographic History* (San Francisco: Richard Abel, 1970), 45.

40. Edward C. Kemble, *A History of California Newspapers, 1846–1858* (Los Gatos, CA: The Talisman Press, 1962; original work published 1858), 117–119.

41. Karl Lo and Him Mark Lai, *Chinese Newspapers Published in North America, 1854–1975* (Washington, DC: Center for Chinese Research Materials, 1977), as cited in Kuei Chiu, *Asian Language Newspapers in the United States: History Revisited,* paper presented at the Round Table on Newspapers, 62nd IFLA Conference, Beijing, China (August 28, 1996).

42. Ibid. See also *The Golden Hills' News,* No. 7, June 24, 1854; No. 8, July 1, 1854; and No. 10, July 29, 1854.

43. L. C. Hirata, "Free, Indentured, Enslaved: Chinese Prostitutes in Nineteenth-Century America," *Signs: Journal of Women in Culture and Society* 5 (No. 1, 1977): 3–29, as cited in both Sucheng Chan, *Asian Americans: An Interpretive History* (Washington, DC: Twain, 1991), and Judy Yung, *Unbound Voices: A Documentary History of Chinese Women in San Francisco* (Berkeley: University of California Press, 1999).

44. Gunther Barth, *Bitter Strength* (Cambridge, MA: Harvard University Press, 1971).

45. Ibid., 174–175.

46. "The Chinese Exodus," *The Golden Hills' News,* May 27, 1854, 1. (Translation of Chinese characters by Stanley Rosen.)

47. Ibid.

48. "The Government, Press, Public and Chinese," *The Golden Hills' News,* July 1, 1854, 1.

49. "The Chinese and the Times," *The Golden Hills' News*, June 10, 1854, 1.

50. "American Preachings Versus Practice," *The Golden Hills' News*, July 29, 1854, 1.

51. "Is There No Help for the Chinese in California?" *The Golden Hills' News*, June 24, 1854, 1.

52. Gunther Barth, *Bitter Strength* (Cambridge, MA: Harvard University Press, 1971).

53. Ibid., 175–176.

54. Edward C. Kemble, *A History of California Newspapers, 1846–1858* (Los Gatos, CA: The Talisman Press, 1962; original work published 1858), 117.

55. Kuei Chiu, *Asian Language Newspapers in the United States: History Revisited*, paper presented at the Round Table on Newspapers, 62nd IFLA Conference, Beijing, China (August 28, 1996), 2, 4–5.

56. Irvine Garland Penn, *The Afro-American Press and Its Editors* (Springfield, MA: Willey & Co., 1891), as cited in Don Dodson and William A. Hachten, "Communication and Development: African and Afro-American" parallels, *Journalism Monographs* 28 (No. 25, May 1973): 25.

57. Tiffany Chan and Emily Woods, "Model Minority," term project and class presentation, Journalism 466M People of Color and the News Media, University of Southern California, Spring 2011.

Epilogue
Thoughts About the Future

Toward the middle of the first decade of this century, the previous edition of this book offered an assessment of what the foreseeable future might hold for people of color, women, and their place in—and out of—communications media in the United States. The assessment, titled "21st Century Challenges and Opportunities," accurately considered its ideas within context of the rapid and evolving technological changes that were sweeping the communications industries at the time.

As this is written, the forces of social media, manifest via personal electronic digital devices, have altered the communications landscape. In earlier editions of this work, it was possible to assess communications phenomena by separately examining their various platform components (e.g., radio, motion pictures, television, or newspapers). The convergence of technologies, multiple content delivery systems, and concentration of media ownership across platforms now renders such analysis less useful. How does one distinguish "entertainment" from "news" or "advertising" from "commentary"? There is also a vigorous debate over the definition of what constitutes journalism to the extent that some have come to believe that everyone with a means of reporting events or expressing personal opinions to an audience is a "journalist." The question is, what do these things mean for racial and cultural minorities in the United States?

As noted in previous editions of this book, the forces of capitalism and media marketing have seen communications firms increasingly adopt the concept of segmenting and targeting content messages for specific audiences. The process has resulted in shifting their focus from what was termed "mass" communication to "class" communication. It was inevitable, therefore, that people of color would become attractive objects of the capitalistic attention of White-owned media conglomerates. Examples include the 2001 purchase of Black Entertainment Television (BET) by Viacom Inc., followed a year later with NBCUniversal assuming control of Telemundo, the Spanish-language cable television operation. Across the nation, several daily newspaper organizations—after decades of undercovering and stereotyping people of color—either purchased or created print and/or online publications targeted at those communities. This circumstance created an identity crisis among many Americans of color wherein media content seemed to emanate from media owned by their group, but in reality these media were merely vehicles designed by hegemonic capitalists to attract them as consumers for corporate advertisers. A case in point: A large portion of African American women believe *Essence* magazine—a fashion- and lifestyle-oriented publication targeted at them—is Black owned, although it is part of the Time Warner media conglomerate. While such enterprises are not necessarily positioned as counter to African American interests, they create the illusion that their content is purposed for the benefit of their market demographic rather than the economic interest of their owners.

This notion was discussed at a 2010 communications symposium at Stanford University where the historical role of cultural diversity in a pluralistic society was considered. From a practical standpoint, the United States operates as a pluralistic democracy encompassing groups (publics) with *unequal* political and economic power. Capitalism is the driving force that powers American society. Communications media operate with the financial "bottom line" as their primary objective, and their content messages are generally motivated by profit incentive and directed toward the marketplace each has determined to exploit. This model is not likely the one envisioned a few centuries ago by John Milton whose theory that an uncensored marketplace of ideas best serves the needs of a free society, a notion that became the philosophical cornerstone of the First Amendment. Neither did Thomas Jefferson foresee that capitalism would undermine the ideal of a free press serving as watchdog over government and business in the best interests of American citizens.

In the 1830s, the penny press era introduced "mass communications" and commercial advertising as the basis for economic viability of newspapers. For practical purposes, the idea that general audience newspapers and their media progeny would exist to serve public interests became a secondary consideration at that time. Although news media in the United States are not generally censored by governmental restraint—as Jefferson had feared—a strong case can be made that they have placed constraints on themselves in the interest of maximizing profits. In 21st-century America, the news media business has become less about news and more about business. In this context, the notion that mainstream newspapers will vigorously champion the cause of equality and justice for marginalized ethnic groups is problematic unless there is some measure of profit incentive.

There seems little hope that 21st-century media in their various platforms will devote significant content attention to advocating for marginalized racial and cultural groups. Theatrical motion pictures, television programs, advertising commercials, and video games will continue to broaden inclusion of racial and cultural groups because it is sound business practice in a multicultural society. Some will be superficial and stereotypical; a few will offer probing and thought-provoking themes. The notion of advocacy for egalitarian social participation will thus be transmitted in subtle ways. While it is true alternative media will continue to voice the aspirations of their constituents for equal access and a fair share of the privileges of American citizenship, their pleas are likely destined to be overwhelmed by a sea of popular culture diversions in the capitalistic marketplace.

Finally, what will be the future of alternative media platforms for marginalized groups? The "traditional" print media platforms continue at this time to be a primary means of communication within the racial and cultural groups under consideration. A few have added online sites to their print publications footprint. On an individual level, journalists and bloggers of color have carved out niches for interpretation and commentary on events that affect their constituencies. Efforts at expanding ownership of media under licensing control of the U.S. Federal Communications Commission (radio, television, cable, satellite, and broadband technology) have proven difficult at best as industry deregulation, lack of financial capital, and conservative political interests in alliance with corporate media conglomerates have worked against minority groups.

Meanwhile, however, the second decade of the 21st century has proven that social media are powerful tools for addressing minority concerns and forging strong bonds for advocacy. The 2011 "Arab Spring" uprisings and the "Occupy Wall Street" movement may portend the future for effective expression of the needs of marginalized groups. The social media tools bypass both governmental and corporate barriers that have muted such voices in the past. They may be a means of realizing the philosophical role of communications envisioned by John Milton who theorized in his *Areopagitica* that an uncensored marketplace of ideas best serves the needs of a free society. Milton vigorously supported the vision of a society wherein "all the winds of doctrine were let loose to play upon the earth, so truth be in the field, we do injuriously by licensing and prohibiting to misdoubt her strength. Let her and falsehood grapple."[1]

Can marginalized racial and cultural groups and women harness the force of social media to speak truth to power and effect change toward equality and fairness in a nation where those ideals served as founding principles? The answer will be found in future interaction between these groups and their application of technology in the new communications environment.

Cultural minority groups are active users of new media age technology that may be key to the future of communication in America.

Source: Comstock Images/Comstock/Thinkstock.

As this is written, individuals in an ever-shrinking global village are utilizing social media to disseminate both positive and negative messages about the experiences of marginalized groups in the United States. This suggests there are more questions than answers when it comes to projecting the long-term benefits of social digital technology in a multicultural society. Negative incidents—such as when Anglo University of California, Los Angeles student Alexandra Wallace posted her now infamous anti-Asian video rants following the 2011 Japanese tsunami—illustrate the consequences of personal intolerant communication via the YouTube and Facebook platforms. Because social media enable participants to believe they are connected to like-minded others, Ms. Wallace's "ching chong ling long ting tong" racist ramblings resulted in such a backlash that she dropped out of UCLA. Her actions, however, spawned other racist offerings including "Ching-Chong-Ling-Long Gourmet Takeout" by fellow UCLA students who pounced on the Internet's power to create a global phenomenon by snatching her most recognizable sound bite to launch what they thought would be a humorous business enterprise. The proliferation of racist "spin-off" activities prompted California politician Mike Eng to sponsor legislation against such activities that "perpetuate misunderstandings about Asian-Americans and intensify hurtful sentiments toward this community."[2]

Perhaps it is not so much that historically marginalized ethnic and cultural groups have lost the ability to poke harmless fun at themselves, but rather that the growing generation of techno-oriented multicultural citizens blurs the lines of distinction between harmless humor and the perpetuation of hurtful, stereotypical messages that fuel racist rhetoric that divides rather than brings Americans closer together. It is possible that the latitude of acceptance and rejection as defined by the younger, technologically savvy generation has grown wider and more tolerant. Yet, daily headlines report a smorgasbord of incidents that remind us that ethnic scapegoating, racial profiling, immigrant bashing, and gender inequities continue to persist. This will remain a challenge for individual Americans as they face an increasingly multicultural future.

Assemblyman Mike Eng (center) sponsored legislation in California to combat racially biased communication against the Asian American community.

Source: United States Government.

Meanwhile, corporate America faces its own challenges. For example, as recounted in Chapter 7, Lowe's Companies Inc., the home improvement retail firm, experienced an unexpected backlash via social media when it decided to pull its advertising from the reality television show *All-American Muslim* on Discovery Communications Inc.'s TLC channel. Lowe's acted after receiving complaints from the Florida Family Association, a conservative Christian group that lobbies companies to promote "traditional, biblical values." But the company immediately drew admonishment from California State Senator Ted Lieu who called the move "bigoted, shameful, and un-American" and demanded an apology. A petition gathered more than 14,000 signatures on SignOn.org that called for companies to continue advertising on the show. In addition, actress Mia Farrow joined the battle in a Twitter post and urged a boycott of Lowe's.[3]

The Lowe's incident is perhaps emblematic of the challenges that lie ahead because there is a troubling lack of diversity in corporate America in general, and media organizations in particular. A 2011 report by Diversity-Inc revealed that of the top 50 "Companies for Diversity" only three media organizations made the list with Cox Communications ranked 20th, Time Warner 28th, and Time Warner Cable 45th. It is true that corporations must walk a fine line and a slippery slope when negotiating the intersections of political correctness, multicultural sensitivity, and freedom of speech, but they must take a leadership role in setting a positive tone for the future as part of their social responsibility in America's capitalistic society. People of color and women must be seen beyond the context of marketing targets that facilitate bottom-line profit margins. More culturally diverse and gender-equitable workforces—at all organizational levels—will ease the transition toward a better communications future. When that becomes a realized objective, the United States will have created a society positioned to test John Milton's theory concerning the marketplace of communicative ideas. In the process, it is likely that economic prosperity will also follow.

Notes

1. John Milton, *Areopagitica: A Speech for the Liberty of Unlicensed Printing to the Parliament of England,* accessed March 22, 2012, http://www.gutenberg.org/files/608/608-h/608-h.htm.

2. Beige Luciano-Adams, "Eng Takes Issue with Name of UCLA Chinese Take-Out Business," *San Gabriel Valley Tribune,* July 14, 2011.

3. Shan Li, "Lowe's Faces Backlash Over Pulling Ads from 'All-American Muslim,'" *Los Angeles Times,* December 13, 2011, accessed March 22, 2012, http://articles.latimes.com/2011/dec/13/business/la-fi-lowes-muslim-20111213.

Suggested Readings

Adare, S. (2005). *"Indian" stereotypes in TV science fiction: First nations' voice speaks out.* Austin: University of Texas Press.

Afzal-Khan, F. (Ed.). (2005). *Shattering the stereotypes: Muslim women speak out.* Northampton, MA: Olive Branch Press.

Ainley, B. (1998). *Black journalists, White media.* Stoke on the Trent, UK: Trentham Books.

Albarran, A. (Ed.). (2009). *The handbook of Spanish language media.* New York: Routledge.

Aleiss, A. (2005). *Making the White man's Indian: Native Americans and Hollywood movies.* Westport, CT: Praeger.

Anderson, L. M. (1999). *Mammies no more: The changing image of Black women on stage and screen.* Lanham, MD: Rowman & Littlefield.

Barlow, W. (1999). *Voice over: The making of Black radio.* Philadelphia: Temple University Press.

Beltran, M. C. (2009). *Latino//a stars in the U.S. eyes: The making and meanings of film and TV stardom.* Champaign: University of Illinois Press.

Ben-Shaul, N. S. (2006). *A violent world: TV news images of Middle Eastern terror and war.* Lanham, MD: Rowman & Littlefield.

Berg, C. R. (2002). *Latino images in film: Stereotypes, subversion, resistance.* Austin: University of Texas Press.

Biagi, S., & Kern-Foxworth, M. (Eds.). (1997). *Facing difference: Race, gender and mass media.* Thousand Oaks, CA: Pine Forge.

Bogle, D. (2001). *Toms, coons, mulattoes, mammies, and bucks: An interpretive history of Blacks in American films.* New York: Continuum International Publishing Group.

Broussard, J. (2004). *Giving a voice to the voiceless: Four pioneering Black women journalists.* New York & London: Routledge.

Brownlee, L. (2007). *Les Brownlee: The autobiography of a pioneering African-American journalist.* Oak Park, IL: Marion Street Press.

Burrell, T. (2010). *Brainwashed: Challenging the myth of Black inferiority.* New York: Smiley Books.

Chilton, K. (2008). *Hazel Scott: The pioneering journey of a jazz pianist from café society to Hollywood to HUAC.* Ann Arbor: University of Michigan Press.

Ching Yoon Louie, M. (2001). *Sweatshop warriors: Immigrant women workers take on the global factory.* Cambridge, MA: South End Press.

Coward, J. M. (1999). *The newspaper Indian: Native American identity in the press, 1820–90.* Urbana: University of Illinois Press.

Cropp, F., Frisby, C., & Mills, D. (2003). *Journalism across cultures.* Ames: Iowa State Press.

Dates, J., & Barlow, W. (1993). *Split image African Americans in the mass media* (2nd ed.). Washington, DC: Howard University Press.

Davila, A. (2008). *Latino spin: Public image and the whitewashing of race.* New York: New York University Press.

Del Valle, E. (2005). *Hispanic marketing & public relations: Understanding and targeting American's largest minority.* Boca Raton, FL: Poyeen Publications.

Dennis, E. E., & Pease, E. C. (1997). *The media in Black and White.* New Brunswick, NJ: Transaction.

Denzin, N. K. (2002). *Reading race: Hollywood and the cinema of racial violence.* Thousand Oaks, CA: Sage.

Diawara, M. (1993). *Black American cinema.* New York: Routledge.

Dines, G., & Humez, J. M. (2010). *Gender, race, and class in media: A critical reader* (3rd ed.). Thousand Oaks, CA: Sage.

Dunn, S. (2008). *"Baad bitches" and sassy supermamas: Black power action films.* Urbana: University of Illinois Press.

Ely, M. P. (2001). *The adventures of Amos 'n' Andy: A social history of an American phenomenon.* Charlottesville: University Press of Virginia.

Entman, R. M., & Rojecki, A. (2001). *The Black image in the White mind: Media and race in America.* Chicago: University of Chicago Press.

Flores, M. (2008). *Hispanics in the media: More than 200 years of Spanish language influence in U.S. communications.* Dubuque, IA: Kendall/Hunt.

Gonzalez, J., & Torres, J. (2011). *News for all the people: The epic story of race and the American media.* New York: Verso.

Graham, A. (2001). *Framing the south: Hollywood, television and race during the civil rights struggle.* Baltimore: Johns Hopkins University Press.

Gutierrez, L. M., & Lewis, E. A. (1999). *Empowering women of color.* New York: Columbia University Press.

Habell-Pallan, M., & Romero, M. (Eds.). (2002). *Latino/a popular culture.* New York: New York University Press.

Hayes, M. E., & Williams, L. F. (Eds.). (2007). *Black women and music: More than blues.* Urbana: University of Illinois Press.

Heider, D. (2000). *White news: Why local news programs don't cover people of color.* Mahwah, NJ: Lawrence Erlbaum.

Hill, G. H., & Raglin, L. (1990). *Black women in television: An illustrated history and bibliography.* New York: Garland.

Hilliard, D. (Ed.). (2007). *The Black Panther: Intercommunal news service.* New York: Atria Books.

Hosokawa, B. (1998). *Out of the frying pan: Reflections of a Japanese American.* Niwot: University Press of Colorado.

Hutton, F. (1993). *The early Black press in America, 1827–1860.* Westport, CT: Greenwood.

Jackson, S., Jieyu, L., & Juhyun, W. (2008). *East Asian sexualities: Modernity, gender, and new sexual cultures.* London: Zed Books.

Jacobs, R. N. (2000). *Race, media, and the crisis of civil society from Watts to Rodney King.* Cambridge, UK: Cambridge University Press.

Jakubowicz, A. (Ed.). (1994). *Racism, ethnicity and the media.* St. Leonards, Australia: Allen & Unwin.

Kamalipour, Y. R. (1995). *The U.S. media and the Middle East: Image and perception.* Westport, CT: Greenwood Press.

Keddie, N. (2007). *Women in the Middle East: Past and present.* Princeton, NJ: Princeton University Press.

Keever, B. A., Martindale, C., & Weston, M. A. (Eds.). (1997). *U.S. news coverage of racial minorities: A sourcebook, 1934–1996.* Westport, CT: Greenwood.

Keith, M. C. (1995). *Signals in the air: Native broadcasting in America.* New York: Praeger.

Kellstedt, P. M. (2003). *The mass media and the dynamics of American racial attitudes.* Cambridge, UK: Cambridge University Press.

Kelton, E. (1993). *The Indian in frontier news.* San Angelo, TX: Talley.

Kern-Foxworth, M. (1994). *Aunt Jemima, Uncle Ben, and Rastus: Blacks in advertising yesterday, today, and tomorrow.* Westport, CT: Praeger.

Korzenny, F., & Korzenny, B. (2011). *Hispanic marketing: Connecting with the new Latino consumer.* Oxford, UK: Butterworth-Heinemann/Elsevier.

Kumake, R., & Moran, J. (2010). *Many cultures one market: A guide to understanding opportunities in the Asian Pacific American market.* Chicago: The Copy Workshop.

Larson, S. (2006). *Media & minorities: The politics of race in news and entertainment.* Lanham, MD: Rowman & Littlefield.

Lee, J., Lim, I. L., & Matsukawa, Y. (2002). *Re-collecting early Asian America: Essays in cultural history.* Philadelphia: Temple University Press.

Lee, R. G. (1999). *Orientals: Asian Americans in popular culture.* Philadelphia: Temple University Press.

Lehrman, S. (2005). *News in a new America.* Miami: John S. and James L. Knight Foundation.

Lind, R. A. (2004). *Race, gender, media: Considering diversity across audiences, content, and producers.* Boston: Allyn & Bacon.

Luther, C., Lebre, C., & Clark, N. (2012). *Diversity in U.S. mass media.* West Sussex. UK: Wiley-Blackwell.

MacDonald, F. J. (1992). *Blacks and White TV: African Americans in television since 1948.* Belmont, CA: Wadsworth.

Marubbio, M. E. (2006). *Killing the Indian maiden: Images of Native American women in film.* Lexington: University Press of Kentucky.

Matsaganis, M., Katz, V., & Ball-Rokeach, S. (2011). *Understanding ethnic media: Producers, consumers, and societies.* Thousand Oaks, CA: Sage.

Mayer, V. (2003). *Producing dreams, consuming youth: Mexican-Americans and mass media.* New Brunswick, NJ: Rutgers University Press.

McGowan, W. (2001). *Coloring the news: How crusading for diversity has corrupted American journalism.* San Francisco: Encounter Books.

Melendez, A. (2005). *Spanish-language newspapers in New Mexico, 1934–1958.* Tucson: University of Arizona Press.

Mendible, M. (Ed.). (2007). *From bananas to buttocks: The Latina body in popular film and culture.* Austin: University of Texas Press.

Meyer, D. (1996). *Speaking for themselves: Neoamericano cultural identity and the Spanish-language press, 1880–1920.* Albuquerque: University of New Mexico Press.

Mills, K. (2004). *Changing channels: The civil rights case that transformed television.* Jackson: University Press of Mississippi.

Moghadam, V. M. (2003). *Modernizing women: Gender and social change in the Middle East* (2nd ed.). Boulder, CO: Lynne Rienner Publishers.

Molina-Guzman, I. (2010). *Dangerous curves: Latina bodies in the media.* New York: New York University Press.

Morgan, A., Pifer, A., & Woods, K. (Eds.). (2006). *The authentic voice: The best reporting on race and ethnicity.* New York: Columbia University Press.

Morgan, R. (2003). *Sisterhood is forever: The women's anthology for a new millennium.* New York: Washington Square Press.

Nama, A. (2008). *Black space: Imagining race in science fiction film.* Austin: University of Texas Press.

Nava, S. (2011). *Working the affect shift: Latina service workers in U.S. film.* Boca Raton, Fl.: Brown Walker Press.

Newkirk, P. (2000). *Within the veil: Black journalists, White media.* New York: New York University Press.

Ono, K., & Pham, V. (2010). *Asian Americans and the media.* Malden, MA: Polity Press.

Ovalle, P. P. (2011). *Dance and the Hollywood Latina: Race, sex, and stardom.* Piscataway, NJ: Rutgers University Press.

Owusu, H. (1997). *Symbols of Native America.* New York: Sterling.

Padgett, G. (2006). *New directions in diversity: A new approach covering America's multicultural communities.* Portland, OR: Marion Street Press.

Pough, G. (2004). *Check it while I wreck it: Black womanhood, hip-hop culture, and the public sphere.* New York: Northeastern.

Pride, A., & Wilson, C., II. (1997). *A history of the Black press in America.* Washington, DC: Howard University Press.

Rhodes, J., & Cary, M. A. S. (1998). *The Black press and protest in the nineteenth century.* Bloomington: Indiana University Press.

Rios, I. D., & Mohamed, A. N. (Eds.). (2003). *Brown and Black communication: Latino and African American conflict and convergence in mass media.* Westport, CT: Praeger.

Rivas-Rodriguez, M. (2003). *Brown eyes on the web: Unique perspectives of an alternative Latino online publication.* New York & London: Routledge.

Rivera, R. Z. (2003). *New York Ricans from the hip hop zone.* New York: Palgrave Macmillan.

Roberts, G., & Klibanoff, H. (2007). *The race beat: The press, the civil rights struggle and the awakening of a nation.* New York: Knopf.

Rodriguez, C. E. (1997). *Latin looks: Images of Latinas and Latinos in the U.S. media.* Boulder, CO: Westview Press.

Rodriguez, C. E. (2008). *Heroes, lovers, and others: The story of Latinos in Hollywood.* New York: Oxford University Press.

Rollins, P. C., & O'Connor, J. E. (Eds.). (1998). *Hollywood's Indian: The portrayal of the Native American in film.* Lexington: The University Press of Kentucky.

Rome, D. (2004). *Black demons, the media's depiction of the African American male criminal stereotype.* Westport, CT: Praeger.

Ross, K., & Playdon, P. (2001). *Black marks: Minority ethnic audiences and the media.* Burlington, VT: Ashgate.

Santa Ana, O. (2002). *Brown tide rising: Metaphors of Latinos in contemporary American public discourse.* Austin: University of Texas Press.

Semmerling, T. J. (2006). *"Evil" Arabs in American popular film: Orientalist fear.* Austin: University of Texas Press.

Shaheen, J. G. (2001). *Reel bad Arabs: How Hollywood vilifies a people.* Northampton, MA: Olive Branch Press.

Shaheen, J. G. (2008). *Guilty: Hollywood verdict on Arabs after 9/11.* Northampton, MA: Olive Branch Press.

Smith, B. (2000). *Home girls: A Black feminist anthology.* New Brunswick, NJ: Rutgers University Press.

Squires, C. (2009). *African Americans and the media.* Malden, MA: Polity Press.

Stephens, L. (1999). *Covering the community: A diversity handbook for media.* Thousand Oaks, CA: Pine Forge Press.

Subervi-Velez, F. A. (Ed.). (2008). *The mass media and Latino politics.* New York: Routledge.

Suggs, H. L. (1996). *The Black press in the Middle West, 1865–1985.* Westport, CT: Greenwood.

Tadiar, N., & Davis, A. (Eds.). (2005). *Beyond the frame: Women of color and visual representation.* New York: Palgrave Macmillan.

Terry, W. (2007). *Missing pages: Black journalists of modern America: An oral history.* New York: Carroll & Graf.

Tovares, R. D. (2002). *Manufacturing the gang: Mexican American youth gangs on local television.* Westport, CT: Greenwood.

Toyoma, N. A., & Gee, T. (2006). *More than serving tea: Asian American women on expectations, relationships, leadership, and faith.* Downers Grove, IL: InterVarsity Press.

Trahant, M. (1995). *Pictures of our nobler selves: A history of Native American contributions to news media.* Nashville, TN: The Freedom Form First Amendment Center.

Trevino, J. (2001). *Eyewitness: A filmmaker's memoir of the Chicano movement.* Houston, TX: Arte Publico Press.

Valdivia, A. N. (2000). *A Latina in the land of Hollywood: And other essays on media culture.* Tucson: University of Arizona Press.

Valdivia, A. N. (2010). *Latinas/os and the media.* Malden, MA: Polity Press.

Vogel, T. (Ed.). (2001). *The Black press: New literary and historical essays.* New Brunswick, NJ: Rutgers University Press.

Waller, L. (Ed.). (1998). *Newspapers, diversity and you.* Princeton, NJ: The Dow Jones Newspaper Fund.

Ward, B. (Ed.). (2001). *Media, culture and the modern African American freedom struggle.* Gainesville: University Press of Florida.

Watkins, M. (2005). *Stepin Fetchit: The life & times of Lincoln Perry.* New York: Pantheon Books.

Watts, J. (2005). *Hattie McDaniel: Black ambition, White Hollywood.* New York: HarperCollins.

Weill, S. (2002). *In the madhouse's din: Civil rights coverage by Mississippi's daily press, 1948–1968.* Westport, CT: Praeger.

Weston, M. A. (1996). *Native Americans in the news: Images of Indians in the twentieth century press.* Westport, CT: Greenwood.

Wilkins, K. G. (2009). *Home/land/security: What we learn about Arab communities from action-adventure films.* Plymouth: Lexington Books.

Wilson, C., II. (1991). *Black journalists in paradox: Historical perspectives and current dilemmas.* Westport, CT: Greenwood.

Wolseley, R. E. (1995). *Black achievers in American journalism.* Nashville, TN: James C. Winston.

Yates, M. (2007). *More unequal: Aspects of class in the United States.* New York: Month Review Press.

Online Resources

A portion of the following list of media diversity online resources was compiled by the Poynter Institute for Media Studies Library.

AAJA Online
http://www.aajaonline.tumblr.com
Media Watch is AAJA's core program to address unfair and inaccurate news coverage of Asian Americans and Pacific Islanders.

Advertising Age
http://www.adage.com/channel/Hispanic-marketing/23
Advertising strategies targeted at African Americans and Hispanics in the media.

American-Arab Anti-Discrimination Committee
http://www.adc.org/
Monitors portrayals of Arabs in the U.S. media.

American Indian Artists Incorporated
http://www.amerinda.org/
Links to other Native American websites to promote authentic representations of Indians in the media.

American Women in Radio and Television (AWRT)
http://www.awrt.org
AWRT is dedicated to advancing the impact of women in electronic media and related fields.

Arab American Institute
http://www.aaiusa.org
Primary national resource on the Arab American experience for the media.

Arab American News Wire
http://www.aams.blogspot.com
American Arab and Muslim news media.

Asian American Journalists Association (AAJA)
http://www.aaja.org
AAJA was formed in 1981 to provide support for Asian American journalists.

Asian American Justice Center
http://www.advancingequality.org/
Asian Pacific American Media Coalition's Report Card on Television Diversity.

Asian American Media
http://bulldog2.redlands.edu/dept/AsianStudiesDept/
Annotated list of resources on Asian American media.

Asian-Nation
http://www.asian-nation.org/
This is an information source on the historical, political, social, economic, and cultural elements that make up today's Asian American community.

ASNE Diversity Resources
http://www.asne.org/kioskdiversity/index.htm
These are diversity resources from the American Society of News Editors.

Association for Women in Communications (AWC)
http://www.womcom.org/
AWC champions the advancement of women across all communications disciplines.

Black PR
http://www.blackpr.com/
Extensive press release and column distribution to the Black media.

Black Press USA
http://www.blackpressusa.com
An independent source of news for the African American community.

Borderzine
http://www.borderzine.com/about-us/
A web community for Latino student journalists connecting the classroom to the newsroom.

CCNMA: Latino Journalists of California
http://www.ccnma.org/
For Latinos pursuing careers in the news media, and to foster accurate and fair portrayals of Latinos in the news media.

California Tomorrow
http://www.californiatomorrow.org/media/images.pdf
Stereotypes of African Americans in television.

Center for Asian American Media (CAAM)
http://www.caamedia.org
A nonprofit organization dedicated to presenting stories in the media that convey the richness and diversity of Asian American experiences.

Columbia Workshop on Journalism, Race & Ethnicity
http://www.jrn.columbia.edu/workshops/
The aim of the Columbia University workshop is to encourage candid and complete coverage of race and ethnicity.

Contacto PR News
http://www.contactonews.com/prnews.htm
Understanding the U.S. Hispanic news media.

Cultural Survival
http://www.culturalsurvival.org/
Native American stereotypes in popular media.

Diversity Toolbox (Society for Professional Journalists)
http://www.spj.org/dtb.asp
These are diversity resources from the Society for Professional Journalists.

DiversityInc.com
http://www.diversityinc.com/
DiversityInc.com offers information on how diversity affects companies' relationships with their employees, suppliers, customers, and investors.

DiversityWeb
http://www.diversityweb.org/
DiversityWeb was designed by the Association of American Colleges and Universities and the University of Maryland at College Park.

Fairness & Accuracy in Reporting (FAIR)
http://www.fair.org/index.php?page=1431
FAIR challenges media bias and censorship since 1986.

Foundation for Asian American Independent Media
http://www.faaim.org/
Promotes film, video, and other media by and about Asian Americans.

Freedom Forum: Newsroom Diversity
http://www.freedomforum.org/diversity/default.asp
This website contains links to news, commentary, and analysis.

Heinz Endowments African American Men and Boys Task Force
http://www.heinz.org/secondary.aspx?SectionID-255
Study on news media reporting on African American men and boys.

International Association of Women in Radio and Television
http://www.iawrt.org/

International Women's Media Foundation (IWMF)
http://www.iwmf.org/
IWMF was founded to strengthen the role of women in the media.
National study on the obstacles and opportunities of women of color in
the U.S. media.

Journalism and Women Symposium (JAWS)
http://www.jaws.org/
JAWS supports the personal growth and professional empowerment of
women in newsrooms.

Journalist's Toolbox
http://www.journaliststoolbox.org./archive/writing-with-numbers/
Society of Professional Journalists' resource guide and web links to
various media organizations addressing diversity issues.

Latin Heat Entertainment
http://www.latinheat.com/
Covering Latino Hollywood since 1992.

Latinos and Media Project
http://www.latinosandmedia.org
This website contains information and resources about a variety of
issues related to Latinos and the media.

Longhouse Media & Native Lens
http://www.longhousemedia.org/programs.html
Native Lens was developed as a result of the absence of indigenous
experiences and perspectives in the media.

Maynard Institute
http://www.maynardije.org/
The institute is dedicated to increasing racial and ethnic diversity in
news coverage, staffing, and business operations.

Media Action Network for Asian Americans (MANAA)
http://www.manaa.org
Dedicated to fighting racism and stereotypes of Asian Americans in the media.

Media Awareness Network
http://209.29.148.33/english/issues/stereotyping/aboriginal_people/aboriginal_portrayals.cfm
Native Americans are virtually invisible on television.

Media Monitors Network
http://www.mediamonitors.net/anayat2.html
Racial profiling of Muslims and Middle Easterners in America.

MIBTP
http://www.thebroadcaster.com/
The mission of the Minorities in Broadcasting Training Program is to ensure diversity in newsrooms at television and radio stations across the United States.

Model Minority
http://www.modelminority.com
Gender, race, and class stereotypes of Asian Americans in the media.

NAA's Diversity and Education Resources
http://www.naa.org/
This website contains resources from the Newspaper Association of America diversity department.

National Arab American Journalists Association (United States)
http://www.naaja-us.com
Network of professional American Arab journalists working in mainstream American news media.

National Asian Pacific American Legal Consortium (NAPALC)
http://www.mediaengage.org/planDesign/partners/fact_sheets/NAPALC.pdf
Participates in the Multi-Ethnic Media Coalition to advocate for representation of Asian Pacific Americans in the media.

National Association of Black Journalists (NABJ)
http://www.nabj.org
NABJ was founded with the purpose of promoting and communicating the importance of diversity in newsrooms.

National Association of Hispanic Journalists (NAHJ)
http://www.nahj.org/
NAHJ is dedicated to the recognition and professional advancement of
Hispanics in the news industry.

National Association of Minority Media Executives (NAMME)
http://media411.tvjobs.com/cgi-bin/search.cgi?Z=&c=75&k=1922
NAMME is an organization for media managers and executives of color
working in newspapers, magazines, radio, television, cable, and new media.

National Association for Multi-Ethnicity in Communications (NAMIC)
http://www.namic.com/
NAMIC educates, advocates, and empowers for the cause of diversity in
the telecommunications industry.

The National Black Programming Consortium (NBPC)
http://www.blackpublicmedia.org/about/
Founded in 1979, the NBPC distributes unique stories of the Black
experience in the new media age.

National Center on Disability and Journalism (NCDJ)
http://www.ncdj.org/
NCDJ's mission is to educate journalists and educators about disability
reporting issues in order to produce more accurate, fair, and diverse news
reporting.

National Coalition on Racism in Sports and Media
http://www.aimovement.org/ncrsm/
Widely held misconceptions and stereotypes of American Indians in
sports teams' imagery and identities.

National Diversity Newspaper Job Bank
http://www.artistsresourceguide.org/National_diversity_newspaper_
job_bank_the
This job bank is devoted to diversifying the news media industry and is
primarily aimed at women and minorities.

National Federation of Press Women (NFPW)
http://www.nfpw.org/
NFPW promotes the highest ethical standards and the professional
development of women.

The National Hispanic Media Coalition
http://www.nhmc.org

A nonpartisan, nonprofit media advocacy and civil rights organization promoting equity throughout the entertainment industry and advocating for fair policies for Latinos and other people of color in the media.

National Lesbian and Gay Journalists Association (NLGJA)
http://www.nlgja.org
NLGJA works to ensure equal benefits and conditions for lesbian and gay employees in news organizations.

National Organization for Women (NOW)
http://www.now.org/issues/media/women_in_media_facts.html
The Women in Media Fact Sheet shows inequality and lack of diversity in media organizations.

Native American Journalists Association (NAJA)
http://www.naja.com/
NAJA was formed to encourage, inspire, enhance, and empower Native American communicators.

Native News Network
http://www.nativenewsnetwork.com/
Discussion on how the media cover American Indians.

Native Public Media
http://www.nativepublicmedia.org
Thoughts about the future of Native Americans in television.

Native Web
http://www.nativeweb.org/papers/essays/franki_webb.html
Stereotypical representations of Native Americans in commercial media.

Native Web Resources
http://www.nativeweb.org/resources/art_artisans_galleries/films_videos/
Explores the uneasy relationship American Indians have had with the media since the origins of film.

The Network Journal
http://www.tnj.com/news/black-american
The Network Journal covers all stories on Black newspapers in America that are based on African American people.

New America Media
http://www.newamericamedia.org
The country's first and largest national collaboration of journalism schools and more than 2,000 ethnic news media organizations.

NewsOne
http://www.newsone.com/
Breaking news for Black America features the latest news from a Black perspective.

The Pew Charitable Trusts
http://www.pewtrusts.org/our_work_detail.aspx?id-240
Includes information on media and journalism, media analysis, news coverage index, and news interest index.

Pew Research Center's Project for Excellence in Journalism
http://www.stateofthemedia.org/2011/African-american/
Annual report on American journalism and the role of ethnic media.

Poynter Online's Column: Journalism With a Difference
http://www.poynter.org/column.asp?id=58
The featured columnists include Aly Colon, Thomas Huang, Keith Woods, and Jodi Rave.

Poynter Online's Diversity Resources
http://www.poynter.org/uncategorized/780/diversity-bibliography/
This is a broad range of articles and source materials about diversity from the Poynter Institute.

Public Broadcasting System
http://www.pbs.org/
PBS programs periodically address issues related to media coverage of cultural minorities and women at both the local and national levels.

Queer Women of Color Media Arts Project
http://www.qwocmap.org/
Promotes the creation, exhibition, and distribution of new films and video that increase the visibility of lesbian women of color.

Radio Advertising Bureau
http://www.rab.com/public/hm/hm.cfm
Information and sources in the Latino community for fair and accurate coverage of issues.

RTDNA Diversity
http://www.rtdna.org/pages/best-practices/diversity.php
This website contains links to diversity resources from the Radio Television Digital News Association and Foundation.

Social Media Today
http://www.socialmediatoday.com/
Developed to understand social media's diversity problem, with a statistical breakdown of social media use by race and ethnicity.

South Asian Journalists Association
http://www.saja.org
This group's goal is to foster ties among South Asian journalists in North America and improve standards of journalistic coverage of South Asia and South Asian America.

TVJobs
http://media411.tvjobs.com
A comprehensive media directory for broadcast television that includes minority organizations.

UNITY: Journalists of Color, Inc.
http://www.unityjournalists.org/
UNITY is a strategic alliance of journalists of color acting as a force for positive change in the fast-changing global news industry.

U.S. Census Bureau Minority Links
http://www.census.gov/pubinfo/www/hotlinks.html
This website contains data on racial and ethnic populations in the United States.

USAsianwire
http://www.usasianwire.com
Provides an array of distribution and content solutions for PR, marketing, media, and journalism specialists.

Women of Color Media Justice
http://www.womenofcolormediajustice.blogspot.com
Dedicated to improving media representations of young women of color in film, television, print media, and music industries.

Women and Minority Employment Survey
http://asne.org/article_View/ArticleID/1788/Newsroom-employment-up-slightly-minority-numbers-plunge-for-third-year.aspx

Annual survey about the career progress of women and minorities in the news media.

Women's Institute for Freedom of the Press
http://www.wifp.org/
This nonprofit organization works toward media democracy and justice for women.

Women's Media Center
http://www.womensmediacenter.com
Studies of women in the U.S. Media (2012).

Index

About the Authors

Clint C. Wilson II is Professor of Journalism and Graduate Professor of Communication at Howard University. He has also held faculty and administrative positions at the University of Southern California, California State University, Los Angeles, and Pepperdine University. He has lectured at other colleges and universities and has been a seminar leader at the American Press Institute. He has written four books on subjects related to the Black press and the relationship between people of color and the general audience media in the United States. His scholarly work has been published in such periodicals as *Journalism Educator*, *Columbia Journalism Review*, *Quill*, and *Change*. He is a founder of the Black Journalists Association of Southern California and has written for various news media organizations, including the Associated Press, *Los Angeles Times*, *The Washington Post*, *Pasadena Star-News*, *St. Petersburg Times*, and the *Los Angeles Sentinel*. *Journalism and Mass Communication Quarterly* cited his book *A History of the Black Press* as among the 35 "most significant books of the 20th century," and he is a recipient of the Honor Medal for Distinguished Service in Journalism from the University of Missouri. Wilson holds an AA degree in Journalism from Los Angeles City College; a BA degree in journalism and public relations from California State University, Los Angeles; and an MA in journalism from the University of Southern California (USC). He also earned a doctorate in higher education administration from USC. In addition, he has completed fellowships with the Freedom Forum Media Studies Center at Columbia University, the Poynter Institute for Media Studies, and the American Society of Newspaper Editors.

Félix F. Gutiérrez is Professor of Journalism and Communication in the Annenberg School for Communication and Journalism and Professor of American Studies and Ethnicity in the Dana and David Dornsife College of Letters, Arts and Sciences at the University of Southern California. A former senior vice president of the Newseum and Freedom Forum, his publication credits include five books and more than 50 articles or book chapters on diversity and the media. He received the 2011 Lionel C. Barrow Jr. Award for Distinguished Achievement in Diversity Research and Education of the Association for Education in Journalism and Mass Communication. The National Association of Hispanic Journalists named him the "Padrino

(Godfather) of Hispanic Journalists" in 1995. He held faculty or administrative positions at the University of Southern California; California State University, Northridge; Stanford University; and California State University, Los Angeles; and visiting appointments at the University of Texas-Austin; Columbia University and The Claremont Colleges. In addition to writing freelance articles, he worked during summers and on a weekly basis for the *Pasadena Star-News* and the Associated Press during the 1980s. His advocacy on behalf of people of color and their inclusion in the media has been recognized by the Asian American Journalists Association, Association for Education in Journalism and Mass Communication, Black College Communication Association, California Chicano News Media Association, National Association of Hispanic Journalists, and others. He is in the National Association of Hispanic Journalists Hall of Fame and the Stanford University Alumni Association Multicultural Hall of Fame, received the Honor Medal from the University of Missouri School of Journalism, and was an inaugural member of the Northwestern University Medill School of Journalism Hall of Achievement. He is a trustee of the Freedom Forum Diversity Institute at Vanderbilt University. His education includes a BA degree from California State University, Los Angeles, an MSJ from the Medill School of Journalism at Northwestern University, and an MA and a PhD from the Department of Communication at Stanford University.

Lena M. Chao is Associate Professor of Communication Studies at California State University, Los Angeles (CSULA), where she also serves as Director for the Asian and Asian American Institute. Prior to joining the faculty at CSULA, she was on the administrative staff of the Media Institute for Minorities at the University of Southern California and worked as a Public Service Coordinator at KFWB News radio in Los Angeles. She also has worked at Radio Español and served as Media Director for the American Civil Liberties Union of Southern California. Her areas of scholarly specialization include public relations, mass communication, and intercultural and interpersonal communications. Her academic work has been published in journals such as *Human Communication, California Politics and Policy*, and *Feedback*, among others. She was on the founding board of the Media Action Network for Asian Americans (MANAA), a watchdog group that monitors the communication media in the United States for fair, balanced, and accurate portrayals of Asian Pacific Americans. Her public service activities also include membership on the advisory boards of two nonprofit organizations, The Coalition of Brothers and Sisters Unlimited and the Estelle Van Meter Multipurpose Center, which are both located in South Central Los Angeles. She is Faculty Director for Service Learning at California State University, Los Angeles, promoting curriculum development and faculty and student involvement in community service learning opportunities. Dr. Chao received her BA in English literature from the University of California, Los Angeles, and her MS in print journalism and PhD in communication arts and sciences from the University of Southern California.

⑤SAGE research**methods**

The essential online tool for researchers from the world's leading methods publisher

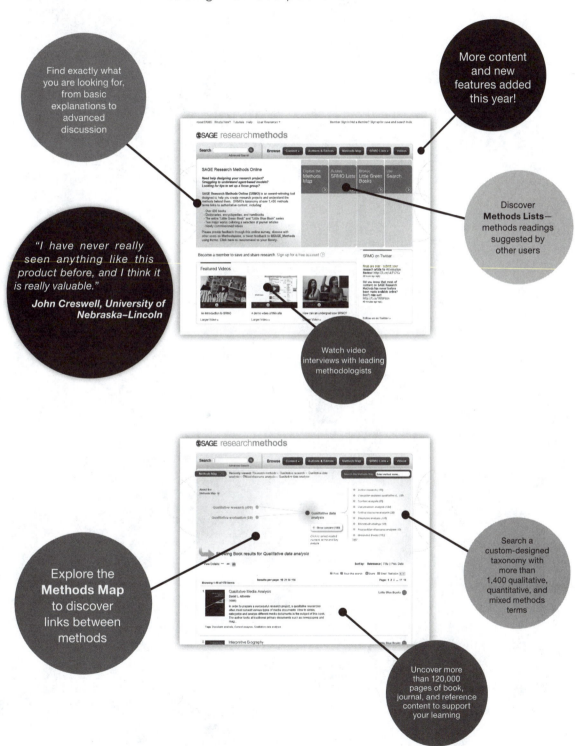

Find exactly what you are looking for, from basic explanations to advanced discussion

More content and new features added this year!

"I have never really seen anything like this product before, and I think it is really valuable."

John Creswell, University of Nebraska–Lincoln

Discover **Methods Lists**— methods readings suggested by other users

Watch video interviews with leading methodologists

Explore the **Methods Map** to discover links between methods

Search a custom-designed taxonomy with more than 1,400 qualitative, quantitative, and mixed methods terms

Uncover more than 120,000 pages of book, journal, and reference content to support your learning

Find out more at
www.sageresearchmethods.com